AIRLINES WORLDWIDE

More than 300 Airlines Described and Illustrated in Colour

B I HENGI

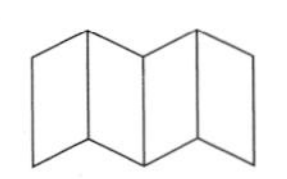

Midland Publishing
Limited

Airlines Worldwide

ISBN 1 85780 067 2

First published in 1997 by
NARA-Verlag, Postfach 1241, D-85388 Allershausen,
Germany, as 'Fluggesellschaften Weltweit'

This English language edition published 1997 by
Midland Publishing Limited
24 The Hollow, Earl Shilton
Leicester, LE9 7NA, England.
Telephone: 01455 847 256 Fax: 01455 841 805
E-mail: midlandbooks@compuserve.com

Worldwide distribution (except North America):
Midland Counties Publications (Aerophile) Limited
Unit 3 Maizefield, Hinckley Fields,
Hinckley, Leics, LE10 1YF, England.
Telephone: 01455 233 747 Fax: 01455 233 737
E-mail: midlandbooks@compuserve.com

North American trade distribution:
Specialty Press Publishers and Wholesalers
11481 Kost Dam Road, North Branch, MN 55056, USA
Telephone: 612 583 3239 Fax: 612 583 2023
Toll free telephone: 800 895 4585

Design concept and layout

Printed in Hong Kong.

Photograph on previous page:
Boeing 777-236 G-RAES in one of the many
variations of the British Airways colour scheme.
(Martin Bach)

More than 300 Airlines Described and Illustrated in Colour

Introduction

This book is an English-language version of the successful German 'Fluggesellschaften Weltweit', now in its third edition.

It aims to give an overview and illustrate 301 of the world's leading or more interesting airlines, with their history, routes, aircraft fleet and operations.

It is not a comprehensive guide to every operator; adding together all the scheduled airlines, holiday and charter and local service operators gives an answer in the region of 5,000, which if included, would clearly result in a very large and extremely expensive publication.

The German edition was compiled by B. I. Hengi, edited by Josef Krauthäuser and published in January 1997. It has been translated, edited and updated by Neil Lewis so that it is as current as possible at press-time in August 1997.

Fleet quantities must be regarded as approximate only. With aircraft being delivered, retired, temporarily stored, or leased between operators every day, it is impossible to be definitive. We have also omitted some small aircraft which may be in an airline's fleet for training, communications or other purposes and are not in general passenger service. Likewise, future orders range from firm through 'rolling options' to such nebulous things as letters of intent for up to 15 years hence! However we have done our best to ensure that the information in these pages is as up-to-date as possible and forms a valid and useful guide to the operations of the airlines described.

We hope that you will enjoy this book, and welcome your comments for future editions.

Midland Publishing
August 1997

Contents

Airport Abbreviations/Codes

Europe

Aalborg (AAL)
Aalesund (AES)
Aarhus (AAR)
Aberdeen (ABZ)
Adana (ADA)
Adler/Sochi (AER)
Ajaccio (AJA)
Alghero (AHO)
Alicante (ALC)
Almeria (LEI)
Altenrhein (ACH)
Amsterdam (AMS)
Ancona (AOI)
Ankara (ANK)
Antalya (AYT)
Antwerp (ANR)
Arad (ARW)
Arrecife (ACE)
Athens (ATH)
Augsburg (AGB)
Avignon (AVN)
Barcelona (BCN)
Bari (BRI)
Basle/Mulhouse (BSL/MLH)
Bastia (BIA)
Belfast (BFS)
Belgrade (BEG)
Bergamo (BGY)
Bergen (BGO)
Berlin-Schönefeld (SFX)
Berlin-Tegel (TXL)
Berlin-Tempelhof (THF)
Bern (BRN)
Bervelag (BVG)
Bilbao (BIO)
Billund (BLL)
Birmingham (BHX)
Bodo (BOO)
Bologna (BLQ)
Bordeaux (BOD)
Borlange (BLE)
Bratislava (BTS)
Braunschweig (BWE)
Bremen (BRE)
Brest (BES)
Brindisi (BDS)
Bristol (BRS)
Brno (BRQ)
Brussels (BRU)
Budapest (BUD)
Bucharest-Otopeni (OTP)
Burgas (BOJ)
Caen (CFR)
Cagliari (CAG)
Cardiff (CWL)
Catania (CTA)
Clermont-Ferrand (CFE)
Cologne/Bonn (CGN)
Copenhagen (CPA)
Corfu (CFU)
Cork (ORK)
Dalaman (DLM)
Dijon (DIJ)
Dinard (DNR)
Dortmund (DTM)
Dresden (DRS)
Dublin (DUB)
Dubrovnik (DCA)
Düsseldorf (DUS)
East Midlands (EMA)
Edinburgh (EDI)
Eindhoven (EIN)
Elba (EBA)
Ercan (ECN)
Erfurt (ERF)
Erzurum (ERZ)
Esbjerg (EBJ)
Faro (FAO)
Faroes(FAE)
Florence (FLR)
Frankfurt (FRA)
Friedrichshafen (FDH)
Fuerteventura (FUE)
Funchal (FNC)
Gdansk (GDN)
Geneva (GVA)
Genoa (GOA)
Gerona (GRO)
Gibraltar (GIB)
Glasgow (GLA)
Gothenburg (GOT)
Granada (GRX)
Graz (GRZ)
Guernsey (GCI)
Hamburg (HAM)
Hammerfest (HFT)
Haugesund (HAU)
Hannover (HAJ)
Helsinki (HEL)
Heraklion (HER)
Hof (HOQ)
Horta (HOR)
Hudiksvall (HUV)
Humberside (HUY)
Ibiza (IBZ)
Innsbruck (INN)
Inverness (INV)
Isle of Man (IOM)
Istanbul (IST)
Ivalo (IVL)
Izmir (ADB)
Jersey (JER)
Jerez de la Frontera (XRY)
Jonköpping (JKG)
Kalamata (KLX)
Kaliningrad (KGD)
Katowice (KTW)
Kaunas (KUN)
Kefalonia (EFL)
Keflavik (KEF)
Kharkov (HRK)
Kiel (KEL)
Kiev-Borispol (KBP)
Kirkenes (KKN)
Klagenfurt (KLU)
Kos (KGS)
Kristiansund (KSU)
La Coruna (LCG)
Larnaca (LCA)
Las Palmas (LPA)
Leeds/Bradford (LBA)
Le Havre (LEH)
Leipzig (LEJ)
Lille (LIL)
Linz (LNZ)
Lisbon (LIS)
Liverpool (LPL)
Ljubljana (LJU)
London-City Airport (LCY)
London-Gatwick (LGW)
London-Heathrow (LHR)
London-Luton (LTN)
London-Stansted (STN)
Lourdes (LDE)
Lvov (LWO)
Lugano (LUG)
Luxembourg (LUX)
Lyon (LYS)
Maastricht (MST)
Madrid (MAD)
Mahon (MAH)
Milan-Linate (LIN)
Milan-Malpensa (MXP)
Malaga (AGP)
Malmö-Sturup (MMX)
Malta (MLA)
Manchester (MAN)
Marseille (MRS)
Minsk (MSQ)
Montpellier (MPL)
Moscow-Sheremetyevo (SVO)
Moscow-Domodedovo (DME)
Moscow-Vnukovo (VKO)
Mostar (OMO)
Munich FJS (MUC)
Münster/Osnabrück (FMO)
Murmansk (MMK)
Mykonos (JMK)
Nantes (NTE)
Narvik (NVK)
Naples (NAP)
Newcastle (NCL)
Nimes (FNI)
Nice (NCE)
Norrköpping (NRK)
Norwich (NWI)
Nürnberg (NUE)
Odense (ODE)
Odessa (ODS)
Ohrid (OHD)
Olbia (OLB)
Oslo-Fornebu (FBU)
Oslo-Gardermoen (GEN)
Ostrava (OSR)
Oulu (OUL)
Paderborn/Lippstadt (PAD)
Palermo (PMO)
Palma de Mallorca (PMI)
Pamplona (PNA)
Paphos (PFO)
Perpignan (PGF)
Paris-Charles de Gaulle (CDG)
Paris-Orly (ORY)
Pisa (PSA)
Ponta Delgada (PDL)
Porto (OPO)
Porto Santo (PXO)
Prague (PRG)
Prestwick (PIK)
Pula (PUY)
Reggio Calabria (REG)
Rennes (RNS)
Reykjavik (RKV)
Reus (REU)
Rhodes (RHO)
Riga (RIX)
Rijeka (RJK)
Rimini (RMI)
Rome-Ciampino (CIA)
Rome-Leonardo da Vinci (FCO)
Rostov (ROV)
Rotterdam (RTM)
Rouen (URO)
Rovaniemi (RVN)
Saarbrücken (SCN)
Salzburg (SZG)
Samos (SMI)
Santa Cruz de la Palma (SPC)
Santa Maria (SMA)
Santander (SDR)
Santiago de Compostela (SCQ)
Santorin (JTR)
Sarajevo (SJJ)
Seville (SVQ)
Shannon (SNN)
Shetland-Sumburgh (LSI)
Simferopol (SIP)
Skiathos (JSI)
Skopje (SKP)
Sofia (SOF)
Sonderborg (SGD)
Southampton (SOU)
Southend (SEN)

Split (SPU)
Stavanger (SVG)
Stockholm-Arlanda (ARN)
Stockholm-Bromma (BMA)
Stornoway (SYY)
Strasbourg (SXB)
St Petersburg (LED)
Stuttgart (STR)
Sundsvall (SDL)
Svolvaer (SVJ)
Tallinn (TLL)
Tampere (TMP)
Teesside (MME)
Tenerife(TFS)
Thessaloniki (SKG)
Thingeyri (TEY)
Timisoara (TSR)
Tirana (TIA)
Tivat (TIV)
Toulouse (TLS)
Trabzon (TZX)
Trieste (TRS)
Tromso (TOS)
Trondheim (TRD)
Turin (TRN)
Turku (TKU)
Umea (UME)
Valencia (VLC)
Varna (VAR)
Vasteras (VST)
Venice (VCE)
Verona (VRN)
Vienna (VIE)
Vilnius (VNO)
Visby (VBY)
Warsaw (WAW)
Westerland (GWT)
Wroclaw (WRO)
Zadar (ZAD)
Zagreb (ZAG)
Zakynthos (ZTH)
Zürich (ZRH)

North America

Abbotsford (YXX)
Abilene (ABI)
Akron (AKC)
Albany (ALB)
Albuquerque (ABQ)
Amarillo (AMA)
Anchorage (ANC)
Aspen (ASE)
Atlanta (ATL)
Atlantic City (ACY)
Augusta (AGS)
Austin (AUS)
Bakersfield (BFL)
Baltimore (BWI)
Bangor (BGR)
Bar Harbor (BHB)
Baton Rouge (BTR)
Beaumont/Port Arthur (BPT)
Bellingham (BLI)
Bermuda (BDA)
Bethel (BET)
Billings (BIL)
Bimini (BIM)
Birmingham (BHM)
Blanc Sablon (YBX)
Boise (BOI)
Boston (BOS)
Bozeman (BZN)
Bridgeport (BDR)
Brownsville (BRO)
Buffalo (BUF)
Burbank (BUR)
Calgary (YYC)
Casper (CPR)
Cedar Rapids (CID)
Charleston (CHS)
Charlotte (CLT)
Chattanooga (CHA)
Cheyenne (CYS)
Chicago-O`Hare (ORD)
Chicago-Midway (MDW)
Chico (CIC)
Churchill (YYQ)
Cincinnati (CVG)
Cleveland (CLE)
Colorado Springs (COS)
Columbus (CMH)
Corpus Christi (CRP)
Dallas/Fort Worth (DFW)
Dallas-Love Field (DAL)
Dallas-Meacham Field (FTW)
Dawson City (YDA)
Dayton (DAY)
Daytona Beach (DAB)
Deer Lake (YDF)
Del Rio (DRT)
Denver (DEN)
Des Moines (DSM)
Detroit (DTW)
Duluth (DLH)
Durango (DRO)
Dutch Harbor (DUT)
Edmonton (YEG)
Elko (EKO)
El Paso (ELP)
Eugene (EUG)
Fairbanks (FAI)
Fayetteville (FYV)
Flagstaff (FLG)
Fort Lauderdale (FLL)
Fort Myers (RSW)
Freeport (FPO)
Fresno (FAT)
Gander (YQX)
Goose Bay (YYR)
Grand Canyon (GCN)
Great Falls (GTF)
Great Harbor Cay (GHC)
Greensboro/High Point (GSO)
Greenville/Spartanburg (GSP)
Halifax (YHZ)
Hamilton (YHM)
Hana (HNM)
Harlingen (HRL)
Harrisburg (MDT)
Hartford (BDL)
Hay River (YHY)
Helena (HLN)
Hilo (ITO)
Honolulu (HNL)
Houston-Hobby (HOU)
Houston-International (IAH)
Huntsville (HSV)
Indianapolis (IND)
Inuvik (YEV)
Iqalit-Frobisher (YFB)
Jackson (JAN)
Jacksonville (JAX)
Juneau (JNU)
Kalaupapa (LUP)
Kansas City (MCI)
Kauai Isl.-Lihue (LIH)
Kelowna (YLW)
Ketchikan (KTN)
Key West (EYW)
Knoxville (TYS)
Kodiak (ADQ)
Kona (KOA)
Kotzebue (OTZ)
Kuujjuaq-Ft.Chimo (YVP)
Lafayette (LFT)
Lake Charles (LCH)
Laredo (LRD)
Las Vegas (LAS)
Lexington (LEX)
Little Rock (LIT)
London (YXU)
Long Beach (LGB)
Los Angeles (LAX)
Louisville (SDF)
Macon (MCN)
Madison (MSN)
Marsh Harbor (MHH)
Memphis (MEM)
Miami (MIA)
Midland/Odessa (MAF)
Milwaukee (MKE)
Minot (MOT)
Minneapolis/St Paul (MSP)
Missoula (MSO)
Mobile (MOB)
Monroe (MLU)
Monterey (MRY)
Montgomery (MGM)
Montreal-Dorval (YUL)
Montreal-Mirabel (YMX)
Myrtle Beach (MYR)
Nashville (BNA)
Nassau (NAS)
Natashquan (YNA)
New Bern (EWN)
New Orleans (MSY)
New York-Kennedy (JFK)
New York-La Guardia (LGA)
New York-Newark (EWR)
Nome (OME)
Norfolk (ORF)
Norman Wells (YVQ)
Oakland (OAK)
Oklahoma City (OKC)
Omaha (OMA)
Ontario (ONT)
Orlando (MCO)
Oshkosh (OSH)
Ottawa (YOW)
Palm Springs (PSP)
Pensacola (PNS)
Peoria (PIA)
Philadelphia (PHL)
Phoenix (PHX)
Pittsburgh (PIT)
Pocatello (PIH)
Portland (PDX)
Prince Albert (YPA)
Prince George (YXS)
Prince Rupert (YPR)
Quebec (YQB)
Raleigh-Durham (RDU)
Rapid City (RAP)
Regina (YQR)
Reno (RNO)
Repulse Bay (YUT)
Resolute Bay (YRB)
Richmond (RIC)
Rockford (RFD)
Sacramento (SMF)
Saint John (YSJ)
St Louis (STL)
Salt Lake City (SLC)
San Antonio (SAT)
San Diego (SAN)
San Francisco (SFO)
San Jose (SJC)
Santa Ana John Wayne (SNA)
Santa Barbara (SBA)
Santa Fe (SAF)
Saskatoon (YXE)
Sault Sainte Marie (SSM)
Savannah (SAV)
Schefferville (YKL)
Seattle/Tacoma (SEA)
Seattle-Boeing Field (BFI)

Sept-Iles (YZV)
Sioux City (SUX)
South Bend (SBN)
Spokane ((GEG)
Sun Valley (SUN)
Syracuse (SYR)
Tallahassee (TLH)
Tampa/St Petersburg (TPA)
Toledo (TOL)
Toronto (YYZ)
Toronto-Island (YTZ)
Tri-Cities (TRI)
Tucson (TUS)
Tulsa (TUL)
Valdez (VDZ)
Vancouver (YVR)
Victoria (YYJ)
Waco (ACT)
Washington-Dulles (IAD)
Washington-National (DCA)
West Palm Beach (PBI)
West Yellowstone (WYS)
White Horse (YXY)
Wichita (ICT)
Windsor (YOG)
Winnipeg (YWG)
Winston-Salem (INT)
Yakutat (YAK)
Yellowknife (YZF)
Yuma (YUM)

South America/ Caribbean

Acapulco (ACA)
Acarigua (AGV)
Aguadilla (BQN)
Altamira (ATM)
Andahuaylas (ANS)
Anguilla (AXA)
Antigua (ANU)
Antofagasta (ANF)
Aracaju (AJU)
Araracuara (ACR)
Arequipa (AQP)
Arica (ARI)
Armenia (AXM)
Aruba (AUA)
Asuncion (ASU)
Bahia Blanca (BHI)
Bahia Solano (BSC)
Baranquilla (BAQ)
Barbados (BGI)
Barbuda (BBQ)
Barcelona (BLA)
Belem (BEL)
Belize (BZE)
Belo Horizonte Intl. (CNF)
Belo Horizonte-Pampulha (PLU)
Bogota (BOG)
Bonaire (BON)
Boa Vista (BVB)
Brasilia (BSB)
Bucaramanga (BGA)
Buenos Aires-Pistarini (EZE)
Buenos Aires-J.Newbery (AEP)
Cali (CLO)
Cajamarca (CJA)
Camaguey (CMW)
Cancun (CUN)
Cape Haitien (CAP)
Caracas (CCS)
Cartagena (CTG)
Cayenne (CAY)
Cayman Brac (CYB)
Chihuahua (CUU)
Ciudad Bolivar (CBL)
Ciudad Del Carmen (CME)
Cochabamba (CBB)
Comodoro Rivadavia (CRD)
Cordoba (COR)
Corumba (CMG)
Cozumel (CZM)
Cuiaba (CGB)
Curacao (CUR)
Curitiba (CWB)
Cuzco (CUZ)
Dominica (DOM)
Durango (DGO)
Flores (FRS)
Florianopolis (FLN)
Fortaleza (FOR)
Fort de France (FDF)
Georgetown (GEO)
Grand Cayman (GCM)
Grenada (GND)
Guadalajara (GDL)
Guatemala City (GUA)
Guayaquil (GYE)
Havana (HAV)
Hermosillo (HMO)
Holguin (HOG)
Huanuco (HUU)
Iquassu (IGU)
Iquitos (IQT)
Kingston (KIN)
La Ceiba (LCE)
La Paz (LAP)
La Paz (LPB)
La Serena (LSC)
Lima (LIM)
Managua (MGA)
Manaus (MAO)
Maracaibo (MAR)
Mar del Plata (MDQ)
Matamoros (MAM)
Mayaguez (MAZ)
Mazatlan (MZT)
Medellin (MDE)
Merida (MRD)
Mexicali (MXL)
Mexico City (MEX)
Montego Bay (MBJ)
Monterrey (MTY)
Montevideo (MVD)
Montserrat (MNI)
Mount Pleasant (MPN)
Natal (NAT)
Neuquen (NQN)
Nuevo Laredo (NLD)
Oaxaca (OAX)
Panama City (PTY)
Paramaribo (PBM)
Pointe a Pitre (PTP)
Porlamar (PMV)
Port au Prince (PAP)
Port Elizabeth (BQU)
Port of Spain (POS)
Porto Alegre (POA)
Puerto Ordaz (PZO)
Puerto Plata (POP)
Puerto Vallarta (PVR)
Punta Arenas (PUQ)
Punta Cana (PUJ)
Quito (UIO)
Recife (REC)
Rio de Janeiro (GIG)
- Santos Dumont (SDU)
Rio Gallegos (RGL)
Rio Grande (RGA)
Riohacha (RCH)
St Croix (STX)
St Eustatius (EUX)
St Kitts (SKB)
St Lucia (SLU)
St Maarten (SXM)
St Thomas (STT)
San Andres (ADZ)
San Carlos de Bariloche (BRC)
San Jose (SJO)
San Juan (SJU)
San Pedro Sula (SAP)
San Salvador (SAL)
Santa Cruz (VVI)
Santa Cruz Do Sul (CSU)
Santiago (SCL)
Santo Domingo (SDQ)
Salvador (SSA)
Sao Paulo-Congonhas (CGH)
Sao Paulo-Guarulhos (GRU)
Tampico (TAM)
Tegucigalpa (TGU)
Tijuana (TIJ)
Tortola (EIS)
Trujillo (TRU)
Tuxtla Gutierrez (TGZ)
Union Island (UNI)
Ushuaia (USH)
Valencia (VLN)
Valledupar (VUP)
Veracruz (VER)
Villahermosa(VSA)
Villavicencio (VVC)
Virgin Gorda (VIJ)
Vitoria (VIX)
Zacatecas (ZCL)

Middle East - Asia - Australia - Pacific

Abu Dhabi (AUH)
Aden (ADE)
Adelaide (ADL)
Agartala (IXA)
Agra (AGR)
Aleppo (ALP)
Alice Springs (ASP)
Alma Ata (ALA)
Alor Setar (AOR)
Amman (AMM)
Amritsar (ATQ)
Anadyr (DYR)
Apia (APW)
Ashkhabad (ASB)
Auckland (AKL)
Ayers Rock (AYQ)
Bahrain (BAH)
Baku (BAK)
Baghdad (SDA)
Baku (BAK)
Balikpapan (BPN)
Bandar Abbas (BND)
Bandar Seri Begawan (BWN)
Bandung (BDO)
Bangalore (BLR)
Bangkok (BKK)
Beijing (BJS)
Beirut (BEI)
Bintulu (BTU)
Bishkek (FRU)
Bhopal (BHO)
Bombay (BOM
Bora Bora (BOB)
Brisbane (BNE)
Calcutta (CCU)
Canberra (CBR)
Cebu (CEB)
Cheju (CJU)
Chelyabinsk (CEK)
Chiang Mai (CNX)
Chittagong (CGP)
Christchurch (CHC)
Colombo (CMB)

Dacca (DAC)
Damascus (DAM)
Darwin (DRW)
Delhi (DEL)
Denpasar (DPS)
Dhahran (DHA)
Doha (DOH)
Dubai (DXB)
Dushanbe (DYU)
Fukuoka (FUK)
Goa (GOI)
Guam (GUM)
Guangzhou (CAN)
Hanoi (HAN)
Harbin (HRB)
Hat Yai (HDY)
Ho Chi Minh City (SGN)
Honiara (HIR)
Hong Kong (HKG)
Hyderabad (HYD)
Ipoh (IPH)
Irkutsk (IKT)
Isfahan (IFN)
Islamabad (ISB)
Jakarta-Halim (HLP)
Jakarta-Soekarno (CGK)
Jeddah (JED)
Johur Bahru (JHB)
Jokjakarta (JOG)
Kabul (KBL)
Kaoshiung (KHH)
Karachi (KHI)
Kathmandu (KTM)
Khabarovsk (KHV)
Kota Bharu (KBR)
Kota Kinabalu (BKI)
Krasnoyarsk (KJA)
Kuala Lumpur (KUL)
Kuching (KCH)
Kuwait (KWI)
Lae (LAE)
Lahore (LHE)
Langkawi (LGK)
Luang Prabang (LPQ)
Madras (MAA)
Magadan (GDX)
Majuro (MAJ)
Male (MLE)
Mandalay (MDL)
Manila (MNL)
Medan (MES)
Melbourne (MEL)
Miri (MYY)
Mount Hagen (HGU)
Muscat (MCT)
Nadi (NAN)
Nagasaki (NGS)
Nagoya (NGO)
Nanjing (NKG)
Niigata (KIJ)
Norilsk (NSK)
Noumea (NOU)
Novosibirsk (OVB)
Okinawa (OKA)
Osaka (OSA)
Pago Pago (PPG)
Palembang (PLM)
Papeete (PPT)
Penang (PEN)
Perth (PER)
Phnom Penh (PNH)
Phuket (HKT)
Port Maquarie (PQQ)
Port Moresby (POM)
Port Vila (VLI)
Pusan (PUS)
Pyongyang (FNJ)
Qingdao (TAO)
Queenstown (ZQN)
Rabaul (RAB)
Rarotonga (RAR)
Riyadh (RUH)
Riyan Mukalla (RIY)
Rotorua (ROT)
Sanaa (SAH)
Sandakan (SDK)
Saidpur (SPD)
Semipalatinsk (PLX)
Sendai (SDJ)
Seoul (SEL)
Shanghai (SHA)
Sharjah (SHJ)
Shenyang (SHE)
Sibu (SBW)
Singapore (SIN)
Srinagar (SXR)
Surabaya (SUB)
Suva (SUV)
Sydney (SYD)
Tacloban (TAC)
Taipei International (TPE)
- Sung Shan (TSA)
Tarawa (TRW)
Tashkent (TAS)
Teheran (THR)
Tel Aviv (TLV)
Tianjin (TSN)
Tiflis (TBS)
Tongatapu (TBU)
Tokyo-Haneda (HND)
Tokyo-Narita (NRT)
Townsville (TSV)
Trivandrum (TRV)
Truk (TKK)
Ufa (UFA)
Ujung Pandang (UPG)
Ulan Bator (ULN)
Ulan Ude (UUD)
Ulsan (USN)
Urumqi (URC)
Varanasi (VNS)
Vientiane (VTE)
Vladivostok (VVO)
Wagga Wagga (WGA)
Whangarei (WRE)
Wellington (WLG)
Wenzhou (WNZ)
Wuhan (WUH)
Xiamen (XMN)
Xi An (SIA)
Yangon (RGN)
Yantai (YNT)
Yerevan(EVN)
Zamboanga (ZAM)
Zhengzhou (CGO)

Africa

Abidjan (ABJ)
Abu Simbel (ABS)
Accra (ACC)
Addis Ababa (ADD)
Agadir (AGA)
Algiers (ALG)
Alexander Bay (ALJ)
Alexandria (ALY)
Alula (ALU
Antananarivo (TNR)
Asmara (ASM)
Aswan (ASW)
Bangui (BGF)
Banjul (BJL)
Bamako (BKO)
Beira (BEW)
Bengasi (BEN)
Benguela (BUG)
Bissao (BXO)
Blantyre (BLZ)
Bloemfontein (BFN)
Boa Vista (BVC)
Bouake (BYK)
Brazzaville (BZV)
Bujumbura (BJM)
Bukoba (BKZ)
Bulawayo (BUQ)
Cabinda (CAB)
Cairo (CAI)
Capetown (CPT)
Casablanca (CMN)
Conakry (CKY)
Cotonou (COO)
Dar-Es-Salaam (DAR)
Dakar (DKR)
Denis Island (DEI)
Diredawa (DIR)
Djerba (DJE)
Djibouti (JIB
Douala (DLA)
Durban (DUR)
Entebbe (EBB)
Freetown (FNA)
Gabarone (GBE)
Garoua (GOU)
Harare (HRE)
Johannesburg (JNB)
Juba (JUB)
Kananga (KGA)
Kano (KAN)
Karika (KAB)
Keetmannshoop (KMP)
Khartoum (KRT)
Kigali (KGL)
Kilimanjaro (JRO)
Kinshasa (FIH)
Korhogo (HGO)
Lagos (LOS)
Libreville (LBV)
Lilongwe (LLW)
Livingstone (LVI)
Lome (LFW)
Luanda (LAD)
Lüderitz (LUD)
Lusaka (LUN)
Mahe (SEZ)
Majunga (MJN)
Malindi (MYD)
Marrakech (RAK)
Maputo (MPM)
Maseru (MSU)
Mauritius (MRU)
Mogadishu (MGQ)
Mombasa (MBA)
Monastir (MIR)
Monrovia-Roberts (ROB)
Monrovia-Sprigg Payne (MLW)
Moroni (YVA)
Nairobi (NBO)
Ndjamena (NDJ)
Niamey (NIM)
Nouakchott (NKC)
Oran (ORN)
Ougadougou (OUA)
Port Elizabeth (PLZ)
Port Gentil (POG)
Port Harcourt (PHC)
Port Sudan (PZU)
Praia (RAI)
Pretoria (PRY)
Rabat (RBA)
Sal (SID)
Sao Tome (TMS)
St Denis (RUN)
Tamanrasset (TMR)
Tangier (TNG)
Tripoli (TIP)
Umtata (UTT)
Victoria Falls (VFA)
Walvis Bay (WVB)
Windhoek (WDH)
Yaounde (YAO)
Zanzibar (ZNZ)

Photograph: Boeing 727-200Adv HK-3738X (Josef Krauthäuser/Miami)

ACES COLOMBIA

Calle 49, No.50-21 Piso 34, Ed del Cafe,
Medellin 6503, Colombia
Tel. 4-2517500 Fax. 4-251677

Three letter code	IATA No.	ICAO Callsign
AES	137	Aces

The private Aerolineas Centrales de Colombia – ACES – was formed in August 1971, under the ownership of the United Coffee Growers Co-operative. Regional services began on 1st February 1992 from the base at Medellin to Bogota and Medellin using Saunders ST-27s (modified de Havilland Herons). From September 1976 services to smaller airports were run with de Havilland Twin Otters. Jet equipment was necessary for the development of longer routes, and Boeing 727-100s from Eastern Airlines were bought and flown from 1981. The ST-27 remained in service until 1987, when it was replaced by the Fokker F27. By this time the route network embraced over 20 internal destinations, and was to be further developed.1991 saw the beginning of an extensive re-equipment programme. ATR42s supplanted the F27s, and the Boeing 727-100s were replaced by later series models. The first international service was inaugurated on 1st July 1992 to Miami, and the build up of this route necessitated the acquisition of further Boeing 727-200Adv, leased in 1994 and 1995. ACES was appointed by the postal authorities as a carrier of mail and parcels, and several destinations in the Caribbean were served by charter flights. The long-term fleet plan calls for the replacement of the Boeing 727s with newer aircraft.

Routes

ACES flies to 37 destinations in Columbia, including the island of San Andres, and to Miami.

Fleet

6 ATR42
2 Boeing 727-100
5 Boeing 727-200 Adv
9 De Havilland DHC-6 Twin Otter

Photograph: McDonnell Douglas DC-9-32 S5-ABF (Uwe Gleisberg/Munich FJS)

ADRIA AIRWAYS

Kuzmiceva 7, 61000 Ljubljana
Slovenia
Tel. 61 133 4336 Fax. 61 323356

Three letter code	IATA No.	ICAO Callsign
ADR	165	Adria

Adria Airways was set up in 1960. Flight operations began in March 1961 with a Douglas DC-6, the initial fleet consisting of four DC-6Bs obtained from KLM. In 1968, the airline became a part of the trading company Interexport and from then on it was called Inex Adria Airways. In 1970, new DC-9-32 aircraft flew the first scheduled flights from Ljubljana to Belgrade. From 1985 onwards, Inex also flew to Munich for the first time, as a scheduled service; there were also scheduled flights to Ljubljana. In addition to these scheduled services, charter flights are also provided for various tour operators. The airline's name changed back to Adria Airways in May 1986 when it became independent. When the first Airbus A320 was delivered in 1989, the airline took on a new colour scheme for its aircraft and reassumed its original name. Due to the civil war conditions in Yugoslavia in 1991, Adria's licence to fly was cancelled on 25th October 1991 but was returned on 16th January 1992. In 1992 Adria became the flag carrier of the independent state of Slovenia. As Adria cannot make full use of its aircraft, these are leased out to other companies, for instance an A320 with Air Maldives.

Routes

Athens, Djibouti, Larnaca, London, Munich, Paris, Tel Aviv and Zürich as scheduled services. Charter flights from many European airports to destinations in Croatia and Slovenia; plus special flights carrying foreign workers.

Fleet	Ordered
3 Airbus A320 1 Cessna 441 2 De Havilland DHC-7 2 McDonnell Douglas DC-9-32	2 Canadair Regional Jet

Photograph: BAe 146-300 EI-CLJ (Josef Krauthäuser collection/Birmingham)

AER LINGUS

P O Box 180, Dublin Airport
Republic of Ireland
Tel. 01 705 2222 Fax. 01 705 3832

Three letter code	IATA No.	ICAO Callsign
EIN	053	Shamrock

In 1936, Aer Lingus Teoranta was set up for regional and European services, and Aerlinte Eireann Teoranta for international flights in 1947. The two airlines make up Aer Lingus, which is state-owned. Flights started with a de Havilland DH.84 from Dublin to Bristol. That was on 27th May 1936, and the aircraft took off from the famous Baldonnel airfield, as Dublin at that time did not have its own airport. Soon there were flights to London, Liverpool and to the Isle of Man. In 1947, seven Vickers Vikings were purchased for European services but were sold in 1948 and DC-3s became the main aircraft type in the fleet. Viscounts arrived in 1954 and enabled Aer Lingus to fly to Paris, Amsterdam, Düsseldorf, Frankfurt and Rome, and the Lockheed Constellation made flights across the Atlantic possible. From 28th April 1958 onwards, Aer Lingus flew to New York. Fokker F27s were added in 1958. From 1st January 1960 Aer Lingus and Aerlinte were closely integrated and operated as Aer Lingus – Irish International Airlines. The Boeing 720 was introduced on the transatlantic service in December 1960. After the Boeing 720, the Boeing 747 was used from 1971 onwards. In the eighties Aer Lingus found itself in a severe crisis: numerous destinations were abandoned and the number of aircraft was reduced. Reorganisation took place, linked with a fleet renewal programme. Boeing 737s, first introduced in April1969, have been the backbone of the fleet in recent years, with the 200 series latterly replaced by later models. Aer Lingus Commuter was formed in 1984 to cater for traffic between Ireland and UK regional airports – BAe 146s and Fokker 50s are used, the SAAB 340 fleet having been disposed of. Boeing 747s have been replaced by Airbus A330-300s beginning in March 1994.

Routes

Amsterdam, Birmingham, Boston, Bristol, Brussels, Copenhagen, Cork, Derry, Dublin, Düsseldorf, Edinburgh, Frankfurt, Galway, Glasgow, Jersey, Knock, Leeds/Bradford, London, Madrid, Milan, Manchester, Newcastle, New York, Paris, Rome, Salzburg, Shannon, Sligo, Zürich. Seasonal charters, eg to Lourdes.

Fleet

5 Airbus A330-300
5 BAe 146-300
6 Boeing 737-400
10 Boeing 737-500
6 Fokker 50

Photograph: McDonnell Douglas DC-9-14 XA-BCS (Author's collection)

AERO CALIFORNIA

Apartado Postal 555, Hidalgo 316,
La Paz Baja California Sur 23000, Mexico
Tel. 112-26655 Fax. 112-53993

Three letter code	IATA No.	ICAO Callsign
SER	078	Aerocalifornia

The company was founded in 1960 and operated as an air taxi concern with several Cessnas and Beech 18s. Until the 1980s the indestructible Douglas DC-3 was also in the fleet which was expanded in 1982 with the addition of a DC-9-15. Aero California was initially active it its own neighbourhood, Baja California, and flew charters, but also scheduled services between La Paz, Tijuana and Hermosillo. It was possible to fly the scheduled network with the Convair 340; further routes were added over the years. At the end of the 1980s it was decided to undertake a careful expansion and to give up some of the propeller airliners in favour of more DC-9s. At the beginning of 1990 the first route to the United States was started: to Los Angeles. Since 1995 the fleet has been all jet, with the retirement of the last Cessna and Beech 18. As well as scheduled services, Aero California operates charter flights to Mexican tourist centres.

Routes

Augascalientes, Ciudad Juarez, Ciudad Obregon, Ciudad Victoria, Colima, Culiacan, Guadalajara, Hermosilo, Loreto, Los Angeles, Los Cabos, Los Mochis, La Paz, Manzanillo, Matamoros, Mazatlan, Mexico City, Monterrey, Puebla, Torreon, Tijuana, Tucson.

Fleet

11 McDonnell Douglas DC-9-14/15
5 McDonnell Douglas DC-9-32

Photograph: Ilyushin IL-96-300 RA-96008 (Josef Krauthäuser/Seattle SEA)

AEROFLOT - ARIA

Leningradsky Prospect 37a, 125167 Moscow
Russia
Tel. 095 1556641 Fax. 095 1556647

Three letter code	IATA No.	ICAO Callsign
AFL	555	Aeroflot

Aeroflot was formed in March 1923 as Dobrolet, using de Havilland, Junkers and Vickers aircraft. In 1929 Dobrolet became Dobroflot when it was absorbed into a Ukrainian airline and became responsible for all civil aviation activities in Russia. Dobroflot became Aeroflot in 1932. Regular international services developed only after the Second World War. Aeroflot's first supersonic passenger service was inaugurated on 1st November 1977 between Moscow and Alma Ata but was suspended after several years. Aeroflot's vast fleet of over 7,500 aircraft carried over 100,000,000 passengers for the first time in 1976, while the airline also supplied agricultural, survey, aero-medical, maintenance and training services within Russia and was also responsible for airports. Political changes in the former Soviet Union have been paralleled by changes in aviation. Since 1991, the former Aeroflot directorates became independent and established their own airlines. Newly independent republics also set up their own airlines and took over aircraft belonging to Aeroflot. It was only in the course of 1993 that the new Aeroflot evolved in line with Western ideas, and was renamed as Aeroflot-Russian International Airlines (ARIA). All other services have been delegated to independent airlines. Only a small section of the old fleet was taken over, and for the first time five Airbus A310-300s were leased with the first deliveries from July 1992 especially for use on routes to Japan and East Asia. Further recent fleet changes have seen the introduction of the Ilyushin IL-96 widebody from 1994, and leasing arrangements for US built aircraft, notably Boeing 767-300s from 1995 and a DC-10 freighter, with 10 Boeing 737-400s on order for delivery from April 1998 to October 1999.

Routes

Aeroflot-Russian International Airline flies to about 135 destinations in around 100 countries in Europe, America, Asia and Africa.

Fleet

10 Airbus A310-300
2 Boeing 767-300
22 Ilyushin IL-62M
12 Ilyushin IL-76
20 Ilyushin IL-86
6 Ilyushin IL-96-300
1 McDonnell Douglas DC-10-30F
13 Tupolev Tu-134
30 Tupolev Tu-154
1 Tupolev Tu-204

Ordered

10 Boeing 737-400
19 Ilyushin 96-300
Ilyushin IL-114
Tupolev Tu-204
(no quantities available)

Photograph: Boeing 747-200 LV-OPA (Guido Latz/Paris CDG)

AEROLINEAS ARGENTINAS

Paseo Colon 185, 1063 Buenos Aires
Argentina
Tel. 01 3173000 Fax. 01-3173585

Three letter code	IATA No.	ICAO Callsign
ARG	044	Argentina

Four smaller airlines merged in May 1949 at the instigation of the Argentinian Ministry of Transport to form Aerolineas Argentinas, the national airline to take over the operation of FAMA, ALFA, Aeroposta and Zonda from December 1949. The only other airline left was the Air Force-controlled LADE. Using aircraft such as DC-3s and DC-4s brought in to the airline, not only domestic destinations were served but also, from March 1950 onwards, New York. In 1959, the de Havilland Comet 4B was introduced on international routes and was used until 1966, when the first of a total of ten Boeing 707s was delivered. Boeing 737s were purchased for short-haul flights in 1969 followed by Fokker F28s in 1975. Boeing 747s were first used regularly on the New York route in 1976, and to Europe as well from 1977 onwards. Regional routes are served by Boeing 737s, 727s and Fokker 28s, with the addition of MD-80s from the early 90s onwards. Three Airbus A310s were acquired from Delta Airlines in 1994 for use on services to the USA. In the summer of 1996 a US hub was established at Miami, from which Boeing 727s operate connecting flights to Canada and the Caribbean. Iberia had acquired a 20% stake in Aerolineas Argentinas in 1993, increased to 83% in 1995, the rest being owned by staff and the Argentine government. However, the Iberia stake is being reduced as the Spanish airline is being obliged to sell its shares, with American Airlines taking a stake in Aerolineas Argentinas in July 1997. There are marketing alliances with Iberia, Austral and Malaysia Airlines, and no doubt closer co-operation with American will follow shortly.

Routes

Auckland, Bogota, Caracas, Florianopolis, Frankfurt, Guayaquil, Lima, London, Los Angeles, Madrid, Mexico City, Miami, Montreal, Montevideo, New York, Panama, Paris, Porto Alegre, Punta del Este, Rio de Janeiro, Rome, Santiago, Sao Paulo, Toronto, Zürich.

Fleet

3 Airbus A310
6 Boeing 747-200
3 Boeing 727-200
15 Boeing 737-200
3 Fokker F28
7 McDonnell Douglas MD-80

Photograph: Airbus A320-200 D-ALAA (André Dietzel/Munich FJS)

AERO LLOYD

Lessingstrasse 7-9, 61440 Oberursel
Germany
Tel. 06171 641132 Fax. 06171 641049

Three letter code	IATA No.	ICAO Callsign
AEF	633	Aero Lloyd

Aero Lloyd Flugreisen GmbH is a private airline set up on 20th December 1980, and which started flights in March 1981 with three SE210 Caravelle 10Rs. It is the successor to another company of the same name founded in 1979, but which went out of business under mysterious circumstances at the beginning of December 1980. Initially it ran charter flights to the traditional regions around the Mediterranean. The travel company Air Charter Market also contributed to the utilisation of the aircraft, and this company now owns half of the Aero Lloyd capital. From May to July 1982, Aero Lloyd also had in service a DC-9-32. From May 1986, there was an expansion phase with new MD-80 aircraft; it flew new routes, and also put the first MD-87 into operation in 1988. Over the years, up to 22 MD-82/83/87 have been in service. In addition to charter flights, Aero Lloyd entered the scheduled flights business from Summer 1988. As well as German internal services, routes to London, Paris and Zurich were offered. However, following losses on these services, and the acquisition of a stake in the airline by Lufthansa, Aero Lloyd withdrew from scheduled services in 1992. In late 1993 the last DC-9-32 was sold, and a pointer to the future given with the order from Airbus of the first A320, which arrived at Frankfurt in a new modern colour scheme in January 1996. The Airbus A320 and A321s will form the basis of the new fleet. The airline also maintains an operating base at Munich Airport.

Routes

About 45 destinations around the Mediterranean, Canary Isles, Ireland and Norway are served.

Fleet	Ordered
6 Airbus A320-200 15 McDonnell Douglas MD-82/83	11 Airbus A321

Photograph: McDonnell Douglas MD-88 XA-AMV (Josef Krauthäuser/Miami)

AEROMEXICO

Paseo de la Reforma 445, CP 06500
Mexico City, Mexico
Tel. 327 4094 Fax. 511 9457

Three letter code	IATA No.	ICAO Callsign
AMX	139	Aeromexico

The original Aeromexico was established on 14th September 1934 as Aeronaves de Mexico. Pan American Airways acquired a 40% interest on 12th September 1940 but this passed to the Mexican Government when the airline was fully nationalised in 1950. Its position was strengthened with the takeovers of other Mexican airlines, including Lamsa, Aerovias Reforma and Aerolineas Mexicanas culminating in 1961 with that of Guest Aerovias, then one of the country's largest airlines. It became Aeromexico in February 1972. The present-day Aeromexico has been in operation since 1st October 1988, after its predecessor of the same name was declared bankrupt in April 1988 by its owners the Mexican Government and the airline was compelled to discontinue operations. In November 1988, a consortium of Mexican business interests acquired a controlling interest and services restarted to thirty domestic destinations and five cities in the United States. Aeromexico is one of the country's two national airlines (the other being Mexicana), renamed Aerovias de Mexico, but still marketed under its former name. It acquired a subsidiary, Servicio Aereos Litoral (Aerolitoral) in November 1990 and has a stake in Mexicana and in Aero Peru. It remains privately owned, with 25% held by the Mexican pilots' association. Business recession in Mexico has had its effect on Aeromexico; in 1995 services to Europe were cut back and all the DC-10s sold. Likewise several uneconomic internal routes have been abandoned. Along with these measures has gone a financial restructuring. During 1995 co-operation agreements were reached with British Airways, Air France, Japan Airlines, Delta and America West.

Routes

About 20 destinations in Mexico; further routes to Los Angeles, Dallas, Miami, the Caribbean, Central and South America, Paris and Madrid.

Fleet

6 Boeing 757-200
3 Boeing 767-200
18 McDonnell Douglas DC-9-32
25 McDonnell Douglas MD-82/88
2 McDonnell Douglas MD-87

Photograph: Boeing 757-200 XA-SMD (Björn Kannengiesser/Miami)

AERO PERU

Avenida Jose Pardo, 601 Lima 18
Peru
Tel. 14-478900 Fax. 14-443974

Three letter code	IATA No.	ICAO Callsign
PLI	210	Aeroperu

Aero Peru was set up by the Government of the Andean state on 22nd May 1973 as the new national airline. The new airline replaced Aerolinas Peruanas SA, which ceased operations on 3rd May 1971. Aero Peru brought together APSA and SATCO to form one airline. SATCO was under the administration of the Peruvian Air Force and brought three F28 to the new airline. These aircraft were used to start operations, initially domestic services. The first Boeing 727 was acquired in May 1974. Two DC-8-50s were purchased in 1974 from the Venezuelan airline VIASA for international flights which started on 28th July 1974. From December 1978 to 1982, Aero Peru also used two Lockheed TriStars, but it was not possible to operate them economically and efficiently. The privatisation of Aero Peru was completed in 1981. In 1992, Aeromexico acquired a 47% stake in Aero Peru. The flights of these two airlines are co-ordinated, and Aero Peru also obtains aircraft from Aeromexico.

Routes

From Lima to Bogota, Buenos Aires, Caracas, Mexico City, Miami, Rio de Janeiro, Santiago, furthermore to 20 internal destinations such as Cuzco, Iquitos, Juanjui, Piura, Tacma, and Trujillo.

Fleet

6 Boeing 727
2 Boeing 757-200
1 Fokker F28

Photograph: Airbus A310-300 TU-TAF (Patrick Lutz/Paris-CDG)

AIR AFRIQUE

3, Avenue Joseph Anoma, 01BP 3927 Abidjan, Ivory Coast
Tel. 225203000 Fax. 225203005

Three letter code	IATA No.	ICAO Callsign
RKA	092	Airafric

The airline was established on 28th March 1961 in co-operation with Air France, UAT (now UTA) and the former French colonies of Benin, Burkina-Faso, the Central African Republic, Chad, the Congo, the Ivory Coast, Mauritania, Niger, Senegal, Cameroon and Gabon. The latter two countries withdrew from the consortium in the early 1970s, while Togo joined in January 1968. The objective was the creation of comprehensive internal services within these countries as well as international connections, in the absence of which each of these relatively poor countries would have to establish its own airline.The first service of this multi-national airline took place in August 1961 with DC-4s and DC-6s. In the year the airline was established, a route was set up to Paris using a Lockheed Constellation. A DC-8 leased from UTA was Air Afrique's first jet aircraft on 5th January 1962. In the 1960s and 1970s, DC-8s, leased from Air France and UTA formed the basis of its fleet. In February 1973, a DC-10-30 was delivered, the airline's first widebody aircraft. The Boeing 747 was used from October 1980 to March 1984, but this aircraft turned out not to be flexible enough for Air Afrique's purposes. Airbus A310s were increasingly used; this was obviously the ideal aircraft for the airline, especially with the opening of new routes to South Africa.
An increase in passenger numbers and freight carryings has been established since 1992. This improvement has made possible the acquisition of the Airbus A300-600, the first of which was delivered in 1995 as a replacement for the DC-10 on high-density routes. Air Afrique has code-share agreements with SAA, TAP and Swissair.

Routes

Within the African countries with a stake in the airline; to South Africa, to Europe especially France and to the Middle East.

Fleet

3 Airbus A300B4
2 Airbus A300-600
4 Airbus A310-300
1 Antonov An-12
2 Boeing 707-300F
2 Boeing 737-200

Photograph: Boeing 737-200Adv 7T-VES (Josef Krauthäuser/Frankfurt)

AIR ALGERIE

1, Place Maurice Audiens, Algiers,
Democratic Republic of Algeria
Tel. 644822 Fax. 610553

Three letter code	IATA No.	ICAO Callsign
DAH	124	Air Algerie

In 1946, the Compagnie Générale de Transport Aerien was created while Algeria was still under French rule. It was merged with the Compagnie Air Transport to form the present Air Algerie on 22nd May 1953. Douglas DC-4s and Lockheed Constellations were used on routes to Paris and Marseille. Air Algerie started using their first jet, the SE210 Caravelle in December 1959. In 1972 the airline was nationalised, the Caravelles were subsequently replaced by a large fleet of Boeing 727s and 737s; in 1974 the first Airbus A300B4 was taken over from TEA, before they obtained the first A310s of their own for use on routes to France. A slow growth and renewal took place, marked in 1990 by the delivery of the first Boeing 767; since then nothing much has altered. Air Algerie undertakes governmental flying, for instance agricultural work, for which a large number of helicopters are available. For numerous transport tasks, including services to desert locations, Air Algerie flies the military Hercules transport in civilian guise. For the future, a closer co-operation with Air Afrique is planned by way of a joint venture.

Routes

North Africa, Middle East and Western Europe, especially to destinations in France, Frankfurt, London, Amsterdam and Zürich. A dense internal network.

Fleet

4 Airbus A310-200
15 Boeing 737-200
11 Boeing 727-200
3 Boeing 767-300
7 Fokker F27
2 Lockheed L-382 Hercules

Photograph: McDonnell Douglas DC-9-31 P4-MDD (Josef Krauthäuser/Miami)

AIR ARUBA

P.O. Box 1017, Oranjestad, Aruba,
Netherlands Antilles
Tel. 23151 Fax. 38138

Three letter code	IATA No.	ICAO Callsign
ARU	276	Aruba

The regional area administration of Aruba set up Air Aruba in September 1986. Initially it worked as a ground-handling agent. With the aid of Air Holland and KLM, however, it started flights to the neighbouring islands in 1988, using NAMC YS-11s. For seasonal use a leased Boeing 757 was also used, which was replaced by the larger Boeing 767 leased since 1991. Air Aruba is active today in the business of providing scheduled flights and charters and at times also serves destinations in Europe such as Amsterdam and Cologne. Since the Boeing 767 was not really being used effectively, the European routes were abandoned in 1995, and a co-operation agreement concluded with KLM, to which ALM and Avianca are also participants. Since then, the airline has concentrated above all on the US market, and here Air Aruba works closely together with US Airways, under an alliance signed in May 1995.

Routes

Bonaire, Buenos Aires, Bogotà, Caracas, Curacao, Las Piedras, Maracaibo, Medellin, Miami, New York, Sao Paulo, St Maarten, San José, Tampa.

Fleet

1 McDonnell Douglas DC-9-31
2 McDonnell Douglas MD-88
1 McDonnell Douglas MD-83

Photograph: De Havilland DHC-8 C-GAAM (Jörg Thiel collection)

AIR ATLANTIC

P.O. Box 13190, St Johns, Newfoundland
A1B 4A4, Canada
Tel. 709-570 0791 Fax. 709-570 0870

Three letter code	IATA No.	ICAO Callsign
ATL	574	Air Atlantic

Air Atlantic was set up as a regional airline in St Johns in 1985 and began operations on 28th February 1986 with two Dash 7 aircraft as a Canadian Pacific commuter airline. 1986 saw the delivery of the first DHC-8, and the following year saw Canadian Pacific become Canadian, so that Air Atlantic now flies as a Canadian Partner. Its first international route was from St Johns to Boston in August 1987. In September 1996 the IMP-Group acquired Air Atlantic, and at the same time all Canadian's services to and from St Johns were taken over. Air Atlantic now serves 21 destinations in Atlantic and Central Canada and the eastern USA.
The BAe 146 was brought into the fleet in 1990, and the Jetstream 41s were added from Spring of 1995.

Routes

Boston, Charlottetown, Catham, Churchill, Deer Lake, Fredericton, Gander, Goose Bay, Halifax, Moncton, Montreal, Ottawa, Quebec, St Johns, Stephenville, Wabush, Yarmouth.

Fleet

3 BAe 146-200
5 BAe Jetstream 41
3 De Havilland DHC-8

Photograph: Douglas DC-3 (C-47) G-AMRA (Heinz Kolper/Duxford)

AIR ATLANTIQUE

Coventry Airport, Coventry, CV8 3AZ,
Great Britain
Tel. 1203-307566 Fax. 1203-639037

Three letter code	IATA No.	ICAO Callsign
AAG	-	Atlantic

In 1969 the air taxi company General Aviation Services was founded in Jersey in the Channel Islands. With a Cessna 310, all sorts of tasks were flown, from passengers to freight. Eventually the purchase of several Douglas DC-3s was made, and the company changed its name to Air Atlantique in 1974. The base was moved from Jersey to Coventry in 1984, and in 1986 the British government's attractive pollution control contract and their DC-3s were taken over from Harvest Air. Spectacular actions became increasingly common in the North Sea area during maritime patrol and oil pollution work following incidents to oil rigs or tankers. In 1987 the fleet was increased with the acquisition of a DC-6 for special charter use. In 1994 the company was reorganised into separate groups: Atlantic Cargo is responsible for freight charter and in 1994 received three Lockheed Electras; Air Atlantique Reconnaissance was responsible for maritime patrol and Pollution Control and had at its disposal aircraft with radar and infra-red equipment, but this division has now been sold and the pollution control is operated under contract by Air Atlantique. The two DC-6s have also now been adapted with a 'quick-fit' palletised system so that they can be readily converted from freighters to sprayers on demand. Atlantic Airways was quickly set up for passenger charter work, and here the DC-3s have a special role for airshow work, pleasure and special flights. The newest division in the group is Air Atlantique Historic Flight, whose aim is the restoration, maintenance and operation of historic aircraft; their fleet includes a Scottish Aviation Twin Pioneer which is used for pleasure flying.

Routes

Ad hoc freight and passenger charters, maritime patrol and pollution control.

Fleet

3 Cessna 310
3 Cessna 404
9 Douglas DC-3
2 Douglas DC-6
1 Fairchild Swearingen Metro III
4 Lockheed L-188 Electra
1 Pilatus BN-Islander
1 SAL Twin Pioneer

Photograph: Avro RJ-70 YL-BAL (Patrick Lutz/Frankfurt)

AIR BALTIC

Riga Airport, Riga LV1053,
Latvia
Tel. 207069 Fax. 207369

Three letter code	IATA No.	ICAO Callsign
BTI	657	Air Baltic

Baltic International was founded in 1992 by Texan businessmen and Latvio-Latvian Airlines. The original subsidiary carries out flights into the neighbouring western countries. Alongside the Tu-134s a DC-9 was introduced into the fleet on a loan basis in 1993, but was substituted by a Boeing 727 from 1995. As the company was not developing satisfactorily, a radical cure was decided upon, and in September 1995 Baltic International was merged with Latvian Airlines to create a new national airline Air Baltic. The Latvian government own the majority 51% of the capital, with the rest owned by Baltic International USA, SAS and two investment companies. A fresh start was made with a Saab 340 and in Spring of 1996 three Avro RJ 70s were received. Actually the takeover of Latvio's routes and aircraft, and their disposal had been promised by the Latvian government, but this has been a slow-winded process. Some services are operated in conjunction with SAS and Lufthansa.

Routes

From Riga to Copenhagen, Frankfurt, Helsinki, Kiev, London, Minsk, Moscow, Stockholm, St Petersburg, Tallinn, Vilnius, Warsaw.

Fleet

3 Avro RJ 70
1 Saab 340

Photograph: De Havilland DHC-8-100 C-FABW (Josef Krauthäuser/Vancouver)

AIR BC

5520 Miller Road, Richmond BC, V7B 1A6,
Canada
Tel. 604 224 2603 Fax. 604 224 2675

Three letter code	IATA No.	ICAO Callsign
ABL	742	Aircoach

Air BC (BC being the abbreviation for British Columbia) emerged in 1980 from the merger of various small airlines on Canada's western coast, including Canadian Air Transit, Flight Operation, Gulf Air Aviation, Haida Airlines, Island Airlines, Ominecca Air, Pacific Coastal Airlines, Trans Provincial Airlines and West Coast Air Services. By June 1980, all the airlines had been purchased by Jim Pattison Industries and the first aircraft in the combined fleet, a Twin Otter, was rolled out in Air BC colours. The first Dash 7 arrived in 1983 and the first Dash 8 in 1986. Air Canada acquired a 85% holding in April 1987 and Air BC operates as an Air Canada Connector with an extensive regional network and services to Seattle and Portland in the USA. Its first jet aircraft, the BAe 146 was ordered in 1988. Its main hubs are at Calgary and Vancouver. The airline is now a 100% subsidiary of Air Canada, and following the change in livery of the parent, has altered its aircraft colour scheme in a similar way.

Routes

As a feeder carrier for Air Canada, Air BC serves some 30 destinations in Western Canada, and Portland and Seattle in the USA.

Fleet

5 BAe 146-200
13 De Havilland DHC-8-100
6 De Havilland DHC-8-300

Photograph: Boeing 737-300 OO-ILJ (Xaver Flocki collection)

AIR BELGIUM

Vilvoordelaan 192, 1930 Zaventem,
Belgium
Tel. 2 7160510 Fax. 2-7160511

Three letter code	IATA No.	ICAO Callsign
ABB	-	Air Belgium

Air Belgium is a private charter airline set up on 3rd May 1979 as Abelag Airways. It commenced operations a month later and for marketing reasons became Air Belgium in 1980. The main shareholder was Sun International. Its destinations were well-known regions around the Mediterranean. It used a leased Boeing 737-200. A night charter operation was also operated on behalf of DHL between Brussels and Madrid. In 1988 they obtained a Boeing 737-400 of their own, followed by a Boeing 757 in 1989, and then at the beginning of the 1996 season a Boeing 737-300. The fleet has been variable in extent as aircraft are leased in and out to meet seasonal demand, and the 757 has been on long term lease to Sunways of Sweden. Following heavy losses in 1996, Sun International is trying to sell its 65% shareholding (the balance of 35% is owned by Sobelair).

Routes

Air Belgium flies for various tour organisations to the Mediterranean area and the Canary Isles, plus *ad hoc* charters.

Fleet

1 Boeing 737-300
1 Boeing 737-400
1 Boeing 757-200

Photograph: Boeing 737-400 D-ABAF (Albert Kuhbandner/Munich FJS)

AIR BERLIN

Flughafen Tegel, 13405 Berlin,
Germany
Tel. 030-41012781 Fax. 030-4132003

Three letter code	IATA No.	ICAO Callsign
BER	745	Air Berlin

Air Berlin USA was set up on 11th July 1978 as a wholly-owned subsidiary of the American company Leico. The first charter flights took off from Berlin in April 1979 using a fleet of US-registered Boeing 707s. As is well-known, until German unity was regained on 3rd October 1990, only airlines belonging to the victorious powers of the Second World War were allowed to fly to Berlin. Charter flights with particular departure times were provided by Air Berlin using a Boeing 707 between Berlin and Florida. However, this service, with a stopover in Brussels, was only provided from October 1980 to October 1981. From then on, Air Berlin flew a Boeing 737-300. A 167-seater Boeing 737-400 was placed into service in April 1990 and this variant is now the sole type in the fleet which was considerably extended between 1994 and 1996. After reunification, Air Berlin continued in the charter business but in 1992 became a company registered under German law and thus not restricted to departures from Berlin only. For the future, the airline is an early customer for the new-generation Boeing 737-800 series.

Routes

Charter flights, preferably in the Mediterranean region and to the Canary Isles.

Fleet	Ordered
10 Boeing 737-400	6 Boeing 737-800

Photograph: McDonnell Douglas DC-8-41 N952AX (Josef Krauthäuser/Las Vegas)

AIRBORNE EXPRESS

Airborne Air Park, 145 Hunter Drive,
Wilmington Ohio, 45177 USA
Tel. 513-3825591 Fax. 513-3822452

Three letter code	IATA No.	ICAO Callsign
ABX	832	Abex

Midwest Air Charter of Elyria, Ohio specialised during the 1970s in courier flights for banks and cargo company Airborne Freight Corp., using smaller aircraft types such as the Aerostar, Beech 18, Piper Aztec and LearJet. Then in 1978 five Caravelles were acquired. A year later Airborne took over Midwest and thus acquired its own flight division. Airborne Express received FAA certification in April 1980 and expanded quickly. Alongside the Caravelle the NAMC YS-11 was introduced as a fast turboprop. From its own airport at Wilmington Airpark, where one of the largest packet sorting facilities in the USA has been installed, more and more destinations in the USA are served. DC-9s relieved the ageing Caravelles and soon became numerous. In 1983 43,000 tonnes of freight were forwarded. Increasing amounts of freight and longer distance routes meant the introduction to service in 1984 of the Douglas DC-8. The Airbus consortium offered a freighter version of the A300 as a replacement for the older aircraft in the fleet, but it was decided instead to acquire the Boeing 767-200. These are planned to enter service during 1997, and to lead a fleet renewal until the year 2000, but further DC-9s will also be acquired.

Routes

Freight services within the USA.

Fleet

35 McDonnell Douglas DC-8-61/62/63/63F
69 McDonnell Douglas DC-9-10/30/40
11 NAMC YS-11

Ordered

12 Boeing 767-200

Photograph: ATR42-300 A2-ABC (Jürgen Gleisberg/Maue)

AIR BOTSWANA

P.O. Box 92, Gabarone,
Botswana
Tel. 352182 Fax. 375408

Three letter code	IATA No.	ICAO Callsign
BOT	636	Botswana

Air Botswana was set up as a national airline by a presidential decree of July 1972. After Botswana National Airways (1966-1969) and Botswana Airways (1969-1972), Air Botswana took over operations on 1st August 1972 with Fokker F27s and Britten-Norman Islanders. By 1980 a HS.748 and a Viscount comprised the fleet on scheduled services from Gaborone to Johannesburg and Lusaka and other points. The airline was a unit of the Botswana Development Corporation contracting out maintenance and flight operations control to Safair Freighters of Johannesburg. However in April 1988, it was taken over by the Botswana Government. A fleet renewal programme started in 1988, with new ATR42s taking the place of the F27s. In late 1989 Air Botswana also obtained its first jet, a BAe 146-100. It has formed a subsidiary, Southern Links, to develop regional business. The airline has established regional joint ventures with Air Zimbabwe and Zambia Airways.

Routes

National routes from Gabarone to Francistown, Maun, Maputo, Maseru. International services to Harare, Johannesburg, Luanda, Nairobi, Victoria Falls, Windhoek and Lusaka.

Fleet

2 ATR42
1 BAe 146-100

Photograph: Dornier 228 F-ODYC (Frank Litaudon/Nouméa)

AIR CALEDONIE

BP 212 Aerodrome de Magenta, Noumea,
New Caledonia
Tel. 252339 Fax. 254869

Three letter code	IATA No.	ICAO Callsign
TPC	190	Aircal

Air Calédonie started as Société Calédonienne de Transports Aériens (Transpac) being founded on 25th September 1955, and began operations the same month between Noumea and Lifan. The local government held 76% of the shares in this airline. In 1968 the airline took the name of Air Calédonie. In addition to its own routes, it also provides flights on behalf of UTA. Aircraft used were Cessna 310, Britten-Norman Islanders and de Havilland Twin Otters. In 1983 they carried 135,000 passengers on regional flights, and the number of passengers carried rose to over 180,000 in 1989.

ATR42s and Dornier 228s were added to the fleet from 1987 onwards, serving New Caledonia and other islands which form the Loyalty group. Air France has a small holding of 3% in the airline; the rest is owned by the regional government.

Routes

Belep, Huailon, Kone, Koumac, Lifon, Mare, Noumea, Ovre, Tiga, Touho.

Fleet	Ordered
3 ATR42 2 Dornier Do 228	1 Dornier Do 328

Photograph: Boeing 747-200 C-GAGA (Josef Krauthäuser/Miami)

AIR CANADA

Place Air Canada Montreal, Quebec H2Z 1X5, Canada
Tel. 514-4225000 Fax. 514-4227741

Three letter code	IATA No.	ICAO Callsign
ACA	014	Air Canada

The Canadian government set up Trans Canada Air Lines (TCA) on 10th April 1937, and it was administered by CNR, the Canadian Railways. On 1st September flights between Vancouver and Seattle started with a Lockheed 10A. Setting up a network within Canada was TCA's most important concern in the following years. April 1939 saw the first Vancouver-Montreal flight, and shortly afterwards TCA flew from Montreal to New York. During the Second World War, a regular connection between Canada and Scotland was created using converted Lancaster bombers. After the war, TCA flew to Düsseldorf as early as 1953 as part of the so-called emigrant flights. In addition to the DC-3, Lockheed Constellations, Canadair North Stars, Bristol 170s, Vickers Viscounts and Vickers Vanguards were in use. On 1st April 1960, the first jets, DC-8s, were added to the fleet. In 1964, the name Air Canada and new colours were introduced. In 1967 the first DC-9s arrived. Air Canada expanded globally and introduced the first large-capacity aircraft in 1971. Overseas flights were flown using Boeing 747s and Lockheed TriStars, with the more recent addition of the Boeing 767. It became fully privatised in 1989. The addition of the first Airbus A320 in early 1990 continued the renewal of the fleet and heralded the introduction of a new corporate image and colour scheme. The newest type in the fleet is the Airbus A340, and these are used on the new routes to Seoul and Osaka inaugurated in 1994. It was announced in August 1997 that Airbus A330-300s and A340s will be acquired from 1999 to replace the Boeing 747 'classics'. Air Canada controls five regional companies: Air BC, Air Ontario, Air Alliance, Air Nova and NWT-Air, and works in co-operation with Continental Airlines in the United States.

Routes

Intensive domestic network (64 points), with partner airlines as feeders, USA, Caribbean, European routes have been divided with Canadian since 1989 so that Air Canada serves Athens, Berlin, Düsseldorf, Frankfurt, Geneva, Hong Kong, Lisbon, London, Madrid, Nice, Paris, and Zürich. Osaka and Seoul in the Far East.

Fleet		Ordered
15 Airbus A319	6 Boeing 747-100/200	20 Airbus A319
34 Airbus A320	3 Boeing 747-400	
8 Airbus A340	26 Canadair Regional Jet	
29 Boeing 767-200/300	35 McDonnell Douglas DC-9-32	

Photograph: Airbus A300B4 F-BVGI (Patrick Lutz/Paris CDG)

AIR CHARTER

4, rue de la Couture, Sillic 318,
94588 Rungis, France
Tel. 145603300 Fax. 1-45603399

Three letter code	IATA No.	ICAO Callsign
ACF	-	Air Charter

Air Charter, a subsidiary of Air France and Air Inter Europe, carries package tourists primarily to the holiday regions of the Mediterranean. It was set up on 3rd February 1966 as Air Charter International (ACI). Flights began in July with SE 210 Caravelles taken over from Air France. In May 1979, Air Charter obtained its first Boeing 727s, and in 1988 Airbus A300B4 aircraft were acquired. When needed, Air Charter leases from or to Air France, Air Inter, EAS, and Euralair. In 1995 and 1996 four Airbus A320 were taken over, to replace the older Boeing 727s.

Routes

Charter flights in the Mediterranean area, North Africa and the whole of Europe.

Fleet

2 Airbus A300B4
4 Airbus A320
2 Boeing 737-200

Photograph: Boeing 747SP B-2438 (B.I.Hengi/Zürich)

AIR CHINA

100621 Capital International Airport,
Beijing, Peoples Republic of China
Tel. 1-4563220 Fax. 1-4563348

Three letter code	IATA No.	ICAO Callsign
CCA	999	Air China

Air China International was set up by the CAAC in July 1988 as an independent international division. Some aircraft carry Air China logos; however, further aircraft are leased from CAAC when needed. Air China is responsible for the international service of the People's Republic. It was formerly the Beijing-based international division of CAAC, the Civil Aviation Administration of China and was re-named Air China in July 1988. This was done at a time when the Chinese Government decided to form the airline operating divisions of CAAC into separate airlines, each with its own name, and concentrate on its role as a regulatory body. CAAC itself had been formed on 2nd November 1949 after the creation of the People's Republic. There were new routes to Vienna from 1992 onwards, plus cargo services to Los Angeles and to Copenhagen in 1993. The fleet and route network are being continually enlarged, and after nearly two years of delay due to political and trade disputes with the USA, government approval was given in March 1997 for the acquisition of the first five Boeing 777-200s for delivery commencing late 1998. A significant new service approved in mid-1997 following the handover of Hong Kong to China was a direct service from Hong Kong to London, the first by a mainland Chinese airline, and in direct competition to the established carrier Cathay Pacific. Air China has co-operation agreements with Ariana, Austrian and Korean Airlines, and is a partner with Lufthansa in the aircraft maintenance firm Ameco in Beijing.

Routes

Addis Ababa, Alma Ata, Amsterdam, Bangkok, Berlin, Boston, Brussels, Bucharest, Copenhagen, Frankfurt, Hong Kong, Karachi, Kuwait, London, Los Angeles, Manila, Melbourne, Moscow, New York, Paris, Rome, Seoul, Singapore, Sydney, Toronto, Tokyo, Vienna, Zürich. In addition more than 50 destinations in China.

Fleet

2 Antonov 12
4 BAe 146
4 Boeing 747-200
4 Boeing 747 SP
10 Boeing 747-400
19 Boeing 737-300
10 Boeing 767-200/300ER
2 Lockheed L-382 Hercules
8 Yunshuji Y-5
4 Yunshuji Y-7

Ordered

3 Airbus A340
3 Boeing 747-400
5 Boeing 777-200

Photograph: ATR42-300 F-OHFC (Uwe Gleisberg/Munich FJS)

AIR DOLOMITI

Via Aquilera 45, 34077 Ronchi dei Legionari,
Trieste, Italy
Tel. 481-474479 Fax. 481-477711

Three letter code	IATA No.	ICAO Callsign
DLA	101	Dolomiti

Set up in January 1988, Air Dolomiti started operations in May 1991 with a Dash 8, on the Trieste-Genoa route. Further routes within Italy followed quickly. In November 1992 Air Dolomiti started flights abroad for the first time on the route Verona-Munich. Verona developed into a minor hub for the airline, with numerous connecting flights. With the purchase of the ATR42 from 1994, the DHC-8s left the fleet, and the aircraft adopted the new colour scheme which is currently in use. The airline has worked with Lufthansa since 1995 and is a Lufthansa Partner, with several joint flights, and in sales and marketing. Thus Munich has developed as the most important airport for Air Dolomiti, and passengers from northern Italy have connections here to Lufthansa flights. There is a demand for more direct flights, and in order to provide these two further ATR42s were added in 1995. Additionally since 1996 there has been an alliance with Crossair, and the Basle-Rome service is operated jointly. Seasonal and charter flights are operated as well as schedules to Italian holiday regions and to Sardinia. The airline enjoyed its first profitable year in 1996, paving the way for a share issue and further expansion.

Routes

Barcelona, Basle, Cagliari, Genoa, Munich, Olbia, Parma, Rome, Trieste, Turin, Venice, Verona.

Fleet	Ordered
6 ATR42-300 2 ATR42-500	2 Canadair Regional Jet

Photograph: Dornier Do 328 HB-AEE (B.I.Hengi/Bern)

AIR ENGIADINA

Flughafenstrasse 11, 3123 Belp,
Switzerland
Tel. 9601211 Fax. 9601217

Three letter code	IATA No.	ICAO Callsign
RQX	834	Engiadina

Air Engiadina was formed on 22nd April 1987. The Engadine region of Switzerland is a little off the beaten track as far as air transport is concerned, and would be better served by having its own regional airline. In January 1988 the route from Samedan to Zurich was opened with a single BAe Jetstream 31, and in 1989 a new connection was established between Zurich and Eindhoven, with a Munich route following in 1992. At this point a Dornier 228 was brought into service. With a factory-fresh Dornier 328, the first example of its type delivered into airline service, the Berne-Vienna route was opened. In 1994 followed routes from Berne to London, and Berne to Amsterdam, and the company base was moved to Berne, taking over Sunshine Aviation. In order to finance all this, the company's capital was raised to 10.8 million Swiss Francs. From the beginning of the 1995 summer timetable Berne-Frankfurt was introduced, and service increased to Amsterdam, as well as developing London City Airport, and operating a series of charters to Elba. Air Engiadina received its fourth Dornier 328 on 27th October 1995, and at the same time the Jetstream was sold. In 1995 the airline carried 84,204 passengers. The future will be characterised by consolidation and further developments, particularly of summer charter flights. The arrival of the fifth Dornier 328 in the Autumn of 1996 completed the planned fleet size.

Routes

Amsterdam, Berne, Brno, Dublin, Eindhoven, Elba, Frankfurt, London, Manchester, Munich, Reus, Vienna, Zürich.

Fleet

5 Dornier Do 328

Photograph: Boeing 757-200 EC-FEF (Frank Schorr/Düsseldorf)

AIR EUROPA

Gran Via Asima 23, 07009 Palma de Mallorca, Spain
Tel. 71-178111 Fax. 71-431500

Three letter code	IATA No.	ICAO Callsign
AEA	996	Air Europa

Air Europa is one of the profitable remainders of the former multinational organisation Air Europe and was set up in June 1986 on the island of Majorca. The airline, registered as Air Espana SA, was, at the time it was set up in 1984, 75% owned by two Spanish banks and 25% by the British company ILG, until the time of the latter's failure in 1991. It started flights on 21st November 1986 with a Boeing 737-300. The first flight was from London-Gatwick to Palma de Mallorca, which is also Air Europa's base. Air Europa and Air Europe had an identical livery and fleet, comprising Boeing 737s and 757s, and aircraft switched between the carriers to meet their individual needs at different times of the year. After the failure of its British partner, some tour organisers and banks took over its shares, enabling flights to continue. In 1991, Air Europa obtained three Boeing 757-200s for use on long-distance flights, which include services to and from Scandinavia. Boeing 767s were used briefly during 1994/95, but these larger aircraft were inflexible in their operation, and were mostly exchanged for further 757s. Since 1995 has been successful with scheduled services in competition with Iberia, and operates frequent daily services between Madrid and Barcelona.

Routes

Charters from Great Britain, Scandinavia and Western Europe to destinations on the Spanish mainland; to the Canary Islands and Mallorca. Bangkok, Cancun, Delhi, Halifax, Havana, New York and Santo Domingo are amongst long-distance charter destinations. To New York, and seven Spanish domestic points from Madrid.

Fleet	Ordered
12 Boeing 737-300	10 Boeing 737-800
5 Boeing 737-400	
7 Boeing 757-200	
1 Boeing 767-200	

Photograph: De Havilland DHC-6 PK-OCL (Björn Kannengiesser/Djakarta)

AIRFAST INDONESIA

Kuningan Plaza, Suite 305 Jl HR Rasuna Sard Kar, C11-14 Djakarta, Indonesia
Tel. 6221-5207696 Fax. 6221-5200731

Three letter code	IATA No.	ICAO Callsign
AFE	-	Airfast

Set up in 1971 as a joint venture between Indonesia and Australia with the objective of offering passenger and cargo charters in Southeast Asia, flights started with DC-3s. Fokker F27s and various small aircraft for flights to the Indonesian islands were also used. The airline has been in private Indonesian ownership since 1982 and in addition to its original objectives the tasks now envisaged also include offshore flights to oil rigs, aerial photography and earth resource survey flights. Furthermore there are all sorts of special operations such as logging, and heavy helicopter lift operations. The principal base is Jakarta, but there are others in Singapore and Kalimantan.

Routes

Passenger and freight flights within Indonesia, Singapore, Malaysia, South East Asia and to Australia.

Fleet

3 BAe HS.748
2 Bell 204
4 Bell 206
3 Bell 212
2 Bell 412
3 Boeing 737-200
1 CASA-IPTN 212
3 De Havilland DHC-6 Twin Otter
1 Douglas DC-3
3 Sikorsky S-58T

Photograph: Aérospatiale/BAe Concorde F-BVFF (Stefan Schlick/Hahn)

AIR FRANCE

45 rue de Paris, 95747 Roissy,
France
Tel. 1-41567800 Fax. 1-41567029

Three letter code	IATA No.	ICAO Callsign
AFR	057	Airfrans

On 30th August 1933 Air Orient, Air Union Internationale de Navigation Aérienne and Société Générale Transport Aérien merged to create the national airline Air France and bought the assets of Compagnie Générale Aéropostale. By the Second World War, Air France had consolidated its leading position in Europe and North Africa. There were flights to all the colonies, including Indochina. During the war, flights from 'free' France or from North Africa (Casablanca) were possible. After the war, air transport in France was nationalised and Société Nationale Air France was set up on 1st January 1946, followed by Compagnie Nationale Air France on 16th June when the airline was incorporated by Act of Parliament. In the beginning, the airline made use of French aircraft such as the Bréguet 763, the SE 161 and other lesser known types. In 1953, the Comet was delivered, marking the start of jet transport. Further English aircraft, Vickers Viscounts, were used on short and medium-distance flights, while long-haul routes were served by DC-4s and Lockheed Constellations. The 26th May 1959 saw the successful advent of the SE 210 Caravelle. Boeing 707s and Boeing 747s were introduced as replacements for propeller aircraft on inter-continental flights. From May 1974 Airbus A300s were also used for the first time, and on 21st January 1976 the Concorde was licensed for scheduled services. The latest aircraft in the Air France fleet is the Airbus A340. The operations, routes and aircraft of Aeromaritime and UTA were integrated into Air France in 1992. In the mid-1990s the group entered a financial crisis and restructuring was necessary. Air France and Air Inter Europe are to be fully integrated from September 1997. Air France has close links with many other airlines, particularly in Africa.

Routes

Air France has an intensive worldwide network, especially to its former colonies and overseas dependencies. In Europe all major cities are served.

Fleet

6 Aérospatiale/BAe Concorde
9 Airbus A300
10 Airbus A310-200/300
25 Airbus A320-100/200
3 Airbus A321-200
12 Airbus A340-200/300
43 Boeing 737-200/300/500
44 Boeing 747-100/200/400
6 Boeing 767-300

Ordered

9 Airbus A340-300
10 Boeing 777-200

Photograph: Boeing 747-200 F-ODJG (Christian Volpati/Paris CDG)

AIR GABON

P.B. 2206, Libreville,
Gabon
Tel. 732197 Fax. 731156

Three letter code	IATA No.	ICAO Callsign
AGN	185	Golf November

Set up in 1951 as Compagnie Aérienne Gabonaise. In 1951 it began local services from Libreville with Beech and de Havilland aircraft. The airline was a founder member of Air Afrique and belonged to the consortium from 1961 to 1977. The airline was designated as the national carrier in 1968. In addition to its involvement in Air Afrique and international routes, the present-day Air Gabon operates independently in Gabon; it was known until 1974 as Société Nationale Air Gabon. In 1974 it acquired its first F28, followed by a further aircraft of this type and a Boeing 737. After leaving Air Afrique, Air Gabon then obtained a Boeing 747-200 for scheduled services to Europe in 1978. In 1988 the airline was reorganised and its network of routes tightened up. Its first Fokker 100 was acquired in 1990, but traffic growth on its routes meant that by 1995 this would be exchanged for a Boeing 727. The Boeing 767 was added to the fleet at the end of 1996. London is a recent addition to the network. About 480,000 passengers fly each year with Air Gabon.

Routes

Abidjan, Bangui, Bitam, Cotonou, Dakar, Douala, Fougamou, Franceville, Gamva, Kinshasa, Lagos, Lambarene, London, Lome, Luanda, Marseille, Mekambo, Moanda, Nice, Oyem, Paris, Port Gentil, Rome.

Fleet

1 ATR42-300
1 Boeing 727-200Adv
1 Boeing 737-200Adv
1 Boeing 747-200
1 Boeing 767-200ER
2 Fokker F28

Photograph: Dornier Do 228 F-OGOF (Author's collection)

AIR GUADELOUPE

Aéroport du Raizet 97110 Abymes,
French-Guadeloupe
Tel. 590-915344 Fax. 590-917566

Three letter code	IATA No.	ICAO Callsign
AGU	427	Air Guadeloupe

Air Guadeloupe was set up by Air France and the local government of the French overseas department in 1970. It started operations with a Fairchild FH227 for a shuttle service between Point-a-Pitre and Fort de France. The FH227 was replaced by an ATR42 in 1987, with a second aircraft of the same type joining the fleet later in that year. The Dornier 228 was introduced with three deliveries between 1988 and 1990 After heavy losses in 1992, the airline applied to start insolvency proceedings; but flights continued. Air France took on 45% of the capital, and the rest is owned by the island's government. The first ATR72 was introduced to the fleet at the beginning of 1996, with another expected during 1997, and at the 1997 Paris Air Show in June it was announced that the airline had ordered two more Fairchild Dornier 228-112s for delivery later in the year.

Routes

Marie-Galante, Les Saintes, La Desirade, Saint Bartholmy, Saint Martin, Saint Thomas and San Juan are important destinations in the Caribbean.

Fleet	Ordered
2 ATR42 1 ATR72 2 De Havilland DHC-6 4 Dornier Do 228	1 ATR72 2 Fairchild Dornier 228

Photograph: Boeing 737-300 PH-OZA (Andreas Witek/Graz)

AIR HOLLAND

Schipholweg 291, Postbus 1117,
75116 Badhoevedorp, Netherlands
Tel. 20-6584444 Fax. 20-6598176

Three letter code	IATA No.	ICAO Callsign
AHR	-	Orange

Air Holland was formed in early 1984 by private companies and received its operating licence on 30th July that year. A Boeing 727-200 started flights on 2nd April 1985, and the second aircraft of this type followed as early as May 1985. Air Holland operates for tour operators from Amsterdam, Rotterdam, Maastricht and Eindhoven. From 1988 the 727s were replaced by four new, more modern Boeing 757s, and a further example followed in 1989 and again in 1990. Air Holland itself not only provides charter flights for tour operators but also leases the aircraft to other airlines. In 1992 Air Holland had to suspend flights for financial reasons, but after reorganisation as Air Holland Charter BV it was able to resume charter flights in 1993.

Routes

Charter flights principally in the Mediterranean area and to the Canary Isles; in winter also to the Alpine regions and to the Caribbean.

Fleet

3 Boeing 757-200
3 Boeing 737-300

Photograph: Boeing 747-400 VT-ESM (Frank Schorr/London LHR)

AIR INDIA

A. I. Buildg. 218 Backbay Rec. Nairnam Point,
Bombay 40021, India
Tel. 022-2024142 Fax. 022-2024897

Three letter code	IATA No.	ICAO Callsign
AIC	098	Airindia

Air India can trace its history back to July 1932 when Tata Sons Ltd operated a mail service between Bombay, Madras and Karachi using de Havilland Puss Moths. Name changes followed to Tata Airlines in 1938 and to Air India on 29th July 1946. A further change came in 1948 to Air India International. Regular flights to London commenced in 1948 from Bombay via Cairo and Geneva and in 1953 all Indian air services were placed under state control and the same year Constellation flights served the Far East. Air India obtained its first Boeing 707 on 18th February 1960, enabling the airline to provide flights to New York. In 1962 the airline's name was shortened to Air India. Its first large-capacity aircraft, a Boeing 747, was delivered in 1971. This aircraft flew on scheduled flights to London, and Frankfurt featured on Air India's flight schedule from 1973 onwards. Since the early 1980s Air India has also operated Airbus aircraft. 1989 was the year when India's flag carrier was restructured, with the aircraft also being repainted in a more 'modern' style. In late 1993 Air India obtained its first Boeing 747-400, though this appeared in the 'old' colours which were re-established because of customer dislike of the 'new'. There are co-operation agreements with Air Mauritius, Ethiopian, Gulf Air, Indian Airlines, Lufthansa and Malaysia Airlines.

Routes

From principal bases at Bombay, Calcutta and Delhi to worldwide destinations including Frankfurt, Geneva, Hong Kong, London, Manchester, Mauritius, Moscow, New York, Perth, Rome, Singapore, Sydney, Tokyo and Toronto.

Fleet

3 Airbus A300B4
8 Airbus A310-300
9 Boeing 747-200
2 Boeing 747-300
6 Boeing 747-400

Photograph: Airbus A321-100 F-GMZE (Patrick Lutz/Paris ORY)

AIR INTER EUROPE

1 Avenue Maréchal Devaux, 91550 Paray, Vieille Poste, France
Tel 1-46751212 Fax. 1-46756584

Three letter code	IATA No.	ICAO Callsign
ITF	279	Air Inter

Lignes Aériennes Intérieures was founded on 12th November 1954, but the first flight took place only on 17th March 1958, with a leased aircraft from Paris to Strasbourg. Air Inter operated some scheduled flights until flights were discontinued in 1958, but economic success was denied the airline. After reorganisation, Air Inter resumed operations, again with leased aircraft. The first aircraft owned by the company in 1962 were six Vickers Viscount 708s, and four Nord 262s bought from Air France. The latter also supplied 3 SE 210 Caravelles in 1965. On 16th May 1974, Air Inter took the first of a total of ten Avions Marcel Dassault Mercures, an aircraft which was, however, not a success and Air Inter became the only operators of the type. This aircraft opened the route Paris-Lyon, which in the meantime has become the airline's most successful route. In October 1976, Air Inter obtained Airbus A300 large-capacity aircraft. In 1977, the company agreed with Air France to cease charter operations and received in return a 20% holding in Air Charter. Another Airbus product, the A320, was obtained by Air Inter as a launch customer as early as June 1988. The takeover of UTA on 12th January 1990 enabled Air France to indirectly acquire a majority stake in Air Inter. Since then Air Inter, Air France and UTA have been merged into Groupe Air France. In early 1994 Air Inter was again an Airbus launch customer, this time for the new twin-jet large-capacity jet aircraft, the 330. Two years later, in June 1996, the first Airbus A319 was delivered. As the Air France group is further reorganised, the business of Air Inter Europe is also in the process of change, and it will become fully integrated with Air France beginning in September 1997.

Routes

Connects all important French cities - including the island of Corsica - with Paris. Additionally about 20 European destinations are served.

Fleet

9 Airbus A319
35 Airbus A320
5 Airbus A321
5 Fokker 100

Photograph: Boeing 727-200Adv 6Y-JMM (Josef Krauthäuser/Miami)

AIR JAMAICA

72-76 Harbour Street, Kingston,
Jamaica
Tel. 809-9223460 Fax. 809-9220107

Three letter code	IATA No.	ICAO Callsign
AJM	201	Juliet Mike

Air Jamaica was established by the government of Jamaica (60% share), together with Air Canada (40%) in October 1968. It succeeded an earlier company of the same name established with the help of BOAC & BWIA in 1962 and which had operated a Kingston-New York service with leased aircraft since 1965. Using a DC-9 leased from Air Canada, the new company started flights to Miami on 1st April 1969, and with a DC-8 to New York. From 1974 London was the only European destination in its timetable, in conjunction with British Airways, but this connection was discontinued after a few years. Boeing 727s were acquired in late 1974 for Miami services. The DC-8 was too large for the airline's needs, and it was replaced by Airbus A300s in 1983. These were used for flights to the USA and Canada. In 1980 the airline had become fully state owned but a long-awaited privatisation succeeded in May 1994, with the government disposing of 75% of its holding. The reorganisation brought with it a new colour scheme and new aircraft. The London service was reopened in 1996 using the Airbus A310. There are marketing alliances with Delta, US Airways, TWA and United. The main competition in the area comes from American Airlines, and in order to combat this there is a co-operation agreement with BWIA, and a new hub has been set up in mid-1997 at Montego Bay from which a network is to be developed.

Routes

Atlanta, Baltimore, Curacao, Grand Cayman, London, Miami, Kingston, New York, Philadelphia.

Fleet

6 Airbus A310-300
4 Airbus A320-200
2 Boeing 727-200Adv
2 McDonnell Douglas MD-83

Photograph: Ilyushin IL-18 P-836 (Björn Kannengiesser/Beijing)

AIR KORYO

Sunan District, Pyongyang,
Democratic Republic of Korea
Tel. 37917 Fax. 4571

Three letter code	IATA No.	ICAO Callsign
KCA	120	Airkoryo

Air Koryo, formerly Chosonminhang Korean Airways (CAAK) is the state airline of the Democratic Republic of Korea (North Korea). It was formed in 1954 to succeed SOKAO, the joint Soviet – North Korean airline established in 1950, which started with Li-2s, and operated Ilyushin IL-12s and Antonov An-2s. With the founding of CAAK the Soviet fleet was taken over, and later IL-14s and then IL-18s were brought into service. Only Soviet types were used; thus the first jet was a Tupolev Tu-154 delivered in 1975, with further examples following in 1979 and 1982. These were also used on long-distance routes such as to East Berlin or Prague, with intermediate fuel stops necessary. With the delivery of the Ilyushin IL-62 came an aircraft properly suited to these longer routes, and it was possible to introduce non-stop service from Pyongyang to Moscow. In 1993 came a change, when Choson Minhang became Air Koryo. In addition to passenger services, freight flights are also undertaken, and Air Koryo fulfils various other functions on behalf of the state, and is responsible for handling at all the airports in the country. Its main base is the airport of the capital, Pyongyang. In the autumn of 1996 a new scheduled service to Macau was initiated.

Routes

Regular flights to Beijing, Berlin, Khabarovsk, Macau, Moscow and Sofia. Charters to eastern Europe and the former Soviet Union. Regional services to Chongsin, Kaesong, Wonsan, Hamhun, Kilchu, Kanggyae and Sinuiju.

Fleet

8 Antonov An-24
4 Ilyushin IL-18
4 Ilyushin IL-62
3 Ilyushin IL-76MD
2 Tupolev Tu-134
4 Tupolev Tu-154

Photograph: Airbus A340-300 4R-ADA (Josef Krauthäuser/Frankfurt)

AIR LANKA

37, York Street, Colombo,
Sri Lanka
Tel. 1-735555 Fax. 1-735122

Three letter code	IATA No.	ICAO Callsign
ALK	603	Airlanka

Air Lanka was set up on 10th January 1979 in order to be able to continue the business affairs of Air Ceylon, which had ceased in 1978. The airline was then 60% owned by the Sri Lankan Government and 40% with Sri Lankan businesses. Management and technical assistance was provided by Singapore Airlines. Operations started on 1st September 1979 with two leased Boeing 707s from SIA. The first TriStar owned by the airline flew from Colombo to Paris on 2nd November 1990: Zürich, Frankfurt and London followed soon after. At times there were flights with leased Boeing 747s to London-Gatwick, but the passenger volume – due to the political situation in the country – is somewhat in decline. The Boeing 737 is an addition to the TriStar for regional flights to India and the Maldives. A planned renewal of the long-distance fleet had to be postponed in 1993 as financing the planned Airbus A340s was not initially possible. However this was arranged through an international banking consortium and in the autumn of 1994 the first of a pair of A340s entered service on European routes. A third example followed in 1995, replacing older TriStars.

Routes

Regional network from Colombo, otherwise mainly flights to Europe to destinations such as Amsterdam, Frankfurt, London, Paris, Vienna and Zürich.

Fleet

2 Airbus A320-200
3 Airbus A340-300
2 Lockheed L-1011-500
2 Lockheed L-1011-100

Photograph: McDonnell Douglas MD-83 F-GHEB (Andrè Dietzel/Munich FJS)

AIR LIBERTE

3 rue du Pont des Hallas, 94656 Rungis Cedex, France
Tel. 1-49792300 Fax. 1-46865095

Three letter code	IATA No.	ICAO Callsign
LIB	718	Air Liberté

Air Liberté was set up in July 1987. Flights started in April 1988 with a leased MD-83, especially for Club Aquarius, one of the major tour organisers in France. From its base at Paris-Orly, Air Liberté took on a scheduled service to Montreal from 1993, but principally operated passenger services to both European and Mediterranean holiday resorts from French cities. With the advent of Club Mediterranée as a shareholder in 1994 the French internal network was expanded, and the takeover of AOM was mooted. Routes from Toulouse to Dakar and London were inaugurated, but in a squabble over slot allocations at Paris-Orly, routes were quickly inaugurated and discontinued. At the beginning of 1996 new internal services were started to Nice, which was intended to become a second hub, and in May of that year the entire route network from Paris-Orly of Euralair was taken on. Along with this came Euralair's three Boeing 737-200s, and four DC-10s were taken on long-term lease. The airline had become financially very weak, losing about FFr 1 billion ($181m) in 1996, and 70% of the shareholding was acquired in 1997 by British Airways, who also own TAT. These two airlines are now being integrated under one management, and considerably reorganised. A subsidiary operation in Tunisia known as Air Liberté Tunisie operated for several years using MD-83s seconded from the parent airline; this has now become independent and changed its name to Nouvelair Tunisie (see page 225).

Routes

French domestic services from Paris-Orly; further destinations in the Mediterranean area and North Africa and Réunion as well as in the Caribbean and to South East Asia are principally served as charters.

Fleet

5 Boeing 737-200
8 McDonnell Douglas MD-83
5 McDonnell Douglas DC-10

Photograph: Airbus A321-100 D-AVZG (Patrick Lutz/Hamburg-Finkenwerder)

AIR MACAU

P.O. Box 1910,
Macau
Tel. 3966888 Fax. 396866

Three letter code	IATA No.	ICAO Callsign
AMU	675	Air Macau

The first Airbus A321 landed on 5th November 1996 at the new airport at Macau, the (still) Portuguese colony on China's doorstep. The official opening of the airport followed on 8th November with the handover of the aircraft to Air Macau. The airline had been founded in October 1994 and belongs to the predominantly Chinese Macon Aviation Services Company (MASC) which in turn is owned by CAAC and local investors. A modest part of the capital is also held by TAP-Air Portugal. The airline has been designated as the colony's sole carrier for 25 years. Two Airbus A320s and two A321s are leased from ILFC, with deliveries made in late 1995 and in 1996 for use on regional services. There are plans to acquire longer-range types for Asian routes.

Routes

Bangkok, Beijing, Haikou, Kaoshiung, Qingdao, Shanghai, Taipei, Wuhan, Xiamen.

Fleet	Ordered
2 Airbus A320 2 Airbus A321	2 Airbus A321

Photograph: Boeing 747-200 5R-MFT (Xaver Flocki collection)

AIR MADAGASCAR

31 Avenue de l'Independence, BP 437,
Antanaraivo, Republic of Madagascar
Tel. 22222 Fax. 25728

Three letter code	IATA No.	ICAO Callsign
MDG	258	Madair

Air Madagascar was founded in 1961, a year after the state became independent. It was set up by the Government (51%), Air France (40%) and a predecessor company of the same name which had been in existence since 1947. Prior to 1st January 1962 it had been known as Madair. The first service was inaugurated on 20th October 1961 between Tananarive and Paris with a Douglas DC-7C operated on the airline's behalf by the French carrier Transports Aériens Intercontinentaux (TAI). Air France's involvement in the airline was to bring in the domestic flights it had previously provided along with the corresponding aircraft. The first international route was via Djibouti and Marseille to Paris, on which Boeing 707s were employed. Over the next few years an extensive internal network was established to many points in Madagascar and to the African mainland. Further aircraft used in those early years were DC-3s and DC-4s. In 1979 the Boeing 747-200SCD, its first and only widebody aircraft, was added to the fleet. With the acquisition of a Boeing 737-300 in 1995 the regional network was extended, and the airline now flies to several destinations in southern Africa.

Routes

Djibouti, Kenya, Mauritius, Munich, Paris, Réunion, South Africa and to over 20 internal destinations.

Fleet

2 Boeing 737-200
1 Boeing 737-300
1 Boeing 747-200
4 De Havilland DHC-6
2 HS.748

Photograph: Boeing 737-300 7Q-YKP (Author's collection)

AIR MALAWI

Robins Road, P.O. Box 84 Blantyre,
Malawi
Tel. 265-620811

Three letter code	IATA No.	ICAO Callsign
AML	167	Malawi

Air Malawi was founded in 1964 by the government of the new state upon achieving independence from Great Britain. Central African Airways was responsible for the operation of flights with the Douglas DC-3 and the management of the airline until 1967, when Air Malawi became self-sufficient. Regional routes were served with the Vickers Viscount, and the first jet equipment was the BAC One-Eleven with which routes from Blantyre to Salisbury (now Harare), Johannesburg and Nairobi were flown. A Vickers VC-10 was introduced on 3rd December 1974 for the London service. HS.748s, Britten-Norman Islanders and Short Skyvans were used for shorter range services until the early 1990s when more modern aircraft found their way into the fleet of the small national carrier. There is close co-operation with Air Tanzania. The main base is Blantyre-Chileka, where overhaul work is also carried out for other operators.

Routes

Domestic service to Lilongwe, Mangochi and Mzuzu. Internationally to Beira, Harare, Capetown, Dar-es-Salaam, Durban, Johannesburg, Lusaka, Nairobi and Windhoek.

Fleet

1 ATR42
1 Boeing 737-300
1 Dornier Do 228

Photograph: Airbus A300B4 9M-MHD (Alexander Allwelt/Male)

AIR MALDIVES

P.O. Box 2049 Male,
Maldives
Tel. 322438 Fax.: 325056

Three letter code	IATA No.	ICAO Callsign
AMI	900	Air Maldives

The original Air Maldives was formed in 1974 and began operations in October of that year. The airline served as the flag carrier for the Maldives until May 1977, providing services between Male and Colombo, Sri Lanka with a Convair 440 from the Sri Lankan Air Force, and also covering the internal route to Gan. The airline abruptly halted its Convair operations in 1977, and was succeeded in September 1977 as national flag carriers by Maldives International Airlines, operating between Male and Trivandrum (India) via Colombo from 2nd November 1977. The company had a technical and management agreement with Indian Airlines whose Boeing 737s were used on that service. The arrangement did not last and the new national carrier Maldives Airlines was set up by the Government in 1984 with three DC-8s and three Fokker F27s but it was dissolved in 1986. Air Maldives, operated by the National Travel Bureau, once again launched an air service between Male and Gan via Kaddu Island in South Maldives using a Skyvan. In late 1989 further re-organisation was successfully completed and two new Dornier 228s were added to the fleet. The first large aircraft is an Airbus A300 leased from Malaysian, which ties in with a participation from autumn 1994 of Malaysian Helicopter (which also has holdings in Malaysian Airways and World Airways). An A320 has also been used on long lease from Adria. Increasing tourism has led to the introduction of services to Dubai, Frankfurt and Zurich, and further expansion is envisaged by the year 2000.

Routes

Regular schedules to Colombo, Dubai, Gan, Frankfurt, Kuala Lumpur, Male, Trivandrum, Zurich.

Fleet

1 Airbus A320
1 Airbus A300B4
2 Dornier Do 228
1 De Havilland DHC-8-200

Ordered

1 De Havilland DHC-8-200

Photograph: Avro RJ 70 9H-ACM (Uwe Gleisberg/Munich FJS)

AIR MALTA

Luqa Airport
Republic of Malta
Tel. 662211 Fax. 234149

Three letter code	IATA No.	ICAO Callsign
AMC	643	Air Malta

Air Malta is the national airline of the island republic of Malta, and has been in existence since 30th March 1973, when it was set up by order of the government. The first service was Malta-Rome, from 1st April 1973. Air Malta used only jet aircraft from the beginning. Services were initially flown with leased British Airways Tridents, followed on 1st April 1974 by independent operations. Its network of routes was consolidated and there were regular flights, including charter flights, to London, Amsterdam, Paris, Zürich, Munich, Cairo and Tripoli. Boeing 720s were used, with the addition of Boeing 737-200s from 1978 onwards; these later replaced the 720s. With the introduction of the Airbus A320 in Spring 1990, Air Malta also adopted a new colour scheme for its fleet. With the introduction of the Avro RJ 70 from September 1994, Air Malta has in service its latest modern aircraft type for short and middle-range routes. There is a co-operation agreement signed in August 1995 with Balkan Bulgarian for a proposed joint service to New York.

Routes

Scheduled and charter flights to about 40 European destinations including several UK airports, Frankfurt, Munich and Rome; the Middle East and North Africa.

Fleet

3 Airbus A320-200
4 Avro RJ 70
3 Boeing 737-200
3 Boeing 737-300

Photograph: Dornier Do 228 V7-9206 (Author's collection)

AIR MARSHALL ISLANDS

P.O. Box 1319 Majuro 96960,
Republic of the Marshall Islands
Tel. 6253731 Fax. 6253730

Three letter code	IATA No.	ICAO Callsign
MRS	778	Marshallislands

In 1980 an independent state airline was established with the purpose of creating better air connections between the individual islands of the state territory and the main island of Majuro. It was known as the Airline of the Marshall Islands. The current name was adopted in 1989. The first flights were with GAF-Nomads, but these were augmented in 1982 by a single BAe 748. The most important route is from Majuro to Kwajalein, where an American missile base and air force base is located. A leased DC-8-62 has been used recently to open up a tourist infrastructure; the intention is primarily to bring tourists from the USA to the country. The GAF-Nomads were replaced by Dornier 228s delivered in 1984 and 1985. With the delivery of the first of two fifty-seater Saab 2000s in the middle of 1995 came the introduction of a new generation of regional airliners, which will over time replace the older aircraft in the fleet.

Routes

In the Pacific area, to more than 20 atolls which form part of the state, to Honolulu, Kiribati, Kwajalein, Los Angeles and Tuvalu.

Fleet

1 BAe HS.748
2 Dornier Do 228
2 Saab 2000

Photograph: ATR42 F-WWEA (Author's collection)

AIR MAURITANIE

B.P.41, Nouakchott 174,
Islamic Republic of Mauritania
Tel. 522211 Fax. 53815

Three letter code	IATA No.	ICAO Callsign
MRT	174	Air Mauritania

Air Mauritania was established in September 1962 to take over and expand the small internal network previously provided by Air France and UAT. Operations started in October 1963 with technical assistance and equipment from Spantax and the airline quickly built up its services, particularly in the important agricultural areas in the southern part of the country using Fokker F27s. By the mid-1980's, international services were operated to Dakar and Las Palmas in addition to an extensive domestic network. The airline was owned by the government (60%), Air Afrique (20%) and UTA (20%). Two Fokker F28s have been in use since 1983, and these were renewed in late 1996 with the delivery of two ATR42s. Services to Gran Canaria are operated in partnership with Iberia.

Routes

Aioun Atrouss, Atar, Banjul, Casablanca, Dakar, Gran Canaria, Kaedi, Kiffa, Nouadhibou, Nouakchott, Selibaby, Tidjikja, Zouerate.

Fleet

2 ATR42
2 Fokker F28

Photograph: Boeing 767-200ER 3B-NAL (Andrè Dietzel/Munich FJS)

AIR MAURITIUS

Rogers House 5, President John Kennedy Street, Port Louis, Mauritius
Tel. 2087700 Fax. 2088331

Three letter code	IATA No.	ICAO Callsign
MAU	239	Airmauritius

Air Mauritius was set up on 14th June 1967 although between that date and 1972 its activities were limited to the handling of aircraft operating into and out of Mauritius. It had been formed with the Government having a 51% stake as well as holdings by British Airways and Air France. Air India also became involved. It was August 1972 when operations finally started when a Piper Navajo was leased for a flight from Port Louis to the island of Rodrigues, around 600 km away from the main island. In 1973, a connection to Bombay was set up with the co-operation of Air India and the use of its aircraft. The same procedure was used with flights to London and with Air France to Paris. Only on 31st October 1977 did Air Mauritius obtain a Boeing in its own colours. For a number of years Air Mauritius used Twin Otters on domestic services and a Boeing 707, leased from British Airways, for long-haul flights. In April 1978, Rome was included in its network, and in 1981 Durban, Johannesburg, Nairobi and Antananarivo followed, with Jeddah and Zürich in 1983. A Boeing 747SP was leased from SAA in 1984 in order to be able to provide non-stop flights to Paris. In 1987 Munich and Singapore were included as destinations. The flights to Munich and also more recently to Frankfurt now take place several times a week. The Boeing 707s were replaced by two new Boeing 767s in 1988, with a third added in 1996. The latest type in the fleet is the long-range Airbus A340, the first of six being delivered in mid-1994 These are maintained by Lufthansa with whom there is also a commercial co-operation agreement. For the shorter routes, the first of two ATR42s was delivered at the end of 1986, and there are now two more on order for delivery in mid-1997.

Routes

Antananarivo, Bombay, Brussels, Durban, Frankfurt, Geneva, Harare, Hong Kong, Johannesburg, Kuala Lumpur, London, Madagascar, Manchester, Munich, Nairobi, Paris, Perth, Réunion, Rome, Singapore, Vienna, Zürich.

Fleet	Ordered
2 ATR42 4 Airbus A340-300 2 Boeing 767-200ER 1 Boeing 767-300ER	2 Airbus A340-300 2 ATR42

Photograph: Tupolev Tu-154B ER 85565 (Uwe Gleisberg/Munich FJS)

AIR MOLDOVA

Airport, 277026 Kishinev,
Republic of Moldova
Tel. 0422-524064 Fax. 0422-524040

Three letter code	IATA No.	ICAO Callsign
MLD	572	Air Moldova

The former Soviet republic of Moldavia, bordering on Romania, declared its independence in 1992 and insisted on having its own airline. As early as May 1992 it opened a regular service from Kishinev to Frankfurt. Tupolev 134As and Tu-154s were brought into the fleet, supplemented by Antonov An-24s for regional services. There are occasional charter flights to other destinations in Western Europe such as Munich and Zürich. The airline is also active in the airfreight business, for which Antonov 26s are employed.

Routes

Bucharest, Donetsk, Ekaterinburg, Frankfurt, Krasnodar, Kishinev, Mineralnye Vody, Minsk, Moscow, Murmansk, Samara, Sochi, St Petersburg, Tbilisi and Volgograd.

Fleet

10 Antonov An-24/26
11 Tupolev Tu-134A
7 Tupolev Tu-154B

Photograph: Beechcraft 1900C V5-MMN (Author's collection)

AIR NAMIBIA

P.O. Box 731, Windhoek 9100,
Namibia
Tel. 061-223019 Fax. 061-221910

Three letter code	IATA No.	ICAO Callsign
NMB	186	Namibair

Although the airline was set up as early as 1947 it was only after Namibia, the former South-West Africa, became independent that Air Namibia appeared as Namibia's national carrier. After it was formed as South West Air Transport, regular flights from Windhoek to Swakopmuk began with DC-3s in 1948. Oryx Aviation was taken over in 1959 and the name changed to Suidwes Lugdiens. There was a further takeover at the end of the 60s, the charter airline Namibair Pty Limited. The name of this airline was adopted in 1978 as the airline provided a number of scheduled domestic feeder services to connect with SAA flights at Windhoek. It became the national airline in 1987. On 24th April 1990, Namib Air started regular services to Frankfurt with a Boeing 747SP. The new name was adopted by Air Namibia in the course of 1993. On 6th July 1992 Air Namibia launched a weekly Boeing 747SP service between Windhoek and Heathrow via Johannesburg in competition with SAA and British Airways: flights have since been increased on the route. In 1993 a further Boeing 747SP was acquired from SAA. As well as international routes Air Namibia operates regional services in southern Africa, principally with the Beech 1900, of which three were introduced in the late 1980s, and a single Boeing 737 which entered service in mid-1991. The latest addition to the regional fleet is a single de Havilland Canada DHC-8 which was introduced in mid-1996; two more are on order.

Routes

From Windhoek to Capetown, Frankfurt, Johannesburg, Keetmanshoop, Lilongwe, London, Lüderitz, Luanda, Lusaka, Maun, Swakopmund, Tsumeb, Victoria Falls and Walvis Bay.

Fleet	Ordered
3 Beechcraft 1900	2 De Havilland DHC-8
1 Boeing 737-200Adv	
2 Boeing 747SP	
1 De Havilland DHC-8	

Photograph: Boeing 737-400 C2-RN10 (Author's collection)

AIR NAURU

Nauru International Airport,
Republic of Nauru
Tel. 3310 Fax. 7376

Three letter code	IATA No.	ICAO Callsign
RON	123	Air Nauru

Air Nauru was founded by the government of the Pacific island state in 1970, and inaugurated service on 14th February 1970 with a Dassault Mystère 20 to Brisbane. Further destinations were Honiara and in the following year Majuro, Marshall Islands and Tarawa on the Gilbert Islands. A Fokker F28 replaced the Mystère from 29th January 1972, and with this new routes to Japan and Guam were opened. Boeing 737s and 727s followed the Fokker F28 into service in 1976 and there followed further expansion until 1984 when there were four Boeing 737s and a Boeing 727 in use; however these were taken out of service in 1985. Further routes to Manila, Hong Kong, Auckland, Nadi and Taipei were taken over. Recession and absence of passengers meant that the network was limited by the end of the 1980s. A marketing alliance was made with Air New Zealand and Qantas and the airline shrank to serve only its profitable routes. In 1993 the remaining fleet was exchanged for a new and modern Boeing 737-400, which alone forms the fleet of of the flag carrier of this smallest of independent states. If needed, there is the possibility for aircraft to be rented from Air New Zealand.

Routes

Brisbane, Guam, Honiara, Manila, Melbourne, Nadi, Pohnpei, Suva, Sydney and Tarawa.

Fleet

1 Boeing 737-400

Photograph: Boeing 747-400 ZK-NBU (Uwe Gleisberg/Frankfurt)

AIR NEW ZEALAND

Private Bag 92007, Auckland 1020,
New Zealand
Tel. 9-3662400 Fax. 9-3662667

Three letter code	IATA No.	ICAO Callsign
ANZ	086	New Zealand

The present-day Air New Zealand goes back to 1939, when Tasman Empire Airways Ltd (TEAL) was formed as a joint British (20%), Australian (30%) and New Zealand (50%) company. Short S-30 flying boats were used for regular flights between Australia and Auckland. The flying boats were in use until 1954, and were then replaced by DC-6s. In 1961 the New Zealand Government assumed full control. TEAL entered the jet age in 1965 with the purchase of three DC-8s and in that year the name was changed to Air New Zealand. New routes to the USA were opened up, and the domestic airline NZNAC (formed in 1945) was taken over on 1st April 1978. Larger DC-10s and Boeing 747s were added to the DC-8s, and the last DC-8 left ANZ on 1st September 1989. Frankfurt, apart from London the sole European destination, was first served on 31st October 1987. The airline was privatised in 1988. Boeing 747-400s and Boeing 767-300s were added to the fleet in 1992, although some aircraft have been leased out. Regional services are operated for ANZ by wholly-owned subsidiaries Mount Cook Airlines, Eagle Aviation and Air Nelson. Qantas had a 19% stake in ANZ, which had been acquired in 1988, but this did not sit comfortably with ANZ's acquisition in 1995 of 50% of the capital of the Australian competitor airline Ansett, and so the Qantas stake was sold in the Spring of 1997.

Routes

Air New Zealand connects 19 internal airports. International flights to Australia, Bali, Bangkok, Frankfurt, Hong Kong, Honolulu, Kuala Lumpur, London, Los Angeles, Singapore and the Pacific area.

Fleet	Ordered
12 Boeing 737-200Adv	6 Boeing 737-700
5 Boeing 747-200	1 Boeing 747-400
6 Boeing 747-400	2 Boeing 767-300ER
5 Boeing 767-200ER	
7 Boeing 767-300ER	

Photograph: Airbus A310-300 P2-ANG (Uwe Gleisberg/Cairns)

AIR NIUGINI

Ang House, Jacksons Airport P.O.B. 7186,
7186 Boroko, Papua-New Guinea
Tel. 273200 Fax. 273482

Three letter code	IATA No.	ICAO Callsign
ANG	656	Niugini

Ansett, Qantas, TAA and the government of Papua New Guinea formed Air Niugini jointly in November 1973. With eight Fokker Friendships and twelve DC-3s, the new airline took over operations from Ansett and TAA on 1st November 1973, and carried these out in Australian administered New Guinea until independence. International flights to Sydney and Singapore started in 1975; the international network of flights was extended to Honolulu using Boeing 707s. When it was set up as the national airline of Papua New Guinea, the Government held 60% of the shares, Ansett 16%, Qantas 12% and TAA 12%. In 1976, the Government bought out the Qantas and TAA holdings and in 1980 acquired the Ansett shares to make the airline wholly Government owned. It became the national airline of Papua New Guinea upon the territory's independence from Australia on 16th September 1975. A leased Airbus A300 B4 – beautifully painted – replaced the Boeing 707s in 1984. The first airline-owned Airbus A310s were delivered to Air Niugini in early 1989. The de Havilland DHC-7s are used on internal routes only, but the mainstay of the fleet, the Fokker F28s, the first of which arrived in 1977, serve both domestic and international routes. Two de Havilland Canada DHC-8s are on order for 1997 delivery, also for domestic services.

Routes

Brisbane, Cairns, Hong Kong, Manila, Port Moresby, Port Vila, Singapore, Sydney. About 20 domestic destinations are served.

Fleet	Ordered
2 Airbus A310-300 2 De Havilland DHC-7 8 Fokker F28	2 De Havilland DHC-8-200

Photograph: De Havilland DHC-8-100 C-GANQ (Florian Morasch/Goose Bay)

AIR NOVA

Halifax International. Airport, Enfield,
Nova Scotia, B2T 1E4, Canada
Tel. 902 873 5000 Fax. 902 873 4901

Three letter code	IATA No.	ICAO Callsign
ARN	983	Nova

Three de Havilland DHC-8-100s were used by Air Nova when it started operations in the North-East of Canada in July 1986, having been founded in May 1986. The new airline was so successful in its early years that in addition to further DHC-8s it was also able to purchase BAe 146 jet aircraft. Air Nova is a partner of Air Canada and was one of the first airlines to enter into a relationship of this kind with Air Canada. It is now 100% owned by Air Canada, it feeds Air Canada flights at Halifax and flies to over twenty destinations in eastern Canada and the USA.

Routes

17 destinations including Bathurst, Blanc Sablon, Boston, Deer Lake, Gander, Goose Bay, Halifax, Montreal, Ottawa, Saint John.

Fleet

5 BAe 146-200
14 De Havilland DHC-8

Photograph: Boeing 737-300 DQ-FJD (Jörg Thiel/Brisbane)

AIR PACIFIC

P.O. Box 9266, Nadi Airport,
Fiji
Tel. 386444 Fax. 720512

Three letter code	IATA No.	ICAO Callsign
FJI	260	Pacific

Air Pacific, the flag carrier of Fiji, can trace its history back to 5th April 1947 when Katafanga Estates was formed. In July 1951, the company changed its name to Fiji Airways and operated its first services in September 1951, using de Havilland DH.89 Rapides. With the support of the Australian airline Qantas and in close co-operation with them, the network of routes was extended. In 1957, Qantas took over Fiji Airways as a subsidiary and subsequently opened international services on its behalf. In 1959, de Havilland Herons were added to the fleet, until in 1960 Air New Zealand and BOAC each took over a third of the company. The fleet was renewed in 1967 with HS.748s and Britten-Norman Trislanders. The first jet aircraft was introduced in March 1972, a BAC One-Eleven 400. As early as 1971 the name was changed to Air Pacific, and by 1972 the governments of Fiji, Kiribati, Tonga, Nauru and some private owners acquired a majority interest in the airline. By late 1978, the Fiji Government had purchased shares from Qantas, British Airways and Air New Zealand to control the majority holding. Embraer Bandeirantes were bought in 1980 for regional services. Increased demand in the passenger volume resulted in the purchase of two ATR42s in 1988, but these have been given up in favour of an all-jet fleet of Boeing 737s, 767s and 747s. One 737 is operated jointly with Royal Tongan on joint routes; three of the 'new-generation' 737-700 series have been ordered for delivery in late 1998 and 1999.

Routes

Auckland, Brisbane, Christchurch, Melbourne, Nadi, Suva, Sydney, Tokyo, Tonga, Vila and West-Samoa.

Fleet	Ordered
2 Boeing 737-300/500 1 Boeing 767-300ER 1 Boeing 747-200	3 Boeing 737-700

Photograph: Boeing 767-200ER S7-AAS (Josef Krauthäuser/Frankfurt)

AIR SEYCHELLES

P.O. Box 386,Victoria Mahe,
Seychelles
Tel. 225300 Fax. 225159

Three letter code	IATA No.	ICAO Callsign
SEY	061	Seychelles

In July 1979, the government of the Seychelles bought the two domestic airlines, Air Mahe (formed in 1972) and Inter Island Airways (formed in 1976), in order to form Air Seychelles as the national airline. The routes and aircraft were taken over. Pilatus Britten-Norman Islanders and Trislanders were used for connections with the individual islands. Tourism was heavily promoted, creating a demand for international services. On 1st November 1983, Air Seychelles began scheduled flights to both London and Frankfurt with a weekly DC-10 flight, operated using an aircraft chartered from British Caledonian Airways. In November 1985, Air Seychelles took over an Airbus A300 B4 from Air France, using it for charter flights to Amsterdam, Rome and Frankfurt. In 1989, Boeing 707s replaced the Airbus temporarily until the arrival of the first Boeing 767-200. A Boeing 757-200 was added in 1993, but the need for extra capacity resulted in its exchange for a larger Boeing 767-300 at the end of 1996. The inter-island flights are now served by de Havilland Twin Otters.

Routes

Praslin Island, Bird Island, Denis Island, Frégate Island, Amsterdam, Paris, Rome, London, Frankfurt, Singapore, Bahrain, Nairobi and Zürich.

Fleet

1 Boeing 767-200ER
1 Boeing 767-300ER
4 De Havilland DHC-6 Twin Otter
1 Pilatus BN-Islander

Photograph: Boeing 737-200Adv SU-GAN (Josef Krauthäuser/Frankfurt)

AIR SINAI

12 Kasr el Nil Street, Cairo,
Egypt
Tel. 2-760498 Fax. 2-574711

Three letter code	IATA No.	ICAO Callsign
ASD	903	Air Sinai

Formed in early 1982, Air Sinai started a regular service to Tel Aviv, the same month as Israel completed the final phase of its negotiated return of the Sinai to Egypt. Air Sinai succeeded Nefertiti Aviation as Egypt's flag carrier on the Cairo to Tel Aviv route using Boeing 737s leased from Egyptair. Connections followed to Eilat, Sharm el Sheik, Hurgada, Santa Katharina, in other words, principally to tourist destinations. Fokker F27s were used on domestic services. Air Sinai provides not only scheduled flights but also charter services, e.g. on behalf of Egypt Air and pilgrimage flights for instance to Jeddah. The airline is a subsidiary of Egyptair.

Routes

Al Arish, Hurgada, Mesa Matruh, Ras An Nayb, Sharm el Sheik, Tel Aviv are served from Cairo as schedules.

Fleet

1 Boeing 737-200Adv

Photograph: Boeing 737-200 N159PL (Josef Krauthäuser/Jacksonville)

AIR SOUTH

1500 St Julian Suite 400, Columbia,
South Carolina 29004, USA
Tel. 803-8220502 Fax. 803-8220303

Three letter code	IATA No.	ICAO Callsign
KKB	399	Khaki Blue

This 'low-cost/low-fare' operator was founded in Columbia, South Carolina, and began service on 23rd August 1994 with two leased Boeing 737-200s connecting Atlanta, Miami and St Petersburg. The airline was closely modelled on the successful Southwest Airlines and copied Southwest in many respects – quick turnarounds, multiple daily frequencies to the destinations, no on-board meal service except for drinks and peanuts, and rock-bottom prices. Very quickly new destinations in Florida and on the US east coast were added and further Boeing 737s were added in 1995. Further expansion needed to be slowly and solidly financed. A new investor was found in 1996 though this came in the course of a consolidation of routes and a re-organisation. There is a marketing alliance with Kiwi International Airlines, and as well as schedules, Air South operates *ad hoc* and charter flights. The main base and principal hub is Atlanta-Hartsfield International Airport.

Routes

Atlanta, Columbia, Myrtle Beach, Jacksonville, Raleigh-Durham, Tampa.

Fleet

7 Boeing 737-200

Photograph: ATR42 F-ODUE (Frank Litaudon/Rangiroa)

AIR TAHITI

BP 314 Boulevard Pomare,
Papeete, Tahiti
Tel. 864000 Fax. 864069

Three letter code	IATA No.	ICAO Callsign
VTA	135	Air Tahiti

Air Tahiti, which is partly in private ownership, was formed in 1953 to improve the connections to the individual islands which make up this French province. At that time it was called RAI (Reseau Aérien Interinsulaire) as the Government of French Oceania took over the operations of a small private airline, Air Tahiti, dating from 1950. In 1958 RAI was taken over by the French airline TAI (later UTA). On 1st January 1970 the name was changed to Air Polynesie, after UTA acquired a 62% stake in the airline. Its standard aircraft for many years were Fokker Friendships and Britten-Norman Islanders, as well as Twin Otters. In January 1987, after UTA left, its name was changed to Air Tahiti. To express its independence, and when the ATR42 was introduced in that year, the aircraft were also given the present colours. In 1992 and 1993, the larger ATR72 was integrated into the fleet. A close association has been cultivated with Air France, which has a 7.5% shareholding in Air Tahiti.

Routes

Air Tahiti flies to 35 islands in the archipelago, for example Bora Bora, Hiva Oa, Huahine, Mangareva, Maupiti, Moorea, Nuku Hiva, Raiatea, Rurutu and Tubuai.

Fleet

5 ATR42
3 ATR72
1 Dornier 228-200

Photograph: Boeing 737-200Adv 5H-ATC (Jürgen Gleisberg/Kilimanjaro)

AIR TANZANIA

P.O. Box 543, Dar-es-Salaam,
Tanzania
Tel. 051-38300 Fax. 051-46545

Three letter code	IATA No.	ICAO Callsign
ATC	197	Tanzania

After the break-up of East African Airlines in January 1977, which had been run jointly by Kenya, Uganda and Tanzania, there were practically no air services remaining in Tanzania. Thus in March 1977 Air Tanzania was formed by the government. Fokker F27s and a Boeing 737 were used by Air Tanzania to start flights from Dar-es-Salaam. In 1978 and '79 a further Boeing 737 and a de Havilland Twin Otter, for regional services, were acquired. The departure points for international flights are Dar-es-Salaam and Kilimanjaro International Airport. A Boeing 767 was used for a short while during 1994/95, but this could not be fully utilised. In 1995 the Twin Otter was also taken out of service and the regional network reduced. The airline became a participant in the multi-national Air Alliance, which flies a Boeing 747SP, in 1995.

Routes

Dar-es-Salaam, Kilimanjaro, Bujumbura, Djibouti, Dubai, Entebbe, Harare, Kigali, Lusaka, Mahe, Muscat and Nairobi. About twenty domestic destinations are served.

Fleet

2 Boeing 737-200
3 Fokker F27

Photograph: Fokker F27 TT-AAK (B.I.Hengi collection/Geneva)

AIR TCHAD

27 Avenue du President Tombalbaye, BP 168,
N'Djamena, Chad
Tel. 235-515090

Three letter code	IATA No.	ICAO Callsign
HTT	95	Hotel Tango

Formed on 24th June 1966 as Compagnie Nationale Tchadienne by the Chad government (64% shareholding) and UTA, the new national airline began regional service with the indestructible DC-3 from Fort Lamy (nowadays N'Djamena). A Douglas DC-4 was used to fly via Algiers to Paris, thus creating a swift connection to the former French colony. The state of civil war in Chad, which more or less existed from 1975 onwards, hindered development of the route system, which could only start to be slowly built up following a 1992 peace accord between the conflicting factions. In spite of that a Fokker F27 was bought in 1983, and a further example was received by way of a gift from Libya, but was not registered in Chad. As a replacement for the elderly DC-3 came a de Havilland Canada DHC-6 Twin Otter. Following its takeover of UTA, Air France now has the shareholding in Air Tchad, and there is a co-operation arrangement.

Routes

Scheduled services are only operated domestically to Abecher, Moundou and Sarh; however, there is considerable charter and relief-work flying.

Fleet

1 De Havilland DHC-6 Twin Otter
1 Fokker F27

Photograph: Airbus A320-200 G-JANM (Uwe Gleisberg/Salzburg)

AIRTOURS INTERNATIONAL

Parkway Three, 300 Princess Road,
Manchester, M14 7QU, Great Britain
Tel. 161-2326600 Fax. 161-2326610

Three letter code	IATA No.	ICAO Callsign
AIH	727	Tourjet

Set up in Manchester in 1990 by Airtours, the well-known UK tour operator, to provide it with in-house flying. Flights started in March 1991 with three MD-83s based at Manchester and two others operating out of Birmingham and Stansted. The young airline expanded quickly and acquired three further MD-83s in late 1991 for the 1992 season. In 1993 Airtours bought Aspro Holidays of Cardiff and Aspro's airline, Inter European Airways (formed in 1987) merged into Airtours International on 31st October bringing two Airbus A320s to the fleet. For the 1994 season, the fleet was augmented with further A320s, and two Boeing 767-300s were added for long range services to holiday destinations in the USA, the Caribbean and Thailand. The arrival of the 767s also signalled the adoption of a new colour scheme. The MD-83s were dropped from the fleet from the 1996 summer season and replaced with further A320s. Airtours has a 50% holding in the Danish charter company Premiair, and in the first part of 1997 there was an exchange of A320s between the fleets in order to achieve engine commonality within each airline.

Routes

Charter flights from Manchester, Birmingham, Cardiff, London-Gatwick, Glasgow, Liverpool and Newcastle to the popular Mediterranean destinations; to the Caribbean, USA, Thailand and Australia. Winter charters to – amongst others – Geneva, Salzburg and Munich.

Fleet

10 Airbus A320
7 Boeing 757-200
3 Boeing 767-300 ER

Photograph: Lockheed L-1011 TriStar C-FTNB (Josef Krauthäuser/Amsterdam)

AIR TRANSAT

11600 Cargo Road A 1, Montreal Intl. Airport,
Mirabel, Quebec, J7N 1G9, Canada
Tel. 514-476-1011 Fax. 514-4761038

Three letter code	IATA No.	ICAO Callsign
TSC	649	Transat

Set up in December 1986, Air Transat has become one of Canada's largest charter airlines, after Nationair ceased operations in 1992. Operations started in early 1987 with Boeing 727-200s. Its base is Montreal (where the airline has its own maintenance facility), but Air Transat also serves Toronto, Quebec City and Vancouver. The airline obtained its first Lockheed L-1011 TriStar in late 1987 for flights to the Caribbean. During the summer Air Transat flies regularly to Europe. During 1996 Air Transat took on further TriStars from Air Canada and Cathay Pacific and Boeing 757s have also been steadily added to the fleet since 1992. New routes have been opened to Poland and Portugal. 1.75 million passengers were carried in 1996; Transat flies about a half of all Canada's transatlantic charters.

Routes

The Caribbean and Mexico, South and Central America, plus many cities in the Netherlands, UK, Ireland, Germany, France, Italy, Poland and Portugal.

Fleet

7 Boeing 757-200
12 Lockheed L-1011

Photograph: Boeing 757-200 G-OOOM (Jens Jüngling/Stuttgart)

AIR 2000

First Choice House, London Road, Crawley,
West Sussex, RH10 2GX, Great Britain
Tel. 1293-518966 Fax. 1293-588757

Three letter code	IATA No.	ICAO Callsign
AMM	91	Jetset

The airline was formed in 1986 by the tour operator Owners Abroad, one of the leading British companies, for the purpose of operating intensive charter services outside London. The densely populated region in the north seemed to be perfect and Manchester was selected as the base. Commercial operations commenced with two leased Boeing 757s on 11th April 1987. In 1988, two further Boeing 757s were obtained, one of which was based in Glasgow. Restrictive laws prevented the formation of a Canadian subsidiary (see Canada 3000). The first flights to Mombasa were in the winter season 1988/89, and after the 757s were re-equipped to the ETOPS standard there were also flights to Newark, Boston and Orlando. In October 1990, Air 2000 also received its scheduled air service licence for flights from the United Kingdom to Cyprus and services were finally launched in late 1993 from London Gatwick to Larnaca and Paphos. After regular additions to the fleet with Boeing 757s, the first two Airbus A320s came in April 1992. In 1995 Newcastle and Belfast were added to the operating bases, and from 1996 flights were offered from Dublin. In addition to intensive charter flights, Air 2000 is also involved in the wet-leasing business and leases its aircraft, primarily in winter, to Canada 3000. Air 2000 is now owned by First Choice Holidays and is one of the largest non-scheduled operators in Great Britain.

Routes

Schedules from Birmingham, Glasgow, London-Gatwick, Manchester to Larnaca and Paphos. Charter flights from ten British regional airports to popular Mediterranean destinations, to North Africa, Canada, Caribbean, Mexico, Kenya, Sri Lanka and Thailand. In winter charter flights to the Alpine skiing and holiday destinations.

Fleet

4 Airbus A320-200
13 Boeing 757-200ER

Photograph: Fokker F27 G-BVOB (Frank Schorr/London LHR)

AIR UK

Stansted House, London Stansted Airport,
Essex, CM24 1AE, Great Britain
Tel. 1279-660400 Fax. 1279-660330

Three letter code	IATA No.	ICAO Callsign
UKA	130	Ukay

British Island Airways (formed July 1976), Air Anglia (formed August 1970), Air Wales (formed July 1977) and Air Westward (formed 1976) merged on 16th January 1980 to form the new joint airline, Air UK. The networks of routes were combined and the aircraft fleet co-ordinated. The carrier was a subsidiary of British Air Transport Holdings, in which British and Commonwealth Shipping Group had a 90% shareholding. The merged airline operated scheduled services to twenty-one airports in Britain and to ten international points in mainland Europe. In 1980, inclusive tour flights were also operated but that side of the business was sold to newly-formed British Island Airways, which commenced operations on 1st April 1982. Subsequently, Air UK turned over some domestic routes to Manx Airlines, in which British and Commonwealth held a shareholding. Fokker F27s were the main type in Air UK's fleet and by the mid-1980s the airline was Britain's third largest. In 1987, KLM acquired a 14.9% stake in Air UK, later increased to 45%, and to 100% in mid-1997. Air UK mainly serves airports on the eastern side of Britain and its main international destination is Amsterdam, where it is now the largest foreign user. This activity has been further increased over the last two years, with Air UK taking over KLM's operations to UK airports such as Manchester and Birmingham, and a closer integration of services with KLM. As part of this arrangement further Fokker 100s have been acquired, partly through a swap with KLM of Boeing 737-400s previously operated by Air UK Leisure which had been formed as an autonomous sister charter airline started in 1987, but sold to Unijet who now operate the airline as Leisure International Airways.

Routes

Amsterdam, Aberdeen, Bergen, Birmingham, Brussels, Düsseldorf, Edinburgh, Florence, Frankfurt, Glasgow, Guernsey, Hamburg, Innsbruck, Jersey, Copenhagen, London, Madrid, Manchester, Munich, Newcastle, Nice, Paris, Southampton, Stavanger and Zürich.

Fleet

11 BAe 146-100/300
6 Fokker F27
9 Fokker 50
17 Fokker 100

Photograph: Boeing 737-400 VH-TJI (Björn Kannengiesser/Sydney)

AIR VANUATU

P.O. Box 148,
Port Vila, Republic of Vanuatu
Tel. 23838 Fax. 23250

Three letter code	IATA No.	ICAO Callsign
AVN	218	Air Van

Air Vanuatu was set up as the national airline of this Pacific republic by Ansett Transport Industries and the government in 1981. Ansett held 40% of the shares. Flights started in September 1981 from Vila to Australia, which is where 70% of the passengers come from, using a leased Boeing 737-200 of Polynesian Airlines. Apia in Western Samoa was also served from the start of operations. In November 1987 the government acquired the remaining shares from Ansett. The airline entered a close co-operation with Australian Airlines, receiving aircraft and maintenance support from the latter. In 1989 Auckland and Adelaide were included in the network of routes. When Australian Airlines was taken over by Qantas, it was decided to try to become self-sufficient, even though the sole Boeing 737 came from Qantas. There is close co-operation with Vanair, with joint connecting flights. Thus an Embraer Bandeirante was taken on in July 1995 for regional routes. The main base is Bauerfield Airport near Port Vila.

Routes

From Port Vila to Aniwa, Auckland, Brisbane, Craig Crove, Dillons Bay, Emae, Espiritu Santo, Ipota, Lamap, Lamen Bay, Longana, Melbourne, Nadi, Norsup, Noumea, Sara, Sydney, Valesdir.

Fleet

1 Boeing 737-400
1 Embraer EMB-110 Bandeirante

Photograph: Boeing 767-200 Z-WPE (Stephen Thompsen/London LGW)

AIR ZIMBABWE

P.O. Box AP 1, Harare Airport,
Harare, Zimbabwe
Tel. 4-575111 Fax. 4-575068

Three letter code	IATA No.	ICAO Callsign
AZW	168	Zimbabwe

Air Zimbabwe was established on 1st September 1967 as a statutory body controlled by a board responsible to the Ministry of Transport as Air Rhodesia following the dissolution of Central African Airways Corporation. CAA had served the three territories of Southern Rhodesia, Nyasaland and Northern Rhodesia for some twenty-one years. Due to the political situation it was only possible to fly domestic routes and to neighbouring South Africa until the present government took power and the airline was renamed Air Zimbabwe Rhodesia in 1978. In April 1980, the airline took its present name when the country attained independence and became the Republic of Zimbabwe. It used DC-3s, Vickers Viscounts and Boeing 707/720. It was only after 1980 that the present Air Zimbabwe developed into an airline with flights to neighbouring countries and to Europe. A low-cost 'Sky-Coach' service was operated between Harare, Bulawayo and Johannesburg. In 1983 it took over the cargo airline Affretair. The first Boeing 767s were delivered in 1989 and in 1995 two Fokker 50s were acquired for shorter-range routes.

Routes

Scheduled services from Harare to Athens, Australia, Frankfurt, London, Mauritius, Nairobi, South Africa. Also daily flights to the famous Victoria Falls.

Fleet

1 BAe 146-200
2 Boeing 707-300
3 Boeing 737-200
2 Boeing 767-200ER
2 Fokker 50

Photograph: Boeing 737-400 N779AS (Josef Krauthäuser/Seattle SEA)

ALASKA AIRLINES

P.O. Box 68900, Seattle, Washington 98168, USA
Tel.206-433-3200 Fax. 206-433-3379

Three letter code	IATA No.	ICAO Callsign
ASA	027	Alaska

Alaska Airlines traces its history back to the formation of McGhee Airways in 1932, which merged with Star Air Service in 1934. This airline then became Alaska Star Airlines in November 1943, after the airlines Pollack Flying Service, Mirow Air and Laverny Airways were taken over. These purchases placed more than 75% of the air traffic volume in Alaska under the airline's control. In 1944 the present name was adopted. In addition to scheduled services, Alaska Airlines was also particularly active in the charter business. During the time of the Berlin airlift, and later, during the Korean War, Alaska Airlines aircraft were in use. The first route from Alaska to Seattle was set up in 1951. In 1960 Convair 340s and DC-6s were acquired to replace the DC-3s previously used. On 1st February 1968, Alaska Airlines bought Cordova Airlines, and on 1st April of that year, Alaska Coastal Airlines. In allusion to the opening up of the large oilfields, the airline's first jet aircraft were also called 'golden nugget jets'. In 1970 charter flights from Fairbanks to Khabarovsk in the USSR were flown. In the early 1980s the colour scheme was altered: on the tail of the aircraft a smiling Eskimo appeared. Alaska Airlines became the first customer to order the new extended range MD-83 when it ordered nine aircraft in 1983. There were further purchases of airlines in 1987: Jet America and also Horizon Air which became a feeder operator for Alaska Airlines' services. The routes were extended to California and Mexico. In 1992 direct services to neighbouring Russia became possible. A service to Siberia was opened, with others following in 1994 and 1995. Headlines were made in 1996 when Alaska decided to order Boeing 737-400s instead of the MD-90s which had been on option. By 2000 it is expected that the fleet will be all-737.

Routes

From principal bases at Anchorage, Portland and Seattle to 37 cities in Alaska and the western USA, plus 4 destinations in Mexico and 4 in Russia.

Fleet	Ordered
10 Boeing 737-200Adv	12 Boeing 737-400
24 Boeing 737-400	
44 McDonnell Douglas MD-82/83	

Photograph: Airbus A321-100 I-BIXI (Albert Kuhbandner/London LHR)

ALITALIA

Viale Alessandro Marchetti 111,
00148 Rome, Italy
Tel. 65621 Fax. 65624733

Three letter code	IATA No.	ICAO Callsign
AZA	055	Alitalia

Alitalia (Aerolinee Italiane Internazionali) was founded on 16th September 1946. The Italian government, BEA and some Italian companies formed the company. Operations commenced on 5th May 1947 with Fiat 612s, SIAI Marchetti SM 95s and Lancastrians. In 1948, the first international flights, to Buenos Aires, took place. In 1950, DC-4s were acquired, and in 1953 Convair 340/440s and DC-6s. Its first jet aircraft was a DC-8 in 1960. The further development of Alitalia was preceded by its merger with LAI. Alitalia has been Italy's national airline since November 1957. Vickers Viscounts and Caravelles for short and medium-distance flights joined the fleet. The latter were replaced from August 1967 on by DC-9s.The first Boeing 747 was delivered on 13th May 1970, and the DC-10 in February 1973. In the late 1970s, Alitalia's aircraft orders caused something of a furore with the manufacturers, as Airbus A300s and DC-10s were also ordered in addition to Boeing 727s and 747s; some orders had to be cancelled, however. Since then, the tendency has become to standardise the fleet and the subsidiaries too. For its intercontinental flights Alitalia obtained 11 MD-11s from 1992 onwards, older DC-9s are being replaced with Airbus A321s, the first of which was delivered in March 1994. Another new type was the Boeing 767 in 1995. Following the integration of the subsidiary ATI in 1994, Alitalia is one of the largest European airlines, and it has a shareholding in the Hungarian national carrier, Malev, though this may have to be sold as a condition of the granting of further state aid. A separate operating division has been formed, Team Alitalia, which operates 767s, A321s, F70s, ATR42s and ATR72s, under different cost structures from the main airline.

Routes

Alitalia has a dense network of services worldwide. In Europe over 40 destinations are served.

Fleet

14 Airbus A300B4
17 Airbus A321-100
9 ATR42
4 ATR72
10 Boeing 747-200
6 Boeing 767-300
90 McDonnell Douglas MD-82
8 McDonnell Douglas MD-11

Ordered

3 Airbus A321-100

Photograph: Boeing 747-400 JA8098 (Albert Kuhbandner/Hong Kong)

ALL NIPPON AIRWAYS

3-2-5 Kasumigaseki, Chiyoda-ku, Tokyo 100, Japan
Tel. 3-35823035 Fax. 3-35923119

Three letter code	IATA No.	ICAO Callsign
ANA	205	All Nippon

All Nippon Airways is Japan's largest airline on the basis of the number of passengers carried; most are on domestic flights. Formed in December 1952 as Japan Helicopter and Aeroplane Transport Company, scheduled services began in 1953. It merged in 1958 with Far East Airlines to form All Nippon Airways. The most important route at that time was Tokyo-Osaka. The network of routes was continuously extended using Convair 340s and 440s. In July 1961, two new aircraft were introduced at the same time, the Fokker F27 and the Vickers Viscount 828. After taking over three regional airlines, Fujita in 1963, Central Japan in 1965 and Nagasaki Airlines in 1967, All Nippon grew extremely rapidly. A jet service with Boeing 727s was offered for the first time between Tokyo and Sapporo in 1964. In December 1973, the Lockheed TriStar became the first widebody aircraft to be used. The Boeing 747SR gave ANA – as it also did other Japanese airlines – a jumbo jet with particularly closely spaced seating, making it possible to carry around 500 passengers. The fleet was continually renewed, with Boeing 767s being employed from mid-1984 onwards and Airbus A320s in 1990, as well as Boeing 747-400s. International routes were opened up by ANA relatively late, from the mid-80s onwards. It launched its first scheduled international passenger service in March 1986 with flights to Guam. Services to the USA and Australia soon followed with Beijing added in 1987, Seoul in 1988 and approval to serve London from spring 1989. Fukuoka, Osaka and Tokyo are the main hubs for ANA. There is an impressive re-equipment programme in place for the next five years, included in which is the addition of the Boeing 777, and the retirement of the older 747s.

Routes

Domestic services to 35 points. International to Bangkok, Beijing, Brussels, Dalian, Guam, Frankfurt, Hong Kong, London, Los Angeles, Moscow, Paris, Rome, Seoul, Saipan, Stockholm, Sydney, Washington and Vienna.

Fleet

25 Airbus A320
7 Boeing 737-200Adv
25 Boeing 767-200
40 Boeing 767-300
20 Boeing 747-200/SR
18 Boeing 747-400
6 Boeing 777-200

Ordered

5 Airbus A340
7 Airbus A321
2 Boeing 767-300
22 Boeing 777
2 Boeing 747-400

Photograph: McDonnell Douglas MD-82 PJ-SEG (Josef Krauthäuser/Miami)

ALM

Hato Airport, Willemstad, Curacao,
Netherlands Antilles
Tel. 388888 Fax. 338300

Three letter code	IATA No.	ICAO Callsign
ALM	119	Antillean

Antilliaanse Luchtvaart Maatschappij NV, ALM Antillean Airlines for short, was set up in 1964 to replace KLM in the Caribbean whose West Indian Division had opened a service between Curacao and Aruba in January 1935. Flights started on 1st August 1964 on routes from Curacao with three Convair 340s. On 1st January 1969 96% of the shares in the airline were taken over by the government of the Netherlands Antilles. By 1971 three Douglas DC-9s were in service, acquired from KLM. Windward Island Airways International NV was bought in 1974, the rights to the routes and the aircraft also becoming the property of ALM. In October 1982 two MD-82s came from the makers and a third was leased from Continental in April 1988 and the early DC-9s were disposed of. In 1992 two de Havilland Canada DHC-8s were added to the fleet for the shorter routes. There are marketing and codeshare agreements with United and KLM (who have a 33.5% share in ALM since 1971).

Routes

From the main base at Curacao to Aruba, Atlanta, Bogota, Bonaire, Caracas, Kingston, Medellin, Miami, New York, Port-au-Prince, Port of Spain, Santo Domingo, San Juan and Valencia (Venezuela).

Fleet

3 McDonnell Douglas MD-82
2 De Havilland DHC-8-300

Photograph: Boeing 737-200Adv N808AL (Josef Krauthäuser/Phoenix)

ALOHA AIRLINES

P.O. Box 30028, Honolulu, Hawaii 96820, USA
Tel. 808-8364101 Fax. 808-8360303

Three letter code	IATA No.	ICAO Callsign
AAH	327	Aloha

Aloha Airlines was set up as Trans Pacific-Airlines Ltd on 9th June 1946 and non-scheduled operations began in July of that year. In the first three years of its existence it was a passenger and cargo charterer in the Hawaii islands. Its first aircraft was the DC-3, as with many airlines set up at that time. The first scheduled flights started on 6th June 1949. The airline changed its name to Aloha Airlines in 11th February 1959. Fairchild F27s replaced the DC-3s in June 1959 and in 1963 the larger Vickers Viscounts followed. Altogether, Aloha acquired three Viscounts and six F27s. Its first jet aircraft was also a British product – on 29th April 1966 Aloha started scheduled flights from Honolulu to Maui using BAC One-Elevens. A step towards standardising the fleet was taken with the purchase and delivery of the first Boeing 737s in 1969. Due to the short flight times between destinations the Boeing 737s have very high utilisation figures. In 1987, Aloha became privately owned. With the delivery of the first Boeing 737-400s in early 1993 a new colour scheme was introduced. Since then, only Boeing 737s have been in service and more than 4.7 million passengers have used Aloha Airlines' services. A sister company, Aloha Island Air operates DHC-6s and DHC-8s to smaller islands within the group, and there are marketing alliances with United and Canadian.

Routes

Hilo, Honolulu, Kohnhui, Kona, Lihue with frequent daily services.

Fleet

18 Boeing 737-200Adv
2 Boeing 737-300
2 Boeing 737-400

Photograph: Airbus A320-200 N961LF (Xaver Flocki collection)

AMERICA WEST AIRLINES

4000 East Sky Harbor Building, Phoenix,
Arizona 85034, USA
Tel. 6935732 Fax. 602-6935546

Three letter code	IATA No.	ICAO Callsign
AWE	401	Cactus

America West Airlines was only formed after deregulation and was regarded as one of the most dynamic airlines in the USA. Formed in February 1981, America West started flights from Phoenix on 1st August 1983. In addition to Phoenix, Las Vegas is another major hub. Within six years, the fleet grew from three Boeing 737s at the beginning to over 90 aircraft; with the new routes and destinations the number of employees also rose. They all have a stake in America West Airlines in the form of shares. Initially, as the name indicates, the airline only operated in the western United States, but as the years passed the network of routes was extended to all the states, as well as to Canada and Hawaii. This latter route was opened in November 1989 with Boeing 747s. In 1989 AWE carried over 13.4 million passengers. From 27th June 1991, America West flew under Chapter 11 bankruptcy protection with a reduced fleet, unprofitable routes were given up and a cost reduction programme introduced. This was successful, so that the carrier emerged from Chapter 11 protection in August 1994. The America West Express commuter service was launched in October 1992, with a code-sharing agreement with Mesa Airlines, serving Arizona, California, Colorado and New Mexico. Other associate operators under the America West Express banner are Desert Sun Aviation from Phoenix and Spokane with Fokker 70s and Canadair Regional Jets, Mountain West and Phoenix Airlines. Continental Airlines and Mesa Airlines both have shareholdings in America West, which introduced its new colour scheme in 1996. There are also codeshares with Aeromexico, Continental, Northwest and British Airways.

Routes

Over 90 destinations in 36 states of the USA, Canada and Mexico from main bases at Phoenix and Las Vegas and a minihub at Port Columbus, Ohio.

Fleet	Ordered
28 Airbus A320-200 14 Boeing 757-200 40 Boeing 737-300 20 Boeing 737-200Adv	25 Airbus A320

Photograph: Airbus A300-600 N34078 (Josef Krauthäuser/Miami)

AMERICAN AIRLINES

P.O. Box 619616, DFW International Airport,
Dallas, Texas 75261, USA
Tel. 817-9671234 Fax. 817-967 4318

Three letter code	IATA No.	ICAO Callsign
AAL	001	American

American Airlines came into being on 13th May 1934. Before the DC-3, created to the specifications of American, came into use, Curtiss Condors were mainly used. In 1945 AOA was taken over, an airline specialising in flights to Europe. In 1950 this airline was sold to PanAm and AA concentrated completely on the US market. American was one of America's aircraft manufacturers' most important partners in the period that followed: the DC-3, DC-7, Convair 240 and 990, Lockheed L-188 Electra as well as the DC-10 emerged from specifications and orders placed by American. The DC-7 was used from November 1953 to start the transcontinental non-stop service from New York to Los Angeles. Six years later American's first jet aircraft, the Boeing 707, took over this route. BAC One-Eleven 400s and Boeing 727s were further aircraft in the airline's extensive fleet. 1970 saw the beginning of the era of widebody aircraft when the Boeing 747 was taken into service, followed by DC-10s in August 1971. In that same year American took over Trans Caribbean Airways and has been operating a dense network since then in that area. After deregulation American grew even larger, taking over AirCal in 1987. Numerous routes were purchased from other airlines, preparing the way for an extensive expansion of the routes to the Far East, South America and Europe. In 1984 regional services were consolidated under the 'American Eagle' banner, and these operate extensive services from the major hubs. In 1996 nearly 80 million passengers were carried, and in November a 20-year 630 aircraft purchase plan from Boeing was announced. During 1997 close co-operation with British Airways was planned, which would create a powerful grouping, but this is still subject to government approvals.

Routes

Over 160 destinations worldwide and in the USA (over 250 with American Eagle operations included).

Fleet

35 Airbus A300-600
81 Boeing 727-200
90 Boeing 757-200
72 Boeing 767-200/300
75 Fokker 100
21 McDonnell Douglas DC-10-10/30
14 McDonnell Douglas MD-11
262 McDonnell Douglas MD-80

Ordered

75 Boeing 737-800
11 Boeing 757-200
4 Boeing 767
12 Boeing 777-200

Photograph: Boeing 727-200F N994AJ (Uwe Gleisberg/Miami)

AMERIJET INTERNATIONAL

498 SW 34th Street, Fort Lauderdale, FL 33315, USA
Tel. 305-3590077 Fax. 305-3597866

Three letter code	IATA No.	ICAO Callsign
AJT	810	Amerijet

Amerijet International was set up in 1974 and initially provided only cargo and express goods flights using Learjets and Cessna 401s. In 1985 the first three Boeing 727s were acquired, and further examples followed in 1988 and 1989. A combi version of this aircraft (Boeing 727-100C) was used when the airline moved into the passenger charter business as well as ambulance charters and cargo flights. Amerijet flies regular scheduled cargo flights for DHL and Burlington, both cargo specialists. In 1993 scheduled flights started to Guyana. As the market for medium range freight aircraft has become thin, in 1996 five former PanAm Boeing 727s, which had been stored for years in the Mojave Desert, were bought. Some were taken into service with the airline after extensive overhaul, at the Miami base; others serve as spares sources.

Routes

Antigua, Barbados, Cancun, Dominica, Grenada, Guyana, Mérida, Mexico City, Port of Spain, St Kitts, St Lucia, St Maarten, St Vincent.

Fleet

13 Boeing 727-100/200 C/F
2 Cessna 410/501
1 Dassault Falcon 20F

Photograph: Boeing 737-300 VH-CZL (Jörg Thiel/Sydney)

ANSETT AUSTRALIA

501 Swanston Street, Melbourne,Victoria 3000, Australia
Tel. 3-6231211 Fax. 3-6231114

Three letter code	IATA No.	ICAO Callsign
AAA	090	Ansett

Reginald Ansett set up his company in 1931, starting with bus and lorry journeys in Victoria. ATI Ltd (Ansett Transport Industry) was then formed in 1936 as Ansett Airways, and the first flights were from Melbourne to Hamilton, using a Fokker Universal. Thus began the Ansett-Fokker connection which has been in existence for over fifty years. After buying up various small airlines, Ansett took over Australian National Airways (ANA) on 4th October 1957. Until 1969 the new airline flew under the logo Ansett-ANA. After the merger, aircraft such as the Vickers Viscount and the Lockheed L-188 Electra were used. The first jet aircraft was a Boeing 727, in use from November 1964. Ansett also acquired DC-9s, starting in 1967. In addition to Australia, Port Moresby, at that time in Australian-administered New Guinea, was a focal point of Ansett's activities. In 1981 Ansett ordered new aircraft such as Boeing 767s and 737s. The latest addition to the Ansett fleet is the Airbus A320, known as the Skystar, which came into service from 1988. Ansett today belongs to Air New Zealand and News Corporation and all activities are co-ordinated under the Ansett Holdings banner. The most important recent development has been the consolidation of the aviation activities, as a part of which the former independently-operated subsidiaries East-West Airlines, Ansett WA and Ansett Express have all been merged into the parent. Its first international services were started in 1993 to Bali and Hong Kong. For the latter service a Boeing 747-300 was used, carrying for the first time the new colours currently in use. Rights for other destinations in South East Asia are available; however expansion is being made cautiously. The principal bases are Sydney and Perth, where there are extensive maintenance facilities.

Routes

Extensive Australian network with about 50 destinations. Denpasar, Hong Kong, Jakarta, Kuala Lumpur, Osaka are the first international routes. Additionally there is a service to the Cocos and Christmas Island in the Indian Ocean.

Fleet

19 Airbus A320-200
13 Bae 146-200/300
3 Boeing 747-300
11 Boeing 767-200/300
22 Boeing 737-300
5 Fokker 50

Photograph: McDonnell Douglas DC-10-30 F-GGMZ (Andrè Dietzel/Munich FJS)

AOM - FRENCH AIRLINES

Stategic Orly 108, 13-15 rue du Pont Holles,
94526 Rungis Cedex, France
Tel. 1-49791000 Fax. 1-49791012

Three letter code	IATA No.	ICAO Callsign
AOM	646	French Lines

On 15th December 1988, Air Outre Mer was set up on the island of Réunion in the Indian Ocean. A service was planned to the French overseas provinces on the basis of scheduled-charter flights. Scheduled services with DC-10-30s began on 26th May 1990, initially with three weekly flights from Paris to St Denis de la Réunion. In the autumn of 1990, further DC-10-30s were added to the fleet. In addition, three Dornier 228s were purchased in November 1990 for a newly created domestic service on the island of Réunion. In late 1992, it was merged with the airline Minerve, partly taking over its aircraft. The new airline was re-structured and took on a new colour scheme and revised name. The airline is in intense competition with Air France and TAT ón domestic routes from Paris Orly.

Routes

To the overseas departement of Réunion, in the Caribbean and to over 70 other destinations in over 30 countries.

Fleet

14 McDonnell Douglas DC-10-30
10 McDonnell Douglas MD-83

Photograph: Embraer EMB-120 Brasilia N227AS (Oliver Krauthäuser/Gainesville)

ASA

100 Hartsfield Central Parkway, Suite 800
Atlanta, GA 30354, USA
Tel: 404-7661400 Fax. 404-2090162

Three letter code	IATA No.	ICAO Callsign
ASE	862	Asea

ASA Atlantic Southeast Airlines was founded in March 1979 and started scheduled services in June of that year from Atlanta. De Havilland Canada DHC-7s, Embraer EMB.110 Bandeirantes, and Shorts 360s were all used in the early years. The airline was successful from the start and grew steadily, so that in 1981 over 150,000 passengers were carried to 20 destinations. In 1982 the company went to the market for an increase in share capitalisation, which also allowed the takeover on 1st April 1983 of Southeastern Airlines. Since 1984 there has been an important marketing alliance with Delta Airlines, with many of ASA's flights shown in the schedules as 'Delta Connection' operations. In 1985 the new Embraer 120 Brasilia came into service for the first time, replacing the older Shorts 360 stage by stage, and building up to an extensive fleet. Larger aircraft in the shape of the ATR72 were received by ASA from 1993, and the first jet was the 80-seat BAe 146-200 which has strengthened the fleet since 1995. The trend towards jets, with their greater apparent passenger appeal, has continued, with the 1997 introduction of the Canadair Regional Jet 200ER; this type will slowly replace the Brasilias. The numerous routes are centred on the major Delta hubs of Dallas/Fort Worth and Atlanta, where are located also the company's extensive maintenance facilities.

Routes

From principal hubs at Atlanta and Dallas/Fort Worth to Albany, Abilene, Amarillo, Ashville, Chattanooga, Columbus, Corpus Christi, Evansville, Fayetteville, Gainesville, Greensboro, Huntsville, Jacksonville, Louisville, Mobile, Montgomery, Nashville, Oklahoma City, Pensacola, Texarkana, Tulsa and Waco.

Fleet	Ordered
12 ATR42	25 Canadair Regional Jet 200ER
5 BAe 146-200	
5 Canadair Regional Jet 200ER	
62 Embraer EMB-120 Brasilia	

Photograph: Boeing 727-100 YA-FAU (Author's collection)

ARIANA AFGHAN

P.O. Box 76, Ansari Watt,
Kabul,
Afghanistan

Three letter code	IATA No.	ICAO Callsign
AFG	255	Ariana

Ariana Afghan Airlines Co Ltd was set up on 27th January 1955 as a new national airline. The Indian company Indama Corp. provided the first DC-3 aircraft and held 49% of the shares. These were taken over in 1956 by Pan American World Airways, which considerably expanded the airline. International routes to Delhi and Beirut were set up rapidly, and the Beirut route was extended via Ankara and Prague to Frankfurt. They used DC-4s and later DC-6s. London Gatwick was served by a DC-6. In 1963 its operational base was moved to Kabul from Kandahar, 1967 saw Bakhtar Afghan Airlines formed to begin taking over Ariana's domestic services. In 1968 Ariana obtained its first jet aircraft, a Boeing 727, followed by a DC-10-30 in September 1979. After the invasion by Soviet troops over Christmas 1979, flights collapsed, the DC-10 was sold after being hit by a rocket and Soviet aircraft were added to the fleet. All operations were integrated into Bakhtar on 23rd October 1985 which became the new national carrier. However, by February 1988 it had changed back to its present title. During the ten years of the war, there were only flights to Moscow and Prague, and at times to Berlin-Schönefeld, primarily in order to transport the injured. Flights are only expected to normalise again gradually, as the political situation following the Russian pull-out and the ensuing civil war is still unstable. As a safety precaution, Ariana operates its aircraft principally from Delhi in India.

Routes

Amritsar, Delhi, Dubai, Kabul, Moscow, Prague and Tashkent.

Fleet

2 Boeing 727-100
3 Boeing 727-200
3 Antonov An-26/24
1 Tupolev Tu-154M
1 Yakovlev Yak-40

Photograph: Tupolev Tu-134A EK-6504 (Christian Dougett/Athens)

ARMENIAN AIRLINES

Zvartnots Airport, 375042 Yerevan, Armenia
Tel. 885-2775920 Fax. 885-2151123

Three letter code	IATA No.	ICAO Callsign
RME	956	Armenian

In 1993 the government of this new republic took the initiative and took over the former Aeroflot Directorate in Armenia. The former Soviet republic, where business was once thriving, was at war with the neighbouring republic of Azerbaijan over the Nagorny-Karabakh enclave, as a result of which the delivery of raw materials and energy from this country were cut off. Armenia was dependent on these supplies, and since the start of hostilities business and living conditions had declined. Accordingly the development of air services was to be laborious. Even though the Aeroflot Directorate had carried a meagre two million passengers, the new airline could only manage a third of that. However the airline flies profitably as there are countless expatriate Armenians who use the flights regularly. These should also provide the necessary capital for a privatisation planned for the future. Agreements have been signed with KLM and Air France which should help the airline to develop, especially as the capital, Yerevan, is an attractive tourist city. The Yak-40s are flown by sister company Ararat.

Routes

Adler, Amsterdam, Ashkhabad, Athens, Beirut, Dubai, Ekaterinburg, Kharkov, Minsk, Moscow, Odessa, Paris, Rostov, Simferopol, Teheran, Volgograd.

Fleet

2 Ilyushin IL-86
9 Tupolev Tu-134
10 Tupolev Tu-154
9 Yakovlev Yak-40

Photograph: Lockheed L-1011F TriStar N3066B (Josef Krauthäuser collection)

ARROW AIR

P.O. Box 026062, Miami-Airport,
Fl 33126, USA
Tel. 305-5260900 Fax. 305-5260933

Three letter code	IATA No.	ICAO Callsign
APW	404	Big A

Arrow Airways was set up as a charter airline in late 1946 and was active as an airline until 1954. Only in 1980 was the airline reactivated by its founder George Batchelor, and it started cargo charters on 26th May 1981. A number of DC-8s were acquired for long range charters, contract services for the Military Airlift Command and later for passenger flights. July 1982 saw the first scheduled flight from Los Angeles to Montego Bay. On 18th December 1982 Arrow also flew from Tampa to London. Arrow Airways became Arrow Air in early 1983 and two DC-10s were acquired but were returned due to a cutback in operations. Reorganisation in 1984 resulted in domestic American flights being suspended; on the other hand, some routes to South America were opened. Finally, in 1985, Arrow Air withdrew completely from passenger flights. On 11th February 1986 Arrow Air filed for bankruptcy although charter cargo flights subsequently re-started using the DC-8Fs. Arrow Air made a comeback as a passenger charter airline with Boeing 727s in 1993. Another temporary setback came in the Spring of 1995 when an FAA purge against other operators also grounded Arrow Air on 'safety grounds'. However, the necessary certification and proofs were quickly completed and the airline was able to start up again after just a few weeks, now with a freighter-conversion Lockheed TriStar. This replaced several DC-8s and the Boeing 727s no longer in the slimmed-down fleet.

Routes

Asuncion, Atlanta, Bogota, Caracas, Costa Rica, Guayaquil, Miami, New York, Panama, Quito, San Juan and worldwide charter flights.

Fleet

5 McDonnell Douglas DC-8-62 F
3 McDonnell Douglas DC-8-63 F
3 Lockheed L-1011F

Photograph: Boeing 747-400 HL7415 (Author's collection/Hong Kong)

ASIANA

1 ka Hoehuyn-Dong, Chung Ku, Seoul 100052,
Republic of Korea
Tel. 02-7588114 Fax. 02-7588008

Three letter code	IATA No.	ICAO Callsign
AAR	988	Asiana

The economic boom in South Korea and recently the great mobility of the Koreans led to the formation of this airline. It was originally formed by the Kumho Industrial Group as Seoul Air International and started operations in December 1988, initially only on domestic routes in South Korea. This restriction was soon lifted and international routes opened in 1989, first of all to Fukuoka in neighbouring Japan. Nagoya and Tokyo followed swiftly as well as other Korean domestic destinations; these were served with ten Boeing 737-400s. In 1990 the rights to the routes to Hong Kong and Bangkok were added, as was a new aircraft type, the Boeing 767. New routes to Los Angeles, San Francisco and New York followed in 1992, with the introduction of the Boeing 747-400, and in December 1994 the first all-cargo jumbo, the Boeing 747-400F was introduced. The investments have been colossal, and for the decade beginning 1996 about 60 new aircraft, from Airbus as well as from Boeing are on order or on option, with deliveries commencing in 1998. The leap to Europe was taken in 1995 with service to Brussels, with London following at the end of 1996, and Frankfurt in 1997. Asiana's main base is at Seoul's Kimpo Airport. There are codeshare arrangements with Northwest and Qantas and other co-operation with Air China, China Eastern and Turkish Airlines.

Routes

Bangkok, Beijing, Brussels, Cairns, Detroit, Fukuoka, Guam, Hiroshima, Ho Chi Minh-City, Hong Kong, Honolulu, Khabarovsk, Los Angeles, Macau, Manila, Matsuyama, Nagoya, New York, Okinawa, Osaka, Saipan, San Francisco, Seattle, Sendai, Shanghai, Singapore, Sydney, Takamatsu, Tokyo, Toyama, Vienna and 11 domestic destinations.

Fleet

18 Boeing 737-400
6 Boeing 737-500
16 Boeing 767-300
11 Boeing 747-400/-400F

Ordered

18 Airbus A321-200
3 Boeing 737-400
3 Boeing 767-300
6 Boeing 747-400
15 Boeing 777

Photograph: Boeing 727-200 N1280E (Josef Krauthäuser/Fort Lauderdale)

ATA - AMERICAN TRANS AIR

P.O. Box 51609, Indianapolis,
Indiana 46251, USA
Tel. 317-2474000 Fax. 317-2434165

Three letter code	IATA No.	ICAO Callsign
AMT	366	Amtran

American Trans Air is the largest charter operator in the United States. It was founded in 1973 in Indianapolis, Indiana and started flying for Ambassadair Travel Club with a Boeing 720. In 1981 a permit was received from the Federal Aviation Administration to operate as a charter airline. Further Boeing 707s were acquired, and in 1982 DC-10s and Boeing 727s followed. As there were no DC-10s available for acquisition on the worldwide airliner market, a switch was made to a fleet of Lockheed TriStars, and this type along with the 727 replaced the Boeing 707s. The older 727s were replaced from 1992 with Boeing 757s. A particularly vigorous expansion took place between 1993 and 1995, and a new, bright colour scheme was adopted, along with the change of name to ATA. In 1996 several scheduled services were abandoned and the fleet somewhat reduced.

Routes

Scheduled services from Chicago to Fort Meyers, Honolulu, Maui, San Francisco and in the Caribbean. Worldwide charter flights including to Europe, for instance to Frankfurt, Hamburg, Munich, and Zürich.

Fleet	Ordered
8 Boeing 757-200 24 Boeing 727-200Adv 15 Lockheed L-1011	2 Boeing 757-200

Photograph: Boeing 747-100F N3203Y (Albert Kuhbandner/Hong Kong)

ATLAS AIR

350 Indiana St Suite 640, Golden,
Colorado 80401 USA
Tel. 303-5265050

Three letter code	IATA No.	ICAO Callsign
GTI	369	Giant

In 1992 Atlas Air was formed in New York by Atlas Holding, a sister company of Aeronautics Leasing, as a freight-only carrier, and since then has grown rapidly, with a doubling of the fleet in 1995 alone. With a fleet of Boeing 747 freighters Atlas Air operates worldwide. Scheduled services fly from New York to Hong Kong via Anchorage and via Khabarovsk in Russia back to New York. As well as its own schedules Atlas Air flies scheduled freight charters for other well-known airlines, eg British Airways, China Airlines, Emirates, KLM, SAS and Varig, leasing them both crews and aircraft. In 1996 five Boeing 747s were taken over from Federal Express. However, there are few 747 freighters on the market, so pure passenger aircraft have been acquired and converted to freighters. Thus for instance the whole 747-200 fleet of Thai International has been taken on option and from 1997 onwards these will be converted and brought into service. By the end of 1997 it is expected that the airline will have 24 Boeing 747 freighters ready for service. An order was confirmed in June 1997 for ten new-build Boeing 747-400Fs with options on ten more, the first for delivery in 1998 and the rest between 1999 and 2001. Atlas Air's principal base is New York's JFK International Airport.

Routes

Scheduled, charter and *ad hoc* freight flights. Atlas Air also flies services for SAS, Lufthansa, China Airlines, KLM and other companies.

Fleet	Ordered
1 Boeing 747-100F 19 Boeing 747-200F	7 Boeing 747-200 (for freighter conversion) 10 Boeing 747-400F

Photograph: De Havilland DHC-8-300 D-BMUC (Josef Krauthäuser/Augsburg)

AUGSBURG AIRWAYS

Flughafenstr. 6, 86169 Augsburg,
Germany
Tel, 0821-270970 Fax. 0821-2709766

Three letter code	IATA No.	ICAO Callsign
AUB	614	Augsburg Air

Interot Air Service was employed from 1979 to maintain a regular charter service for members of the Haindl Paper Company and Interot Internationale Spedition. The company aircraft, a Beech 200 Super King Air was used. From 1985 this casual service was improved to become a scheduled service as required and the necessary licence was granted.
A second King Air was added from Autumn 1987, in order to serve Hamburg. The reaction to this service from Augsburg was good, so that in September 1988 a Beechcraft 1900 Airliner could be acquired, with a second following in May 1989. Interot obtained its licence as a scheduled service operator in December 1989 and this gave new perspectives for the future. A leased de Havilland Canada DHC-8 was put into service on the Düsseldorf route from October 1990 Three aircraft of this type were ordered firm, and the reunification of Germany brought with it new destinations, and a change of name to Interot Airways. After the opening of the new Munich Airport, Augsburg saw itself as an alternative to this, and new routes were opened to London and Cologne. From 1st January 1996 the name was changed again to Augsburg Airways, and the aircraft colour scheme changed. Effective from the Winter 1996 timetable, Augsburg Airways became a Lufthansa Partner and flies mainly from Munich on behalf of the national airline. The main base remains however at Augsburg airport.

Routes

Augsburg, Berlin, Dresden, Düsseldorf, Cologne, Leipzig, London City.

Fleet

1 Beechcraft 1900 Airliner
5 De Havilland DHC-8-100
3 De Havilland DHC-8-300

Photograph: McDonnell Douglas MD-83 LV-WGM (Björn Kannengiesser/Buenos Aires AEP)

AUSTRAL

Avenue L.N. Alem 134, 1001 Buenos Aires, Argentine
Tel. 1-3173600 Fax. 1-7784308

Three letter code	IATA No.	ICAO Callsign
AUT	143	Austral

Austral was formed in June 1971 from the merger of two private airlines, Austral Compania Argentina de Transportes Aereos and Aerotransportes Litoral Argentino (ALA). Both airlines were set up in 1957 and had already been working together since 1966, when Austral acquired 30% of the shares in ALA. Thus, for example, new aircraft such as the BAC One-Eleven or the NAMC-YS-11A were bought and technical services carried out jointly. Its first MD-81 was received in January 1981. Austral is today the second largest airline in Argentina and provides both scheduled and charter flights.

Austral is owned by Aerolineas Argentinas. A sister company Inter Austral flies regional services with two CASA CN235s. A further associate company is Patagonia Airlines, which flies freight only.

Routes

Buenos Aires, Bahia Blanca, Cordoba, Mar del Plata, Mendoza, Rosario, Tucuman, Montevideo, Rio Gallegos and Neuquen are the most important points in Austral's route network.

Fleet

2 CASA (IPTN) CN235-200
2 McDonnell Douglas MD-81
2 McDonnell Douglas MD-83
9 McDonnell Douglas DC-9-32

Photograph: Airbus A 321-100 OE-LBC (Albert Kuhbandner/Vienna)

AUSTRIAN AIRLINES

Postfach 50, 1107 Vienna,
Austria
Tel. 1-1766 Fax. 1-685505

Three letter code	IATA No.	ICAO Callsign
AUA	257	Austrian

Austrian Airlines was set up on 30th September 1957 through a merger of Air Austria and Austrian Airways, neither of which had commenced operations. With leased Vickers Viscounts belonging to the AUA partner Fred Olsen, AUA started flights on 31st March 1958 on the route Vienna-London. A short time later, scheduled services began to Frankfurt, Zürich, Paris, Stuttgart and Rome. In early February 1960, AUA bought its own Vickers Viscount 837s. In February 1963 the first Caravelle was brought into service. Domestic routes were still being served by the DC-3s, which were, however, replaced in 1966 by HS.748s. In 1969, the AUA was reorganised, with unprofitable routes and the entire domestic network being discontinued. With the introduction of the new Douglas DC-9 in June 1971 the airline was given a new colour scheme. Between April 1969 and March 1971 trans-Atlantic Boeing 707 schedules were operated in co-operation with Sabena. Attempts to make the transition to long-distance flights failed in 1973. From 1975 onwards, DC-9-51s were ordered, and the AUA was one of the launch customers for the MD-81. From 1988 on, the first MD-87s with extended range were added to the fleet. The third attempt to get involved in long-distance flights was successful in 1989, with the opening of schedules to Tokyo and New York. These use the Airbus A310, which the AUA obtained in 1989. In 1995 three new types were introduced to the fleet – the Fokker 70, Airbus A321 and A340 – and this also heralded the appearance of a new colour scheme for the aircraft. Four new Airbus A330s have been ordered for delivery from August 1998. Swissair owns 10% of AUA, and All Nippon 9%; in turn AUA owns 43% of Tyrolean and 36% of Lauda Air. There are codeshares with about 15 airlines.

Routes

New York, Tokyo, Moscow, Johannesburg; Austrian is strongly oriented towards services to Eastern Europe, but serves also important destinations in Western Europe, Scandinavia and the Middle East. Charter services operate to the Mediterranean area, Kenya, the Maldives and elsewhere.

Fleet		Ordered
4 Airbus A310-300	15 McDonnell Douglas MD-81/82/83	7 Airbus A320-200
3 Airbus A321-100	5 McDonnell Douglas MD-87	3 Airbus A321-100
2 Airbus A340-200		2 Airbus A340-200
4 Fokker 70		

Photograph: Boeing 727-200Adv YV-97C (Josef Krauthäuser/Miami)

AVENSA

Avda. Universidad Torre El Chorro Edif.29,
Piso 2/3 Aptdo 943, Caracas 101, Venezuela
Tel. 2-5623022 Fax. 2-5630225

Three letter code	IATA No.	ICAO Callsign
AVE	128	Ave

Aerovias Venezolanas SA – Avensa for short – was set up on 13th May 1943 by Pan American and a group of Venezuelan businessmen. Freight flights started in December 1943 with Ford Trimotors and Stinson Reliants ferrying much needed supplies to the growing oil industry in the Carteru part of the country; passenger services started in May 1944 with Lockheed 10As. After the Second World War, DC-3s were added to the fleet. In 1953, Convair 340s were ordered in 1953 in order to set up a connection to Miami in 1955. By 1960 Avensa had developed a substantial domestic route network plus a regional international system to Miami, New Orleans, Aruba and Jamaica. However in 1961, the then international services of Avensa and LAV (Aeropostal) were merged to form VIASA, in which Avensa had a 45% holding. The first jet aircraft, a Caravelle, was received in 1964, as was the larger Convair 580 turboprop. In 1976, Pan Am sold its 30% shareholding to the Venezuelan government. Boeing 727s were added to the fleet, and in 1989 a fleet renewal programme was initiated with the arrival of the first Boeing 757s and Boeing 737-300s. Financial difficulties led however to the disposal of these new types, and the backbone of the fleet is now a motley mixture of various models of the Boeing 727.

Routes

Regional and internal schedules to about 20 destinations in Venezuela and to Mexico-City, Panama City and Miami.

Fleet

11 Boeing 727
2 Boeing 737-200
5 McDonnell Douglas DC-9-31/51

Photograph: McDonnell Douglas DC-9-32 EC-CGP (Josef Krauthäuser collection)

AVIACO

Maudes 51, 28003 Madrid,
Spain
Tel. 1-5543600 Fax. 1-5334613

Three letter code	IATA No.	ICAO Callsign
AYC	110	Aviaco

Aviacion y Comercio SA, or Aviaco for short, was founded on 18th February 1948 by a group of Bilbao businessmen to operate all-cargo flights. Bristol 170 Freighters were used to transport agricultural produce from Spain to Northern Europe. As this business was not very profitable, they applied to run passenger flights. 1950 marked the first service from Bilbao, the headquarters of the company, via Madrid to Barcelona; there were further domestic flights to the Canary Islands, the Balearic Islands and to Morocco, which was still Spanish at that time. The first international route was from Bilbao to Marseilles via Palma. They used SE 161 Languedocs, Convair 440s, DC-3s, DC-6s and Constellations. As early as the mid-1950s charters were being flown from Britain to Spain. Iberia bought 65% of the shares in Aviaco in 1960. Using an ATL-98 Carvair in 1964 Aviaco opened a 'ferry service' for cars and their occupants from Barcelona to Palma de Mallorca. After the first Caravelle, bought in 1960 from Sabena, a number of other Caravelles were bought from Iberia, taking the place of the older generation of propeller aircraft. DC-8s and DC-9-32s were also bought, replacing the Caravelles in the early 1980s, and since 1990 modern MD-83s have been in use. Deliveries of its order for thirteen MD-88s commenced in August 1991, the first of the model to enter service in Europe. In 1994 the F27s which had been used for shorter routes were sold to Cuba. In the same year Aviaco gave up its own routes and operated together with Iberia, the routes becoming fully code-shared. The company is now a 100% subsidiary of Iberia, for whom it operates several passenger schedules, and is active also in tourist and freight flights.

Routes

Dense regional network in Spain, the Balearics and Canary Isles, to London and Paris. Charter flights throughout Europe.

Fleet

13 McDonnell Douglas MD-88
20 McDonnell Douglas DC-9-32/34

Photograph: Boeing 757-200 N987AN (Josef Krauthäuser/Miami)

AVIANCA COLOMBIA

Av. Eldorado 93-30 Piso 4, Bogota, Columbia
Tel. 1-4139511 Fax. 1-2699131

Three letter code	IATA No.	ICAO Callsign
AVA	134	Avianca

Avianca is one of the world's oldest airlines, tracing its history back for 75 years and claims to be the first airline in the Americas. The Sociedad Colombo-Alemanos de Transportes Aereos (SCADTA) was formed on 5th December 1919, and started flights from the port of Barranquilla on 12th September 1920. Initially, Junkers F-13s were used for the route to Puerto Berrio. Destinations in neighbouring Ecuador and Venezuela were served with Junkers W34s. In 1930 Pan American acquired a 80% majority interest in SCADTA, took over the international flights itself and exchanged the German aircraft for American ones. SCADTA and SCAO were merged in 1940 to form Avianca. On 14th June 1940 SCADTA became Aerovias Nacionales de Colombia (Avianca) and merged with Servico Aereo Colombiano, which has operated a small network since its foundation in 1933. In 1947 Avianca flew to Miami and two years later to New York as well using DC-4s. This aircraft was also used for flights to Europe, to Paris and Lisbon. On 17th April 1953, Hamburg was added to the network of destinations, and in the following year Frankfurt, using Lockheed Constellations. Jet aircraft were first used for international routes in 1962, Boeing 707s and 720s. Avianca was the first South American airline to purchase Boeing 727s and the first went into service in April 1966. In 1970, all the aircraft were painted in the colours still used today. The first Boeing 747s were delivered in November 1976; since 1988, Avianca has been using new ones, plus Boeing 767s. Older Boeing 727s have also been replaced by Boeing 757s. Avianca has been in Colombian ownership since 1978 after Pan American sold its shareholding. Its home base is the airport of Eldorado in Bogota.

Routes

Dense internal network; international flights to destinations in the Caribbean, USA and Europe.

Fleet

3 Boeing 767-300ER
4 Boeing 757-200
3 Boeing 727-200Adv
10 Fokker 50
11 McDonnell Douglas MD-83

Photograph: ATR72-200 EI-CLD (Wolfgang Grond/Zürich)

AVIANOVA

Via Carlo Veniziano 58,
00148 Roma, Italy
Tel. 6551489 Fax. 6551502

Three letter code	IATA No.	ICAO Callsign
NOV	-	Avianova

After Meridiana (see page 214) sold its stake in Avianova to ATI in 1993, this airline is now also owned by the Alitalia group, a fact which is also clearly apparent from the colours of the ATR42 aircraft. Up until the time the airline was sold, these aircraft still bore the red and blue colours of of the original Avianova. It was set up as a regional airline in Olbia, Sardinia, in December 1986 and started flights in August 1987 with three ATR42s. The Alitalia group acquired a stake in Avianova as early as 1989 and further ATR42s were taken over from ATI. The headquarters was also moved to Rome in 1989. After the merger of Alisarda and Universair to form Meridiana, the latter finally sold its shares. In 1995 the larger ATR72 and the Fokker 70 also came into the Avianova fleet. These are used on developing or poorly-supported services flown for Alitalia, where the aircraft of the parent company could not be used economically. The Avianova identity is being dropped as the operation is absorbed into Team Alitalia.

Routes

Alghero, Bastia, Florence, Geneva, Genoa, Cologne, Milan, Marseille, Munich, Naples, Nürnberg, Olbia, Perugia, Pisa, Stuttgart, Tirana, Turin, Venice, Vienna and Zürich.

Fleet

9 ATR42
4 ATR72
5 Fokker 70

Photograph: Boeing 737-200Adv N125GU (Josef Krauthäuser/Miami)

AVIATECA

Avienda Hincapie 10-12, Aeroporto La Aurora,
Guatemala City, Guatemala
Tel. 318261 Fax. 318222

Three letter code	IATA No.	ICAO Callsign
GUG	240	Aviateca

On 14th March in 1945 the airline Empresa Guatemalteca de Aviacion SA (Aviateca) was set up by the government, to take over the operations of PAA-financed Aerovias de Guatemala SA which had been founded in 1939. DC-3s were used to continue operations. DC-6Bs were added to the fleet in 1961, thus making it possible to extend the network of routes to Miami, New Orleans and other destinations. Its first jet aircraft was a leased BAC One-Eleven in 1970. In 1974 the airline was renamed Aerolinas de Guatemala and 2 Boeing 727s were added to the aircraft fleet. The company was privatised in 1989. Since 1989, Aviateca has been flying with leased Boeing 737-200s. TACA holds 30% of the capital; thus there is co-operation in schedules and aircraft use.

Routes

Cancun, Costa Rica, Houston, Los Angeles, Managua, Merida, Mexico-City, Miami, Managua, New Orleans and other destinations in the Caribbean.

Fleet

5 Boeing 737-200Adv

Photograph: Tupolev Tu-134B 4K-65705 (Björn Kannengiesser/Dubai)

AZERBAIJAN AIRLINES

Bina Airport, 370109 Baku,
Azerbaijan
Tel. 243714 Fax. 254466

Three letter code	IATA No.	ICAO Callsign
AHY	771	Azal

In 1992 the government of the new republic of Azerbaijan in Baku brought into existence the Azerbaijan Airline Concern, organised in three divisions. Azal Avia is responsible for passenger services; it is the national flag carrier and flies under the name of Azerbaijan Airlines. The aircraft were taken over from the former Aeroflot division, and in addition older western aircraft – the Boeing 727 and 707 – were brought into service. Slowly the Tupolev Tu-134s and Tu-154s will be phased out, and there are already preliminary contracts for Boeing 757s. However, the longer-term development of the airline is dependent on the political situation in the country.

Routes

Adler, Aktau, Aleppo, Ankara, Ashkhabad, Athens, Bishkek, Chelyabinsk, Dubai, Ekaterinburg, Frankfurt, Gaziantep, Gomel, Istanbul, Karachi, Kazan, Kharkov, Krasnodar, London, Moscow, Nizny Novgorod, Orenburg, Perm, St Petersburg, Samara, Shimkent, Tiflis, Teheran, Tel Aviv, Trabzon, Ufa, Volgograd, Zaporozhye.

Fleet

9 Antonov An-26/32
2 Boeing 707
2 Boeing 727-200
8 Tupolev Tu-134B
15 Tupolev Tu-154B/M
13 Yakovlev Yak-40

Photograph: De Havilland DHC-8-300 C6-BFN (Josef Krauthäuser/Miami)

BAHAMASAIR

P.O. Box N4881 Nassau,
Bahamas
Tel. 809-3278451 Fax. 809-3277408

Three letter code	IATA No.	ICAO Callsign
BHS	111	Bahamas

Bahamasair was established on 18th June 1973, just prior to Bahamian independence from Britain, and immediately took over the domestic and international routes of Out Island Airways and the domestic routes of Flamingo Airlines to become the national airline. Among the aircraft used were HS.748s and BAC One-Elevens. Bahamasair's main route is the connection from Nassau and Freetown to Miami in Florida, only 45 minutes flying time away. The BAC One-Elevens were replaced by three Boeing 737-200s from 1976, and two Boeing 727-200s followed for the routes to New York and Boston. A co-operation agreement was in place with Eastern Airlines. The Bahamian Government assumed full control of the airline in 1979. Since 1990 the older HS.748s have been replaced by more modern DHC-8s with the last 748 leaving the fleet in 1996 after the acquisition of more Dash 8s. As the operation and acquisition of jet aircraft proved too expensive, all the jets were removed from the fleet in 1992 and the airline became a turboprop-only operator. However as competitors emerged in the brisk market to the eastern USA, a Boeing 737 has again been leased since 1995 for these routes.

Routes

From Nassau and Freetown to Fort Lauderdale, Miami, New York, Orlando, West Palm Beach. Several regional destinations in the Bahamas are served with the Shorts 360.

Fleet

1 Boeing 737-200
6 De Havilland DHC-8-300
2 Shorts 360

Photograph: Tupolev Tu-154M LZ-BTH (Frank Fielitz/Frankfurt)

BALKAN

Vrajdebna Airport Sofia 1540,
Bulgaria
Tel. 02661690 Fax. 02723496

Three letter code	IATA No.	ICAO Callsign
LAZ	196	Balkan

The formation of Balkan-Bulgarian Air Transport goes back to 29th June 1947, when BVS-Bulgarske Vazdusne Solstenie was set up. This airline only served a few domestic destinations up to 1949. In 1949, the involvement of the Soviet Union led to the creation of a new company, TABSO, 50/50 owned by Bulgaria and Russia. The first international service, between Sofia and Budapest was operated on 12th September 1949. Lisunov Li-2s and Ilyushin IL-14s served Paris, Frankfurt and Moscow. In 1954, the Soviet share in TABSO passed into the ownership of the Bulgarian state. The four-engined IL-18 came into service in 1962; this aircraft is still familiar to many holidaymakers to the shores of the Black Sea, as it was particularly used for charter flights. 1968 saw the change of name to the one we know today, and also the acquisition of the first Tupolev Tu-134; then, in 1972, came the larger Tu-154. In 1987 the fleet was given a modern colour scheme, to the surprise of many, and in autumn 1990 it even acquired its first Western aircraft, a Boeing 737. The fleet and the service are being increasingly brought up to the Western level; Airbus 320s and further Boeing aircraft are in use, as are the well-proved Russian types. Balkan has a code-share arrangement and operates some joint flights with Air Malta.

Routes

Abu Dhabi, Accra, Addis Ababa, Algiers, Amsterdam, Athens, Baghdad, Bangkok, Beirut, Berlin, Bratislava, Budapest, Casablanca, Colombo, Damascus, Dubai, Frankfurt, Harare, Helsinki, Istanbul, Copenhagen, Lagos, Lisbon, London, Moscow, Munich, New York, Singapore, Vienna, Zürich plus some 15 internal points.

Fleet

2 Airbus A320
13 Antonov An-24
4 Antonov An-12
3 Boeing 737-500
2 Boeing 767-200ER
6 Ilyushin IL-18
24 Tupolev Tu-154

Photograph: ATR72-200 HS-PGE (Author's collection)

BANGKOK AIR

60 Queen Sirikit National Convention Center,
New Raja-dapisek Road, Klongioey, Bangkok
10110, Thailand Tel. 2-2534040 Fax. 2-2534005

Three letter code	IATA No.	ICAO Callsign
BKP	829	Bangkok Air

Set up in 1985 by the owner of Sahokol Air, an air-taxi company which had been formed in 1968 to operate between Bangkok and the tourist resorts of Samui Island and other points, Bangkok Airways started scheduled operations with an Embraer-110 in January 1986. In addition, a Piper PA-31 Navajo was used. An order for two Saab 340A was announced in September 1986 but did not come to fruition. In 1989 and 1990 de Havilland DHC-8s were added to the fleet, but these were replaced in 1994 and 1995 by two ATR72s, the fleet of which has now grown further. In 1992 approval was given for the first international route, to Phnom-Penh, and in 1993 service to Mandalay in neighbouring Myanmar was inaugurated. Its home base is the Don Muang Domestic Airport in Bangkok.

Routes

Bangkok, Chiangmai, Hua Hin, Loei, Mandalay, Phnom Penh, Phuket.

Fleet

1 ATR42-300
6 ATR72-200

Photograph: Ilyushin IL-76TD EW-76836 (Björn Kannengiesser/Dubai)

BELAIR

5 Kortkevicha, 222039 Minsk,
Belarus
Tel. 225702 Fax. 225045

Three letter code	IATA No.	ICAO Callsign
BLI	-	Air Belarus

Belair is the first private airline in Belarus and was set up in 1992. It is based in Minsk and operated regional routes from there with Yakovlev Yak-40s. However, its main business is operating cargo flights, the only way in this country to earn money or foreign currency from flying. Thus Belair flies charter flights for other airlines, including Western airlines, to Western Europe. Two Tupolev Tu-134s were leased in 1996 for use on passenger charter work. Belair should not be confused with Belavia (Belarussian Airlines) which is a state-owned carrier and follows on from the former Aeroflot division in the Republic of Belarus/ Byelorussia.

Routes

Regional routes and charter flights, *ad hoc* and sub-charter.

Fleet

1 Ilyushin IL-76TD
1 Tupolev Tu-134A

Photograph: McDonnell Douglas DC-10-30 S2-ACP (Josef Krauthäuser/Frankfurt)

BIMAN BANGLADESH

Biman Bangladesh Building, 100 Motijheel
Commercial Aera, Dhaka 1000, Bangladesh
Tel. 2-9560151 Fax. 2-863005

Three letter code	IATA No.	ICAO Callsign
BBC	997	Bangladesh

After independence, a new state airline was set up on 4th January 1972 to represent the state of Bangladesh (formerly East Pakistan) to the outside world when it split from Pakistan. Flights started on 4th February 1972 with scheduled services to Chittagong and several other domestic points using a DC-3 leased from the Bangladesh Air Force. DC-3s were soon replaced by F27s. The first international flights were between Dhaka and Calcutta. A weekly charter service between Dacca and London commenced on 9th March 1972 with a leased Boeing 707. In January 1973, scheduled flights to London started with leased Boeing 707s. Two Fokker F28s were added to the fleet in 1981; the Boeing 707s were taken out of service when the DC-10-30s arrived from Singapore Airlines in 1983. In August 1990, the first BAe ATP arrived, thus introducing the renewal of the regional fleet. In 1996 two Airbus A310-300 were acquired, especially for use on Asian services.

Routes

Internally from Dhaka to Chittagong, Syltet, Jessone and Soidyen. International to Abu Dhabi, Amsterdam, Bahrain, Bangkok, Bombay, Brussels, Calcutta, Delhi, Dubai, Doha, Frankfurt, Hong Kong, Jeddah, Karachi, Kuala Lumpur, Kuwait, London, New York, Paris, Rome, Singapore, Sharjah, Tokyo, Yangon.

Fleet

2 Airbus A310-300
2 BAe Jetstream 61/ATP
2 Fokker F28
4 McDonnell Douglas DC-10-30

Photograph: ATR72-200 EC-383 (Hermann Streuhof/Las Palmas)

BINTER CANARIAS

Apartado de Concos 50, 35230 Telde,
Gran Canaria, Spain
Tel. 28-579601 Fax. 28-579604

Three letter code	IATA No.	ICAO Callsign
IBB	138	Canaria

In January 1988, Iberia, Spain's state airline, set up Binter Canarias in order to reorganise regional Spanish flights to the Canary Islands from mainland Spain, previously operated by Aviaco. The brief hops to the islands were uneconomical for the Iberia jets, and so in mid-1988 Binter Canarias started flights with a CASA CN-235. That same year, another aircraft was acquired, and two further aircraft in spring 1989, followed by the first ATR42s in the autumn of that year. These latter were only used for a short period, and were replaced by the larger ATR72s. For a new route from Tenerife to Funchal on Madeira DC-9-32 jets were leased from the parent company, and these have also been employed on other routes.

Routes

Binter Canarias maintains a scheduled service within the Canary Isles - Lanzarote, Tenerife, Gran Canaria, Fuerteventura and Las Palmas, and externally to Madeira.

Fleet	Ordered
6 ATR72 4 CASA CN-235 4 McDonnell Douglas DC-9-32	3 ATR72

Photograph: Vickers Viscount 843 PK-IVY (Martin Bach/Denpasar)

BOURAQ AIRLINES

P.O. Box 2965, Jalan Angkasa 1-3,
Jakarta Pusat 10720, Indonesia
Tel. 21-655289 Fax. 21-6298651

Three letter code	IATA No.	ICAO Callsign
BOU	666	Bouraq

PT Bouraq Indonesian Airlines is a private company founded in the middle of 1970. With three DC-3s it flew from Jakarta to Banjarmasin, Balikpapan and Surabaya. In the following year it was able to re-equip with turboprops in the form of the NAMC YS-11. BN-2 Islanders were used to provide services to destinations far from the main cities where only grass strips were available. Later came Fokker Friendship, Dornier Do28, HS.748 and the Vickers Viscount replaced the DC-3 from 1980. The tasks for the airline were many and varied and freight and charter flights were also undertaken. These were to Malaysia, Thailand and to Manila. In 1973 Bouraq founded the subsidiary company Bali Air, which established its own network with aircraft from the parent company. As the turboprop fleet is ageing, the transition to jets is slowly being made. The Boeing 737-200 was first used in 1993, with further examples added in 1994 and 1995. There is a co-operation agreement with Philippine Airlines. For the future there are expansion plans, particularly for regional international services.

Routes

Balikpapan, Bandung, Banjarmasin, Batu Besar, Berau, Denpasar, Jakarta, Manado, Medan, Palembang, Palu, Pangkalpinang, Pontianak, Samarinda, Semarang, Surabaya, Tarakan, Tawau, Ujung Pandang, Yogyakarta.

Fleet	Ordered
5 BAe HS.748 8 Boeing 737-200Adv	5 IPTN N-250-100

Photograph: Boeing 737-500 LN-BRC (Florian Morasch/Innsbruck)

BRAATHENS S.A.F.E.

Okseneyveien 3, 1330 Oslo,
Norway
Tel. 67-597000 Fax. 67-591309

Three letter code	IATA No.	ICAO Callsign
BRA	154	Braathens

Ludvig G. Braathen, a Norwegian shipowner, formed his airline, Braathens South-America and Far East Air Transport, on 26th March 1946, and started flight operations with Douglas DC-4s. As can be seen from the name, the airline operated charter flights to South America and Hong Kong. On 5th August 1949 a scheduled service from Oslo via Amsterdam-Cairo-Basra-Karachi-Bombay-Calcutta-Bangkok to Hong Kong was introduced. It was only in April 1954 that SAS took over this route. As early as 1952 a network was also built up in Norway, first with de Havilland Herons, and later (1958) with Fokker F27s. The first jet aircraft, Boeing 737s came in 1969; the F27s and Douglas DC-6s were replaced by Fokker F28s. In 1984 Braathens obtained its first widebody aircraft, the Boeing 767; however, this aircraft was sold again because it was not being fully used. The introduction of the new Boeing 737-400/500 generation, to which will be added the -700, provides Braathens with a very modern and homogeneous fleet. Braathens carries each year about 4.5 million passengers, equivalent to the entire population of Norway. In June 1996 Braathens took over 50% of the shares of Transwede with the option of acquiring the rest at the end of 1997. The main bases are Oslo and Stavanger, where there are also maintenance facilities.

Routes

Alesund, Bergen, Billund, Bodo, Evenes, Haugesund, Kristiansund, London, Molde, Murmansk, Newcastle, Oslo, Roros, Stavanger, Svalbard, Tromsö and Trondheim. Charter flights throughout Europe.

Fleet	Ordered
2 Boeing 737-200 23 Boeing 737-500 7 Boeing 737-400	7 Boeing 737-700

Photograph: Boeing 767-200ER G-BNYS (Florian Morasch/Salzburg)

BRITANNIA AIRWAYS

Luton Airport, Bedfordshire, LU2 9ND,
Great Britain
Tel. 1582-424155 Fax. 1582-458594

Three letter code	IATA No.	ICAO Callsign
BAL	754	Britannia

From modest beginnings, Britannia grew into the largest charter airline in the world. On 1st December 1961, Euravia (London) was set up, and it started flight operations on 5th May 1962 with an L-1049 Constellation under contract to Universal Sky Tours, then the principal shareholder. When a Bristol Britannia 102 was commissioned on 6th December 1964, the present name of the airline was also adopted. The Thomson Organisation, one of the major tour operators, took over the airline on 26th April 1965, and Boeing 707s were used for charter flights to Hong Kong, Kuala Lumpur and other faraway destinations. Its first Boeing 737 was put into service in 1968, the first European airline to operate the type. But Britannia withdrew from the long-distance business between 1973 and 1985, as the Boeing 737 – the sole type in the fleet for many years – was deemed unsuitable. Boeing 757s eventually provided this capability, and the first Boeing 767 was delivered in February 1984. In 1988 Orion Airways was bought when Thomson's acquired its parent company, Horizon Travel and six Boeing 737-300s were taken over. By 1989, Britannia had 34 Boeing 737s in service but by 1992 this number had been reduced to 20 and its last 737 was disposed of in 1994 as it has increased its fleet of Boeing 757s and 767s. About 7.5 million passengers are carried each year. A new German subsidiary will start operations in November 1997 with two Boeing 767-300ERs, to compete with LTU and Condor.

Routes

Worldwide charter flights to the Caribbean, Australia, New Zealand, USA; within Europe to summer and winter holiday resorts and to North Africa.

Fleet

6 Boeing 757-200ER
14 Boeing 757-200
6 Boeing 767-200ER
4 Boeing 767-300ER

Ordered

5 Boeing 767-300ER

Photograph: Boeing 747-400 G-BNLO (Martin Bach/London LHR)

BRITISH AIRWAYS

P.O. Box 10 London-Heathrow Airport
Hounslow, Middx. TW6 2JA Great Britain
Tel.181-759-5511 Fax. 181-5629930

Three letter code	IATA No.	ICAO Callsign
BAW	125	Speedbird

British Airways is the result of the merger of BEA and BOAC, following a government decision bringing together British aviation interests under government control. BA came into being on 1st April 1972. Until 1974, BEA and BOAC were still apparently operating separately; the merger became visible on the aircraft in 1974. In 1988, the second largest private airline, British Caledonian, was taken over, after British Airways had been partly privatised in 1984. A major re-equipment programme was begun in 1989. In 1992 and 1993 British Airways featured often in the headlines. First it acquired a stake in US Air, then in the Australian airline Qantas and finally in the French airline TAT and Deutsche BA. Dan Air was taken over for the symbolic amount of one pound. BA set up 'profit centres' in 1993, forming the regional airlines BA Manchester and BA Birmingham. In 1995 British Asia Airways was formed for operations to Taiwan. BA also owns Brymon Airways, operating principally from West Country airports in BA colours. Similar 'franchise' services have been greatly developed over the last two or three years, and are operated in BA colours by CityFlyer from Gatwick, Maersk Air from Birmingham, TAT in France, Deutsche BA in Germany, British Regional Airlines (formerly Manx and Loganair), Comair in South Africa, SunAir in Denmark and GB Airways. Air Liberté in France was acquired in 1997 and is being merged with TAT. Awaiting government approvals is a major alliance with American Airlines (following the acrimonious disposal of the holding in US Air). The latest major addition to the fleet is the Boeing 777, and services from London-Gatwick are being significantly expanded. A controversial new colour scheme was unveiled in June 1997.

Routes

British Airways flies worldwide to over 160 destinations.

Fleet

10 Airbus A 320
7 AS/BAe Concorde
10 BAe ATP/Jetstream 61
35 Boeing 737-200
35 Boeing 737-400
45 Boeing 757-200
25 Boeing 767-300
38 Boeing 747-400
31 Boeing 747-100/200
14 Boeing 777-200
8 McDonnell Douglas DC-10-30

Ordered

10 Boeing 777-200
14 Boeing 747-400
4 Boeing 757-200
3 Boeing 767-300ER

Photograph: Boeing 737-500 G-BVZE (Xaver Flocki collection/Frankfurt)

BRITISH MIDLAND

Donington Hall, Castle Donington,
Derbyshire, DE7 2SB, Great Britain
Tel. 854000 Fax. 854662

Three letter code	IATA No.	ICAO Callsign
BMA	236	Midland

BMA was originally formed in 1938 as Derby Air Schools, a flying school which provided pilot and navigator training for the RAF during the Second World War. It was registered as Derby Aviation in 1948 and local services started on 16th February 1949 using a DH Rapide. The name British Midland Airways was adopted in July 1964. Scheduled services were offered from Derby, Birmingham and Manchester. It made use of DC-3s, Handley Page Heralds, BAC One-Elevens, Vickers Viscounts and Boeing 707s. In 1965 the airline moved base from Derby to the new East Midlands Airport. In addition to charter and scheduled services, BMA also offered aircraft leasing in the 1970s. It was bought in 1968 by an investment group Minster Assets, and in 1978 under its present managing director Michael Bishop it again became privately owned, since which time it has been flourishing. Manx, formed in 1982, was a joint venture between British Midland and British and Commonwealth (owners of Air UK) and Loganair became a subsidiary of BMA in December 1983. British Midland is a main shareholder in Manx Airlines and Loganair. The holding company for these three airlines is the Airlines of Britain Group formed in March 1987, in which SAS also has a 40% stake. In 1985 the colours of the aircraft were also changed. The DC-9 fleet was retired from April 1994 with the advent of the Fokker 70 and 100 fleet. The main element of the current fleet is the Boeing 737, but it was announced in mid-1997 that a mixture of up to 20 Airbus A320/321s would be acquired from 1998 and will largely replace the 737s. More and more code-share and partnership arrangements have been developed, including those with SAS, Air Canada, Alitalia, American, Austrian, Iberia, Malaysian, TAP, Gulf Air and Cathay Pacific.

Routes

Amsterdam, Brussels, Belfast, Birmingham, Dublin, Edinburgh, Frankfurt, Glasgow, Jersey, Leeds/Bradford, Liverpool, Luton, Nice, Palma de Mallorca, Paris, Teesside, Zürich.

Fleet		Ordered
7 Boeing 737-300	2 Saab 340	12 Airbus A320
6 Boeing 737-400		8 Airbus A321
13 Boeing 737-500		
3 Fokker 70		
6 Fokker 100		

Photograph: BAe BAC 1-11 500 G-OBWD (Patrick Lutz/Faro)

BRITISH WORLD AIRLINES

Viscount House, Southend Airport,
Essex, SS2 6YL, Great Britain
Tel. 702-354435 Fax. 1702-331914

Three letter code	IATA No.	ICAO Callsign
BWL	762	Britworld

British United Air Ferries Ltd was set up in Southend in January 1963. It was the result of a merger between Silver City Airways (formed in 1948) and Channel Air Bridge (established as Air Charter in 1954). The airline became famous for its ferry services with Carvair aircraft. The cars were loaded onto them through a large front door, while the passengers also boarded and flew from England to France, Belgium and Holland. Handley Page Heralds were used for charter flights, to which larger Vickers Viscounts were added. In September 1967 the airline changed its name to British Air Ferries. BAF was purchased by the Keegan family in 1971 and sold to Jadepoint in March 1983. In the 1980s it was involved in worldwide aircraft leasing, contract and flight support, and tour group charter activities. It had stopped flying its own scheduled service in 1978 but continued such services in the 1980s for British Caledonian, Air UK and British Midland using its own aircraft, mainly Viscounts. It also operated the Virgin Atlantic Gatwick-Maastricht service. In the late 1980s it had financial problems but came out of administration, a form of bankruptcy protection, in May 1989 and was then acquired by Mostjet. The present name was adopted in 1993. New names also involve different colours, and so the British World aircraft were also given an attractive new scheme. The operational base is primarily London-Stansted, with a further base at Aberdeen. British World's activities are extensive, for example flying scheduled services on behalf of other airlines, charter flights, cargo services and supply flights. In the second half of 1997, new BAe ATPs are to be added to the fleet as partial replacements for the Viscounts being finally retired, and a Lockheed TriStar is also to join the fleet, to be operated from Stansted for a tour operator.

Routes

Charter flights within Britain and Europe. Freight flights on behalf of the Post Office and other companies. Oil-rig support flights for BP.

Fleet	Ordered
2 ATR72 5 BAe BAC 1-11 500 1 BAe 146-300 4 Vickers Viscount 800	2 BAe ATP 1 Lockheed L-1011

Photograph: McDonnell Douglas DC-3 C-GPNR (Josef Krauthäuser collection)

BUFFALO AIRWAYS

P.O. Box 1479, Hay River, NW Territories
X0E 0R0, Canada
Tel. 403-8743333 Fax. 403-8743572

Three letter code	IATA No.	ICAO Callsign
BFL	-	Buffalo

This Northern Canadian company was founded in 1959 in Fort Smith. Its principal tasks are supply flights in the North West Territories and the Yukon. Several helicopters and smaller aircraft were used. However, the ideal aircraft for these varied tasks is not surprisingly the ubiquitous Douglas DC-3, built in 1942, and brought into service here in 1979. At the beginning of the eighties a regional scheduled service was begun, serving Hay River, Uranium City or Chipewyan. The DC-3s are operated with wheeled undercarriages in summer and on skis in the winter, an advantage of one of the few aircraft of this size which can be used to such remote and snow-covered places. Over the course of time, and following the relocation of the company at Hay River, further DC-3s, and the larger DC-4 were added to the fleet, along with another veteran, the Curtiss C-46 Commando. Aerial firefighting duties are also undertaken on behalf of the North-West Territories government as the first line of defence against forest fires.

Routes

Scheduled flights with DC-3 to Yellowknife; *ad hoc,* charter- and special flights in the region.

Fleet

4 Canadair CL-215
3 Consolidated PBY-5A Canso
2 Curtiss C-46 Commando
9 Douglas DC-3/C-47
4 Douglas DC-4/C-54
1 Noorduyn Norseman

Photograph: McDonnell Douglas MD-83 9Y-THW (Josef Krauthäuser/Miami)

BWIA INTERNATIONAL

Administration Building, International Airport,
Port of Spain, Trinidad and Tobago
Tel. 809-6693000 Fax. 809-6643540

Three letter code	IATA No.	ICAO Callsign
BWA	106	West Indian

Set up in November 1939, daily flights started on 17th November 1940 with a Lockheed Lodestar between Trinidad and Barbados. Two more Lodestars were added in 1942. In 1947, BWIA was sold to BSAA but a new airline was set up with the old name, 'BWIA' in 1948. Five Vickers Vikings were used to serve almost all the islands in the Caribbean. In June 1949, BSAA was merged with BOAC, so that BWIA was now a subsidiary of BOAC, taking over flights and aircraft from it. Four Vickers Viscounts were added in 1955, and in 1960 leased Bristol Britannias were first used to fly to London, via New York. In November 1961 the government of Trinidad and Tobago bought back 90% of the shares, and the other 10% in 1967. BWIA used Boeing 727s for the first time to Miami in 1965, replacing the Viscounts. On 14th December 1968, Boeing 707s were first used on the route to New York. Flights to London-Heathrow started in 1975. On 1st January 1980 Trinidad and Tobago Airways Corporation (BWIA International Airways) was formed as the national airline of the Caribbean, through the merger of BWIA and Trinidad and Tobago Air Services, itself formed in 1974. The first L-1011 TriStar reached Trinidad on 29th January 1980, with a further example in August. In 1994 the airline was partially privatised, with the Acker Group and local investors participating; along with this came a fundamental reorganisation of BWIA. Routes were dropped, with London and Frankfurt remaining as the only European destinations. New Boeing 757s and 767s were ordered, but dropped in favour of Airbus A321s and A340s. Two A321s were delivered late in 1996 but operated only briefly, and the A340s were cancelled. A new operating partnership with Air Jamaica was announced in May 1997.

Routes

Scheduled services to 16 destinations in the Caribbean, from Trinidad, Tobago, Aruba, Curacao and Martinique to Miami and New York. In Europe London and Frankfurt are served. Charter flights from points in the USA to Trinidad and Tobago.

Fleet

4 Lockheed L-1011-500
5 McDonnell Douglas MD-83

Photograph: Airbus A320-200 G-BVYC (Christian Dougett/London LGW)

CALEDONIAN AIRWAYS

Caledonian House, Crawley,
West Sussex, RH6 OLF, Great Britain
Tel. 1293-536321 Fax. 1293- 6683331

Three letter code	IATA No.	ICAO Callsign
CKT	885	Caledonian

British Airways bought the traditional airline British Caledonian in 1987. The charter activities of British Caledonian and the British Airways subsidiary British Airtours were combined and Caledonian was set up in late 1987. British Airtours had been set up by British Airways in 1969 and used a fleet of Boeing 737s and TriStars. British Caledonian had been created on 30th November 1970 when a previous Caledonian Airways (formed in 1961) took over British United Airways and was known as Caledonian/BUA until September 1972. The new Caledonian was owned 100% by British Airways. The fleet consisted initially of TriStars and Boeing 737s, but some Boeing 757s were taken over from the parent company in 1988. The fleet was expanded to cope with additional business following the collapse of Air Europe and Dan Air. In November 1995 British Airways sold the airline to the Inspirations travel group for £16 million. Included in the price were five Lockheed TriStars. With a single DC-10 Caledonian carried out flights for BA to the Caribbean, but this task has been passed to Flying Colours for the 1997 season. After Caledonian's first season under the new ownership, the Boeing 757s were returned to the lessors, as the airline added its own Airbus 320s to the fleet. The main operating base remains at London-Gatwick.

Routes

From London and other English cities to the Mediterranean area, USA, Canada, Kenya, and Bangkok. Winter charters also to Salzburg, Zürich, Geneva and Munich.

Fleet

3 Airbus A320
3 Boeing 757-200
6 Lockheed L-1011
2 McDonnell Douglas DC-10-30

Photograph: Boeing 747-200 TJ-CAB (Patrick Lutz/Paris CDG)

CAMEROON AIRLINES

BP 4092, Avenue General de Gaulle, Douala, Cameroon
Tel. 422525 Fax. 423459

Three letter code	IATA No.	ICAO Callsign
UYC	604	Camair

Cameroon Airlines was set up on 26th July 1971 by the Cameroon Government in order to be able to withdraw from the multinational airline Air Afrique and its interest in the consortium ended on 2nd September 1971. It began its own flight operations, between Douala and Yaounde, with Boeing 737s on 1st November 1971. A Boeing 707 was acquired from Air France for long-distance flights, and was used for service to Paris via Rome. In 1982 it was replaced by a Boeing 747. With its own maintenance and base facilities in Douala, Cameroon Airlines has the necessary infrastructure to look after its own aircraft. Air France now has only 4% of the capital, the rest being owned by the Cameroon government. Co-operation agreements are in place with Nigeria Airways, Air France, Air Gabon and Oman Air.

Routes

Abidjan, Bamako, Bangui, Bata, Brazzaville, Brussels, Bujumbura, Cotonou, Garoua, Harare, Jeddah, Johannesburg, Khartoum, Kinshasa, Lagos, Libreville, Lome, London, Malabo, Maroua, Nairobi, N'Djamena, Ngaoundere, Paris, Sao Tome and Yaounde.

Fleet

1 BAe HS.748
2 Boeing 737-200Adv
1 Boeing 747-200

Photograph: Airbus A320-200 C-GVXC (Josef Krauthäuser/Vancouver)

CANADA 3000 AIRLINES

27 Fasken Drive, Toronto, Ontario, M9W 1K6, Canada
Tel. 416-6740257 Fax. 416-6740256

Three letter code	IATA No.	ICAO Callsign
CMM	570	Elite

Founded in 1988 as Air 2000 Airline Ltd, a subsidiary of the British airline Air 2000, the Canadian Ministry of Transport suspended its licence a few days before flight operations were due to commence. The reason was massive objections on the part of other airlines from Canada. Consequently, local investors took over the British shares, and logically enough the name was changed to the present one. Flight operations started in 1989 using Boeing 757s leased from Air 2000. The airline is based in Toronto, but Canada 3000 also operates from Vancouver on the west coast, Calgary, Edmonton, Montreal and Winnipeg. In addition to regular charter flights, the airline also leases aircraft outside the season. In 1992, for the first time, over 1 million passengers were carried. The first Airbus A320 was delivered on 29th May 1993, giving Canada 3000 one of the most modern and up-to-date fleets. In 1996 the fleet was again expanded with an Airbus A320 and a Boeing 757. Air 2000 has continued to supply Boeing 757s to Canada 3000 on lease each winter in an arrangement which benefits both airlines. Plans for the next century foresee the need for widebody airliners, and thus Canada 3000 has options on Airbus A330s.

Routes

Acapulco, Amsterdam, Antigua, Barbados, Belfast, Birmingham, Cancun, Costa Rica, Dublin, Düsseldorf, Edinburgh, Fort Lauderdale, Glasgow, Honolulu, Manchester, Nice, Nassau, Las Vegas, London, Paris, Shannon and many destinations in the Caribbean.

Fleet	Ordered
6 Airbus A320-200 6 Boeing 757-200	2 Airbus A330

Photograph: Boeing 737-200Adv C-GQBH (Uwe Gleisberg/Fort Lauderdale)

CANADIAN

Scotia Center 2800, 700-2nd Street SW, Calgary, Alberta, T2P 2W2, Canada
Tel. 403-294-2000 Fax. 403-294-2066

Three letter code	IATA No.	ICAO Callsign
CDN	018	Canadian

Canadian Airlines International was only set up in January 1988 on a legal basis but it had been formed the previous January and the name came into use in March 1987. Prior to that, the former Canadian Pacific Airlines had been taken over by the slightly smaller Pacific Western Airlines, which had already absorbed Nordair and Eastern Provincial Airways during the preceding year. Before the merger Canadian Pacific was Canada's second largest airline and PWA one of the country's largest regional carriers. In order to strengthen its position with regard to Air Canada, the largest private Canadian airline, Wardair, was taken over in 1989. Canadian acquired its first Boeing 767 in 1988, and at the end of 1990 its first Boeing 747-400. Also, the Airbus A320 was put into service. Canadian operated regular services to Frankfurt and Munich since 1988, but withdrew completely from the German market at the end of 1996. After the approval of the regulatory authorities in 1995, AMR Corporation, the parent of American Airlines, took a 33% interest in the Canadian Airline Corporation, which also has holdings in various other Canadian regional operators such as Air Atlantic, Ontario Express, Canadian Regional and Time Air. A separate division of the airline, Canadian North, serves the wide expanses of Canada's remote northern areas. Since 1st July 1995 there have been code-share arrangements for several routes with American Airlines, and there are marketing alliances with nine other international airlines.

Routes

Auckland, Bangkok, Beijing, Boston, Buenos Aires, Hong Kong, Honolulu, Ho Chi Minh, Kuala Lumpur, London, Los Angeles, Manila, Melbourne, Mexico, Nagoya, Nadi, Paris, Rio de Janeiro, Rome, San Francisco, Santiago, Sao Paulo, Shanghai, Sydney, Taipei, Tokyo, Washington. Additionally about 100 US cities are served in partnership with American Airlines and in Canada.

Fleet

14 Airbus A320-200
46 Boeing 737-200Adv
11 Boeing 767-300ER
4 Boeing 747-400
9 McDonnell Douglas DC-10-30

Ordered

8 Airbus A320

Photograph: Boeing 747-200F LX-ECV (Gottfried Auer/Luxembourg)

CARGOLUX

P.O. Box 591, Luxembourg Airport,
L-2015, Luxembourg
Tel. 42111 Fax. 435446

Three letter code	IATA No.	ICAO Callsign
CLX	172	Cargolux

Cargolux Airlines International SA, Europe's largest scheduled all-cargo airline, was set up on 4th March 1970. The shareholders were Luxair SA, the Icelandic airline Loftleidir and the Swedish shipping company Salenia AB. Flight operations began in May 1970 with a Canadair CL-44. Altogether five CL-44s were used, augmented in 1971 by a DC-8-61. In 1973 the first Boeing 747-200C was acquired. After the Salenia and Loftleidir shares had been taken over by Luxair in the late 1970s, Lufthansa joined Luxair as a shareholder, thus becoming a shareholder of Cargolux as well. Over 40% of the capital is owned by a Luxembourg banking institution. The first Boeing 747-400F in the world, a cargo aircraft of the latest generation, was delivered in November 1993, with a second following at the beginning of 1994, as Cargolux's services to the USA and South East Asia were strengthened. There is a code-share agreement with China Airlines, with an exchange of freight space on the Taipei-Luxembourg route, and there is a similar code-share arrangement with Lufthansa.

Routes

Worldwide freight services, both scheduled and charter.

Fleet	Ordered
4 Boeing 747-200C/F 3 Boeing 747-400F	2 Boeing 747-400F

Photograph: Boeing 737-400 N405KW (Josef Krauthäuser/Fort Lauderdale)

CARNIVAL AIR LINES

1815 Griffith Road, Dania, Florida 33004, USA
Tel. 305-9238672 Fax. 305-9233350

Three letter code	IATA No.	ICAO Callsign
CAA	521	Carnival Air

Carnival Air Lines is a company belonging to Carnival Cruise Lines in Fort Lauderdale, Florida. Formed in 1988, the company bought the aircraft and services of Pacific Interstate Airlines, the present name was adopted in 1989. Carnival Air Lines flies a feeder service to the cruise liners in the Caribbean from various airports in the USA. An agreement with Iberia has been in place since 1992, under which Carnival operates scheduled services from Miami to Chicago, Los Angeles, New Orleans and Houston. In 1996 a new route was inaugurated from Miami to Lima, Peru in co-operation with Faucett, and in co-operation with Ladeco, a route to New York is flown under the same flight number as an extension of the Chilean airline's Santiago service. The operating and maintenance base is at Hollywood International Airport in Fort Lauderdale. In the summer of 1997 it was announced that long-term 'on-off' negotiations for a merger with the 'new' Pan Am were to come to fruition.

Routes

Charter flights, principally in the Caribbean. Scheduled services from Miami as an Iberia partner to Los Angeles, New York, Orlando, Tampa, and White Plains.

Fleet

9 Airbus A300B4
7 Boeing 727-200Adv
7 Boeing 737-400
2 Boeing 737-200

Photograph: Boeing 747-200 VR-HIF (Florian Morasch/Hong Kong)

CATHAY PACIFIC

Swire House, 9 Connaught Road,
Hong Kong
Tel. 27475000 Fax. 27618586

Three letter code	IATA No.	ICAO Callsign
CPA	160	Cathay

Cathay Pacific Airways Ltd was set up on 24th September 1946, and started setting up a connection from Shanghai via Hong Kong and other stopovers to Sydney using a DC-3. In 1948, the Swire Group bought its way into the airline, acquiring 45% of the capital. A small fleet of DC-3 and Catalina amphibians began to fly a regional network from the Crown Colony, with routes increasing as DC-6s were acquired in the early 1950s. The BOAC subsidiary, Hong Kong Airways, was taken over in 1959. In April 1959, Lockheed L-188 Electras were acquired, and three years later Convair 880s as well. Boeing 707s were added to the fleet, until the decision was made to acquire the first widebody aircraft, the Lockheed TriStar. These aircraft opened up new routes in the Middle East. In order, as a British airline to be able to fly to London as well, Boeing 747s were bought, and the first of these was employed on the route to London on 17th July 1980. By 1980 the Swire Group, through its company Cathay Holdings, had increased its shareholding to 70%. In addition to London, there were direct flights to Frankfurt in 1984, which were quickly changed to non-stop flights after the Boeing 747-300 had been introduced. Cathay's fleet replacement continues steadily with the introduction of the Boeing 747-400 in 1989 and the Airbus A340-300 in 1995 and large orders for aircraft of the latest generation including the Boeing 777. The company's colour scheme was completely revised in Autumn of 1994 to reflect a more 'Chinese' influence, which is in tune with the handover of Hong Kong to China which took place in the summer of 1997, and as an adjunct to which Swire group has sold part of the shareholding to Chinese investors. Cathay has majority shareholdings in Dragonair and Air Hong Kong.

Routes

Cathay flies to some 45 destinations such as Adelaide, Amsterdam, Auckland, Bahrain, Bangkok, Beijing, Bombay, Brisbane, Cairns, Chicago, Colombo, Dubai, Frankfurt, Fukuoka, Ho Chi Minh, Johannesburg, Kuala Lumpur, Los Angeles, London, Manchester, Manila, Mauritius, Melbourne, New York, Osaka, Paris, Rome, Seoul, Tokyo and Zürich.

Fleet

11 Airbus A330-300
6 Airbus A340-300
4 Boeing 747-200F
7 Boeing 747-200
6 Boeing 747-300
19 Boeing 747-400
2 Boeing 747-400F
4 Boeing 777-200

Ordered

2 Airbus A330-300
5 Airbus A340-300
8 Boeing 777-300

Photograph: Boeing 737-200Adv VR-CYB (Uwe Gleisberg/Tampa)

CAYMAN AIRWAYS

P.O. Box 1101, Georgetown, Grand Cayman, British West Indies
Tel. 9498200 Fax. 9497607

Three letter code	IATA No.	ICAO Callsign
CAY	378	Cayman

Cayman Airways Ltd was formed in July 1968 to take over the affairs of Cayman Brac Airways Ltd, which in turn had been set up by the Costa Rican airline LACSA. LACSA owned 49% of the shares in Cayman Airways until December 1977 when the airline came under the control of the government of Cayman. Flight operations to Jamaica and Miami started with BAC One-Elevens. Britten-Norman Trislanders flew the service between the islands of Grand Cayman, Brac and Little Cayman. Boeing 727-200s replaced the BAC One-Elevens, and also a DC-8 which had been in service up to the mid-70s. In 1989 the first leased Boeing 737-400s were added to the fleet as a replacement for the Boeing 727s. In 1993 the fleet was reduced, as the 737-400s were seen to be too large and too expensive. Since then flights have been concentrated on those to Jamaica and to the USA.

Routes

Atlanta, Houston, Miami, Montego Bay, Tampa, and within the Caribbean.

Fleet

2 Boeing 737-200Adv

Photograph: Boeing 747-200F B-1864 (Stefan Schlick/Luxembourg)

CHINA AIRLINES

131, Nanking East Road, Taipei 104,
Republic of China
Tel. 02-7152626 Fax. 02-7175120

Three letter code	IATA No.	ICAO Callsign
CAL	297	Cal

On 16th December 1959, some former members of the national Chinese air force set up CAL. PBY Catalina flying boats were initially used for charter flights. Domestic scheduled flights were also operated using DC-3s and Curtiss C-46s. In 1965 the airline became the official flag carrier of the Republic of China. Lockheed Constellations were used to start a scheduled connection to Saigon in December 1966, primarily in order to transport members of the US Armed Forces and cargo to Vietnam. Connections to Hong Kong and Tokyo also came into existence in 1967 using two new Boeing 727s. 1970 saw the first trans-Pacific flight to San Francisco, via Tokyo and Honolulu. CAL obtained its first jumbo jet aircraft, a Boeing 747, in 1975. The 747 was followed in June by Airbus A300s for regional services in 1982 when a Boeing 767 was also delivered making China Airlines the first airline in the world to operate the A300 and B767 together. It was the first airline in Asia to purchase the latter type. In 1983 a route to Amsterdam was set up, the only destination in Europe for many years; this situation is for political reasons, however. MD-11s and Boeing 747-400s have been added to the fleet or have been used to replace older aircraft. With Mandarin Airlines (100%) and Far Eastern Air Transport (20%), CAL has powerful subsidiaries, which are in sharp competition with private enterprises. In October 1995 the current aircraft colour scheme was introduced. There are codeshares with Continental, Garuda and Vietnam Airlines.

Routes

From Taipei to Dallas, San Francisco, New York, Los Angeles, Honolulu, to Japan, South Korea, Manila, Singapore, Djakarta, Hong Kong, Bangkok, Dhahran, Johannesburg, Luxembourg and Amsterdam.

Fleet

6 Airbus A300B4
6 Airbus A300-600
3 Boeing 737-400
3 Boeing 747-200
3 Boeing 747-200F
5 Boeing 747-400

Ordered

2 Airbus A300-600
15 Boeing 737-800
3 Boeing 747-400

Photograph: Airbus A340-300 B-2381 (Klaus Brandmaier/Munich FJS)

CHINA EASTERN

2550 Hongqiao Road, International Airport,
200335 Shanghai, Peoples Republic of China
Tel. 21-2558899 Fax. 21-2556039

Three letter code	IATA No.	ICAO Callsign
CES	781	China Eastern

In May 1988 China Eastern separated from CAAC, which had previously had air traffic under its sole control and initially shared ten MD-82s with China Northern Airlines acquired from CAAC. Since then it has assumed responsibility for its flights from Shanghai. China Eastern has developed continuously and has also been expanding considerably internationally. MD-11s delivered in 1992/93 allowed routes to be flown to Bahrain, Brussels, Chicago, Madrid, Los Angeles and Seattle. Chinese-assembled MD-82s form the backbone of the modern fleet, which was also expanded with Airbus A310s introduced in 1987. Even during the CAAC era the Shanghai district had acquired Western aircraft types such as the Shorts 360, DHC-8, Lockheed Hercules and BAe 146, though only in small numbers. With the upsizing of the fleet came an expansion of the network. Hong Kong, Nagoya and Seoul were served with Airbuses, and in 1996 the newly-delivered Airbus A340-300s allowed the introduction of services to European destinations such as Munich. On the Shanghai-Seoul route a codeshare arrangement with Asiana is in place. With its own MD-11 freighters there are scheduled services to the USA. The main base of China Eastern for international operations is the Hongqiao Airport in Shanghai, but domestic services are also flown from Nanchang. The centre for all operations such as agricultural flying and crop-spraying is in Hefei. It was announced in August 1997 that the Airbus A320 has been selected to replace the Fokker 100s.

Routes

Bahrain, Bangkok, Beijing, Brussels, Changsha, Chicago, Fukuoka, Fuzhou, Guangzhou, Guilin, Haikou, Hong Kong, Hefei, Jinan, Kunming, Los Angeles, Madrid, Munich, Nagasaki, Nanchang, Nanjing, Osaka, Seattle/Tacoma, Shanghai, Shenzen, Singapore, Tokyo, Tunxi, Wuhan, Xian, Xiamen.

Fleet

10 Airbus A300-600
5 Airbus A340-300
10 Fokker 100
6 McDonnell Douglas MD-11
13 McDonnell Douglas-SAIC-MD-82
6 Yunshuji Y-7

Ordered

10 Airbus A320
10 McDonnell Douglas-SAIC-MD-90

Photograph: Yakovlev Yak-42 B-2756 (Björn Kannengiesser/Beijing)

CHINA GENERAL AVIATION

Wu-Su Airport, Taiyun, Shanxi 030031,
Peoples Republic of China
Tel. 351-7040600 Fax. 351-7040094

Three letter code	IATA No.	ICAO Callsign
CTH	-	Tonghang

The former industrial flying service of CAAC was tasked with various functions including aerial photography, reconnaissance, pipeline patrol, oil-platform support flying, crop-spraying in the countryside and passenger transport. These jobs were all taken over by China General Aviation on its foundation in 1987. From four bases – Taiyun, Changzhi, Tianjin and Handan – various types of aircraft and helicopters are used, almost exclusively Russian produced, or Chinese licence-built versions of Russian designs. Well known to tourists are the Mil-8 helicopters which are used from Changping for flights over the Great Wall of China. In 1991 China General Aviation acquired its first Yakovlev Yak-42 for passenger work, at the same time the current colour scheme was introduced. Three Boeing 737-300s were due to be introduced to the fleet in mid-1997.

Routes

Scheduled services to – amongst others – Beijing, Changsha, Chongqin, Guangzhou, Haikou, Hangzhou, Nanjing, Qinhuangdao, Shanghai, Shenyang, Shenzen, Tianjin, Wenzhou, Wuhan, Xiamen, Zhengzhou.

Fleet

3 Antonov An-30
9 Bell 212
5 De Havilland DHC-6 Twin Otter
2 Eurocopter Bo-105
5 Harbin Y-12
10 Mil-Mi-8
8 Yunshuji Y-5
3 Yunshuji Y-7
7 Yakovlev Yak-42D

Ordered

3 Boeing 737-300

Photograph: McDonnell Douglas MD-82 B-2106 (Björn Kannengiesser/Beijing)

CHINA NORTHERN AIRLINES

Dongtha Airport, Shenyang, Liaoning 110043,
Peoples Republic of China
Tel. 24-8294231 Fax. 24-8294433

Three letter code	IATA No.	ICAO Callsign
CBF	782	China Northern

This company was founded in 1988 to serve the furthest Northern regions of the People's Republic, taking on the mantle of the former CAAC Shenyang administration. Its home base is the airport at Shenyang-Taoxin. Yunshuij Y-7 and MD-82 form the main body of the fleet; indeed China Northern is the largest user of the MD-82 in China. Included in the fleet are MD-82s assembled in China under a licence agreement with McDonnell-Douglas. As well as scheduled and charter flights, Mil-8 helicopters are used for industrial work and various other tasks including heavy-lifting or the erection of masts. In 1993 two Airbus A300-600s were leased and these proved to be successful in service, so that six further examples were ordered, entering service during 1994-95. An arrangement for Chinese licence production of the McDonnell Douglas MD-90 has been agreed, and China Northern is to be the launch customer. Since the Spring of 1996 the airline has flown its first international route from Shenzen to the new international airport at Macau.

Routes

Extensive network in China: Beijing, Changchun, Changhsa, Chengdu, Chongqing, Dalian, Dandong, Fuzhou, Guangzhou, Haikou, Hangzhou, Hefei, Jilin, Jinan, Macau, Nanjing, Nanning, Shanghai, Shantou, Shenyang, Shenzen, Tianjin, Urumqi, Wenzhou, Ziamen, Xian, Yantai and Zhengzhou.

Fleet

5 Airbus A300-600
26 McDonnell Douglas MD-82
5 McDonnell Douglas MD-90
11 Yunshuij Y-7

Ordered

6 McDonnell Douglas MD-90

Photograph: Tupolev Tu-154M B-2609 (Björn Kannengiesser/Beijing)

CHINA NORTHWEST AIRLINES

Laodong Nanlu, Xiguan Airport, 710082 Xioan, Shaanxi, Peoples Republic of China
Tel. 29-4263029 Fax. 29-4262022

Three letter code	IATA No.	ICAO Callsign
CNW	783	China Northwest

The former CAAC regional directorate of Xian has been flying under the name of China Northwest Airlines since 1989 and has been given the task of operating regional scheduled and charter flights. The fleet taken over from CAAC was based in Lanzou and Xiguan and still consisted of Soviet-built aircraft, mainly Tupolev 154s. China Northwest has a modern maintenance centre at the new Xian-Xianyang Airport. Conditions were therefore right for a successive replacement of the fleet with aircraft up to Western standards. Thus in 1990/91, BAe 146s were delivered for regional services as a replacement for the An-24. In the following year Airbus 300-600s and A310s were brought into service. As well as scheduled and charter passenger services, the airline also undertakes agricultural and forestry aerial work.

Routes

Dense regional scheduled network to over 70 points. Several daily flights Beijing, Shanghai and Hong Kong. Nagoya, Singapore and Tashkent are further international destinations.

Fleet	Ordered
3 Airbus A310-200	3 Airbus A300-600
5 Airbus A300-600	10 Airbus A320-200
10 BAe 146-100/300	
9 Tupolev Tu-154M	
13 Yunshuji Y5	

Photograph: Boeing 757-200 B-2811 (Florian Morasch/Hong Kong)

CHINA SOUTHERN

Baiyun Intl.Airport, 510405 Guangzhou,
Peoples Republic of China
Tel. 20-6678901 Fax. 20-6667637

Three letter code	IATA No.	ICAO Callsign
CSN	784	China Southern

This airline also came into existence in 1989 after the reorganisation of Chinese airlines and the CAAC. The second largest Chinese international airline, based in Guangzhou, is growing and undergoing an enormous boom, increasing at annual rates of over 40%. In two years more than $600 million was invested in the fleet and its replacement. From 1990, Boeing 737s, 757s and more recently 767s were being delivered continually. The super-modern Boeing 777 came into service in 1995. Twenty A320s were ordered in 1997, the first Airbuses to be sold directly to a Chinese operator, with the first delivery made in July. In 1996 China Southern founded its own business airline, operating Lear Jets. In common with other Chinese airlines, China Southern also inherited responsibilities for agricultural and offshore flying for which it employs a diverse fleet of light aircraft and helicopters.

Routes

Include Bangkok, Beijing, Changsa, Guangzhou, Hanoi, Hefei, Hong Kong, Jakarta, Kuala Lumpur, Kunming, Manila, Nanning, Penang, Qindo, Shantou, Shasai, Surabaya, Vientiane, Xiamen, Yichang, Zhanjiang.

Fleet

1 Airbus A320
23 Boeing 737-300
12 Boeing 737-500
20 Boeing 757-200
6 Boeing 767-300
2 Boeing 777-200
4 Saab 340
21 Yunshuji Y5

Ordered

19 Airbus A320
4 Boeing 777

Photograph: Boeing 737-300 B-2522 (Albert Kuhbandner/Hong Kong)

CHINA SOUTHWEST AIRLINES

Shuangli Airport, Chengdu - Sichuan 610202,
Peoples Republic of China
Tel. 28-5814466 Fax. 28-5582630

Three letter code	IATA No.	ICAO Callsign
CXN	785	China Southwest

A further airline which has been separated from the CAAC is China Southwest, which was also set up to run its own flight operations in 1987. Initially the main airliner types used were the Antonov 24, Boeing 707 and Tupolev 154. Since 1992 impressively large fleets of Boeing 737s and 757s have been increasingly used to meet passenger demand. About 30 destinations are served from the Chengdu-Shuangli airport, including more international points. Hong Kong, Kathmandu and Singapore were given service from 1989. Freight services were also flown with the former CAAC Boeing 707s, but this type has been almost completely replaced in the fleet with the delivery of new 757s. The fast growing airline has its maintenance base at Chewngdu, and is building up its staff and experience as Boeing specialists.

Routes

Bangkok, Beijing, Dalian, Guangzhou, Hong Kong, Kunming, Lhasa, Shanghai, Singapore, Urumqi, Wuhan, Xiamen, Zhengzou and other destinations in China.

Fleet

1 Boeing 707-300C
20 Boeing 737-300
13 Boeing 757-200
5 Tupolev Tu-154M
4 Yunshuji Y-12

Photograph: Ilyushin IL-86 B-2018 (Björn Kannengiesser/Beijing)

CHINA XINJIANG AIRLINES

Diwobao International Airport, Urumqi,
Xinjiang 830016, Peoples Republic of China
Tel. 991-335688 Fax. 991-335688

Three letter code	IATA No.	ICAO Callsign
CXJ	651	Xinjiang

Xinjiang Airlines was founded in 1985, its forebear being the CAAC Xinjiang regional administration. It is owned 50% each by CAAC and the Xinjiang regional government. This far western Chinese region borders on Kyrgystan, Mongolia and India, and many places are not quickly accessible other than by air. Thus it is not surprising that for such routes the de Havilland Canada DHC-6 Twin Otter was introduced into service in February 1985. Xinjiang Airlines acquired a further Western aircraft type, the Boeing 737-300, in 1993 and 1994. These are used on international services to Hong Kong and Islamabad. For the high-frequency scheduled service to Beijing, three Ilyushin IL-86 widebodies were acquired at the end of 1993, and at that time the name of the airline was changed to China Xinjiang Airlines. The principal operating and maintenance base is at Urumqi.

Routes

Aksu, Almaty, Beijing, Changsha, Chengdu, Chongqing, Dalian, Fuyun, Guangzhou, Guilin, Harbin, Hong Kong, Hotan, Islamabad, Jinan, Karamy, Kashi, Korla, Kunming, Kuqa, Lanzhou, Moscow, Novosibirsk, Qiemo, Qingdao, Shanghai, Shenyang, Shenzen, Tianjin, Xian, Xiamen, Yinning, Zhengzhou.

Fleet

3 Antonov An-24
4 Boeing 737-300
2 De Havilland DHC-6
3 Ilyushin IL-86
8 Tupolev Tu-154M

Photograph: Boeing 737-300 B-2958 (Martin Bach/Singapore)

CHINA YUNNAN AIRLINES

Wujiabao Airport, Kunming,
Yunnan 650200, Peoples Republic of China
Tel. 871-7177528 Fax: 871-3138675

Three letter code	IATA No.	ICAO Callsign
CYH	592	Yunnan

Like all Chinese airline companies Yunnan has its ancestry in the CAAC, in this case the Yunnan regional administration. It became independent in July 1992 and began a daily Boeing 737-300 service from its base at Kunming-Wujiabao to Beijing and Shanghai. From 1993 international flights were introduced to Bangkok and Singapore. In mid-1996 the totally 737-300 fleet was augmented with two 263-seat Boeing 767-300s in order to accommodate steeply rising traffic levels, and more aircraft of both types are scheduled for delivery over the next year or two.

Routes

Bangkok, Baoshan, Beijing, Chengsha, Fuzhou, Guilin, Hefei, Lijang, Shanghai, Shenzen, Singapore, Wuhan, Zhengzhou.

Fleet	Ordered
10 Boeing 737-300 3 Boeing 767-300ER	3 Boeing 737-300

Photograph: Embraer EMB-120 N159A (Josef Krauthäuser/Fort Lauderdale)

COMAIR

P.O. Box 75021, Cincinnati International Airport, Ohio 45275, USA
Tel. 606-5252550 Fax. 606-5253420-3

Three letter code	IATA No.	ICAO Callsign
COM	886	Comair

Comair began regional service in March 1977 with a Piper Navajo between Cincinnati and Cleveland. The larger Embraer EMB-110 Bandeirante came into service from 1981, following which more destinations were served. The further addition of Shorts 360, Swearingen Metro and in 1984 the Saab 340 aircraft were indicators of expansion and increasing demand. At the beginning of 1984 some 30 destinations were being served from Cincinnati and the airline was already a 'major' amongst regional carriers. In September 1984 Comair became a partner in the newly formed 'Delta Connection' system, under which marketing banner Delta brought together the feeder and regional services which had previously been operated by individual airlines under their own identities. In 1989 Comair Holdings was founded to bring together the by now substantial activities of the group. From 1988 the Embraer 120 Brasilia, a fast turboprop, was introduced; Comair was the first customer for this type. Likewise it was the launch customer for the Canadair Regional Jet, which began deliveries in 1993, and represented the first jet in the fleet. The delivery of the first order for 50 is just about complete, and now 30 more have been ordered for delivery commencing September 1997, with options on yet a further 45, some of which could be taken up as the larger 70-seat CRJ700 model. Comair has two hubs, the principal one in Cincinnati and a secondary one at Orlando in Florida. With over 100 aircraft, 2,500 employees and an increasing annual passenger total, Comair is one of the world's largest regional carriers.

Routes

From the two hubs at Cincinnati and Orlando, 85 towns and cities in 28 US states are served, along with destinations in Canada and in the Bahamas.

Fleet	Ordered
50 Canadair Regional Jet 2 Embraer EMB-110 Bandeirante 39 Embraer EMB-120 Brasilia 10 Saab 340A	30 Canadair Regional Jet

Photograph: McDonnell Douglas DC-10-30 D-ADCO (Uwe Gleisberg/Munich FJS)

CONDOR FLUGDIENST

Am Grünen Weg 3, 65440 Kelsterbach,
Germany
Tel. 06107-939 0 Fax. 06107-939 440

Three letter code	IATA No.	ICAO Callsign
CFG	881	Condor

Condor is the traditional charter-flight subsidiary of the German Lufthansa. Set up in 1955 as Deutsche Flugdienst GmbH, German Federal Railways, two shipping companies and Lufthansa were shareholders in DF. The first aircraft were Vickers Vikings. After DF's considerable initial successes, it suffered a setback in 1959 and was completely taken over by Lufthansa with the aid of the state, thus averting the threat of bankruptcy. In October 1961, Lufthansa bought the Condor Luftreederei (formed in 1957) from the Oetker group and merged it with the DF to form the new Condor Flugdienst GmbH. Vickers Viscounts were bought in 1961 and two Fokker F27s in 1963; in 1965 the first Boeing 727 entered service. Condor had a purely jet fleet as early as 1968. Condor obtained a Boeing 747-100 in 1971, plus another in 1972. These aircraft opened up new routes to Bangkok and to the USA. In the late 1970s, the first oil crisis resulted in excess capacity being reduced. From then on, the smaller DC-10-30 replaced the jumbo on long-distance flights. Boeing 737-300s and Airbus A310s have been in use since 1987. In 1989 the Boeing 757 in the Condor colours was first seen at Europe's airports, the 757s replacing the 727s. In order to be able to meet the rising demand, but also for a while to be able to operate scheduled flights for Lufthansa, the fleet is being expanded. Noteworthy in this connection is that Condor is the launch customer for the new stretched Boeing 757-300, with 12 on order. In 1995 Condor allied itself with various tour companies in order to offer them capacity on their own flights. It is today one of the world's largest charter airlines operating an all-jet fleet out of Frankfurt, Düsseldorf, Munich, Stuttgart and other German cities.

Routes

Flights to USA, Caribbean, the Near and Far East, India, Nepal and destinations in the Mediterranean, Canary Islands, North Africa and Kenya, also to the former Soviet Union and Taipei.

Fleet	Ordered
4 Boeing 737-300	6 Airbus A320-200
18 Boeing 757-200	12 Boeing 757-300
9 Boeing 767-300ER	
5 McDonnell Douglas DC-10-30	

Photograph: De Havilland DHC-8-300 D-BELT (Uwe Gleisberg/Munich FJS)

CONTACT AIR

Postfach 230442, 70624 Stuttgart
Germany
Tel. 0711-167650 Fax. 0711-1676565

Three letter code	IATA No.	ICAO Callsign
KIS	-	Contactair

Contact Air was set up in 1969 and worked as a non-scheduled air carrier, operating among other things ambulance flights and charter flights. It served some routes from Stuttgart, Münster and Hamburg for DLT for some years, using BAe Jetstream 31s. In 1989 Contactair obtained a de Havilland DHC-8 leased from Tyrolean; since then the airline acquired its own DHC-8s and continued to expand its fleet. Contactair took over all propeller-driven aircraft operations from Lufthansa during 1996/97, and along with this transfer came the Fokker 50 fleet. A further rationalisation among Team Lufthansa operators has recently led to a phasing out of the Dash 8s in favour of an all Fokker 50 fleet, most of which are flown in 'Team-Lufthansa' colours.

Routes

Scheduled flights on behalf of Lufthansa to various internal and regional points.

Fleet

11 Fokker 50

Photograph: McDonnell Douglas DC-10-30 N12061 (Andrè Dietzel/Munich FJS)

CONTINENTAL

2929 Allen Parkway, Houston Texas, 77019, USA
Tel. 713-834-5000 Fax. 713-639-3087

Three letter code	IATA No.	ICAO Callsign
COA	005	Continental

Continental can trace its history back to July 1934 as the southwest division of Varney Speed Lines; its name was changed to Varney Air Transport on 17th December 1934, and in 1937 to Continental Air Lines. A network of routes was established using various Lockheed aircraft, mainly in the western USA. After the Second World War, Convair 240s, DC-6s and DC-7Bs were employed. Pioneer Airlines was taken over in 1954. Boeing 707s started 'golden jet' flights on 8th June 1959. The first Boeing 747 took place on 18th May 1970; the DC-10 followed two years later. In October 1981, Texas International acquired a stake in Continental, and the merger of the two companies followed in October 1982 under the Continental name. 1983 brought enormous financial problems and collapse under Chapter 11 bankruptcy protection in September. More than half of the staff were made redundant, many aircraft grounded and routes discontinued. It emerged from Chapter 11 in 1986. In February 1987, the parent company bought up PeoplExpress, New York Air and Frontier, and these airlines were also merged with Continental. The airline's operations doubled as a result, with considerable difficulties during the consolidation. The airline placed itself once again under Chapter 11 in December 1990, emerging in May 1993, at which time a new colour scheme was adopted. In 1994 a 'low-cost' operation was set up as 'Continental Lite' but abandoned after heavy losses. Continental Micronesia is a separate division for Pacific island services, and an extensive network of feeder services is operated by partner airlines under the name 'Continental Express'. Air Canada owns 19% of the capital. A long-term sole supply contract was made with Boeing for new aircraft in June 1997.

Routes

Continental has an intensive internal US network, based on Cleveland, Houston and Newark, and flies to Canada, South America, the South Pacific, to Manila, Guam, Hong Kong, and Taipei. In Europe Birmingham, Düsseldorf, Frankfurt, London, Madrid, Manchester and Paris are served.

Fleet

42 Boeing 727-200
132 Boeing 737-100/200/300/500
20 Boeing 757-200
30 McDonnell Douglas DC-9-32
59 McDonnell Douglas MD-80
25 McDonnell Douglas DC-10-30

Ordered

30 Boeing 737-500
48 Boeing 737-600
30 Boeing 737-800
21 Boeing 757-200
30 Boeing 767-400ER
10 Boeing 777-200

Photograph: Boeing 737-200Adv HP-1163-CMP (Josef Krauthäuser/Miami)

COPA PANAMA

Apartado Postal 1572, Panama City, Panama
Tel. 2272522 Fax. 2271952

Three letter code	IATA No.	ICAO Callsign
CMP	230	Copa

The Compania Panameña de Aviacion SA – COPA – was formed on 21st June 1944. As was the case with many other South and Central American airlines, Pan American Airways set up COPA, together with business people from Panama; Pan American provided 32% of the capital. Scheduled services to neighbouring countries commenced on 15th August 1947 with DC-3s. A Convair CV240 was added to the fleet in 1952. Up until the time when jet aircraft came into use, an HS.748 and a Lockheed L-188 were in the service of COPA. International services had been introduced from 1965 and in 1981 COPA discontinued scheduled Panamanian domestic services. In 1971 Pan American withdrew from Copa Panama and sold its shares. New services were started to Mexico City in October 1991 and to Cali, Montego Bay and San Juan (Puerto Rico) in 1992. In 1995 service to the Dominican Republic was added. There are various joint marketing ventures with TACA.

Routes

Panama, Costa Rica, Dominican Republic, El Salvador, Guatemala, Nicaragua, Jamaica, Haiti and Miami.

Fleet

11 Boeing 737-200Adv

Photograph: Boeing 737-400 F-GFUG (Andrè Dietzel/Munich FJS)

CORSAIR

24 rue Saarinen, Silic 221,
94528 Rungis Silic Cedex, France
Tel. 1-49794980 Fax. 1-49794998

Three letter code	IATA No.	ICAO Callsign
CRL	-	Corsair

Formed in 1981 as Corse-Air International, Corsair started operations on 1st July 1981 and acquired four SE 210 Caravelles. There were charter flights from Paris and Ajaccio within Europe and to North Africa. A characteristic feature of the fleet was a striking head with a headband on the tail of the aircraft. The first Boeing 737s were obtained in 1987, marking the start of a fleet replacement programme. In 1990 a Boeing 747 followed. There were alterations to the airline's name and to the colours of the aircraft in 1991, after a leading French tour operator, Nouvelles Frontières, acquired a stake in the airline. Several Boeing 747s were brought into the fleet to meet the needs of this new partner; the other aircraft are used for scheduled and charter services.

Routes

Abidjan, Bangkok, Cayenne, Dakar, Fort de France, Los Angeles, Mombasa, Montreal, New York, Noumea, Papeete, Point a Pitre, Rome, San Francisco, St Louis, St Martin. To various destinations in Europe and the Mediterranean area.

Fleet

1 Boeing 737-200Adv
2 Boeing 737-400
2 Boeing 747-100
2 Boeing 747-200
1 Boeing 747- 300
1 Boeing 747SP
1 McDonnell Douglas DC-10

Ordered

2 Boeing 747-300

Photograph: ATR42-300 9A-CTU (Andreas Hainzel/Graz)

CROATIA AIRLINES

Savska Cesta 41, 1000 Zagreb,
Croatia
Tel. 6160066 Fax. 530475

Three letter code	IATA No.	ICAO Callsign
CTN	831	Croatia

After the collapse of Yugoslavia the Republic of Croatia was formed in the north of the country with Zagreb as the capital. The national airline formed in 1989 was initially called Zagal-Zagreb Airlines using Cessna and Piper aircraft, but took the present name in 1990. The scheduled services formerly belonging to JAT were taken over using DC-9s from Adria Airways and operations commenced on 5th May 1991 between Zagreb and Split. Due to the UN embargo and the continued fighting, the airspace over the country was closed from September 1990 until 1st April 1992. After it was reopened, Croatian Airlines expanded its flights and has been operating since then with Boeing 737-200s. ATR42s also came into use in 1993 for internal and short-range international flights. With the opening of the airports at Mostar and Sarajevo in the summer of 1996, these points were also served. As well as scheduled flights there are charter flights to meet the needs of Croatians working abroad, and also to serve the slowly reviving Adriatic tourist market.

Routes

Amsterdam, Berlin, Bol, Brussels, Copenhagen, Dublin, Dubrovnik, Düsseldorf, Frankfurt, Istanbul, London, Moscow, Munich, Paris, Prague, Pula, Rome, Skopje, Split, Stockholm, Stuttgart, Tirana, Vienna, Zagreb, Zadar and Zürich.

Fleet	Ordered
1 Airbus A320-200 3 ATR42-300 5 Boeing 737-200Adv	6 Airbus A319-100

Photograph: Saab 2000 HB-IZE (B.I.Hengi/Zürich)

CROSSAIR

Postfach 4002, Basel-Flughafen,
Switzerland
Tel. 61-3252525 Fax. 61-3253268

Three letter code	IATA No.	ICAO Callsign
CRX	724	Crossair

Crossair started a charter service from Zürich to Nuremberg with a Swearingen Metro II on 2nd July 1979. A predecessor had originally been in existence since 14th February 1975 called Business Flyers Basle. This airline operated as a non-scheduled air carrier. When scheduled services started, the name Crossair was used, a name by now well known beyond the borders of the Swiss Confederacy. Crossair had further rights to scheduled routes for Innsbruck and Klagenfurt. Under the guidance of their President Moritz Suter, Crossair made great contributions to European regional services and it provided pioneer crews and ideas for the Saab 340 regional aircraft, for which the airline was a launch customer with an order for ten aircraft in October 1980. In Switzerland, Crossair opened up new services from Basle, Berne and Lugano over the years. On 15th June 1984 a Crossair Saab 340 entered service on the Basle-Paris route which it had taken over on behalf of Swissair. Crossair's achievements were rewarded with many awards, eg that of 'Commuter Airline of the Year'. In 1990, over 1 million passengers were carried for the first time, and the Fokker 50 and its first jet aircraft, the BAe 146, were introduced. On 30th March 1992, a BAe 146 service between Zürich and London City commenced.
The airline, in which Swissair now has a majority stake, was a launch customer for the Saab 2000 50-seat regional airliner which was introduced in 1994 after some delivery delays. As part of a re-organisation within the Swissair group, Crossair has also taken over the parent airline's MD-80s which are flown on scheduled and charter services.

Routes

From Basle, Zürich, Geneva, Berne and Lugano Crossair has its own schedules to Italy, France, Austria, Germany, Belgium, the Netherlands and the UK. Also operations on behalf of Swissair.

Fleet

16 Avro RJ 85/100
16 Saab 340A/B
26 Saab 2000
8 McDonnell Douglas MD-82/83

20 Saab 2000

Photograph: Tupolev Tu-154M OK-UCF (Andrè Dietzel/Munich FJS)

CSA - CZECH AIRLINES

Ruzyne Airport, 16008 Prague,
Czech Republic
Tel 362614 Fax. 3162774

Three letter code	IATA No.	ICAO Callsign
CSA	064	CSA Lines

CSA was founded on 6th October 1923 and flew its first service from Prague to Bratislava with a Hansa Brandenburg Aero A-14. In mid-1930 the exclusively internal service was expanded internationally with a Prague-Bratislava-Vienna-Zagreb route, and connections to Romania and the USSR followed. By the mid-1930s CSA was one of the leading European airlines. However closure was enforced from 1938 to 1946 by the war. A new start was made in 1947 with the Douglas DC-3, but following political change in 1948 came the influx of Soviet technology, and CSA flew Ilyushin IL-12s and 14s, and from 9th December 1957 the Tupolev Tu-104A, with which service to Jakarta was introduced. The IL-12s were replaced by IL-18s and a schedule to Havana initiated. For long-range routes the Ilyushin IL-62 was acquired in 1969 and in 1970 New York and Montreal were first served. The Tupolev Tu-134A was employed for many years on European routes, but replaced gradually with more modern Tu-154Ms from April 1988. The political swing during 1989 made it possible for the first time in 40 years to order western aircraft; Airbus A310-300s were thus delivered in 1990, to replace the Ilyushin IL-62s. Since then the fleet has been constantly renewed and upgraded to western standards, including Boeing 737s and ATR42s and 72s. Following the division of the erstwhile Czechoslovakia into two republics, a change of name (effective from 26th March 1995) and a new colour scheme have been introduced. There are joint services/codeshares with Luxair, KLM, LOT and Lufthansa.

Routes

Internal network serving 5 cities. Additionally CSA flies from Prague to 50 destinations in 4 continents.

Fleet

2 Airbus A310-300
2 ATR42
4 ATR72
9 Boeing 737-400/500
3 Tupolev Tu-134A
4 Tupolev Tu-154M

Ordered

3 Boeing 737-400/500

Photograph: Yakovlev Yak-42 CU-T1277 (Xaver Flocki collection)

CUBANA

23-64 Vedado, Havana 1040C
Cuba
Tel. 7 36 775 Fax 7 36 190

Three letter code	IATA No.	ICAO Callsign
CUB	136	Cubana

Cubana had been formed originally on 8th October 1929 as Compania Ñacional Cubana de Aviacion Curtiss by the Curtiss Aviation Group and started operations on 30th October 1930 using a Ford 4-AT-E. On 6th May 1932, the carrier was purchased by Pan American and the name 'Curtiss' was removed from its title. In 1945 the word 'Ñacional' was also removed and Cuban interests took a 46% shareholding. Its first international service under its own name took place on 15th May 1946 to Miami flown by a DC-3. Cubans gained a 52% interest in 1948 and Pan American sold its remaining shares in 1954. For the past few years socialist Cuba has been opening its doors to western tourists, after tourism had been discovered as a way of earning foreign currency. Since that time, Cubana IL-62s are occasionally to be seen at European airports. The Empresa Consolidada Cubana de Aviacion was established by the Cuban government in 1959 when its predecessor, Compania Cubana de Aviacion SA was taken over, reorganised and merged with smaller airlines. At that time the fleet consisted of English and American aircraft such as Constellations, Britannias and Viscounts and the majority were offered for sale in 1961. After the USA's economic blockade, only Soviet-built aircraft were used and IL-14s, IL-18s, An-12s and An-24s arrived between 1961 and 1967. In 1974 Cubana's first pure jet, an IL-62, arrived and went into service in November between Havana and Madrid. Since the collapse of the 'Warsaw Pact' more services have been introduced to the West, some now flown with leased DC-10s. The acquisition of six Fokker F27s from Aviaco in 1994 was another sign of the easing of relations with the non-communist world, and marked the introduction of a new colour scheme.

Routes

Intensive internal network; Caribbean, Latin America and several destinations in Europe such as Basle, Berlin, Brussels, Frankfurt, Cologne, London, Moscow, Munich, Paris and Prague.

Fleet

12 Antonov An-24/26
8 Fokker F27
14 Ilyushin IL-62M
2 Ilyushin IL-76
7 Tupolev Tu-154
5 Yakovlev Yak-40
4 Yakovlev Yak-42D

Photograph: Airbus A320-200 5B-DAV (Frank Fielitz/Frankfurt)

CYPRUS AIRWAYS

21 Alkeou Street, Engomi 1903, Nicosia,
Cyprus
Tel.443054 Fax. 443167

Three letter code	IATA No.	ICAO Callsign
CYP	048	Cyprus

Cyprus Airways was set up on 24th September 1947 by British European Airways, Cypriot business people and the government. British registered DC-3s were used to start flight operations to Athens on 18th April 1948. There were further routes to Haifa, Istanbul, Rome, Beirut and Cairo. Vickers Viscounts opened the London route in the 1950s after BEA, on behalf of Cyprus Airways, began the world's first sustained turboprop passenger service on 18th April 1953 when a Viscount flew the London Heathrow-Nicosia route. Cyprus became an independent nation in August 1960 and BEA signed a deal with Cyprus Airways in 1961 to operate its services, initially for a five year period, with BEA aircraft. The arrangement finally ended in late 1969. Its first jet aircraft were two Hawker-Siddeley Tridents bought in November 1969 from BEA. In July 1974 Cyprus Airways had to close down operations, as Turkish troops had occupied Nicosia Airport and a Trident was destroyed in fighting. The first Boeing 707 service took off on 8th February 1975 from the new base at Larnaca airfield in the south of Cyprus. BAC One-Elevens were acquired, one each in 1977, 1978 and 1980; and in 1984 the first Airbus A310 arrived, followed at the end of 1989 by the new Airbus A320. In 1990 Cyprus Airways created a wholly-owned subsidiary Eurocypria Airlines to operate charter flights from Europe to Larnaca and Paphos using three Airbus A320s. In 1991 all aircraft were repainted in a new colour scheme, which is still worn today by what is now an all-Airbus fleet.

Routes

Amman, Amsterdam, Athens, Bahrain, Beirut, Berlin, Birmingham, Brussels, Damascus, Dubai, Frankfurt, Helsinki, Heraklion, Jeddah, Kuwait, Linz, London, Lyon, Manchester, Munich, Paris Rome, Riyadh, Salzburg, Tel Aviv Vienna and Zürich.

Fleet

8 Airbus A320
4 Airbus A310-200

Photograph: Boeing 757-200 N638DL (Josef Krauthäuser/Fort Lauderdale)

DELTA AIR LINES

Hartsfield Atlanta Airport, Georgia 30320, USA
Tel. 404-7152600 Fax. 404-7678499

Three letter code	IATA No.	ICAO Callsign
DAL	006	Delta

Delta Air Lines is not only the world's leading carrier in terms of passenger numbers (97 million in 1996), it is also one of the oldest, tracing its history back to Huff Daland setting up in 1924 to spray cotton fields in Mississippi Delta. The name Delta Air Services was taken in 1928. A Travelair was used on its first scheduled passenger service on 17th June 1929 from Dallas to Jackson. The company was sold to the Aviation Corporation in 1930 and became Delta Air Corporation. In 1940, there were already ten Lockheed Electras and five DC-3s in the fleet. A further name change came in 1945 to the present title. In 1953 Delta merged with Chicago and Southern Airlines and for a short time was known as Delta C&S Air Lines. Northeast Airlines was taken over in 1972, and finally Western Airlines was acquired in April 1987; thus the network of routes was continually expanded. In 1959 DC-8s, in 1960 Convair 880s and in 1965 DC-9s came into service. Delta was a launch customer with all of these aircraft. Boeing 747s were in service from 1970-77, plus DC-10s from 1972-75. However, the airline eventually settled on the Lockheed TriStar. In 1978 flights started across the Atlantic to London, and to Frankfurt a year later. In November 1991, Pan Am was bought up and all the routes and aircraft were integrated. There are shareholdings in and partnership arrangements with Swissair and Singapore Airlines, and the 'Delta Connection' is a network of airlines providing feeder and regional services. New colours, the first for 35 years, were unveiled in April 1997 and will be applied over the next three years. In Spring 1997 Delta signed an exclusive 20-year fleet acquisition plan with Boeing, with planned purchase of up to 644 aircraft and launching the 767-400. It includes 106 firm orders initially.

Routes

Delta Air Lines has over 2600 flights each day to about 250 destinations worldwide. The principal US hubs are at Atlanta, Dallas/Fort Worth and Cincinnati.

Fleet

129 Boeing 727-200Adv
54 Boeing 737-200Adv
13 Boeing 737-300
90 Boeing 757-200
15 Boeing 767-200
56 Boeing 767-300/300ER
31 Lockheed L-1011
17 Lockheed L-1011-500
14 McDonnell Douglas MD-11
120 McDonnell Douglas MD-88
16 McDonnell Douglas MD-90

Ordered

70 Boeing 737-600/700/800
9 Boeing 757
21 Boeing 767-300ER
21 Boeing 767-400
15 McDonnell Douglas MD-90
1 McDonnell Douglas MD-11

Photograph: Fokker 100 D-ADFB (Uwe Gleisberg/Munich FJS)

DEUTSCHE BA

Wartungsallee 13, 85356 Munich-Flughafen, Germany
Tel. 089-97591 500 Fax. 089-97591 503

Three letter code	IATA No.	ICAO Callsign
BAG	944	Speedway

Delta Air from Friedrichshafen was set up by the Scholpp transport group in Stuttgart in March 1978 and started flights between Friedrichshafen and Stuttgart with a DHC-6 Twin Otter in April 1978, as well as Friedrichshafen-Zürich. In 1982 a Swearingen Metro III was added to the fleet. A second Metro III was added in 1984 as well as a Dornier 228, the latter being used on the route Friedrichshafen-Oberpfaffenhofen. In 1985 Delta Air was converted into a private limited company, with the involvement of the Swiss airline Crossair. In May 1987 it was given the status of a scheduled airline and since then has been flying some routes with Saab 340s, added to the fleet in 1986, on behalf of the German airline Lufthansa. In March 1992 three German banks bought 51% of the shares and British Airways the remaining 49% stake in Delta Air and the name was changed to Deutsche BA on 5th May 1992. The new scheduled airline used not only Saab 340s but also Boeing 737-300s, introducing the Saab 2000 and Fokker 100 from 1995. During 1992 and 1993 scheduled services were inaugurated, amongst others to Moscow and Ankara. The company headquarters were moved to Munich from 1st January 1995. During 1997 regional services are being withdrawn and the propeller-driven aircraft sold on to another operator. The Fokker 100s, which cannot now be augmented with new aircraft following the demise of the Dutch manufacturer, are to be replaced from August 1997 by Boeing 737-300s.

Routes

Deutsche BA has a dense internal network and connections to major European cities. Charter flights operate to the classic Mediterranean region.

Fleet	Ordered
12 Boeing 737-300 4 Fokker 100	6 Boeing 737-300

Photograph: Boeing 727 N722OH (Josef Krauthäuser/Miami)

DHL AIRWAYS

P.O. Box 75122, Cincinnati, Ohio 45275, USA
Tel. 606-2832232 Fax. 606-5251998

Three letter code	IATA No.	ICAO Callsign
DHL	423	Dahl

DHL Airways is an undertaking of the internationally active DHL Worldwide Express, founded in 1969. The DHL name stems from the first letters of the surnames of the three founders. Initially its task was the carriage of courier packages between California and Hawaii, carried on scheduled flights, and then on other routes within the USA. In time the company acquired its own smaller aircraft such as the Swearingen Metro II and Cessna 402. At the beginning of the 1980s business had developed so that packages were carried on their own aircraft only and within the USA there were 12 hubs and 76 so-called gateways where freight could be accepted. DHL now operates worldwide with 14 international hubs. Boeing 727s formed the bulk of the fleet, with DC-8s for long-range services, and even a helicopter in New York. Lufthansa and Japan Airlines both have 25% shares in, and marketing alliances with, DHL. Other operators fly services on behalf of DHL, for instance European Air Transport of Belgium for various European services. For the expanding Asian market, DHL has Sinotrans as a partner in China, with service building up to 26 centres. A memorandum of understanding was signed in April 1997 for the acquisition of 7 used Airbus A300B4 freighters for the US network for delivery between the second half of 1998 and the end of 1999.

Routes

Scheduled freight services within the USA to 88 points; internationally to 14 destinations on all continents.

Fleet

1 Bell 206-L1 Long Ranger
24 Boeing 727-100/200
10 Fairchild SA 227 Expediter
1 Learjet 35
7 McDonnell Douglas DC-8-73F

Photograph: Airbus A320-200 VR-HYT (Florian Morasch/Hong Kong)

DRAGONAIR

22 F Devon House, Taikoo Place, 979 Kings Road, Quarry Bay, Hong Kong
Tel. 25901328 Fax. 25901333

Three letter code	IATA No.	ICAO Callsign
HDA	043	Dragonair

Dragonair became active in April 1985, mainly in order to serve destinations in the People's Republic of China from Hong Kong. The airline started flight operations with two Boeing 737-200Adv although during the first year of operations much of the time the aircraft were grounded due to opposition from Cathay Pacific. However over the next few years some scheduled routes were awarded to Dragonair and several more Boeing 737s were leased as the network of scheduled routes was expanded. Dragonair was a wholly-owned subsidiary of Hong Kong Macau International Investments until late 1989. China International Trust and Investment and the Swire Group now own most of the shares. Since 1989, destinations outside the People's Republic of China are also being served and a charter department has been set up. In mid-1990 a Lockheed L-1011 TriStar was acquired from Cathay Pacific. When the first Airbus A320 was delivered in late 1992, a new aircraft colour scheme was adopted. Four Airbus A330s were introduced in 1995/96 as replacements for the TriStars, thus completing a most modern fleet.

Routes

Bandar Seri Begawan, Beijing, Chengdu, Dalian, Guilin, Hangzhon, Haikon, Hiroshima, Kagoshima, Kathmandu, Kuching, Nanjing, Phuket and Shanghai are served from Hong Kong.

Fleet	Ordered
7 Airbus A320-200 4 Airbus A330-300	2 Airbus A320-200 2 Airbus A330-300

Photograph: BAe 146-100 A5-RGD (Josef Krauthäuser/Bangkok)

DRUK AIR

P.O. Box 209, Thimpu,
Kingdom of Bhutan
Tel 22825 Fax. 22775

Three letter code	IATA No.	ICAO Callsign
DRK	787	Royal Bhutan

Druk Air was established on 1st April 1981 by decree of the King of Bhutan. After the infrastructure for air traffic had been created, a Dornier 228 started operations with a flight to Calcutta on 12th February 1983. In mid-1983 a second aircraft of the same type was acquired. Charters were flown for the Indian domestic carrier, Vayudoot, on routes in eastern India. When a BAe 146 was delivered, the airline entered the jet age. Druk Air intends to expand its network using this aircraft. The first new service point was Bangkok. The BAe 146 is also available to the King of Bhutan for personal flights. With the delivery of a further BAe 146 in 1992 all flights are now jet-operated.

Routes

Bangkok, Calcutta, Dhaka, Delhi, Kathmandu, and Yangon.

Fleet

2 BAe 146-100

Photograph: McDonnell Douglas MD-83 HB-IKN (B.I.Hengi/Zürich)

EDELWEISS AIR

Postfach 8055, Zürich-Flughafen,
Switzerland
Tel. 1-8165060 Fax. 1-8165061

Three letter code	IATA No.	ICAO Callsign
EDW	-	Edelweiss

On 19th October 1995 a new charter company was set up in the Zürich area. The Kuoni travel company and the Greek Venus Airlines were shareholders. It was set up as a joint stock company and thus could take on further participants; the capital was raised to 3.5 million Swiss Francs on the acquisition of the aircraft in December 1995. At the end of January 1996 the first MD-83 arrived, with the second following at the end of March. Edelweiss tries to live up to its claim to be 'more than an airline', and creates a very Swiss atmosphere with cabin crews in 'Heidi' uniforms (yodelling captains?), and for a meal comes a wurst and cheese salad with yoghurt and butter braids. Milk and chocolates are also offered. The aircraft colour scheme reflects the name and is very striking.

Routes

Djerba, Faro, Fuerteventura, Ibiza, Lanzarote, Larnaca, Las Palmas, London, Mahon, Naples, Palma de Mallorca, Tenerife, Vienna.

Fleet

3 McDonnell Douglas MD-83

Photograph: Airbus A320-200 SU-GBF (Uwe Gleisberg/Munich FJS)

EGYPT AIR

International Airport, Cairo,
Egypt
Tel. 23902444 Fax. 23901557

Three letter code	IATA No.	ICAO Callsign
MSR	077	Egyptair

Misr Airwork was founded on 7th June 1932 and services started in July 1933 with de Havilland Dragons. In 1949 the then wholly Egyptian-owned operation was renamed Misrair. Following a political union between Egypt and Syria in February 1958, Misrair was re-named United Arab Airlines and in December 1958, Syrian Airways was merged into UAA. However, in September 1961 Syria withdrew from the amalgamation. The UAA used Comet 4Bs and Vickers Viscounts. Egypt carried on the airline under the name of UAA.
In 1964 Misrair was revived as a domestic airline, and both airlines were brought together on 10th October 1971 to form the new Egypt Air. For political reasons UAA/Egypt Air also flew Soviet aircraft in the 1960s and '70s, including An-24s, IL-18s, IL-62s and Tu-154s. In April 1975 the airline switched to Airbus A300s and Boeing 737s. Boeing 707s followed for long-distance routes, and later Boeing 747s as well. In November 1980, Egyptair was financially re-organised and the share capital is now held equally by the National Bank of Egypt and Misr Insurance. An extensive fleet replacement began with Boeing 767s and Airbus A300-600s in 1989. In 1991 Airbus A320s followed for short and medium range routes, and at the end of 1996 the new Airbus A340 was introduced as an eventual replacement for the Boeing 747s on some long-range services. The three new Boeing 777-200IGWs (Increased Gross Weight) were delivered in mid-1997, taking over the transatlantic service from July.

Routes

Egypt Air's route network stretches from Los Angeles and New York in the USA to Tokyo. In total about 60 destinations are served.

Fleet

9 Airbus A300-600
4 Airbus A300B4
7 Airbus A320-200
4 Airbus A321-200
4 Airbus A340-200
7 Boeing 737-200/500
2 Boeing 747-300
2 Boeing 767-300ER
3 Boeing 767-200ER
3 Boeing 777-200IGW

Photograph: Boeing 747-400 4X-ELB (Albert Kuhbandner/Munich FJS)

EL AL ISRAEL AIRLINES

P.O. Box 41, Ben Gurion Airport 70100 Tel Aviv, Israel
Tel. 3-9716111 Fax. 3-9716040

Three letter code	IATA No.	ICAO Callsign
ELY	114	EL AL

El Al took the initiative after the founding of the State of Israel with aircraft belonging to the Israeli Air Force and started building up services. These were and are vital for the state of Israel, which is surrounded by potential enemies. The aircraft used after the airline was set up on 15th November 1948 were transports, Curtiss C-46 and DC-4s (C-54s). Operations began on 31st July 1949. The first flights were to Switzerland and Paris. London was served from 1949.
A regular service to New York was established as early as 1950 using Lockheed Constellations. Bristol Britannias were acquired in 1957 and the changeover to jet aircraft began in 1960, initially with leased Boeing 707s. The backbone of the El Al fleet for many years was Boeing 707s/720s. In 1971 the first Boeing 747 arrived; in 1983 Boeing 767s replaced 707s, followed in 1987 by Boeing 757s. El Al was the first airline to use the twin engined Boeing 767 on trans-atlantic flights when it started a Montreal-Tel Aviv service in 1984. In the mid-1980s, El Al was restructured, as the danger of economic collapse threatened. After the peace treaty with the PLO and further easing of tension in the Middle East, El Al is also awaiting a regional boost and opportunities to fly to new destinations in this region. New Boeing 747-400s arrived in 1994 and 1995, rejuvenating the fleet. Aircraft are loaned from time to time to another Israeli airline, Arkia.

Routes

Scheduled flights to USA, Canada, South Africa, Kenya, Amsterdam, Athens, Berlin, Brussels, Budapest, Cologne, Frankfurt, London, Munich, Paris, Vienna, Zürich and other destinations in Europe, the Middle and Far East.

Fleet

2 Boeing 737-200
7 Boeing 747-200
3 Boeing 747-200F
3 Boeing 747-400
9 Boeing 757-200
4 Boeing 767-200

Ordered

1 Boeing 747-400

Photograph: Boeing 777-200 A6-EME (Christian Dougett/London LHR)

EMIRATES

P.O. Box 686, Dubai,
United Arab Emirates
Tel. 4-822511 Fax. 4-822357

Three letter code	IATA No.	ICAO Callsign
UAE	176	Emirates

The independent state airline was formed in 1985 with the support of the Sheikh of the United Emirates and operations commenced on 25th October 1985 with a flight between Dubai and Karachi. Emirates had been formed by the Dubai Government under a management agreement with Pakistan International airlines and initially used a leased PIA Boeing 737 and Airbus A300. The first services were to India and Pakistan, followed by Dacca, Colombo and Cairo in 1986. 1987 saw the first flights to London, Frankfurt and Istanbul, using the newly delivered Airbus A310, of which further examples followed in 1988 and 1990. The larger Airbus A300-600 was ordered however, and the last two Boeing 727s taken out of service in 1995. Emirates is expanding purposefully, but always with caution in new markets. In 1996 a new service to Melbourne was added, using the new Boeing 777, first delivered in June 1996. Emirates has a very modern fleet and uses only widebody aircraft. A330s are to replace the A300s and A310s from 1999. There are code-share agreements with KLM and United Airlines.

Routes

Abu Dhabi, Amman, Bangkok, Beirut, Bombay, Colombo, Comores, Damascus, Delhi, Dacca, Dhahran, Doha, Dubai, Frankfurt, Ho Chi Minh City, Hong Kong, Istanbul, Jakarta, Jeddah, Johannesburg, Cairo, Karachi, Kuwait, Larnaca, London, Male, Manila, Manchester, Melbourne, Muscat, Paris, Riyadh, Rome, Shiraz, Singapore, Teheran and Zürich.

Fleet	Ordered
10 Airbus A310-300	16 Airbus A330-200
6 Airbus A300-600	2 Boeing 777-200
5 Boeing 777-200	

Photograph: Boeing 737-500 ES-ABC (Patrick Lutz/Hamburg)

ESTONIAN AIR

2 Lennujaama Str, Tallinn EE0011, Estonia
Tel. 401101 Fax. 312740

Three letter code	IATA No.	ICAO Callsign
ELL	960	Estonian

Estonian Air was set up by the government of the newly formed state of Estonia on 1st December 1991 and declared to be the country's flag carrier. Estonian Air started the first scheduled service to Helsinki with Tu-134s in the same month. Further routes, especially to Scandinavia, were established in quick succession. In 1995 the state privatisation commission permitted the conversion into a public company. 34% of the capital remains with the government, the rest is with various private investors led by the Danish airline Maersk Air, who now give considerable management assistance. The first step after privatisation was the sale of several Tu-134s and the acquisition of two Boeing 737-500s decorated in a new modern colour scheme, along with an expansion of the route network. Two Fokker 50s have also been leased from Maersk, and the four modern Western aircraft now forming the fleet carry more passengers (about 216,000 expected in 1997) than did the whole fleet of 13 Tu-134s, 4 Yak-40s and 12 An-2s inherited from Aeroflot. The main base is in Tallinn, where there are also maintenance facilities. Seasonal charter flights are operated throughout Europe as well as the regular schedules.

Routes

Amsterdam, Copenhagen, Frankfurt, Hamburg, Helsinki, Kiev, London, Minsk, Moscow, St Petersburg, Stockholm, and Vilnius.

Fleet

2 Boeing 737-500
2 Fokker 50

Photograph: Lockheed L-100-30 ET-AKG (Patrick Lutz/Frankfurt)

ETHIOPIAN AIRLINES

P.O. Box 1755, Bole Airport, Addis Ababa,
Peoples Democratic Republic of Ethiopia
Tel. 612222 Fax. 611474

Three letter code	IATA No.	ICAO Callsign
ETH	071	Ethiopian

Ethiopian Airlines was set up on 26th December 1945 by proclamation of the emperor of the time, Haile Selassie, to develop international Services and to establish connections from the capital to communities in isolated mountainous regions, where little or no surface transport existed. Scheduled flights started on 8th April 1946 with five DC-3s. The first service was between Addis Ababa and Cairo. A management contract was concluded with the American airline TWA assuring long-term support. DC-6Bs were used to operate regular flights to the first European destination, Frankfurt, in June 1958 followed by Athens, Rome, Paris and London. Boeing 720 jet aircraft were introduced in 1962, followed by further Boeing 707s and 720s. Its first Boeing 727 arrived in December 1981. Boeing 767s replaced the 707s and 757s supplanted the 727s, and the DC-3s were largely replaced by the first modern ATR42s in 1989. The airline took delivery in 1997 of a fleet of new Fokker 50s for use on internal and regional services, to some extent replacing the Twin Otters. The airline's slogan is 'Bringing Africa Together' which is especially apposite to the extensive African network centred on Addis Ababa.

There are marketing partnerships with Air India and Nigeria Airways.

Routes

Over 40 internal destinations ; 30 destinations in Africa, to Athens, Bombay, Beijing, Aden, Abu Dhabi, Berlin, Jeddah, Frankfurt, London, Rome and Moscow.

Fleet

3 ATR42
1 Boeing 707-320
1 Boeing 737-200Adv
5 Boeing 757-200
3 Boeing 767-200/300
1 De Havilland DHC-5
4 De Havilland DHC-6
3 Fokker 50
2 Lockheed L-100-30 Hercules

Ordered

2 Fokker 50

Photograph: BAe 146-200 D-AJET (Andrè Dietzel/Munich FJS)

EUROWINGS

Flughafenstrasse 100, 90411 Nürnberg, Germany
Tel. 0911-36560 Fax. 0911-522452

Three letter code	IATA No.	ICAO Callsign
EWG	104	Eurowings

NFD and RFG were merged on 1st January 1993 to form Eurowings. After the majority shareholder, Albrecht Knauf, had insisted on a concentration and division of tasks of the two airlines, the result was a joint operation. At the same time the aircraft were also given a new corporate image. NFD and RFG operated extensive regional services from Dortmund and Nuremberg, in both cases with ATRs, Metroliners and Do 228s. An all-cargo BAe 146-200 QT is operated for TNT. The good characteristics of this type led to its use for passenger work on selected routes from 1995, and for charters. With its own tourist subsidiary EWG has been strong in this market since the autumn of 1995. For that reason two Airbus A319s were ordered. As well as its own services Eurowings also flies on behalf of other airlines. There are co-operation agreements with Air France, KLM and Northwest Airlines. The bases are at Nuremburg and Dortmund.

Routes

Intensive internal network, and to Amsterdam, Brussels, Guernsey, Jersey, London, Lyon, Nice, Prague, Warsaw, Vienna and Zürich.

Fleet	Ordered
2 Airbus A319	1 Airbus A319
17 ATR42	
10 ATR72	
6 BAe 146-200	

Photograph: Boeing 767-300ER B-16605 (Björn Kannengiesser/Phuket)

EVA AIR

376 Hsin-nan Road, Sec. 1 Luchu,
Taoyuan Hsien, Taiwan, Republic of China
Tel. 3515167 Fax. 3352093

Three letter code	IATA No.	ICAO Callsign
EVA	695	Evaair

In March 1989, Evergreen, the largest container shipping line in the world, set up its own airline. But state-imposed conditions, quarrels concerning the airline's name (confusion with the names of other companies) and new aircraft that were not immediately available prevented them from starting flights straightaway. Finally, EVA Air, provided with US$370 million, started flights on 1st July 1991. It used Boeing 767-300ERs on routes to Bangkok, Manila, Hong Kong and Seoul. It has been serving Vienna since November 1991, and London since April 1993. There are also important connections to the USA since the carrier's first trans-Pacific service, from Taipei to Los Angeles, started in December 1992. EVA Air is growing rapidly and is becoming one of the top Taiwanese airlines, and has acquired stakes in Makung Airlines and Great China Airlines, thus giving a regional dimension to its network. The first MD-11 was introduced into the fleet in the Autumn of 1994, and further Boeing 747-400s have been added. The first MD-11 freighter service took place in October 1995 from Taiwan to Amsterdam. New routes to Brisbane, Paris and San Francisco are also being developed. In 1996 a further acquisition of a domestic carrier was made, this time of Taiwan Airlines which flies several Britten-Norman Islanders and Dornier 228s and operates non-scheduled services, with seasonal flights to Far Eastern holiday centres.

Routes

Amsterdam, Anchorage, Bangkok, Dubai, Fukuoka, Ho Chi Minh City, Jakarta, Hong Kong, Kaoshing, Kuala Lumpur, Los Angeles, London, Manila, Maldives, New York, Paris, Penang, Seattle, Seoul, Singapore, Sydney, Taipei, Vienna.

Fleet

5 Boeing 767-300ER
4 Boeing 767-200
12 Boeing 747-400
6 McDonnell Douglas MD-11
2 McDonnell Douglas MD-90

Ordered

2 Boeing 747-400
6 McDonnell Douglas MD-11

Photograph: Boeing 747-200 N482EV (Peter Zierfels/Düsseldorf)

EVERGREEN INTERNATIONAL AIRLINES

3850 Three Mile Lane, Mc Minnville,
OR 97128-9496, USA
Tel. 503-4720011 Fax. 503-4344221

Three letter code	IATA No.	ICAO Callsign
EIA	494	Evergreen

Evergreen International Airlines is a division of Evergreen Aviation. This holding company also owns one of the largest helicopter companies in the USA, Evergreen Helicopter, and also the famous Marana Airpark in Arizona, where aircraft are parked when temporarily out of use. Here Evergreen also has a large maintenance facility and performs storage and overhaul work on most airliner types. The airline was set up on 28th November 1975 when Evergreen Helicopters acquired the operator's certificate from Johnson Flying Service. Operating as Johnson International, the company was founded as early as 1924 and was awarded one of the first supplemental certificates in 1957. Evergreen operates a domestic American cargo service as a subcontractor of UPS and other companies, but it also has its own cargo routes to China and Hong Kong. In addition, aircraft are wetleased, i.e. with crew, to other airlines. In 1995 the fleet was slimmed down and the Boeing 727s sold to a customer for re-engining. The airline itself also operates scheduled and *ad hoc* charter flights, both freight and passenger work, and undertakes troop transportation for the United States Army.

Routes

Scheduled freight flights from Hong Kong to New York. Worldwide freight charters.

Fleet

12 Boeing 747-100/200
8 McDonnell Douglas DC-9-15/30

Photograph: Boeing 727-200 N573PE (Björn Kannengiesser/Fort Lauderdale)

EXPRESS ONE INTERNATIONAL

3890 West Northwest Highway, Suite 700,
Dallas TX 75220, USA
Tel. 214 912 2500 Fax. 214 350 1399

Three letter code	IATA No.	ICAO Callsign
LHN	-	Longhorn

Express One is a US supplemental air carrier and a subsidiary of Wikert and Wikert. The airline began in 1975 as Jet East International with air taxi services from Dallas Love-Field Airport, using Beech King Airs and Learjets moving more into the 'airline' business from 1980. It also flew five Boeing 727s on behalf of UPS, the well-known 'parcel flyer'. Its name was changed to Express One in 1989, and it had contracts with Emery and DHL, also package freight carriers. It used five further Boeing 727s also for passenger flights on a charter basis, adding DC-9s to these in 1991/92. Express One made it across the Atlantic for the first time in July 1993 using leased DC-10s for charter flights to Frankfurt. In June 1995 all aircraft were voluntarily grounded after the FAA had expressed safety concerns during a routine inspection. At the same time the company sought Chapter 11 bankruptcy protection to enable a restructuring to take place. The company recommenced operations with a smaller fleet and now concentrates on freight work, including European operations for DHL.

Routes

US domestic freight flights with hubs at Indianapolis, Dallas/Fort Worth, Minneapolis/St Paul and Terre Haute. European hub at Brussels for DHL.

Fleet	Ordered
6 Boeing 727-100F	2 Boeing 727-200Adv
7 Boeing 727-200Adv	
11 Boeing 727-200F	

Photograph: Boeing 737-200 OB-1476 (collection Jörg Thiel)

FAUCETT PERU

Apartedo 1429, Lima 100,
Peru
Tel. 14-643424 Fax. 14-641114

Three letter code	IATA No.	ICAO Callsign
CFP	163	Faucett

Elmer J. Faucett, an American citizen and pilot, set up the Compania de Aviacion Faucett SA on 15th September 1928. A true flying pioneer, he established a connection from Talara in the north to Arequipa in the south via Lima. He used Stinson Detroiters. Stinson designed the F-19 specially for Faucett's needs. Aircraft were produced by Faucett under licence and used in flight operations. In addition to aircraft operations, the airports in many places in Peru were laid out or expanded by Faucett. In 1938 Aerovias Peru was taken over; after the Second World War, DC-3s and DC-4s were bought, followed in 1960 by DC-6s and in April 1968 the first jet aircraft, a Boeing 727. BAC One-Elevens were added to the fleet; the first was delivered in 1971. Aeronaves del Peru, a cargo airline has been the main shareholder in Faucett since 1982. In 1984 the main international service to Miami by DC-8 was discontinued for some time or only flown as far as the Cayman Islands due to political differences with the USA. Mainly cargo is carried with a somewhat aged fleet; Faucett also provides aircraft for APA of the Dominican Republic since this airline has no aircraft of its own.

Routes

Arequipa, Ayachucho, Chiclayo, Chimbote, Cuzco, Iquitos, Juliaca, Miami, Piura, Pucallpa, Porto Maldonado, Rioja, Tacna, Talara, Tarapoto, Truijillo, Tumbes, Yurimagues.

Fleet

2 Boeing 727-200
6 Boeing 737-100/200
1 McDonnell Douglas DC-8-62F
1 Lockheed L-1011

Photograph: McDonnell Douglas DC-10-30 N302FE (Patrick Lutz/Los Angeles LAX)

FEDEX

P.O. Box 727,
Memphis TN 38134-2424, USA
Tel. 901-369 3600 Fax. 901-332 3772

Three letter code	IATA No.	ICAO Callsign
FDX	023	Fedex

Frederick W. Smith set up Federal Express in June 1971, and it started flight operations on 17th April 1973 using Dassault Falcon 20s. Up to 60 of these aircraft were in use. In 1978 it was floated on the stock exchange and became a joint-stock company. The FedEx system revolutionised the entire cargo market 20 years ago and has found a lot of imitators since then. The shipments are distributed from a central hub in Memphis with US regional sorting centres, using the hub-and-spoke distribution system which it invented. After air cargo deregulation in November 1977, FedEx was also able to operate larger aircraft. They bought Boeing 727s in large numbers, and later DC-10s and Boeing 747s as well. In 1989 Flying Tiger Line, which had been established and well-known for many years, was bought and its DC-8s and Boeing 747s integrated. Although only express shipments were transported at the beginning, other cargo shipments are also transported. 1995 was a year of particular innovation, when FedEx opened its own hub at the former US military base at Subic Bay in the Phillipines, and in July started Asia One, the first overnight delivery service in Asia, From Subic Bay the whole Asian region is accessible to FedEx. Second development in the year was the introduction of a new corporate identity, with the adoption of the former colloquial acronym of FedEx as its official name. The new colour scheme was introduced for the aircraft, including the newly delivered Airbus A310 freighters. Many A300s and A310s are being acquired from other carriers for full freight conversion, and older Boeing 747-200Fs sold off. Already the world's largest airfreight carrier, this increase in capacity will ensure further growth. Numerous smaller companies fly feeder services to smaller towns and cities for FedEx with Cessna 208s and Fokker F27s.

Routes

Federal Express serves over 100 cities in USA, and over 200 countries worldwide.

Fleet

20 Airbus A300-605F
37 Airbus A310
162 Boeing 727-100/200
264 Cessna 208 Caravan
32 Fokker F27
35 McDonnell Douglas DC-10
26 McDonnell Douglas MD-11

Ordered

15 Airbus A310
42 Airbus A300-605F
50 Cessna Caravan
19 McDonnell Douglas DC-10
8 McDonnell Douglas MD-11

Photograph: McDonnell Douglas MD-11 OH-LGD (Björn Kannengiesser/Beijing)

FINNAIR

PL 15, 01053 Finnair Vantaa,
Finland
Tel 81881 Fax 8188736

Three letter code	IATA No.	ICAO Callsign
FIN	105	Finnair

Set up on 9th October 1923 as Aero OY, the German company Junkers had a 50% stake. The first flight was from Helsinki to Tallinn on 20th March 1924 with a Junkers F-13. Until 1936, seaplanes were used until airports were built in Finland. Flights to Berlin and Paris were added. Aero OY had to discontinue operations on 21st September 1944, until spring 1945, when eight C-47s were bought. The first flights were to Stockholm and Copenhagen. Convair 340/440s replaced the C-47s (DC-3s). A new service to Moscow in 1956 was followed by Frankfurt, Cologne, Basle and Geneva in 1957. The Caravelle was introduced in 1960, and Finnair started to change over to jets. KarAir, a private Finnish airline, founded in 1957, was taken over in 1962. DC-8s were ordered for new long-distance flights to the USA, and the first arrived in 1969. They were also used for charters to the Mediterranean. In 1968 the name Finnair was adopted as the sole valid designation of the airline. DC-10-30s were delivered from 4th February 1975 and used primarily for flights to the American west coast, to Tokyo and New York. For medium-distance flights the Caravelles were replaced by DC-9s. The first MD-11 was acquired in December 1990. For cost reasons, KarAir, which had operated independently, was integrated in 1993. Likewise, a subsidiary, Finnaviation, operating Saab 340s on domestic services was integrated in 1996. Also in 1996 a co-operation agreement was concluded with Lufthansa, but this has been weakened by SAS's co-operation with Lufthansa and new agreements were made in spring 1997 with Maersk and Braathens to strengthen Finnair's Stockholm hub. An order was placed in mid-1997 for Airbus A319/320/321s which will replace the DC-9s beginning early 1999 – initially 12, with 24 options.

Routes

From Helsinki to Amsterdam, Athens, Baltimore, Bangkok, Barcelona, Beijing, Bergen, Bodo, Brussels, Budapest, Copenhagen, Düsseldorf, Frankfurt, Geneva, Gothenburg, Hamburg, Istanbul, Kiev, London, Milan, Manchester, Moscow, Munich, Murmansk, New York, Nice, Osaka, Paris, Prague, Riga, Rome, St Petersburg, San Francisco, Singapore, Stockholm, Tallinn, Tokyo, Toronto, Vienna, Vilnius, Warsaw and Zürich. Charter flights also.

Fleet

2 Airbus A300B4
6 ATR72
4 McDonnell Douglas MD-11
25 McDonnell Douglas MD-82/83/87
12 McDonnell Douglas DC-9-51
7 Saab 340

Ordered

12 Airbus A319/320/321
4 Boeing 757-200

Photograph: Boeing 727-100C C-GVFA (Henry Tenby/Yellowknife)

FIRST AIR

Carp Airport, 352 Carp Road,
Carp, Ontario, KOA ILO, Canada
Tel. 613-8393340 Fax. 613-8395690

Three letter code	IATA No.	ICAO Callsign
FAB	245	First

Bradley Air Services is Canada's largest independent regional carrier and provides scheduled charter and cargo flights from various points in Canada. The scheduled flights go under the name of First Air. Bradley Air Services was set up in 1954 having originally started as Bradley Flying School in 1946 and started flight operations with DC-3s the same year. The first scheduled services were flown in the 1970's by DC-3s followed by HS.748s, a type especially well suited to operation in the extreme climatic conditions found where the company flies, from 1978 onwards. Its first Boeing 727 was acquired in 1986 and was introduced on Frobisher Bay to Ottawa services. The operating profile is quite unusual; principally carrying freight in the far north of Canada and on to Greenland, and even on occasion to Europe, but with the possibility of carrying passengers on some sectors. For this reason the aircraft are configured in combi versions. The main base is Ottawa, where the company has maintenance facilities, and there is a further base at Yellowknife, which is also the base of a subsidiary company Ptarmigan Airways. Since 1995 First Air has been a part of the Makivik Corporation.

Routes

First Air is principally active on freight and passenger charters and schedules in the north of Canada. Various flights operate to Greenland and to the USA. There is also charter activity, particularly to Florida.

Fleet

8 BAe HS.748
6 Boeing 727C/F
10 DHC-6-300

Photograph: Dornier Do 228-200 B-12259 (Matthias Ebbers /Taipei TSA)

FORMOSA AIRLINES

340 Tun Hwa North Road, Taipei 10592,
Taiwan
Tel. 2-5149811 Fax. 2-5149817

Three letter code	IATA No.	ICAO Callsign
FOR	-	Formosa

Formosa Airlines, which is in private ownership, has been in existence since 1966 as an agricultural concern although from 1972 to 1975 a DC-6B acquired from Far Eastern Air Transport was employed on charter work. At this time the airline was known as Yung Shing Airlines. In 1978 a group of businessmen took control to develop a variety of air work. Domestic, charter and ambulance flights started with Britten-Norman Islanders. Two Dornier 228s came into operation in 1983, and a further three followed in 1985. In 1987 the name was changed to the present Formosa Airlines and an order for two Saab 340s was placed in December 1987 and both were delivered in 1988, with more of the type added later. The fleet has been further developed with the addition of Fokker 50s, and in 1995 the first jet type, the Fokker 100. Today Formosa operates the largest commuter network in booming Taiwan. The main base of this regional airline is Sung Shan Airport in Taipei, where the airline also has its own maintenance facilities.

Routes

Formosa Airlines operates a network of flights to 25 points in Taiwan and the neighbouring islands.

Fleet

4 Dornier Do 228-200
5 Fokker 50
2 Fokker 100
1 Pilatus-BN Islander
7 Saab 340A/B

Ordered

3 Dornier Do 328

Photograph: Boeing 737-300 EI-CHH (collection Josef Krauthäuser)

FRONTIER AIRLINES

2015 East 46th Avenue, Denver,
Colorado 80239, USA
Tel. 303-3717400 Fax. 303-3717007

Three letter code	IATA No.	ICAO Callsign
FFT	422	Frontierflight

Shortly after the opening of Denver's new airport Continental Airlines reduced its services there by 80%. To fill this vacuum local investors and business people created a new airline with the traditional name of 'Frontier'. The first Frontier Airlines was formed, also in Denver, in 1948 and was active until 1986 when deregulation in the US airline industry led to the creation of mega-carriers taking over the smaller companies, and thus Frontier was taken over by Continental and the name disappeared from the skies. And so on 5th July 1994 the new Frontier, operating two leased Boeing 737-200s , began service from Denver again, with service to Bismarck and Fargo. Two further Boeing 737s were leased from August 1994 and the network expanded, with the addition of even more 737s, now including -300 models. The tail fins of Frontier's aircraft are decorated with attractive animal motifs. There is a marketing alliance with Continental Airlines, and to allow for further expansion a share issue is planned, but with no shareholder holding more than 10% of the shares. As well as scheduled services, Frontier operates charters, especially to holiday destinations. In June 1997 talks were held with Western Pacific (see page 307), also a Colorado-based 737 operator, with a view to a merger to enable the airlines jointly to better compete with United; this is expected to become effective by October 1997.

Routes

From its Denver base to Albuquerque, Bismarck, Chicago-Midway, El Paso, Fargo, Las Vegas, Los Angeles, Minneapolis/St Paul, Omaha, Phoenix, Salt Lake City, San Francisco.

Fleet	Ordered
7 Boeing 737-200 4 Boeing 737-300	3 Boeing 737-300

Photograph: Boeing 737-400 EC-FLD (Andrè Dietzel/Munich FJS)

FUTURA INTERNATIONAL AIRWAYS

Gran Via Asima 17, Poligono Son Castello,
07009 Palma de Mallorca, Spain
Tel. 71-755196 Fax. 71-202014

Three letter code	IATA No.	ICAO Callsign
FUA	-	Futura

Futura International Airways was set up in 1989 as a joint venture between Aer Lingus (initially 25%, now 85%) and Spanish investors based at Palma with the objective of providing package tours from Ireland to Spain. In February 1990, flights started from Dublin to Palma de Mallorca with two Boeing 737-300s leased from Guinness-Peat Aviation (GPA). Other airports such as Basle, Düsseldorf, Manchester, Munich and Vienna followed quickly. Larger Boeing 737-400s were acquired in 1991 and 1992. With the opening up of markets in the former Warsaw Pact states, Futura has been able to take a slice of this business, and thus flies tourists from Hungary, Ukraine and Russia to Spain. During 1995 more Boeing 737-400s were acquired, trading in the -300s. About 1.3 million passengers fly with Futura each year.

Routes

Charter flights from Ireland, Israel, Great Britain, Germany, Austria, Ukraine, Hungary, Czech Republic, and Switzerland to Spain, especially Mallorca and the Canary Isles.

Fleet

8 Boeing 737-400

Photograph: Boeing 737-300 PK-GWH (Martin Bach/Yokyakarta)

GARUDA INDONESIA

Jalan Merdeka Selastan 13, Jakarta 10110, Indonesia
Tel. 3801901 Fax. 368031

Three letter code	IATA No.	ICAO Callsign
GIA	126	Indonesia

26th January 1949 is the official date when Garuda was founded. On this day, a DC-3 flew from Calcutta to Rangoon registered under the name of 'Indonesian Airways'. It was the first civil aircraft of the new Republic of Indonesia, but could not fly in Indonesia for political reasons. It was only after the official declaration of independence at the end of 1949 that the airline was also installed by the government in Indonesia; however, at the beginning it needed the assistance of KLM. The airline was nationalised in March 1954. In addition to DC-3s, Convair 240/340s were in use, plus Lockheed L-188 Electras from 1961 onwards. In 1963, De Kroonduif, an airline in the Indonesian part of New Guinea, was taken over. Convair CV990s were Garuda's first jet aircraft to fly to Amsterdam, in 1965. These aircraft were replaced in 1968 by DC-8s. Sydney was served for the first time in 1969, via Bali, and DC-9s were also bought in that year, with some Fokker F27s for domestic services. These were, however, taken out of service in 1971 and sold, due to the purchase of F28s. Large-capacity aircraft were added to the Garuda fleet in the form of DC-10-30s in 1973, initially leased from KLM. In early 1980 the airline put Boeing 747s into service and flew with them to Frankfurt. In the late 1980s, on the occasion of the airline's fortieth anniversary, the entire fleet was repainted in new attractive colours. Starting with the summer schedule in 1992, after the delivery of the MD-11s, Garuda opened up a weekly Medan-Jakarta-Munich flight and Madrid and Berlin were added to the network in 1993. There are codeshare agreements with KLM, China Airlines and Iberia, and a shareholding in the domestic and regional carrier Merpati.

Routes

Amsterdam, Brussels, Zürich, Vienna, Rome, London and Paris in Europe. Cairo, Jeddah, Riyadh, Abu Dhabi, Singapore, Kuala Lumpur, Hong Kong, Manila, Taipei, Tokyo, Los Angeles, Darwin, Perth, Sydney, Melbourne and over 30 destinations in Indonesia are served by Garuda.

Fleet

9 Airbus A300B4
5 Airbus A300-600
4 Airbus A330-300
7 Boeing 737-400
8 Boeing 737-300
6 Boeing 747-200
3 Boeing 747-400
5 Fokker F28
5 McDonnell Douglas DC-10-30
8 McDonnell Douglas MD-11

Ordered

5 Airbus A330-300
12 Boeing 737-300
5 Boeing 737-500
6 Boeing 777-200

Photograph: Boeing 737-300 4L-AAA (Andrè Dietzel/Munich FJS)

GERMANIA

Flughafen Tegel, Gebäude 23, 13405 Berlin, Germany
Tel. 030-41013610 Fax. 030-41013615

Three letter code	IATA No.	ICAO Callsign
GMI	-	Germania

In 1986, exactly ten years after it had been set up, the SAT (Special Air Transport) airline changed its name to Germania. Operations with jet aircraft had begun in September 1978 with three former LTU Caravelle 10Rs. The first SAT aircraft was an F27. As well as the Caravelles, the airline owned two Boeing 727s, but these were only flown in Germania's colours after the airline had been renamed. The Caravelles were replaced from 1989 onwards and the first Boeing 737-300s were bought. Germania flies subcharters today for other airlines and for various tour operators. Some of Germania's aircraft flew in DFD colours. Germania has a considerable number of flights from Berlin, including scheduled services from Berlin to Heringsdorf/Baltic Sea. Six further Boeing 737-300s were brought into use from the spring of 1992, at which point the colour scheme was also modified. The airline was taken over by the Hetzel travel company in 1995. Several aircraft have been leased to Condor and fly for that airline, but with Germania crews. For the future, Germania is amongst the first airlines to receive the very latest model Boeing 737-700, with 12 on order for delivery commencing in October 1997.

Routes

Charter flights to the Mediterranean area, to North Africa, the Canary Isles, and Turkey. 'Civil service' shuttle between Cologne/Bonn and Berlin

Fleet	Ordered
14 Boeing 737-300	12 Boeing 737-700

Photograph: McDonnell Douglas DC-10-30 9G-ANA (Frank Schorr/Düsseldorf)

GHANA AIRWAYS

Ghana Airways Avenue 9, P.O. Box 1636,
Accra, Ghana
Tel. 21-773321 Fax. 21-777078

Three letter code	IATA No.	ICAO Callsign
GHA	237	Ghana

With the support of BOAC, the government of Ghana set up the national airline on 4th July 1958 with the government having a 60% stake and BOAC 40% to take over the operations of West African Airways Corporation in the British colony formerly known as the Gold Coast. Soon, on 16th July, a scheduled service to London began, using Boeing 377 Stratocruisers leased from BOAC. Domestic services were taken over from WAAC on 1st October 1958. The Stratocruisers were later replaced by Bristol Britannias. On 14th February 1961 Ghana took over sole control of the airline. Soviet IL-18s were bought as part of a further expansion. As these were not particularly economical to use, all eight aircraft were returned to the manufacturer after a period of time. Ghana Airways' first jet aircraft was a Vickers VC-10, and for short-range routes the BAe HS.748 was also acquired. In 1983 the Douglas DC-10 arrived and was used for long distance flights, and regional routes were flown with Fokker F28s and DC-9s, but currently an F27 is in use. In time the DC-10 is expected to be replaced by the MD-11. The main base is the international airport at Accra-Kotoka.

Routes

Abidjan, Banjul, Conakry, Cotonou, Dakar, Düsseldorf, Freetown, Harare, Johannesburg, Kuassi, Lagos, Lome, London, New York and Rome.

Fleet

1 Fokker F27-600
2 McDonnell Douglas DC-10-30
1 McDonnell Douglas DC-9-51

Photograph: Airbus A 320-200 A40-EC (Björn Kannengiesser/Dubai)

GULF AIR

P.O. Box 138, Manama,
Bahrain
Tel. 231166 Fax. 220677

Three letter code	IATA No.	ICAO Callsign
GFA	072	Gulfair

Gulf Air is the national carrier of the Gulf state co-operation of Bahrain, Qatar, the United Arab Emirates and Oman. This airline was set up as Gulf Aviation on 24th March 1950, with flights in the region using Avro Ansons starting on 5th July 1970. De Havilland Dove and Heron aircraft followed and DC-3s and F27s were added to the fleet, partly under British sponsorship. These were replaced from 1969 onwards with BAC One-Elevens. 1970 saw the start of regular flights to London with leased Vickers VC-10s. On 1st April 1974 the four states took Gulf Aviation over, giving the airline a new legal status and the present name of Gulf Air. Boeing 737s replaced the BAC One-Elevens from 1977. For long-distance flights, Gulf Air used Lockheed L-1011 TriStars starting in 1976. Fleet replacement and expansion started with the arrival of the first Boeing 767-300ERs. In the long term these are intended to replace the older TriStars. However, the Gulf War led to this programme being suspended for the time being, and it was only resumed in 1993 with the delivery of Airbus A320s. During 1994/95 the last Boeing 737-200s were retired and the Airbus A340 introduced. One of the four Gulf states, the United Arab Emirates comprises a number of smaller individual states and most of these do not recognise Gulf Air as their official carrier. One, Dubai set up its own official airline, Emirates, in 1985 and Gulf Air then ceased services to Dubai. Gulf Air has been suffering from over-capacity and thus has been making some disposals, and leasing out aircraft to other airlines. Stored TriStars have been returned to service following sales of 767s. Operating partners include American Airlines and British Midland.

Routes

From six Gulf airports, scheduled services to Amsterdam, Amman, Athens, Bangkok, Beirut, Bombay, Brussels, Casablanca, Colombo, Damascus, Delhi, Dharan, Entebbe, Frankfurt, Hong Kong, Istanbul, Jakarta, Johannesburg, Karachi, Kuala Lumpur, Kuwait, London, Namibia, Nairobi, Rome, Paris, Singapore, Sydney, Zanzibar and Zürich.

Fleet	Ordered
14 Airbus A320-200	6 Airbus A330-300
4 Airbus A340-300	
9 Boeing 767-300	
5 Lockheed L-1011-200	

Photograph: BAe 146-300 D-AHOI (Patrick Lutz/Hamburg)

HAMBURG AIRLINES

Terminal 4, Flughafen, 22335 Hamburg, Germany
Tel. 040-50752902 Fax. 040-50751490

Three letter code	IATA No.	ICAO Callsign
HAS	099	Hamburg Air

Hamburg Airlines was set up on 15th April 1988 in order to take over Hanse Express, which had gone bankrupt. Hanse Express had been founded as Hadag Air on 1st March 1974 and was known as Holiday Express until August 1986 when its final name was adopted. In addition to the route rights, two Dornier 228s were also taken over by the new airline. In September 1988 the first DHC-8 was leased in order to be able to overcome capacity bottlenecks. New routes to Amsterdam and Rotterdam, as well as to London-Gatwick were opened. After the reunification of Germany, Hamburg Airlines was also active in the new federal states. Scheduled services were expanded in early summer 1990 with the use of Fokker 100s for charter flights. In 1992 the airline was sold in its entirety to Saarland Airlines. After the collapse of a tour operator – Saarland Airlines got into financial difficulties – Hamburg Airlines also had to apply to open insolvency proceedings in autumn 1993. Flights continued in the hope of consolidation after a new partner had been found, resulting in a change to the legal form of the company's organisation. During 1994 the first BAe 146 was introduced, with further examples following in 1995 and 1996. Also in 1996 the capital base was increased in order to give a firmer foundation. As well as schedules, charter work is undertaken.

Routes

Athens, Berlin, Dresden, Dublin, Hamburg, Leipzig, Oporto, Riga, Rome, Saarbrücken, Stuttgart, Thessaloniki, Vilnius.

Fleet

2 BAe 146-200
2 BAe 146-300
3 De Havilland DHC-8-100
2 De Havilland DHC-8-300

Photograph: Boeing 737-400 D-ALHK (Oliver Krauthäuser/Frankfurt)

HAPAG-LLOYD FLUG

Postfach 420240, 30662 Hannover, Germany
Tel. 0511-97270 Fax. 0511-9727494

Three letter code	IATA No.	ICAO Callsign
HLF	617	Hapaglloyd

The well-known German shipping company Hapag-Lloyd set up the airline with its traditional name in July 1972. Flights started in March of the following year with three Boeing 727-100s acquired from All Nippon Airlines and its 727 fleet subsequently increased to eight aircraft by 1979. After lengthy negotiations Bavaria-Germanair was taken over in late 1978. This takeover provided Hapag-Lloyd with various BAC One-Eleven and Airbus A300B4 aircraft. While the latter were integrated into the existing fleet, the One-Elevens were sold and new Boeing 737-200s were ordered. A replacement of the fleet and its adaptation to future needs was decided in 1987. A total of six Airbus A300B4s were exchanged for Airbus A310s and Boeing 737-400s were ordered, the first of which arrived in Hanover in autumn 1990. When the Airbus A310 was introduced, Hapag-Lloyd was then in a position to provide flights to the USA and Caribbean as well. The airline is to be the launch customer for the latest model Boeing 737-800 and when deliveries of the 16 aircraft on order are made from 1998 onwards it will have the most modern of the German charter fleets. The main base is Hannover, where there are maintenance facilities, but flights are operated from all the main German airports.

Routes

Charter flights to the Mediterranean, to the Canary Isles, to Africa, Middle East, Far East, USA and Caribbean.

Fleet	Ordered
4 Airbus A310-200	16 Boeing 737-800
4 Airbus A310-300	
12 Boeing 737-400	
5 Boeing 737-500	

Photograph: McDonnell Douglas DC-10-10 N148AA (Patrick Lutz/Los Angeles)

HAWAIIAN AIR

P.O. Box 3008, Int.Airport Honolulu,
96820 Hawaii, USA
Tel. 808-525-5511 Fax 808-5253299

Three letter code	IATA No.	ICAO Callsign
HAL	173	Hawaiian

Founded on 30th January 1929 as Inter Island Airways in Honolulu by the Inter Island Steam Navigation Company, flights started on 11th November 1929 between Honolulu and Hilo with Sikorsky S-36 amphibian flying boats, replaced later by larger S-43 versions. Air mail contracts were obtained in 1934 and during the following years the fleet included the still larger Sikorsky S-34 amphibians. A permanent route certificate was awarded on 16th June 1939. On 1st October 1941, the airline assumed its present name, Hawaiian Airlines, known now as Hawaiian Air and flight operations were changed over to DC-3s. Increased expansion in the tourist business and route additions led to the acquisition of larger aircraft in 1952 such as Convair 340s, and from 1958 Douglas DC-6s. In 1966 the airline switched over to jet aircraft with the introduction of the DC-9-30. DC-8s were added to the fleet in 1983 and Lockheed TriStars in 1987, for charter flights to the American continent, the Pacific and Europe. A Honolulu-Los Angeles service was introduced on 12th June 1985 and was later extended to Las Vegas. In early 1991, Northwest Airlines paid $20 million for a 25% holding in the airline. Hawaiian Air sought Chapter 11 protection in 1993 as the result of financial difficulties, sought new financial partners and re-organised the whole airline. The DHC-7s were sold, the DC-8s taken out of service, the TriStars exchanged for DC-10s and a number of routes abandoned. By September 1994 financial health had been restored to allow emergence from Chapter 11. A marketing agreement was made with American Airlines, with whom Hawaiian now works closely. There is an intensive and frequent network of flights amongst the Hawaiian islands.

Routes

Hilo, Honolulu, Hoolehua, Kahului, Kauai, Kona, Lanai City, Las Vegas, Los Angeles, Pago Pago, Papeete, Portland, San Francisco, Seattle.

Fleet

13 McDonnell Douglas DC-9-51
9 McDonnell Douglas DC-10-10

Photograph: McDonnell Douglas MD-87 EC-EXF (Josef Krauthäuser/Düsseldorf)

IBERIA

130 Calle Velazquez, 28006 Madrid, Spain
Tel. 5874747 Fax. 5857682

Three letter code	IATA No.	ICAO Callsign
IBE	075	Iberia

The present-day Iberia was formed in 1940 as the result of the merger of several airlines. After the Spanish Civil War, the German influence on the airline was still quite considerable, with Lufthansa holding 49% of the capital. In 1944 the Spanish government acquired all the shares and ordered DC-3s to add to the Ju-52 fleet. Iberia, as a pioneering European airline after the Second World War, opened up important routes to Buenos Aires (1946), Caracas and San Juan (1949), Havana, New York and Mexico (1954), Bogota (1958), Santiago and further destinations in early 1960. South America is thus traditionally one of the most important markets. DC-4s and Lockheed Constellations were used, and the first jet aircraft was a DC-8 in 1961. The Caravelle was acquired in 1962 for short-distance and medium-distance flights; these were passed on to the subsidiary Aviaco in 1967 and DC-9s were bought. Iberia obtained its first large-capacity aircraft, the Boeing 747, in October 1970. In 1972 Boeing 727s were bought, and a year later DC-10-30s. A large-scale fleet replacement programme is underway in the 1990s. MD-87s and A320s are replacing older DC-9s and Boeing 727s. Iberia has a stake in various companies such as VIASA, Aerolineas Argentinas, Viva, Aviaco, Ladeco and Royal Air Maroc. The first Airbus A340s were introduced in 1996 as replacements for the DC-10 on long-range routes.

Routes

Intensive internal network with hubs at Madrid and Barcelona. Schedules to the USA, Caribbean, South and Latin America, the Middle East, Africa and important destinations in Europe are regularly served.

Fleet

8 Airbus A300B4
22 Airbus A320-200
4 Airbus A340-300
28 Boeing 727-200Adv
8 Boeing 757-200
7 Boeing 747-200
7 McDonnell Douglas DC-10-30
3 McDonnell Douglas DC-8-62F
15 McDonnell Douglas DC-9-32
24 McDonnell Douglas MD-87

Ordered

4 Airbus A340-300
8 Boeing 757-200

Photograph: Boeing 737-400 TF-FID (Uwe Gleisberg/Salzburg)

ICELANDAIR

Reykjavik Airport, 101 Reykjavik,
Iceland
Tel. 690100 Fax. 690391

Three letter code	IATA No.	ICAO Callsign
ICE	108	Iceair

Icelandair, or Flugfelag Islands HF, was formed on the north coast of Iceland as Flugfelag Akureyar on 3rd June 1937, and began service to Reykjavik with a Waco YKS. In 1940, the headquarters of the airline was moved to the capital Reykjavik, and a Beech 18, two de Havilland Dragon Rapides and a further Waco YKS were bought. After the end of the Second World War, a scheduled service from Iceland via Prestwick to Copenhagen was set up for the first time in 1946. In April 1948, Flugfelag obtained its first Douglas DC-4, using it for a second route to London. The first flights to Germany took place as early as 1955; in 1965 its present title was adopted and Fokker F27s were put to use, and two years later Boeing 727s. Icelandair was set up in its present form on 20th July 1973 as the holding company for Flugfelag Islands and Loftleidir (Icelandic Airlines formed on 10th March 1944). The company was a holding company after the merger but did not assume all operating responsibility until 1st October 1979. Since 1973 it had been Icelandic flying transatlantic services and Icelandair flying domestic and European services. In 1988 836,000 passengers flew with Icelandair. The DC-8s were replaced by modern Boeing 757s in 1989, the rest of the fleet was continually replaced and Boeing 737s added. The F27s were replaced by modern F50s for regional routes, giving Icelandair an entirely new fleet. More Boeing 757s are on order, including the new stretched -300 for delivery in 2001 and 2002, with options on eight more for delivery up to 2006.

Routes

Internal Icelandic service to 10 points. International routes to Amsterdam, Baltimore, Berlin, Boston, Copenhagen, Faroe Islands, Frankfurt, Glasgow, Gothenburg, Halifax, Hamburg, London, Luxembourg, Milan, Munich, New York, Orlando, Oslo, Paris, Salzburg, Stockholm, Vienna and Zürich.

Fleet	Ordered
5 Boeing 757-200ER	2 Boeing 757-200
4 Boeing 737-400	2 Boeing 757-300
4 Fokker 50	

Photograph: Airbus A300B2 VT-EDZ (Stefan Hartmann collection)

INDIAN AIRLINES

113 Gurdwara Rakabganj Road, Parliament Street, New Delhi, India
Tel. 11-3718951 Fax. 11-3719333

Three letter code	IATA No.	ICAO Callsign
IAC	058	Indair

Indian Airlines Corporation was set up on 28th May 1953 by the central government in Delhi and on 1st August 1953 formally acquired the routes and assets of eight independent airlines – Airways (India), Bharat Airways, Himalayan Aviation, Kalinaga Airlines, Indian National Airways, Deccan Airways, Air India and Air Services of India. They were all nationalised and combined to form Air India and Indian Airlines, with Indian Airlines being responsible for regional services. The airline's first flights were on 1st August 1953, and it used DC-4s, Vickers Vikings and DC-3s. Daily night airmail services were inaugurated on 5th November 1955 between the major Indian cities. In 1957 these aircraft were partly replaced by Vickers Viscounts, and by Fokker F27 from May 1961 onwards. The airline's first jet aircraft was the Caravelle, acquired in February 1964. HS.748s manufactured under licence in India were also used, as were Airbus A300s, the first widebody aircraft. When the latest generation of aircraft, the Airbus 320, was introduced at the end of 1989/ beginning of 1990, some operational problems arose which had an effect on flights and on passenger numbers. Indian Airlines' flights are regionally divided up, from Delhi, Bombay, Calcutta and Madras. The airline was partially privatised in 1994, but it still remains under strong government influence. The regional carrier Vayudoot formed with Air India in 1981 has now been integrated into Indian Airlines.

Routes

Over 70 destinations in India are served, and in addition international flights to Kabul, Dhaka, Chittagong, Male, Karachi, Kathmandu, Lahore, Colombo, Bangkok and Singapore.

Fleet

10 Airbus A300B2/B4
30 Airbus A320-200
12 Boeing 737-200Adv

Photograph: Boeing 747SP EP-IAD (Frank Schorr/Geneva)

IRAN AIR

P.O. Box 13187, Head Office, Mehrabad Airport,
Teheran, Islamic Republic of Iran
Tel. 979111 Fax. 903248

Three letter code	IATA No.	ICAO Callsign
IRA	096	Iranair

Iran Air came into existence in February 1962 as the result of the fusion of Iranian Airways and Persian Air Service, by order of the government of the time. Iran Air had been established as a private company in 1944 and was known as Iranair. Persian, also in private hands, had initially begun freight services in 1955 with Avro Yorks. The routes and aircraft were taken over from Iran Air's predecessors. In 1965 Iran Air acquired Boeing 727s to open new routes to London and Frankfurt. In March 1976 a Boeing 747SP started scheduled flights to New York. The first Airbus A300s were used in 1978, mainly on much travelled routes to neighbouring countries. Political developments in the early 1980s following Ayatollah Khomeini's rise to power in 1979 and the departure of the Shah and war lasting several years with neighbouring Iraq resulted in considerable changes. Prior to 1979 Iranair had been one of the world's fastest growing airlines scheduling over 100 weekly international departures from Teheran to 29 foreign cities from New York to Tokyo. It was the last airline to cancel its order for Concorde. In the mid-1980s, the number of weekly international flights had reduced to less than 30 from Teheran. It was only from 1989 onwards that Iran Air was able to restructure itself. Fleet modernisation began in September 1990 with the delivery of the first Fokker 100s for regional flights. Further modernisation is presently hindered because of the US economic embargo, which also applies to civil aircraft. In 1992 Iran Air Tours was established as a subsidiary, jointly with Tajik Air.

Routes

Iran Air flies to destinations in the Middle East and to Frankfurt, London and Paris. An internal service connects the major towns and cities with Teheran. There are also intensive Hadj pilgrim charters to Saudi Arabia.

Fleet

5 Airbus A300B2
2 Airbus A300-600
3 Boeing 737-200
6 Boeing 727-200
4 Boeing 707-300
3 Boeing 747-200
1 Boeing 747-100
4 Boeing 747SP
6 Fokker 100

Photograph: Boeing 737-400 TC-ADA (Frank Schorr/Munich FJS)

ISTANBUL AIRLINES

Firuzköy Yolu 26, Avcilav, Istanbul 34850, Turkey
Tel. 212-5092100 Fax. 212-5938742

Three letter code	IATA No.	ICAO Callsign
IST	-	Istanbul

Istanbul Airlines (or Istanbul Hava Yollari) was set up in December 1985 by Turkish and West German interests in order to meet the increased demand for seats in aircraft to Turkey. Flights started on 14th March 1986 with SE 210 Caravelles. Two BAC One-Eleven aircraft were also leased from Tarom. The first Boeing 737s were introduced in November 1988. This type of aircraft was also used to set up a scheduled service providing better connections from Istanbul to other Turkish centres. The airline developed very quickly and further Boeing 737-400s were bought. In order to meet the demand for charter flights, Boeing 727s were also used, replacing the Caravelles. In 1995 Istanbul Airlines received two Boeing 757-200s.

Routes

Istanbul Airlines flies to over 50 destinations within Europe and to Israel.

Fleet

6 Boeing 737-400
7 Boeing 727-200
3 Boeing 757-200

Photograph: Boeing 737-400 JA8992 (Björn Kannengiesser/Nagoya)

JAPAN AIRLINES

Tokyo Bld., Marunouchi 2-7-3, Chiyoda-ku,
Tokyo 100, Japan
Tel. 3-32842610 Fax. 3-32842659

Three letter code	IATA No.	ICAO Callsign
JAL	131	Japanair

JAL was set up on 1st August 1951 as Japanese Air Lines when civil aviation was re-activated in Japan after the Second World War. The first flight took place with a leased Martin 202 from Tokyo-Haneda to Osaka on 25th October 1951. Exactly a year later the first flight with a DC-4 owned by the airline took place. In 1953 the DC-6 was introduced, and 2nd February 1954 saw the first international flight from Tokyo to San Francisco; in August 1960 the DC-8 was introduced for this route. The following year the Tokyo-London polar route and Paris/Copenhagen to Tokyo was opened with DC-8s. Convair 880s were introduced in 1962 and used for the first time to Frankfurt via South-East Asia. In 1967 a flight 'around the world' was set up. The first flights over Siberia to Europe were in March 1970, saving several hours compared to the polar route. In the same year, on 1st July the Boeing 747 was used, initially on Pacific routes. The DC-10-40 was specially designed for JAL and used from the mid-1970s onwards. In 1979 Zürich became a new destination and in 1985 Düsseldorf. The airline also expanded to the USA in the eighties, with Atlanta as a new destination. The first Boeing 767 was integrated into the fleet in 1987. The Japanese Government sold its remaining 34.5% stake in JAL in November 1987 giving JAL a new corporate identity and resulting in the introduction of new colours. The MD-11 came into the fleet from 1993, joined in 1995 by the Boeing 737-400 and in 1996 by the Boeing 777. JAL has interests in the following other companies: Japan Asia (see page 179), Japan Air Charter, Japan Trans Ocean, Air New Zealand, DHL and Hawaiian Airlines. Another subsidiary Japan Air Express is planned to start in July 1998 with two Boeing 737-400s. The JAL fleet should be 153 aircraft by the end of 1999.

Routes

Internal services link Tokyo with Osaka, Komatsu, Kagoshima, Okinawa, Fukuoka, Hakodate and Sapporo. 63 international destinations in 27 countries are served including Australia, New Zealand, Brazil, USA, Canada, Korea, China, Hong Kong, Singapore, Manila, Jakarta, Bangkok, the Far East and Europe.

Fleet		Ordered
21 Boeing 767-200/300	4 Boeing 737-400	17 Boeing 737-400
32 Boeing 747-400	5 Boeing 777-200	18 Boeing 747-400
13 Boeing 747-300	13 McDonnell Douglas DC-10-40	3 Boeing 767-300
35 Boeing 747-100/200	10 McDonnell Douglas MD-11	5 Boeing 777-200
		5 Boeing 777-300

Photograph: McDonnell Douglas MD-90 JA8062 (Jörg Thiel collection)

JAPAN AIR SYSTEM - JAS

37 Mori Building, 5-1 Toranomon,
3-Chome, Minato-ku, Tokyo, Japan
Tel. 3-54734000 Fax. 3-54734009

Three letter code	IATA No.	ICAO Callsign
JAS	234	Air System

Japan Air System (JAS) is the new name adopted since 1st April 1988, for the former TOA-Domestic (TDA). Toa Domestic Airlines resulted from the merger of Japan Domestic and TOA Airways on 15th May 1971; the latter was founded on 30th November 1953. Japan Domestic had been formed in March 1964 through the amalgamation of North Japan Airlines, Nitto Aviation and Fuji Airlines. Toa Domestic operated flights with NAMC YS-11s until the introduction of the first DC-9 jet aircraft in 1973; these were in turn phased out during a fleet modernisation in the 1990s. Airbus A300s have also been in use since 1980. The name was changed in 1988 and adapted to the new situation, as flights outside Japan had now also become possible. The first international flight was to Seoul in Korea. The first DC-10-30 was delivered to JAS on 30th March 1988. For the first time JAS had an aircraft for intercontinental flights, and it is used for charter flights to Hawaii and Singapore. With the delivery of the new MD-90s has come a colourful new paint scheme, and Boeing 777s are slated for delivery also during 1997. JAS is Japan's third largest airline. In July 1997 it was announced that it was planned to re-structure up to 30% of the loss-making domestic network, and to expand services within Asia, especially to China. Commuter services in Japan's southern western Island are operated by Japan Air Commuter, which was set up in 1983 and in which JAS has a 60% stake and the government 40%. This uses principally Saab 340s.

Routes

To over 40 internal destinations such as Fukuoka, Akita, Hiroshima, Nagasaki, Osaka, Sapporo, Tokyo, Yakusima, Okinawa. Charters in South East Asia, and to Siberia, Hawaii and Australia.

Fleet

17 Airbus A300B4
17 Airbus A300-600
2 Boeing 777-200
2 McDonnell Douglas DC-10-30
1 McDonnell Douglas DC-9-41
26 McDonnell Douglas MD-81
8 McDonnell Douglas MD-87
8 McDonnell Douglas MD-90

Ordered

2 Airbus A300-600R
5 Boeing 777-200
8 McDonnell Douglas MD-90

Photograph: McDonnell Douglas DC-10-40 JA8532 (Albert Kuhbandner/Hong Kong)

JAPAN ASIA

Yurakucho Denki Building, 7-1 Yurakucho,
1-Chome, Tokyo, Japan
Tel. 32842974 Fax. 32842980

Three letter code	IATA No.	ICAO Callsign
JAA	688	Asia

Japan Asia Airways is a wholly-owned subsidiary of Japan Airlines being established on 8th August 1975. The airline was set up for political reasons, as Japan Airlines wished to open up connections to the People's Republic of China, but only received permission when it gave up its Taiwan services. However, as the Taiwan flights are so lucrative, Japan Asia was formed as a face-saving operation and politicians in China and Japan were kept happy. Japan Air Lines had suspended Taiwan services in April 1974 following the problems resulting from the Japanese Government's recognition of the Republic of China (Taiwan). Jet operations started on 15th September 1975 between the two countries. Expansion of services, to Manila and Hong Kong, took place in the mid-1980s. Japan Asia obtained the aircraft, first DC-8s, then later DC-10s and Boeing 747s, from its parent company. As well as scheduled services, charters are carried out to popular holiday destinations.

Routes

From Tokyo, Osaka, Nagoya to Hong Kong, Kaoshiung, Taipei, Manila, Okinawa.

Fleet

4 McDonnell Douglas DC-10-40
4 Boeing 747-100/200/300

Photograph: McDonnell Douglas DC-9-32 YU-AJL (Jörg Thiel collection/Frankfurt)

JAT - YUGOSLAV AIRLINES

Jat Poslouni Centar, Ho Shi Minova 1670,
Novi Beograd 11070, Yugoslavia
Tel. 11-133535 Fax. 11-137756

Three letter code	IATA No.	ICAO Callsign
JAT	115	JAT

The predecessor of JAT was Arpout, founded in 1927, but which was forced to terminate operations at the outbreak of the Second World War. Then JAT was founded on 1st April 1947, and started operations with the ubiquitous Douglas DC-3. The jet era arrived with the Caravelle in 1963 and marked an expansion of services. In Europe especially, destinations such as Moscow, Amsterdam and Stockholm could now be reached non-stop. In 1969 the DC-9 was introduced, and a year later the Boeing 707, with which for the first time it was possible to offer transatlantic service to the USA and Canada, and destinations in the Far East and Australia were also taken on. In 1974 the Caravelles were retired and the Boeing 727 introduced for middle-range services, and in 1978 the DC-10 became the long-range successor to the Boeing 707s. A further fleet renewal began in 1985 with the acquisition of Boeing 737-300s. However on 31st May 1992 JAT was forced to give up its international flights as a result of United Nations sanctions because of the political situation in what was by then the former Yugoslavia and the ongoing civil war in Bosnia. The embargo was lifted and international flights resumed on 6th October 1994. As a reflection of the new situation, a new colour scheme was adopted, with the 'Yugoslav Airlines' inscription. Routes were flown from Belgrade principally to European cities, but there was no demand for long-range services and three DC-10s were sold. Other aircraft from the formerly extensive fleet were leased to other operators. The main base, with a major maintenance operation, is Belgrade Airport.

Routes

Amman, Amsterdam, Athens, Barcelona, Brussels, Bucharest, Copenhagen, Düsseldorf, Frankfurt, Istanbul, Kiev, Larnaca, London, Moscow, Paris, Rome, Stockholm, Stuttgart, Tel Aviv, Vienna and Zürich.

Fleet

3 ATR72
8 Boeing 727-200Adv
9 Boeing 737-300
1 DC-10-30
9 McDonnell Douglas DC-9-32

Photograph: Fokker F27 G-JEAD (Author's collection)

JERSEY EUROPEAN AIRWAYS

Terminal Building, Exeter Airport, EX5 2BD, Great Britain
Tel. 1392-366669 Fax. 1392-366151

Three letter code	IATA No.	ICAO Callsign
JEA	267	Jersey

Jersey European Airways was founded on 1st November 1979 in order to take over the activities of two companies, Intra Airways and Express Air Services. Intra (Jersey) Airways goes back to 1969 when several British United Airline (BUA) pilots decided to start their own airline. With a DC-3 they flew services from Jersey to the other Channel Islands, to northern France, and later to Ostend in Belgium. For several years Intra flew passengers from Staverton to Jersey, and other charter destinations followed. In 1974 a Britten-Norman Islander was acquired and a service to London-Gatwick commenced. As well as schedules Intra undertook charter and freight work and had up to six DC-3s in service. Express Air Services had several Piper PA-31 and flew passenger and courier flights with these. After acquisition by the Walker Group, in 1983 the operations of both were brought together under the Jersey European name. Twin Otters and Embraer Bandeirantes saw the departure of the smaller types, and with the start of a new service to Birmingham the Fokker F27 was introduced. 1989 saw the HS.748 also added for use on other UK domestic services such as Belfast to Birmingham. Further F27s, Shorts 360s and then the first jets, BAe 146s, were added and these three types now form the basis of the fleet. The latter type has been particularly prominent in recent acquisitions, following a major increase in the network, including some code-share and partnership work with Air France.

Routes

Scheduled services from the two principal bases at Belfast and Jersey to Birmingham, Blackpool, Bristol, Derry, Exeter, Glasgow, Guernsey, Isle of Man, Leeds/Bradford, London-Gatwick, Manchester, Paris and Stansted. Charter flights within Europe and flights on behalf of the British Post Office.

Fleet

10 BAe 146-100/200/300
8 Fokker F27-500
2 Shorts SD-360

Photograph: Boeing 747-100F N701CK (Andreas Witek/Graz)

KALITTA AMERICAN INTERNATIONAL AIRWAYS

842 Willow Run Airport,Ypsilanti,
Michigan 48198, USA
Tel. 313-4840088 Fax. 313-4849812

Three letter code	IATA No.	ICAO Callsign
CKS	571	Connie

Founded as Connie Kalitta Services, named after the owner, this private company began its services in November 1972 from its base at Detroit-Willow Run Airport, from which it still operates today. An unrestricted licence allowed passenger and freight charter services within the United States. In 1984 Connie Kalitta took over another Detroit-based charter company, Jet Way, and in the same year permission was given for international freight services. The fleet consisted of Douglas DC-8s for international services, DC-9s for passenger charters, and assorted Lear Jets, Beech 18s and HFB Hansas for courier flights. With the takeover of the Zantop routes in May 1993 the name was changed to Kalitta American International Airways and the company reorganised. Alongside the freight business, aircraft are leased out to other operators and subcharters flown. In July 1994 Kalitta received their first Lockheed L-1011 TriStar freighter conversion, from Marshall Aerospace of Great Britain, and put it into service on international charter work: several further aircraft of this type have since been added. There are also Boeing 747s in the fleet, mostly freighters, but a couple configured for passenger duties. At the beginning of 1995 MGM Grand Air was taken over; this company had operated luxuriously appointed DC-8s and Boeing 727s on passenger work. Another subsidiary company under the same own ownership is Kalitta Flying Service Inc.

Routes

Charter and freight services within the USA and worldwide.

Fleet

20 Boeing 727-200F
8 Boeing 747-200F
10 Lockheed L-1011
21 McDonnell Douglas DC-8

Photograph: Ilyushin IL-86 UN-86077 (Patrick Lutz/Hannover)

KAZAKHSTAN AIRLINES

Zholtoksan St 59, Almaty 48300,
Kazakhstan
Tel. 3272-336349 Fax. 3272-336383

Three letter code	IATA No.	ICAO Callsign
KZA	736	Kazair

Kazakhstan, a state rich in mineral resources, became independent from the Soviet Union in 1991, and since then has progressed positively, though there are dangerous wastes from the past to be found in large parts of the country and in the ground. The powerful directorate of the former Aeroflot region was disbanded and broken up into new companies. Thus there are about 15 airlines, of which Kazakhstan Airlines is the largest and the flag carrier. There are about 25,000 employees and scheduled services and charters are flown. Freight operations are a successful part of the company, flying *ad hoc* and subcontract cargo, particularly to Western Europe and the Far East. Most of the staff are employed in the agricultural aviation division, where there are Mil Mi-8 and other helicopters along with Antonov An-2 biplanes in service. The base for all operations is Almaty, formerly Alma Ata. In this vast country the movement of people and goods by air plays a decisive role. For services to western Europe a Boeing 747SP has been used since 1994, and a VIP Boeing 757 has been in use since 1995. A 1996 order for five Boeing 767s does not seem to have been consummated.

Routes

Akmola, Aktau, Aktyubinsk, Arkalyk, Atyrau, Balkhask, Beijing, Delhi, Dushanbe, Ekaterinburg, Frankfurt, Hannover, Kaliningrad, Karaganda, Kiev, Kokshetau, Kostanay, Mineralnye Vody, Moscow, Novosibirsk, Omsk, Osh, Petropavlovsk, Samara, Semipalatinsk, Sharjah, Shimkent, Teheran, Tel Aviv, Ufa, Ulgii, Uralsk, Urumqi, Vienna, Zhambyl, Zhezkazgan.

Fleet

1 Antonov An-12
36 Antonov An-24
10 Antonov An-26
9 Antonov An-30
1 Antonov An-72
1 Boeing 747SP
1 Boeing 757-200
4 Ilyushin IL-76TD
7 Ilyushin IL-86
11 Tupolev Tu-134A
26 Tupolev Tu-154
30 Yakovlev Yak-40
6 Yakovlev Yak-42D

Photograph: Saab 340A VH-EKD (Jörg Thiel/Adelaide)

KENDELL AIRLINES

86 Baylis Street OR, Wagga Wagga, NSW 2650, Australia
Tel. 69- 220100 Fax. 69-220116

Three letter code	IATA No.	ICAO Callsign
KDA	678	Kendell

Set up in 1966 as a non-scheduled air carrier with the name PremiAir Aviation. The first aircraft was a Piper Apache for air-taxi work, followed by a Piper Cherokee Six. The name was changed to Kendell Airlines in 1971. Regular scheduled flights from Wagga Wagga to Melbourne started on 18th October 1971 using a Piper Navajo. De Havilland Herons arrived in 1975 and Swearingen Metros by 1979. Over the years Kendell developed in southern Australia into a regional airline now flying to four federal states. In 1985 the Saab 340 was introduced. TNT/News Corp, owners of Ansett, increased its shareholding in Kendell over the years and in 1986 when Ansett closed down Airlines of South Australia, Kendell took over a number of its routes. In October 1990, TNT/News Corp acquired 100% ownership after buying out Dan Kendell, the airline's founder. Ansett remains an important partner for Kendell, and Kendell flies supplementary and feeder flights for Ansett. Over the last two years three new Saab 340B have been added, along with three more 340As, bringing the total of this type in service to fifteen.

Routes

Albury, Ayers Rock, Broken Hill, Burnie, Ceduna, Coober Peddy, Coona, Devonport, King Island, Kingscote, Mildura, Mount Gambier, Port Lincoln, Portland, Sydney, Tumut, Wagga Wagga and other points in south-eastern Australia.

Fleet	Ordered
7 Fairchild Swearingen Metro 23	1 Fairchild Swearingen Metro 23
15 Saab 340A/B	

Photograph: Airbus A310-300 5Y-BEL (Albert Kuhbandner/Zürich)

KENYA AIRWAYS

Kenyatta International Airport, P.O. Box 19002,
Nairobi, Kenya
Tel. 2-823000 Fax. 2-823488

Three letter code	IATA No.	ICAO Callsign
KQA	706	Kenya

After the collapse of the multinational airline East African Airways, the flag carrier for Kenya, Tanzania and Uganda in 1976, the Kenyan government was compelled to set up its own national airline. With the aid of British Midland Airways and two leased Boeing 707s, flight operations started from Nairobi to London, Frankfurt, Athens and Rome in February 1977, one month after it was formed on 22nd January 1977. The leased aircraft were replaced by Boeing 707s of their own. The airline acquired modern aircraft from 1986 onwards, when it was possible to replace the Boeing 707s with Airbus A310s. Fokker 50s were introduced for shorter-range services from 1988. In the early 1990s the airline declined, earning a poor reputation for reliability and service, but the problem was tackled; reorganisation and rationalisation made, and in 1996 the airline was partly privatised with the participation of KLM, holding 26% of the shares. In April 1997 a daily service to Amsterdam was started, to feed into the KLM network. The earlier model Boeing 737s have been replaced during 1997 by two new -300 series. Charter flights are conducted under the name Kenya Flamingo Airlines.

Routes

Amsterdam, Athens, Bombay, Frankfurt, Copenhagen, Cairo, Karachi, London, Mombasa, Nairobi, Paris, Rome, Zürich. In Africa between 15 and 20 destinations are served.

Fleet	Ordered
3 Airbus A310-300 2 Boeing 737-300 3 Fokker 50	1 Boeing 737-300

Photograph: Boeing 727-200 N267US (Josef Krauthäuser/Tampa)

KIWI INTERNATIONAL AIRLINES

Hemisphere Centre, US 1 & 9 South Newark, NJ 07114, USA
Tel. 201-6451133 Fax.201-6451161

Three letter code	IATA No.	ICAO Callsign
KIA	538	Kiwiair

What were one-time employees of the once so famous but no longer active airlines such as Eastern Airlines, Midway Airlines and PanAm to do? First a group led by former Eastern pilot R W Iverson tried to take over the Pan Am New York-Boston-Washington shuttle, but were were prevented from doing so by Delta Airlines. A projected takeover of Midway Airlines met equal lack of success, and so they formed their own airline, Kiwi International. The Federal Aviation Administration granted the necessary operating licence and on 21st September 1992 service was started from Newark to Atlanta, Chicago and Orlando. Within eighteen months there were 30 daily departures in the expanded schedule, and more than ten Boeing 727s were in use. In 1993 Kiwi sprang a surprise by ordering 16 Rombac One-Elevens (Airstar 2500s). As delivery of these from the Romanian manufacturer was indefinitely delayed, the order was cancelled, and the airline set about the modernisation of its 727s with new engines. As a result of the closer FAA inspection of 'low-cost' airlines, some problems emerged which led to a brief grounding in December 1995 in order to give the authority a complete control. As a result of this, Boeing 727 pilot training has been improved and the airline has taken on responsibility for its own maintenance. Chapter 11 bankruptcy protection had been entered in September 1996, but the airline emerged from this in July 1997 and is set to re-commence expansion, with an eye also to fleet modernisation.

Routes

Atlanta, Chicago/Midway, Las Vegas, New York/Newark, Orlando, Tampa, West Palm Beach.

Fleet

9 Boeing 727-200

Photograph: McDonnell Douglas MD-11 PH-KCD (Oliver Krauthäuser/Amsterdam)

KLM ROYAL DUTCH AIRLINES

P.O. Box 7700, 1117 ZL Amsterdam,
Airport Schiphol, Netherlands
Tel. 20-6492227 Fax. 20-6488391

Three letter code	IATA No.	ICAO Callsign
KLM	074	KLM

Formed on 7th October 1919, KLM is the oldest operating airline in the world. The first scheduled flights were from Amsterdam to London on 17th May 1920 with a DH 16. Mainly Fokker aircraft were used until the outbreak of the Second World War. In 1929 the route to Batavia (today called Djakarta) was opened, at that time the longest route. Its first transatlantic link came in 1934 with a route to Curacao using a Fokker F XVIII. Operations in the West Indies started in 1935. DC-2s were introduced in 1935, followed by DC-3s in 1936. KLM had one of the densest networks in Europe until 1940. Services around the West Indies continued during the Second World War and allows KLM to claim over 75 years of continuous operations. After 1945, reconstruction commenced with DC-3 aircraft. Convair 240s followed, replaced by the Convair 340 in 1953. The Vickers Viscount took over important routes in Europe from 1957 onwards, and was replaced by the Lockheed Electra in 1959. Overseas flights were initially operated using DC-4s, Lockheed Constellations and DC-6s and DC-7s as the last of the propeller aircraft. The first DC-8 was used to New York on 4th April 1960. Boeing 747s, introduced in 1971, and DC-10s took over the long-distance routes in the 1970s. On the short-distance and medium-distance routes, KLM initially used DC-9s, which were later replaced by Boeing 737s and Airbus A310s added. The present flagship of KLM is the Boeing 747-400, which came into service in May 1989. KLM acquired a minority interest in Northwest Airlines in 1993 and will continue to work closely with this US partner, though the shareholding is to be sold in the later part of 1997. KLM also has stakes in ALM-Antillean, Air UK (now 100%), Martinair, Transavia and KLM-Cityhopper.

Routes

From its home base of Amsterdam-Schiphol KLM has a dense European network, and serves over 120 cities on all continents.

Fleet

19 Boeing 737-400
16 Boeing 737-300
18 Boeing 747-400
3 Boeing 747-300
10 Boeing 747-200SUD
10 Boeing 767-300
10 McDonnell Douglas MD-11

Ordered

2 Boeing 737-300
4 Boeing 737-800
2 Boeing 747-400

Photograph: Fokker 50 PH-KVC (Josef Krauthäuser/Düsseldorf)

KLM-CITYHOPPER

Postbus 7700, 1117 2L Schiphol Oost,
Netherlands
Tel. 6492227 Fax. 6488154

Three letter code	IATA No.	ICAO Callsign
KLC	195	City

The present KLM Cityhopper is the successor in name to NLM Dutch Airlines, which was set up in 1966 and started scheduled flights between Amsterdam, Eindhoven and Maastricht on 29th August 1966. It used the proven Fokker F27 Friendship. Regional international scheduled flights began in April 1974. In 1976 the name was changed to NLM Cityhopper and KLM acquired a majority interest. Netherlines was set up in 1984 and started flights between Amsterdam and Luxembourg on 8th January 1985. Further scheduled routes were opened up between 1985 and 1988 using Jetstream 31s. By 1987, Netherlines was owned by the Nedlloyd Group, who also owned Transavia. In 1988, KLM decided to buy Netherlines with the intention of asking NLM, which operated Fokker F27s and F28s, to merge the airlines together. The merger subsequently brought about the formation of KLM Cityhopper in early 1990 although the joint airline did not officially come into being until April 1991. Fleet renewal has taken place in the 1990s with Saab 340s and Fokker 50s being introduced at the beginning of the decade, and then Fokker 70 jets supplanting the older Fokker F28s from 1996. Its base is Amsterdam-Schiphol, where the entire KLM infrastructure is used.

Routes

Amsterdam, Antwerp, Belfast, Berlin, Bremen, Bristol, Brussels, Cardiff, Düsseldorf, Eindhoven, Frankfurt, Guernsey, Hannover, Jersey, London, Luton, Luxembourg, Maastricht, Malmö, Paris, Rotterdam, Southampton, Strasbourg, Stuttgart.

Fleet

10 Fokker 50
7 Fokker 70
11 Saab 340

Photograph: Boeing 747-400 HL-7496 (B.I.Hengi/Zürich)

KOREAN AIR

C.P.O. Box 864, Seoul,
Republic of Korea
Tel. 02-7517114 Fax. 02-7555220

Three letter code	IATA No.	ICAO Callsign
KAL	180	Koreanair

Korean Air Lines had been formed in June 1962 by the South Korean Government to succeed Korean National Airlines which was established in 1947. The private company Hanjin Transport Group took over Korean Air Lines, which up to that time had been state-owned, with eight aircraft on 1st March 1969. Its international routes were to Hong Kong and Osaka. In 1973, KAL obtained its first Boeing 747, used from May 1973 for the trans-Pacific services via Tokyo and Honolulu to Los Angeles. In the same year a weekly service to Paris started, the first destination in Europe, with Boeing 707s. The Airbus A300B4 came into service in 1975, and was used for the East Asian market. DC-10 deliveries also started in 1975. In 1984 the name Korean Air was introduced and all their aircraft were given the present colour scheme. Frankfurt became the third destination in Europe that same year. In December 1986, KAL was a launch customer for the MD-11, and is also taking on the Boeing 777 alongside an impressive and growing fleet of 747-400s. Korean Air is developing into one of the largest airlines in the world with scheduled services to all five continents. It is also developing an extensive freighter fleet, with five MD-11s converted to dedicated freighters during 1995/96. The main base is at Kimpo Airport, Seoul, and there are marketing alliances with ten other international airlines.

Routes

Korean internal flights to 10 points, and international service to Australia, USA Los Angeles and New York; several destinations in Japan, Singapore, Hong Kong, Bangkok, the Middle East and Europe.

Fleet

25 Airbus A300-600
2 Airbus A300F4
8 Airbus A300B4
2 Airbus A330-300
2 Boeing 747SP
25 Boeing 747-400
2 Boeing 747-300
11 Boeing 747-200F
4 Boeing 747-200
2 Boeing 777-200
12 Fokker 100
14 McDonnell Douglas MD-82/83
5 McDonnell Douglas MD-11F

Ordered

7 Airbus A330-300
8 Boeing 747-400
2 Boeing 777-200
8 Boeing 777-300

Photograph: Airbus A340-300 9K-ANC (Andrè Dietzel/Munich FJS)

KUWAIT AIRWAYS

P.O. Box 394, 13004 Safat,
Kuwait
Tel. 4345555 Fax. 4319204

Three letter code	IATA No.	ICAO Callsign
KAC	229	Kuwaiti

Kuwait Airways Corporation came into existence in 1953 as a national airline set up by local businessmen as Kuwait National Airways. Its first route was from Kuwait City to Basra, flown for the first time in April 1954 with DC-3s. The present name was adopted in 1958 when in May 1958 the British airline BOAC took over the management of the airline and managed it until independence in 1962. Vickers Viscounts replaced the DC-3s. Kuwait Airways operated a de Havilland Comet 4C on the routes to London, Paris and Frankfurt. The airline became wholly-Government owned on 1st June 1963 and took over Trans Arabia. On 20th March 1966 the first of a total of three HS Tridents was introduced. Three Boeing 707s followed two years later and took over all routes gradually. In 1978 Kuwait Airways acquired its first Boeing 747 Jumbo. Airbus aircraft were ordered as successors to the Boeing 707s, with three Boeing 767s being added from 1986 onwards as part of continued fleet replacement. After the Iraqi occupation of Kuwait in summer 1991 flights were discontinued; some aircraft were destroyed, some were seized by Iraq , whilst others were transferred abroad for lease. Restricted flights were provided by Kuwait Airways from Cairo. Since the end of the Gulf War KAC has resumed flights from Kuwait to Europe, such as to Geneva, Frankfurt, London and Munich. Kuwait Airways' colours were slightly altered in 1993, and by 1995 more or less the whole fleet had been renewed. Some Kuwait Airways aircraft are used for government flights.

Routes

Alexandria, Amsterdam, Athens, Abu Dhabi, Bahrain, Bangkok, Bombay, Colombo, Dakar, Damascus, New Delhi, Dubai, Istanbul, Jeddah, Cairo, Karachi, London, Madrid, Manila, Munich, New York, Paris, Rome, Singapore and Teheran.

Fleet		Ordered
6 Airbus A300-600	2 Boeing 747-200	2 Boeing 777-200
4 Airbus A310-300	1 Boeing 747-400	
3 Airbus A320-200		
4 Airbus A340-300		

Photograph: Antonov An-26 EX-26036 (Björn Kannengiesser/Moscow)

KYRGHYZSTAN AIRLINES

720062 Bishkek, Manus Airport,
Kyrghystan
Tel. 3312-313084

Three letter code	IATA No.	ICAO Callsign
KGA	758	Kyrgyz

Although independent since 1991, Kyrghystan has remained a member of the CIS. The former Aeroflot directorate was taken over to form the only airline, to develop future services and to function as the national carrier. The transformed airline named itself Kyrgyzstan Aba Yoldoru National Airline, with Bishkek Air Enterprises as its main shareholder. It also has a subsidiary in the second largest city – Osch-Karakol Air Enterprises. Additionally the airline still works with Aeroflot for ticketing and marketing and as a code-share partner. Furthermore the company has responsibilities for government duties including ambulance and relief flights. Kyrghystan is one of the poorest states of the CIS; increased business relationships with neighbouring Kazakhstan, Uzbekistan and China bring an increased need for air services in this remote region. As well as scheduled services, charter flights are operated and efforts are made to fill aircraft with cargo. The first service to western Europe, specifically Frankfurt, was inaugurated in summer 1996.

Routes

Almaty, Baku, Ekaterinburg, Frankfurt, Istanbul, Kaliningrad, Karakol, Krasnoyarsk, Moscow, Novosibirsk, Omsk, Osch, Samara, St Petersburg, Tashkent and charters amongst others to Irkutsk, Khabarovsk, Ulan Bator and Yumen.

Fleet

1 Antonov An-26
1 Antonov An-28
1 Ilyushin IL-76TD
14 Tupolev Tu-154
6 Tupolev Tu-134
11 Yakovlev Yak-40

Photograph: Boeing 727-200 CP-1276 (Author's collection)

LAB - LLOYD AEREO BOLIVIANO

Casilla Correo 132,
Cochabamba, Bolivia
Tel. 42-25903 Fax. 42-50744

Three letter code	IATA No.	ICAO Callsign
LLB	051	Lloyd Aereo

Set up by German immigrants on 15th September 1925, following an historic proving flight with an imported Junkers F-13, on 25th July from Cochabamba to Sucre as part of the centennial celebrations of Bolivia's independence. A regular service, with the F-13, began a few months later, on 24th December, between Cochabamba and Santa Cruz. The Bolivian government had a stake in the airline, which got into financial difficulties in 1928, however. Company shares were sold to the Junkers company and the latter brought three further F-13s into the airline. The network of routes was steadily extended as far as the Brazilian and Argentinian border. Over the years further Junkers aircraft such as W 34s and Ju 52s were employed in the service of LAB. German influence disappeared in 1941 as the result of American pressure and the company was nationalised on 14th May 1941 and Lodestars were introduced on flights after Panagra took an interest in operations. In 1948 Curtiss C-46s were added to the fleet. The first DC-4s were used on the new route to Asuncion or Porto Vila, followed in 1961 by DC-6s. In the late 1960s LAB was reorganised and Fairchild FH227s were acquired for regional routes, as well as a Lockheed Electra for international routes. In 1970 the change was made to Boeing 727s, and there were flights to Miami in the USA for the first time in 1975. Further routes to Santiago and Caracas followed. Airbus A310-300s were introduced to the fleet, the first in 1991 and a second in 1996. At the end of 1995 the Brazilian airline VASP took a 49% interest in LAB, and at the same time the colour scheme was modified.

Routes

As well as Bolivian internal services there are flights to Arica, Asuncion, Belo Horizonte, Buenos Aires, Caracas, Quito, Lima, Manaus, Mexico-City, Miami, Montevideo, Panama, Rio de Janeiro, Santiago and Sao Paulo.

Fleet

2 Airbus A310-300
1 Boeing 707-320F
7 Boeing 727-100/200
1 Boeing 737-300
2 Fokker F27

Photograph: Boeing 737-200Adv N28ILF (Xaver Flocki collection)

LACSA

P.O. Box 1531, San Jose,
Costa-Rica
Tel. 2316064 Fax. 2329185

Three letter code	IATA No.	ICAO Callsign
LRC	133	Lacsa

Pan American set up Lineas Aereas Costarricenses SA in December 1945 with the support of the government of Costa Rica and private interests. Flights started in 1950, to Miami. In June 1946 some domestic destinations were linked up for the first time to form a network of scheduled routes. They used Convair CV440s, Curtiss C-46s and DC-6s. It became the national flag carrier in 1949. In 1952 TACA de Costa Rica, their only competitor in the country, was bought up. In 1967 LACSA acquired its first jet aircraft, a BAC One-Eleven 400. These were replaced by Boeing 727s in late 1970. The airline's domestic network was transferred in September 1979 to Servicios Aereos Nacionales (SANSA). A fleet acquisition programme has earmarked the Airbus A320 as the aircraft of the 1990s and the first one was delivered in late 1990. TACA holds 10% of the shares and thus there is a close working relationship. The main operating and maintenance base is in San Jose.

Routes

Barranquilla, Cancun, Caracas, El Salvador, Guatemala, Los Angeles, Mexico City, Miami, New Orleans, New York, Panama, Quito, Rio de Janeiro, San Juan.

Fleet

4 Airbus A320
7 Boeing 737-200Adv

Photograph: Boeing 757-200 CC-CYH (Author's collection)

LADECO

Av. Bernardo O'Higgins 107, Santiago, Chile
Tel. 6395053 Fax. 639727

Three letter code	IATA No.	ICAO Callsign
LCO	145	Ladeco

Linea Aerea del Cobre Ltda., abbreviated as LADECO, was set up as a private company on 3rd September 1958 to serve the copper mining region of northern Chile. Flight operations began on 1st November 1958, initially on the Santiago to El Salvador route. LADECO took over the rights to the routes from CINTA-ALA, as well as DC-3 aircraft. The DC-3s were equipped with more powerful Twin Wasp engines in order to be able to take off more easily from the high-altitude airport at Santiago. In 1965 the larger DC-6s were added to the DC-3s and the network of routes expanded. In 1975 LADECO bought its first Boeing 727-100. When the DC-6s were taken out of service, more aircraft of this type were added. Two Boeing 707s were bought for long-distance routes in 1978 and 1979 and were used for flights to Miami and New York. From 1992 there was evidence of a fleet renewal programme, with the acquisition of a Boeing 737-300 and two 757-200s, but these did not stay in the fleet for very long, and the work is again being done using the old faithful 737-200s. In 1995 LAN-Chile took over Iberia's former shareholding in LADECO, and took the majority shareholding in 1996. Since then the airlines have worked closely together and shared the route network.

Routes

15 destinations in Chile. International services to Asuncion, Sao Paulo, Rio de Janeiro, Guayaquil, Bogota, Mendoza, Miami and Washington.

Fleet

8 Boeing 737-200

Photograph: Lockheed L-1011-500 CS-TEA (Henrique Belinha/Lisbon)

LAM

P.O. Box 2060, Maputo,
Peoples Republic of Mozambique
Tel. 1-465137 Fax. 1-735601

Three letter code	IATA No.	ICAO Callsign
LAM	068	Mozambique

DETA – Direccao de Exploracao dos Transportes Aereos – was set up in August 1936 as a department of the railways and harbours and airways administration in Laurenco Marques, the capital at that time of Mozambique, which was under Portuguese administration. An airfield was set up on the outskirts of the city for the first time and DETA's first flight, and also the first scheduled flight, was on 22nd December 1937 to Johannesburg with a Junkers Ju 52. De Havilland Moths and Dragonflies were also used. Further Ju 52s were used, but these were replaced after the end of the Second World War by Douglas DC-3s. July 1962 saw the first use of Fokker F27s. The arrival of two Boeing 737s in December 1969 also heralded the start of the jet age for DETA. During the revolution in the 1970s, flights practically came to a standstill. After independence in June 1975 and reorganisation, the national airline also received a new name: LAM – Lineas Aereas de Mocambique – in May 1980. In 1993 Boeing 737-300s and briefly the Boeing 767 came into use. With the arrival of these aircraft, the colours of the airline were also changed. TAP-Air Portugal is an important partner of LAM and the Lisbon to Maputo route is jointly operated. The other routes to Europe were abandoned in 1995 on economic grounds.

Routes

Beira, Durban, Harare, Johannesburg, Lichinga, Lisbon, Luanda, Lusaka, Madrid, Manzini, Nampula, Tete.

Fleet

3 Boeing 737-200Adv
2 Beech 200C
3 CASA 212-200
5 Cessna 402C
4 Partenavia P.68C
1 Lockheed L-1011-500

Photograph: Boeing 767-300ER CC-CEY (Josef Krauthäuser/Miami)

LAN CHILE

Estado 10, Piso 21, Casilla 147-D,
Santiago de Chile, Chile
Tel. 2-6394411 Fax. 2-6383884

Three letter code	IATA No.	ICAO Callsign
LAN	045	Lan

LAN Chile (Lineas Nacional de Chile) is one of the oldest airlines in South America. Set up on 5th March 1929 as Linea Aeropostal Santiago-Africa under the command of the Chilean Air Force, it initially provided mail flights. The airline was nationalised in 1932 when the present name was adopted. Lockheed Lodestars were used in 1948 to open a scheduled service to Buenos Aires, and also to Miami from 1958 with DC-6s. The SE 210 Caravelle was LAN's first jet aircraft, and was delivered in March 1964. In 1967 the Boeing 707 followed, and was used to open up a route to the Easter Islands and on to Tahiti. In 1974 the South Pole route was opened to Australia, the first airline to link South America with Australia. Three DC-10s were added to the fleet in 1980 and were used for flights to the USA and Europe. Boeing 767s were added in 1986 and later replaced the DC-10s. LAN Chile carried out the first ever Twinjet (Boeing 767-200ER) revenue service across the South Atlantic in September 1986. The airline was privatised in 1989 and the Cueto family became the principal shareholder. Regional and national flights were further improved and extended from 1990 with leased BAe 146s. In 1996 the Cueto family also acquired the majority shareholding in Ladeco, and there has been a sharing of routes. The main base is at Santiago de Chile, and there is a marketing agreement with Air New Zealand.

Routes

Buenos Aires, Caracas, Frankfurt, La Paz, Lima, Madrid, Mexico City, Miami, Montevideo, New York, Papeete, Rio de Janeiro, Santa Cruz, Sao Paulo as well as about 30 domestic destinations in Chile and to the Easter Islands.

Fleet	Ordered
2 BAe 146-200	3 Boeing 767-300ER
15 Boeing 737-200Adv	
10 Boeing 767-300ER	

Photograph: ATR72-200 F-OLAO (Author's collection)

LAO AVIATION

2 Rue Pan Kham, Vientiane,
People's Republic of Laos
Tel. 212057 Fax. 212056

Three letter code	IATA No.	ICAO Callsign
LAO	627	Lao

As a result of the Vietnam War, in which the Kingdom of Laos of that time was also involved, three airlines were active in the early 1970s: Royal Air Lao, Lao Air Lines and Civil Aviation Co. The last of these was operated by the Pathet Lao movement for a free Laos. This airline received help from North Vietnam. After the final takeover of power, the remaining aircraft belonging to the airlines were brought together to form Lao Aviation. It was established on 19th January 1976 by the People's Republic of Laos and took over from Royal Air Lao as the national flag carrier. The fleet consisted of Vickers Viscounts, Lockheed Hercules, Sikorsky S-58 helicopters, Douglas DC-3s and DC-4s. As there was no need for flights in Laos, these aircraft were sold or scrapped. Spare parts were not available to maintain these aircraft, so a new fleet was built up favouring Soviet aircraft. International flights between Vientiane and Bangkok and Hanoi were introduced and to Phnom-Penh, operated by Antonov An-24s. The present name of the airline was introduced in 1979. Since the government allowed foreign investors to take a stake in 1995, ATR72 and Boeing 737 aircraft have been introduced for international routes.The fleet policy has also included the operation of Chinese-built aircraft.

Routes

Bangkok, Chiangmai, Hanoi, Ho Chi Minh City, Luang Prabang, Pakse, Phnom Penh, Xieng Khouang, Yangon.

Fleet

1 Antonov An-24
1 ATR72
1 Boeing 737-200
6 Yunshuji Y 12
3 Yunshuji Y 7

Photograph: Boeing 737-300 OE-ILF (Uwe Gleisberg/Munich FJS)

LAUDA AIR

Postfach 56, 1300 Flughafen Vienna-Schwechat, Austria
Tel. 70072081 Fax. 70073157

Three letter code	IATA No.	ICAO Callsign
LDA	231	Laudaair

Lauda Air was set up in April 1979, when Niki Lauda, the former Formula One motor racing world champion, took over a licence to operate non-scheduled flights from Alpair. Lauda had a 51% stake and Itas Austria 49%. Flight operations started on 24th May 1979 with two Fokker F27s. After a phase of restructuring and conversion into a joint-stock company, the airline leased two Rombac One-Elevens from Tarom in 1985. Boeing 737-200s and -300s were added and were later used to replace the Rombacs. At that time Lauda Air was primarily flying to Greece and Spain. In 1986 Lauda Air applied for a licence to operate scheduled flights to Australia, which it finally obtained in 1988. In that year Lauda Air obtained its first Boeing 767-300ER, followed by a second one in November 1989. Scheduled services to Sydney, Hong Kong and Singapore were further expanded. The airline has the rights to scheduled flights worldwide. The first European scheduled routes were started in late 1990, from Vienna to London-Gatwick and in the same year licences were obtained for international services which had previously been reserved for Austrian Airlines. In the autumn, Lufthansa acquired a 25% share in Lauda Air via Condor, and this was increased to 39.7% in 1994. Lauda Air flies in co-operation with the latter to Miami. In another example of co-operation with Lufthansa Lauda now flies Canadair Regional Jets between Vienna and several European cities on behalf of the German airline. In 1993, it formed an Italian subsidiary, Lauda Air SpA, which operates from Milan-Malpensa. The Lufthansa/Condor shareholding was reduced on sale to Austrian Airlines in March 1997, the national carrier now owning 36% of Lauda Air as part of its ambition to create a grouping of all Austrian carriers.

Routes

Lauda Air flies schedules to Bangkok, Phuket, Hong Kong, Singapore and Sydney. For Lufthansa Miami and several European destinations are served. Charters are flown especially to the Mediterranean area also from Salzburg, Graz and Linz near Vienna.

Fleet	Ordered
5 Boeing 767-300ER 2 Boeing 737-300 2 Boeing 737-400 8 Canadair Regional Jet	4 Boeing 777-200 2 Boeing 737-800

Photograph: De Havilland DHC-8-100 V2-LCX (Xaver Flocki collection)

LIAT

P.O. Box 819, V.C.Bird International Airport,
St Johns, Antigua
Tel. 268-4620700 Fax. 268-4623455

Three letter code	IATA No.	ICAO Callsign
LIA	140	Liat

Leeward Island Air Transport Services Ltd, LIAT for short, was set up in 1956 by two American businessmen. LIAT started flights from Antigua to Montserrat with a Piper Apache. A year later LIAT became part of British West Indian Airways who took a 75% stake. Beech Bonanzas and DH Herons were the ideal aircraft for short island hops to other islands in the Virgin Islands. The first HS.748 was acquired on 1st February 1965. In November 1971 the British company Court Line Aviation took over the airline and introduced the BAC One-Eleven and BN-Islanders. In 1974, after the collapse of Court Line in August, a rescue company was set up in November known as LIAT (1974) Ltd and it still has that company name. Its partners were the governments of six Caribbean island states, with further states acquiring a stake over the years. The first DHC-8s were bought in 1987, contributing to the expansion of the route network. At the beginning of 1995 the last HS.748 was retired and in November 1995 the company was privatised. The main operating and maintenance base is Antigua.

Routes

Anguilla, Antigua, Barbados, Barbuda, Caracas, Carriacou, Grenada, Guadeloupe, Guyana, Martinique, Montserrat, Nevis, San Juan, St Croix, St Kitts, St Lucia, St Maarten, St Thomas, St Vincent, Tobago, Tortola, Trinidad and Union Island.

Fleet

6 De Havilland DHC-6
9 De Havilland DHC-8-100
3 De Havilland DHC-8-300

Photograph: Boeing 727-200Adv 5A-DID (Author's collection)

LIBYAN ARAB AIRLINES

Haiti Street, P.O. Box 2555, Tripoli,
Socialist Peoples Libyan Arab Jamahiriya
Tel. 21-602083 Fax. 21-602085

Three letter code	IATA No.	ICAO Callsign
LAA	148	Libair

The merger of Libiavia and United Libyan Airlines resulted in the formation of the the state-owned Kingdom of Libya Airlines in September 1964 in order to have a state airline. August 1965 saw the start of flights to Europe and North Africa as well as to the Middle East with two Caravelles. In 1969 some Fokker F27s were added to the fleet for domestic services. 1969 also saw political changes in the country following the September revolution, as a result of which the airline changed its name to Libyan Arab Airlines on 1st September 1967. Boeing 707s, 727s and later Airbus A310s were added. Political and trade sanctions meant that the western-built fleet could only be partly used. For this reason the fleet was expanded using Soviet Tupolev 154M aircraft from 1990 onwards. As a result of these political sanctions, since 15th April 1992 Libya no longer has any flight rights abroad. An independent division of the airline, Libyan Arab Air Cargo, has a fleet of Ilyushin 76 and Lockheed L-100 Hercules active on freight work.

Routes

Services to several internal destinations from Tripoli and Benghazi.

Fleet

15 Fokker F27
3 Fokker F28
9 Boeing 727-200
1 Boeing 707-300

Photograph: Yakovlev Yak-42 LY-AAW (Björn Kannengiesser/Moscow)

LITHUANIAN AIRLINES

8 Radunes, Vilnius Airport, 232038 Vilnius, Lithuania
Tel. 2-630116 Fax. 2-266828

Three letter code	IATA No.	ICAO Callsign
LIL	874	Lithuania Air

Lithuanian Airlines was the first airline of the Baltic republics which obtained independence from the former Soviet Union; it started its own flights in 1991. The aircraft were taken over from the former directorate of Aeroflot. Lithuanian immediately turned towards western Europe and Scandinavia and started flights to those countries first. A leased Boeing 737 was first used to Copenhagen on 20th December 1991. Malev assisted in building up flights and trained the pilots on Boeing 737s. In late 1992 Lithuania was accepted into IATA. Lithuanian served London Gatwick and Heathrow with a weekly service to each starting on 3rd August 1992 but from 25th October the service became twice weekly to Heathrow from Vilnius. With the delivery of further Boeing 737s several Tupolev Tu-134s were sold, and customers were also found for the Antonov 24s and Yak-40s, so that the fleet is now rationalised. A new colour scheme was introduced in 1994. It is intended that the fleet will in time become all-Boeing, either purchased or leased. An alliance with Finnair was signed in May 1996.

Routes

Amsterdam, Berlin, Copenhagen, Ekaterinburg, Frankfurt, Hamburg, Kiev, London, Moscow, Odessa, Paris, Samara, St Petersburg, Stockholm, Tallinn, Tashkent, and Warsaw all have scheduled service. Regular charter flights to Athens and Istanbul.

Fleet

3 Boeing 737-200Adv
1 Saab 340B
11 Yakovlev Yak-42

Photograph: ATR72 SP-LFB (Björn Kannengiesser/Frankfurt)

LOT

Uliczka 17, Stycznia 39, 00906 Warsaw,
Poland
Tel. 6066565 Fax. 460909

Three letter code	IATA No.	ICAO Callsign
LOT	080	LOT

Aerolloyd Warsaw (subsequently Aerolot) and Aero were united to form the future state airline Polskie Linie Lotnicze – LOT on 1st January 1929 by order of the government. Aerolloyd had begun regular flights in September 1922 and started international services in 1925, Aero was formed in 1922. LOT Junkers F-13s flew to Vienna, Berlin, Moscow and Helsinki. As a result of the Second World War, a fresh start with Soviet aircraft could only be made in 1946. While the Ilyushin IL-14 was part of the fleet in the 1950s, Western aircraft such as the Convair 240 or Vickers Viscount were also used. Tu-134 and Tu-154 jet aircraft were the mainstay of the short and medium-distance routes, while the IL-62M was used for long hauls. Western Boeing 767s have also been in use since 1989. The fleet is being brought up to Western standards as quickly as possible. LOT is also working on its services and is increasingly becoming a competitor for established airlines. In December 1992, LOT became a joint stock holder company, a transitional step towards privatisation. For regional routes ATR72s were added from 1991, and the addition of Boeing 737s from 1993 to 1996 also signalled the departure of the last of the Russian-built jets. Its transatlantic services to the USA and Canada (where there are large expatriate Polish populations) bring in a significant part of its revenue and LOT has co-operation agreements with American Airlines. A loss of $12.7 million was shown in 1996, and a part of a plan to ameliorate this situation, a low-cost regional subsidiary EuroLOT, operating the ATR72s, was started in July 1997.

Routes

Dense network within Poland, to major European cities and to Bangkok, Beijing, Singapore, Delhi, Montreal, Chicago, and New York.

Fleet	Ordered
8 ATR72 3 Boeing 737-300 6 Boeing 737-400 6 Boeing 737-500 6 Boeing 767-200/300ER	1 Boeing 737-400 2 Boeing 737-800

Photograph: Boeing 757-200 EC-EGH (Author's collection Palma de Mallorca)

LTE INTERNATIONAL AIRWAYS

Calle del Ter 27, Poligono de Son Fuster,
07009 Palma de Mallorca, Spain
Tel. 71-475700 Fax. 71-478874

Three letter code	IATA No.	ICAO Callsign
LTE	-	Fun Jet

LTE – Lineas Transportadores Espanola was set up on 29th April 1987. 25% of the shares were held by LTU; more was not legally possible, and the rest were held by Spanish shareholders. Flights started on 1st November 1987 with a Boeing 757 from Palma to Hamburg. A second 757 followed in December 1987. The aircraft came from the LTU-subsidiary LTS and their colours were a slightly altered blue and white. LTE operates domestic flights to Barcelona and Madrid. It has also been providing long-distance charters to Mombasa and the Dominican Republic from these airports since 1990. In 1991 the colour scheme was changed, and since then it has been expanded to a total of five Boeing 757s. LTE has been particularly active in the new federal states in Germany after reunification and operates from airfields with low passenger volume such as Dresden or Berlin. From 1st January 1993 LTE was 100% taken over by LTU, flights are co-ordinated, and the aircraft fleet is interchangeable with the parent.

Routes

Charter flights from Germany, Austria, Switzerland, and from Finland and Italy to the Spanish mainland, the Balearics and Canary Islands.

Fleet

3 Boeing 757-200

Photograph: Airbus A 330-300 D-AERK (Andrè Dietzel/Munich FJS)

LTU INTERNATIONAL AIRWAYS

Halle 8, Flughafen, 40474 Düsseldorf, Germany
Tel. 0211-941808 Fax. 0211-9418881

Three letter code	IATA No.	ICAO Callsign
LTU	266	LTU

LTU was formed as Lufttransport Union on 20th October 1955 by an Englishman, Mr Dromgoole, but the chief partner, and soon to become sole owner, was the Duisburg building contractor Conle. The present name was adopted in 1956. Frankfurt was the first base but transferred to Düsseldorf in 1960. The first aircraft, Vickers Vikings, were in use until 1963. Further aircraft used were Bristol 170s, Fokker F27s and DC-4s, until flights with jet aircraft started, in the form of the first Caravelles in 1965. From 1969 onwards LTU was one of the first charter airlines to use solely jet aircraft. In addition to the Caravelles, Fokker F28 Fellowships were also used from 1968. 1973 saw the start of the age of widebody aircraft, with the acquisition of the first Lockheed L-1011 TriStars. This was also the aircraft which enabled LTU to make the breakthrough to become Germany's largest charter airline. Up to eleven TriStars were used by LTU, allowing it to include faraway tourist destinations. In 1989 it also applied for a licence to operate as a scheduled air carrier; the licence was granted on some routes from autumn 1990 onwards. Also in this year the Westdeutsches Landesbank took a 34% shareholding in LTU. The purchase of the first MD-11s in late 1991 began a renewal of the fleet, which was completed in 1996 with the introduction of the newest widebody, the Airbus A330. These two types replaced the TriStars, the last of which left the fleet in May 1996. In the Spring of 1996 LTU took over Rheinland Air Service, and LTU-Süd was integrated into the parent company, thus giving a uniform appearance to all the LTU aircraft. A restructuring announced in July 1997 following losses, calls for the dropping of some long-haul routes and the removal of the MD-11s from the fleet during 1998.

Routes

Long distance destinations are Miami, New York, Los Angeles, Phoenix, Bangkok, Bali, Colombo, Mombasa, Male, Havana, Puerto Plata and other Caribbean points. From Düsseldorf, Berlin, Frankfurt, Hamburg, Stuttgart and Munich to tourist destinations in the Mediterranean, Canary Isles, Turkey, Greece and North Africa.

Fleet

6 Airbus A330-300
10 Boeing 757-200
5 Boeing 767-300ER
4 McDonnell Douglas MD-11

Photograph: Airbus A319-100 D-AILA (Uwe Gleisberg/Munich FJS)

LUFTHANSA

von Gablenz-Str 2-6, 50679 Cologne, Germany
Tel. 0221-8260 Fax0221 8263818

Three letter code	IATA No.	ICAO Callsign
DLH	220	Lufthansa

The 'old' Lufthansa, founded in 1926, was put into liquidation by the victorious powers in the Second World War. In early 1950 the German government made efforts to acquire air sovereignty and set up an independent national airline. For this purpose 'Luftag' was set up in 1953, which was renamed after the old Lufthansa in 1954. The first flight with a Convair 340 was on 1st April 1955, and the first flight abroad was to New York on 8th June 1955 with a Lockheed Constellation. In 1960 Lufthansa made use of Boeing 707s on transatlantic flights for the first time; Boeing 720s were acquired for routes to Africa and the Middle East. Lufthansa was the first customer outside the USA to obtain the Boeing 727 for medium-distance routes in April 1964. Lufthansa was the first to order the Boeing 737, delivered from 1967; it has been the 'workhorse' of the airline on short-distance routes for many years and is being replaced with the latest model. The age of widebody aircraft started in March 1970 with the introduction of Boeing 747s. With orders for DC-10s and for Airbus A300s in the mid-1970s Lufthansa demonstrated the politics of its fleet renewal policy. It is well known for its constant fleet updating and in 1988 the Boeing 747-400 and the Airbus A320 were introduced, in 1993 the Airbus A340, in 1994 the A321 (for which it was launch customer) and in 1996 the 'short' Airbus A319. Lufthansa Cityline operates regional flights using aircraft up to 80 seats – Canadair and Avro Regional Jets – for the parent. Lufthansa has a stake in Lauda Air, and co-operation agreements with United Airlines, Thai Airways, Varig, SAS and South African Airways. In Europe, regional partners are Augsburg Airways, Contact Air, Tyrolean, Air Dolomiti, and from June 1997 Air Littoral in France.

Routes

Lufthansa flies to over 190 destinations in 90 countries worldwide.

Fleet

8 Airbus A319
33 Airbus A320-200
16 Airbus A321-100
8 Airbus A310-300
13 Airbus A300-600
16 Airbus A340-200/300
17 Avro RJ 85
10 Boeing 737-200Adv
46 Boeing 737-300
30 Boeing 737-500
8 Boeing 747-200
22 Boeing 747-400
33 Canadair Regional Jet

Ordered

12 Airbus A319
4 Airbus A321
1 Airbus A340-300

Photograph: Boeing 747-200F D-ABYZ (Albert Kuhbandner/Frankfurt)

LUFTHANSA CARGO

Postfach 1244, 65451 Kelsterbach,
Germany
Tel. 6965437 Fax. 6966886

Three letter code	IATA No.	ICAO Callsign
GEC	020	Lufthansa Cargo

Lufthansa Cargo Aktiengesellschaft was established on 1st January 1995 as a 100% subsidiary of Lufthansa, to take over its worldwide airfreight activities. Its predecessor was Lufthansa Cargo Airlines, one of the many restructurings with Lufthansa, and German Cargo Services GmbH. The latter owed its existence to the withdrawal in 1977 of an anachronistic statute which had until then forbidden full-freight charter in the Federal Republic. The driving force behind this change was Lufthansa, who were seeing losses of tons of freight to neighbouring countries. Thus on 10th March 1977 German Cargo Services GmbH was founded in Frankfurt, and made its first flight on 15th April 1975 with a Boeing 707 to Hong Kong. By the middle of 1979 four Boeing 707s were in use, such was the growth of freight business. With the introduction of the Douglas DC-8, GCS's structure was altered, having until then been reliant on Lufthansa for the provision of crews and maintenance, it now employed its own pilots and had its own maintenance facility. German Cargo had four DC-8-73s in service, transporting everything which could travel by air, specialising particularly in services to Africa, South America and the Far East, as well as worldwide charters. In the course of a re-organisation in 1994/95 its activities were brought into those of Lufthansa Cargo, who now have a major specialist cargo fleet, principally consisting of Boeing 747Fs, with dedicated MD-11 freighters on order for 1998 delivery.

Routes

Worldwide scheduled and charter freight services.

Fleet	Ordered
3 Boeing 737-200F 11 Boeing 747-200F	5 McDonnell Douglas MD-11F

Photograph: Boeing 737-500 LX-LGR (Josef Krauthäuser/Frankfurt)

LUXAIR

BP 2203, 2987 Luxembourg-Airport,
Grand Duchy of Luxembourg
Tel. 4-7982311 Fax. 4-4432482

Three letter code	IATA No.	ICAO Callsign
LGL	149	Luxair

The Société Luxembourgeoise de Navigation Aérienne, or Luxair for short, was set up in 1961 as Luxembourg Airlines with the support of the government, of banks and Radio Luxembourg and technical assistance provided by KLM. Regular flights started on 2nd April 1962 with a Fokker F27 to Amsterdam, Frankfurt and Paris. Luxair started using Vickers Viscounts in 1966 and SE 210 Caravelles in March 1970. These were replaced in 1977 by Boeing 737s. Leased Boeing 707s were added to the fleet in 1980 for long-distance flights. One Airbus A300B4 was used at Luxair, but only for a short time, as it proved too large for the airline's needs. The Airbus was then exchanged for a Boeing 747SP, which was used from then on for long-distance flights. A fleet replacement programme started in 1989 with the delivery of the first Fokker 50s. The long-distance routes were given up in 1995. Luxair Commuter is a subsidiary company which operates with Embraer 120s (though the actual 'Commuter' titling has recently been removed from the aircraft themselves). Luxair has a 24.5% holding in Cargolux, while Lufthansa is a shareholder in Luxair, with 13% since December 1992.

Routes

From Luxembourg for example to Amsterdam, Frankfurt, Geneva, Hamburg, Copenhagen, London, Malaga, Manchester, Munich, Nice, Palma de Mallorca, Paris, Rome, Saarbrücken and other destinations in Europe. Charters are flown as well as scheduled services.

Fleet

2 Boeing 737-400
4 Boeing 737-500
4 Fokker 50

Photograph: Boeing 737-500 OY-MAC (Klaus Brandmaier/Innsbruck)

MAERSK AIR

Airport Dragoer South, 2791 Copenhagen, Denmark
Tel. 32314444 Fax. 32314490

Three letter code	IATA No.	ICAO Callsign
DAN	349	Maerskair

The A.P. Moeller shipping company set up Maersk Air as a subsidiary in February 1969. It was originally intended purely as a charter business. Flight operations started in December 1969 with a HS.125 and a Fokker F27. The young airline's urge to expand resulted in it taking over Falckair, a domestic airline, plus its routes to Odense and other destinations in 1970. In November 1971, Maersk joined with SAS and Cimber Air to create Danair, based at Copenhagen. Maersk now has a 38% stake in Danair. Air Business, another regional airline, was acquired in May 1983; it had been operating between Esbjerg and Stavanger. The route from Billund to Sonthad was opened with de Havilland DHC-7s. Further scheduled services connect Copenhagen with Billund and Ronne. In addition to scheduled and charter flights, Maersk Air has also earned considerable turnover from the aircraft leasing business. Maersk Air UK was established in July 1993 to take over the activities of Birmingham European Airways (previously Birmingham Executive Airways until 1989), which operated BAC One-Elevens and Jetstream 31s from the UK airport. This has now become a British Airways franchise operation, using Boeing 737s supplied by the Danish parent and a Jetstream 41. A further subsidiary is Star Air in Denmark, and there is a holding of 49% in Estonian Air. Maersk is one of the first airlines in the world to order the latest generation Boeing 737-700 which will be delivered from late 1997 onwards, joining an existing and growing fleet of -300 and -500 models.

Routes

Scheduled services from Billund and Copenhagen to Amsterdam, Brussels, Esbjerg, Faroe Islands, Frankfurt, Kristiansund, London, Odense, Paris, Ronne, Stockholm and Vojens. Seasonal charters are flown to the Mediterranean or winter sports destinations.

Fleet	Ordered
4 Boeing 737-300	4 Boeing 737-500
11 Boeing 737-500	6 Boeing 737-700
6 Fokker 50	

Photograph: Boeing 747-400 9M-MPH (Josef Krauthäuser/Frankfurt)

MALAYSIA AIRLINES

Jalan Sultan Ismail Bangunan MAS,
50250 Kuala Lumpur, Malaysia
Tel. 7464555 Fax. 7463027

Three letter code	IATA No.	ICAO Callsign
MAS	232	Malaysian

Malaysian Airline System came into existence on 3rd April 1971 after the former MSA (Malaysia-Singapore Airlines) was split up. Its history dates to Malayan Airways formed in 1937 but operations only started in May 1947 with two Airspeed Consuls. After the formation of the Federation of Malaysia in November 1963, Malayan became Malaysian Airways, with BOAC and Qantas the majority shareholders. Malaysian absorbed Borneo Airways in 1965. When Singapore separated from Malaysia in 1967 the airline changed its name to Malaysian-Singapore Airlines. Singapore's Government pushed for extension of international routes while Malaysia wanted greater emphasis on Malaysian domestic expansion. The rift brought about the new MAS which started operations on 1st October 1972. Destinations in Malaysia were served with nine F27s and three Britten-Norman Islanders. Weekly flights to London started in 1974 with Boeing 707s. Further destinations in Europe such as Amsterdam, Zürich and Frankfurt were soon to follow. In 1976 the first DC-10-30 was delivered, and in 1982 two Boeing 747-200s were added, which were also used for flights to the US from 1985 onwards. On 15th October 1987 MAS introduced new colours, and 'System' was dropped from the name, following the sale by the government of its shares. Malaysian expanded worldwide and invested in new technology and aircraft. In 1994 the A330 was introduced as a DC-10 replacement, with MD-11s following in 1995. MAS Cargo flies freight-only operations with MD-11s and Boeing 747-200Fs, and regional services are operated with Fokker 50s and Twin Otters. Malaysian is one of the largest Asian airlines, with almost unfettered expansion potential. By the year 2000 it is expected to have increased capacity by 50%.

Routes

Some 35 internal destinations, and connections to Australia, Japan, Korea, Hong Kong, Indonesia, Philippines, Thailand, Taiwan, the Middle East, USA, Africa and Europe.

Fleet

12 Airbus A330-300
2 Boeing 737-300F
40 Boeing 737-400
9 Boeing 737-500
16 Boeing 747-200/300/400
2 Boeing 777-200
6 De Havilland DHC-6
11 Fokker 50
2 McDonnell Douglas DC-10-30
4 McDonnell Douglas MD-11

Ordered

10 Boeing 747-400
9 Boeing 777-200
4 Boeing 777-300

Photograph: Boeing 767-200ER HA-LHB (Andrè Dietzel/Budapest)

MALEV-HUNGARIAN AIRLINES

V Roosevelt ter 2, 1051 Budapest,
Hungary
Tel. 1-2669033 Fax. 1-2662685

Three letter code	IATA No.	ICAO Callsign
MAH	182	Malev

Malev was originally established on 26th April 1946 as a joint Hungarian/Soviet undertaking with the title Maszovlet, with a fleet of eleven Lisunov Li-2s and six Polikarpov Po-2s. Flight operations began on 15th October 1946 on domestic routes and international flights started the next year. On 25th November 1954 the Hungarian government gained complete control and the airline adopted the name Magyar Legiközlekedesi Vollat (MALEV). When Ilyushin Il-18s were delivered, in May 1960, flights started to European destinations such as Amsterdam, Vienna and Moscow. With the development of Hungary's road system, domestic services were gradually trimmed through the late 1950s and 1960s, with the last flights operated in 1969. The Tupolev 134 was the first jet aircraft in 1968, followed by the Tu-154 in 1973. Replacement of Soviet-built aircraft with Boeing 737s started in 1989 and Malev was one of the first eastern bloc countries to acquire western airliners. Boeing aircraft are also used for long-distance routes. The first Boeing 767 was acquired by Malev at the end of 1992. The airline became a public limited company from 30th June 1992. Alitalia acquired 30% of the capital and started to work closely with Malev. During 1995 the first Fokker 70 was received for use on the shorter European routes, and several of the older Tupolevs were disposed of. A codeshare deal was agreed with Delta from May 1996. In May 1997 the Hungarian government decided to sell another 39% of the Malev shares, and Alitalia may also be forced to sell as a condition of further state aid being given in Italy. Cash from this privatisation would be used to replace the rest of the Tupolevs.

Routes

From Budapest scheduled flights to Amsterdam, Athens, Barcelona, Berlin, Beirut, Brussels, Cairo, Kiev, London, Moscow, Munich, Paris, Rome, Warsaw, Vienna, Zürich and other European destinations. Charters are flown as well as schedules.

Fleet

6 Boeing 737-200
4 Boeing 737-300
2 Boeing 737-400
2 Boeing 767-200ER
3 Fokker 70
3 Tupolev Tu-134
5 Tupolev Tu-154

Photograph: BAe 146-100 G-MIMA (Xaver Flocki collection)

MANX AIRLINES

Ronaldsway Airport, Ballasalla, Isle of Man,
IM9 2JE, Great Britain
Tel. 1624-826000 Fax. 1624-826001

Three letter code	IATA No.	ICAO Callsign
MNX	916	Manx

Manx Air Charter was founded immediately after the Second World War, in 1947. It went bankrupt in 1948 and was integrated into Silver City. It was only in 1982 that the fine-sounding name of this airline was revived. Manx Airlines was founded on 1st November of that year by British Midland Airways with a 75% stake and the rest held by British and Commonwealth Shipping Line. Flights started from Ronaldsway to London-Heathrow using Fokker Friendships and Vickers Viscounts. The airline also acquired a Saab 340 and BAC One-Elevens, plus a BAe 146 as its first jet aircraft which replaced the Saab 340 in 1988. The Viscount 800 was replaced by BAe ATPs in 1989. British Midland assumed full control of the airline in 1988 and Manx Airlines became a member of the Airlines of Britain group. In 1993 Manx acquired the new Jetstream 41. On 28th March 1994, Manx became the largest regional airline in Europe based on the size of its network of routes following the takeover of a number of routes and aircraft from group airline Loganair. During 1995 the airline started to operate partly as a British Airways franchise, with some aircraft painted in the flag carrier's colours, and in summer 1996 BA's Scottish operations were also taken over by Manx along with its aircraft. This close alliance with BA was not entirely comfortable in the light of parent company British Midland's competitive position with British Airways, and thus the grouping has been distanced by the formation of a new operating identity, British Regional Airlines. The newest addition to the fleet, being delivered during mid to late 1997, is the Embraer 145 regional jet.

Routes

Aberdeen, Belfast, Birmingham, Cardiff, Dublin, Edinburgh, Glasgow, Jersey, Liverpool, London, Luton, Manchester, Southampton and other destinations in the British Isles are served, plus shorter range European flights.

Fleet

British Regional:
12 BAe Jetstream 41
10 BAe ATP
1 BAe 146-200
2 Embraer 145
8 Shorts SD360

Manx:
1 BAe Jetstream 41
5 BAe ATP
1 BAe 146-100

Ordered

3 Embraer 145 *(British Regional)*

Photograph: Boeing 767-300ER PH-MCM (Josef Krauthäuser/Miami)

MARTINAIR

Postbus 7507,1118 ZG Schiphol,
Netherlands
Tel. 20-6011222 Fax. 20-6011303

Three letter code	IATA No.	ICAO Callsign
MPH	129	Martinair

Martin Air Holland – or to be very precise – Martin's Luchtvervoer Maatschaappij N.V, was founded on 24th May 1958 by Martin Schröder using a single Douglas DC-3. The airline was originally called Martins Air Charter, until the present name was introduced in April 1968. Sightseeing and air taxi flights were provided. A smaller airline, Fairways Rotterdam, was taken over in January 1964. KLM acquired a 25% stake in the airline, and further shares were sold to a shipping company. Martinair obtained DC-7s, Lockheed Electras and DC-8s from KLM. Using these aircraft, Martinair went into the charter business in a big way. In 1973 Martinair acquired DC-10s, in 1984 it obtained Airbus A310s and introduced the first Boeing 747 in a combi version in 1988. Further fleet renewal was undertaken and the Boeing 767 supplanted the Airbus, and the first MD-11 convertible freighter arrived at the end of 1994; this type was to replace the DC-10s. The word 'Holland' was dropped from the title in 1995. Martinair continues to expand with a very modern fleet, and yet continues to undertake its traditional activities of aerial photography, survey and aerial advertising. It is also particularly active in air freight. The main base is at Amsterdam-Schiphol, where the airline has its own maintenance facilities.

Routes

Holiday destinations in the Mediterranean, Caribbean, USA, Canada, South-east Asia. Worldwide freight flights.

Fleet	Ordered
3 Boeing 747-200 6 Boeing 767-300ER 5 McDonnell Douglas MD-11	2 McDonnell Douglas MD-11

Photograph: Boeing 747-200 N204AE (Albert Kuhbandner/Munich FJS)

MEA - MIDDLE EAST AIRLINE

P.O. Box 206, Beirut,
Lebanon
Tel. 629250 Fax. 629260

Three letter code	IATA No.	ICAO Callsign
MEA	076	Cedar Jet

MEA, whose full title is Middle East Airline SA, was founded in May 1945 as a private company by a group of Lebanese businessmen and started a de Havilland Rapide service between Beirut and Nicosia on 20th November and to Baghdad on 15th February 1946. In 1949 Pan American acquired a stake, and the first thing it did was to replace the three DH.89As with DC-3s in order to obtain more capacity for the transportation of cargo. Pan American withdrew from the airline in 1955, its stake being acquired by BOAC. Scheduled services started on 2nd October 1955 to London using Vickers Viscounts; Karachi and Bombay followed. Its first jet aircraft was the de Havilland Comet 4B, used for the route to London from 6th January 1961 onwards. Further expansion came in March 1963 when an agreement was reached for joint development with Air Liban. The two companies formally merged in November 1965 and Air Liban's DC-6s and Caravelles joined the fleet. Boeing 707s came into service in 1968, and in 1969 Lebanese International Airways (LIA) together with its fleet, route and staff was taken over. This merger was desired by the government, as several of LIA's and MEA's aircraft had been completely destroyed during an Israeli attack on Beirut airport in 1968. MEA acquired its first Boeing 747 in May 1975. Flight operations were badly disrupted by the fighting – verging on civil war – which went on for more than ten years, but MEA maintained the link with the outside world in the face of all adversity. Now that peace has returned to the Lebanon, business is being rebuilt and the fleet renewed, such as two Airbus A310s, which were leased in order to be able to take Boeing 707s out of service. The three 747s are being disposed of and up to four more A310s will be added. Air France has taken a shareholding.

Routes

The official timetable for Autumn 1993 showed over 30 destinations in the Middle East, Europe, Asia and Africa.

Fleet

2 Airbus A310-300
3 Airbus A310-200
2 Airbus A320-200
1 Airbus A321-200
8 Boeing 707-300
3 Boeing 747-200

Ordered

2 Airbus A310-300

Photograph: McDonnell Douglas MD-80 I-SMET (Henrique Belinha/Lisbon)

MERIDIANA

193 Corso Umberto, Zona Industrialle A,
07026 Olbia, Italy
Tel. 789-52600 Fax. 789-23661

Three letter code	IATA No.	ICAO Callsign
ISS	191	Merair

Meridiana resulted from the strategic merger of the Italian airline Alisarda and the Spanish airline Universair in 1991. Up until the Spanish airline Meridiana went bankrupt in late 1992, the two partners had co-ordinated their operations while remaining relatively independent. Alisarda was founded on 24th March 1963 in Olbia as an air taxi and general charter company using two Beech-C-45s and began operations that same year. Scheduled passenger services were added on 1st June 1966 initially with Nord 262s, later replaced by Fokker Friendships. Later services took place to destinations in France, Switzerland and within Italy using DC-9s from 1975. Other destinations followed seasonally such as Frankfurt or Munich, initially with charter and later with scheduled flights. Two MD-82s were acquired in 1984, and the fleet of this type has gradually increased. A third-level company, Avianova was established in 1986, but sold to the Alitalia group in 1991. On 1st September 1991 Alisarda changed its name to Meridiana and by 1992 it had become the largest privately owned airline in Italy. Four BAe 146-200s were added to the fleet in 1994. There are plans to double the MD-80 fleet over the next three years. The main base is Olbia, but Florence is being built up as an important point in the network. The airline has links with Alitalia, and with KLM for Amsterdam services.

Routes

Amsterdam, Barcelona, Bologna, Cagliari, Catania, Florence, Frankfurt, Geneva, Genoa, London, Milan, Munich, Naples, Nice, Olbia, Palermo, Paris, Pisa, Turin, Verona, Zürich.

Fleet

4 BAe 146-200
6 McDonnell Douglas DC-9-51
8 McDonnell Douglas MD-82

Photograph: IPTN CN-235-10 PK-MNL (Björn Kannengiesser/Jakarta)

MERPATI

Jolan Angkasa 2, Kotak pos 323,
Jakarta 10002, Indonesia
Twl. 4243608 Fax. 4246616

Three letter code	IATA No.	ICAO Callsign
MNA	621	Merpati

The Indonesian government founded Merpati Nusantara Airlines on 6th September 1962 to take over the network of internal services developed by the Indonesian Air Force. Initial flight operations started on 11th September 1962 connecting Jakarta with domestic points. In 1964, Merpati took over the routes previously operated by the KLM subsidiary de Kroonduif, which had been flown by Garuda since 1962. This predecessor had been particularly active in West Guinea. Scheduled services had started in January 1964. Merpati used the following aircraft: DC-3s, HS.748s, Vickers Viscounts, Vickers Vanguards, NAMC-YS 11s, Dornier 28s, Pilatus Porters. Numerous CASA aircraft manufactured in Indonesia under licence are also used, such as the IPTN 235s, replacing older aircraft. On 28th October 1978 the airline was taken over by Garuda, although Merpati continues to operate as part of the Garuda group under its own name. When the first DC-9s arrived in autumn 1990, new, modern colours were introduced for the aircraft. Five BAe ATPs were added in 1992. The first Fokker 100 was introduced in 1993, and Boeing 737-200s taken over in 1994 as replacements for DC-9s. There are continuing supplies of the CN-235 still being delivered, and the latest local product, the 64-seat IPTN N-250 is also on order, with deliveries to start in 1998. Merpati has the most intensive domestic network in Indonesia.

Routes

Over 130 points including Balikpapan, Bandar Lampg, Bandung, Banjarmasin, Denpasar, Dumai, Ketapang, Kupang, Maumere, Medan, Padang, Palankarya, Paembang, Pekanbaru, Pontianak, Rengat, Semarang, Surabaya, Tanjung Pinan, Waingapur.

Fleet		Ordered
1 Airbus A310	13 Fokker F27	5 Fokker 100
4 BAe ATP	29 Fokker F28	16 IPTN CN-235
1 BAe 146-100	6 Fokker 100	14 IPTN N-250-100
3 Boeing 737-200	14 IPTN CN-235-10	
8 De Havilland DHC-6 Twin Otter	11 IPTN 212 AB4/CC44 Aviocar	

Photograph: Airbus A320-200 XA-RJZ (Josef Krauthäuser/Miami)

MEXICANA

Xola 535, Piso 30, Colonia de Valle 03100
Mexico City, Mexico
Tel. 5-2270260 Fax. 5-6878786

Three letter code	IATA No.	ICAO Callsign
MXA	132	Mexicana

The Compania Mexicana de Aviacion is one of the oldest airlines in the world. It was founded on 12th July 1921 initially in order to fly wage payments to the oilfields near Tampico, as transporting this money overland was no longer safe. The airline adopted its present name on 20th August 1924. In March 1929, Charles Lindbergh piloted the carrier's first international flight between Mexico City and Brownsville, USA via Tampico, its base. From 1929 to 1968 Pan American had a majority interest in Mexicana. Aerovias Centrales was bought in 1935, and Transportes Aereos de Jalinco in 1955. In addition to DC-3s and DC-6s, Comet 4Cs were used on routes to Havana, Los Angeles and New York starting in 1960. The Boeing 727 was introduced in 1966 and the DC-10 in 1981. The Mexican Government became the major shareholder on 15th July 1982 when it increased its stake to 58%. However on 22nd August 1989 it became a private company. A necessary reorganisation involved changes to flight operations and to the network of routes. Airbus A320s were added to the relatively old Mexicana fleet from mid-1991. The Fokker 100 jet was introduced at the end of 1992 for routes with low passenger volume. At this time a new aircraft colour scheme was introduced, with the tailplane of each aircraft in a different hue, Mexicana has interests in various regional companies such as Aerocaribe, Aerocozumel, Aeromonterrey and Turboreactores. Conversely, Aeromexico has a 45% holding in Mexicana, and schedules are thus co-ordinated in order to save unnecessary costs.

Routes

Mexicana operates scheduled and charter services in the Caribbean, Central America, South America and 13 cities in the USA. A dense internal network serves about 30 points within Mexico.

Fleet	Ordered
14 Airbus A320-200 22 Boeing 727-200Adv 3 Boeing 757-200 10 Fokker 100	8 Airbus A320

Photograph: Boeing 727-200 MT-1036 (Björn Kannengiesser/Ulan Bator)

MIAT - MONGOLIAN AIRLINES

Buyant-Ukhaa 43, Ulan Bator 210734,
Mongolia
Tel. 379701

Three letter code	IATA No.	ICAO Callsign
MGL	289	Mongolair

The airline, founded in 1956, is known under a variety of names such as 'Mongolian Airlines', 'Mongoflot' or 'Air Mongol'. MIAT was built up with the aid of the USSR and Aeroflot. The first flight was on 7th July 1956 from Ulan Bator to Irkutsk using an Antonov 24. Equipment in the shape of Lisunov Li-2s (Soviet built Douglas DC-3s) and crews were initially supplied by the Soviet airline and international routes were opened to Peking and Irkutsk to connect with Aeroflot's service to Moscow. A service to Peking was soon discontinued due to lack of demand. The bulk of the fleet built up since the 1960s consists of Antonov An-24s and -26s, but five Chinese-built 17-seater Yunshuji Y-12s were added in 1992. Also in 1992 MIAT obtained a Boeing 727 from Korean Airlines as part of 'development aid' and co-operation. Two further 727s followed in 1994 and allowed the disposal of the Tupolev 154s. Other activities of the airline include agricultural flying and air ambulance work.

Routes

From Ulan Bator to destinations in Mongolia such as Darchan and Eerdenet. There are also services to Moscow and Irkutsk. Charter flights to Korea, Japan, the Middle East and to Beijing.

Fleet

17 Antonov An-24/26/30
3 Boeing 727-200
5 Yunshuji Y-12

Photograph: Fokker 100 N130ML (Björn Kannengiesser/Fort Lauderdale)

MIDWAY AIRLINES

South Cargo 4, Raleigh-Durham International Airport, Raleigh NC 27623, USA
Tel. 800-4464392 Fax. 800-4501909

Three letter code	IATA No.	ICAO Callsign
JEX	878	Jetex

Created as Bader Express Service in 1983, operations began from Bader Field in Atlantic City with charter flights for casinos and air taxi work using a CASA 212. In 1985 plans were laid for a 'low-fare' service to Chicago-Midway, Los Angeles, Phoenix and New York, and with this in mind the company was renamed as Jet Express. The hoped-for acquisition of three Boeing 727s failed for lack of capital. However, another CASA 212 was acquired in order to become a feeder carrier as a TWA-Partner. From 1992 with the Swearingen Metro III the company became a US Air-Express partner. In 1993 the group bought the name Midway Airlines from the bankruptcy of a former airline of that name, leased five Fokker 100s and opened service from Chicago-Midway to New York. The possibility of building a network from Chicago's second airport as a niche carrier as its predecessor had done was however more difficult. Thus after only six months Midway was facing another closure, but at the beginning of 1994 an investment company took 90% of the shares, reorganised the company and installed new management. At the beginning of 1995 the American Airlines former hub at Raleigh-Durham was taken over when American drastically reduced operations there, and Midway moved its headquarters there to concentrate on East Coast services. Alongside more leased Fokker 100s, leased A320s came into service as there was a need for an aircraft for holiday flights to Las Vegas and Cancun. The rapid growth of the earlier years gave way to consolidation and quality improvement. In March 1995 Midway Connection was started with Beech 1900s and Embraer Brasilias providing connecting flights; these are operated by subcontractors.

Routes

Scheduled services within the USA including Atlanta, Boston, Chicago, Fort Lauderdale, Hartford, Islip, Newark, New York, Orlando, Philadelphia, Raleigh-Durham, Tampa, Washington, West Palm Beach.

Fleet	Ordered
1 Airbus A320	4 Airbus A320
12 Fokker 100	

Photograph: McDonnell Douglas DC-9-32 N203ME (Björn Kannengiesser/Fort Lauderdale)

MIDWEST EXPRESS

4915 South Howell Avenue, Milwaukee, Wisconsin 53207, USA
Tel. 414-7474000 Fax. 414-7471499

Three letter code	IATA No.	ICAO Callsign
MEP	453	Midex

Midwest was established after deregulation in November 1983 to provide passenger service in the Midwest and Southeast of the USA. The airline is a subsidiary of KC Aviation, which is itself the established aviation division of Kimberley-Clark, the major paper products company. The initial fleet was a DC-9 and a Convair 580 but more DC-9s soon followed. Flight operations started on 29th April 1984 with a DC-9, on the route Milwaukee to Boston. Over the years a fleet of DC-9-10s and -32s was built up and the routes were extended as far as Dallas and to Los Angeles. Two MD-88s were added in 1989. In 1994/95 the company's capital base was increased in order to finance further expansion. More DC-9-32s were acquired and new routes opened or service frequency increased on existing routes. At the same time a modified colour scheme was introduced for the aircraft.

Routes

Milwaukee, Dallas, Minneapolis, Appleton, Atlanta, Boston, Detroit, Fort Lauderdale, Grand Rapids, Indianapolis, Lansing, Los Angeles, Madison, New York, Philadelphia, Phoenix, San Francisco, Tampa, Washington.

Fleet

8 McDonnell Douglas DC-9-14/15
16 McDonnell Douglas DC-9-32
2 McDonnell Douglas MD-88

Photograph: Airbus A320-200 G-MONY (Gottfried Auer/Salzburg)

MONARCH

Luton Airport, Luton, Bedfordshire, LU2 9NU,
Great Britain
Tel. 1582-400000 Fax. 1582-401306

Three letter code	IATA No.	ICAO Callsign
MON	974	Monarch

Monarch Airlines, a well-known British charter airline, was founded on 5th June 1967 by Cosmos Tours. Flight operations started on 5th April 1968 with a Bristol Britannia flying between Luton and Madrid. Its initial fleet was two Britannia aircraft and its destinations were Mediterranean holiday regions. In 1971 the first jet aircraft was acquired, a Boeing 720. BAC One-Elevens followed in 1975, Boeing 707s in 1978 and the first Boeing 737 in 1980. Its first Boeing 757 arrived in 1983. Licences to operate scheduled services from Luton to Mahon, Palma and Malaga were awarded in the mid-1980s and its first service to Mahon, started on 5th July 1986. Long-haul charter services to the USA were introduced in 1988. Apart from the charter business, Monarch is also very active in aircraft leasing. For example, the entire Euroberlin fleet was leased from Monarch for some years. The fleet is kept up to date, with Airbus A300-600s introduced from 1990, and Boeing 737s were largely replaced by Airbus 320s from the beginning of 1993. Boeing 767s were also acquired, but these were leased to Alitalia. The first Airbus A321 was delivered in April 1997, and two Airbus A330-200s are on order for delivery in 1999. The main base is Luton, but aircraft are detached for operation from the main British airports such as Birmingham, Gatwick, Liverpool and Manchester.

Routes

Schedules to Alicante, Malaga, Menorca, Tenerife, Palma. Charter flights, especially to the Mediterranean, the Alpine region, the Caribbean, East Africa, the Far East and USA.

Fleet

4 Airbus A300-600
7 Airbus A320-200
1 Airbus A321-200
7 Boeing 757-200/200ER
1 McDonnell Douglas DC-10-30

Ordered

2 Airbus A321-200
2 Airbus A330-200

Photograph: Fokker F28 XY-AGA (Klaus Brandmaier/Hong Kong)

MYANMA AIRWAYS

104 Strand Road, Yangon,
Myanmar (Burma) Socialist Republic
Tel. 1-84566 Fax. 1-89583

Three letter code	IATA No.	ICAO Callsign
UBA	209	Unionair

Originally established in 1948 by the Burmese government as the 'Union of Burma Airways', the airline changed its name in December 1972 to Burma Airways Corporation, and finally on 1st April 1989 to Myanma Airways. In between lie more than 40 years of flight operations, which started in 1948 with de Havilland Doves. These were followed by DC-3s and Vickers Viscounts, and the introduction of national and international services. The first F27 was delivered in October 1963. In 1969 a Boeing 727 replaced the Vickers Viscount on international flights. After the first F28 was delivered in 1976 Myanma only used Fokker aircraft. A co-operation was agreed with Royal Brunei in 1993 which provides for international flights to be operated by a separate joint airline; this has been active since the beginning of 1994 as Myanmar Airways International with two leased Boeing 737s.

Routes

Yangon, Akyab, Bangkok, Bhamo, Cebu, Dacca, Hong Kong, Kalemyo, Kawthaung, Kengtung, Khamti, Kuala Lumpur, Mandalay, Manila, Penang, Singapore, Taipei and about ten further internal destinations.

Fleet

7 Fokker F27-100/400/600
3 Fokker F28

Photograph: Boeing 737-200Adv N501NG (Josef Krauthäuser/Miami)

NICA AIRLINES

P.O. Box 6018, Managua,
Nicaragua
Tel. 2-631929 Fax. 2-631822

Three letter code	IATA No.	ICAO Callsign
NIS	930	Nica

Following the collapse of Aeronica there was no longer an international airline active in the still politically unstable Nicaragua. Soon after the elections in 1992 a new company was established with the help of TACA – Nicaraguenses de Aviacion SA – or NICA for short. TACA held 49% of the shares, the rest being with private investors and the Nicaraguan government. In July 1992 it was possible to open the first service to Miami with a leased Boeing 737-200. The main base is Managua, from where an internal network was also run with a CASA 212. As well as passenger schedules, charters and freight services are also flown. NICA has joined in the frequent-flier programme with TACA, LACSA and Aviateca, and these airlines are building up a marketing alliance.

Routes

Bluefields, Corn Island, Guatemala City, Miami, Panama City, Puerto Cabezas, San Jose, San Salvador.

Fleet

1 Boeing 737-200Adv

Photograph: Airbus A310-200 5N-AUH (Patrick Lutz/London LHR)

NIGERIA AIRWAYS

P.O.B 1024, Ikeja,
Nigeria
Tel. 01-900810 Fax. 4936347

Three letter code	IATA No.	ICAO Callsign
NGA	087	Nigeria

West African Airways Corporation started operations in the former British colony in West Africa in 1946. Nigeria Airways was established in 1958 to take over the Nigerian operations of WAAC with the name WAAC (Nigeria) Ltd. The Nigerian Government assumed full ownership of the airline on 1st May 1959. Flight operations in the new independent state of Nigeria were started with the aid of BOAC using aircraft leased from the latter on 1st October 1958. Boeing 377 Stratocruisers were used to open a route from Lagos to London, and from 1st April 1962 the de Havilland Comet 4B was used on this route.

In 1971 the state took control of the company, and a Boeing 707 was the first aircraft owned by the recently established airline. The present title was formally adopted on 22nd January 1971 although it had been used for commercial purposes since 1958. A Boeing 707 took over operating the Lagos-London service in 1971 from ex-BOAC Vickers VC-10 aircraft which had been introduced in 1969. When the first Douglas DC-10s arrived in October 1976, Nigeria Airways had its first widebody aircraft. Two Airbus A310s were delivered in 1983 and another two in 1984. They are primarily used on African routes.

Over the last few years Nigeria Airways has been in decline. Massive financial problems have led to the abandonment of routes, redundancies and the sale of aircraft.

Routes

Abidjan, Abuja, Accra, Banjul, Calabar, Conakry, Cotonou, Douala, Enugu, Jeddah, Jos, Kaduna, Kano, Libreville, Lome, London, Makurdi, Port Harcourt, Rome, Sokoto and Yola.

Fleet

4 Airbus A310-200
2 Boeing 707-300
6 Boeing 737-200Adv
1 McDonnell Douglas DC-10-30

Photograph: Boeing 757-200 N507US (Josef Krauthäuser/Portland)

NORTHWEST AIRLINES

Minneapolis/St Paul International. Airport,
St Paul, MN 55111, USA
Tel. 612 726-2111 Fax. 612 726-6599

Three letter code	IATA No.	ICAO Callsign
NWA	012	Northwest

This airline was founded on 1st August 1926 in Minneapolis/St Paul as Northwest Airways. In the early years it operated flights with a Stinson Post from Chicago to St Paul. Regular passenger services began in 1933 using DC-3s. In 1934 Northern Air Transport was taken over and the name changed to Northwest Airlines. On 15th July 1947 the first polar route was opened using DC-4s. This route was from Seattle via Anchorage to Tokyo and on to Manila. From that time on the airline was called Northwest Orient Airlines. Boeing Stratocruisers were used on the routes to South East Asia. Lockheed Constellations, DC-6s, DC-7s and Lockheed L-188 Electras were the most important aircraft during the propeller age until the first DC-8s arrived. They were used for the route from Seattle to Chicago, and were then used to replace the propeller aircraft on the Asia routes. On 30th April 1970, NW acquired its first widebody aircraft, a Boeing 747, followed by DC-10-40s in late 1972. In 1979 Northwest crossed the Atlantic to Copenhagen and Stockholm and in 1980 to London. Unlike many other airlines, Northwest's growth was solely internal until 1986, when Republic was bought. In 1988 the old name, Northwest Airlines, was adopted again. When the first Airbus A320s were delivered in late 1989, Northwest also introduced the new colour scheme. Though there has been some fleet renewal, expansion has notably been by the purchase of second-hand DC-9s in recent years, and the emphasis has been on the refurbishment of older aircraft rather than new purchases. Northwest works in close co-operation with KLM, which holds voting shares and has feeder arrangements with other airlines including Mesaba and Express Airlines I, who fly as 'Northwest Airlink' and with NW flight numbers.

Routes

Over 240 destinations in over 20 countries, with over 100 in the USA alone. Principal hubs are at Minneapolis/St Paul, Detroit, Memphis and Tokyo-Narita. Many regional flights are operated by Northwest Airlink.

Fleet

50 Airbus A320-200
43 Boeing 727-200
34 Boeing 747-100/200
10 Boeing 747-400
48 Boeing 757-200
22 McDonnell Douglas DC-9-14/15
115 McDonnell Douglas DC-9-31/32
12 McDonnell Douglas DC-9-41
35 McDonnell Douglas DC-9-51
8 McDonnell Douglas MD-82
37 McDonnell Douglas DC-10-30/40

Ordered

20 Airbus A320-200
16 Airbus A330-300
25 Boeing 757-200
4 Boeing 747-400

Photograph: McDonnell Douglas MD-83 EI-CGI (Albert Kuhbandner/Munich/FJS)

NOUVELAIR TUNISIE

BP 66 Aéroport International,
Monastir 5025, Tunisia
Tel. 3-467100 Fax. 3-467110

Three letter code	IATA No.	ICAO Callsign
LBT	-	Nouvelair

The French airline Air Liberté established a subsidiary of the same name in Tunisia in 1990 and began regular charter flights from Monastir with a MD-83 supplied by the parent company. Destinations in the former East Germany, newly part of the unified country, were served. Further aircraft could be used on loan from the parent in case of need. The company developed satisfactorily and another MD-83 was added in 1991. However, financial crisis overtook the parent, and things looked black for the Tunisian arm until it was sold in 1996 to Tunisian Travel Service. There was to be increased co-operation with Tunisair and with Air Liberté until the latter was sold to British Airways. With the sale of shares Air Liberté Tunisie became a company under Tunisian law, and a renaming as Novelair Tunisie followed in March 1996. Hand in hand with the new name went a new colour scheme for the aircraft. Two more MD-83s have been added, one each in March 1996 and March 1997.

Routes

Charter flights from airports in countries including Belgium, France, Germany, Holland, Ireland, Italy, Austria, Russia, Scandinavia, Hungary, Czech Republic and the UK to Tunisia.

Fleet

4 McDonnell Douglas MD-83

Photograph: Boeing 727-200 5N-MML (Josef Krauthäuser collection)

OKADA AIR

17 B Sapeh Road, Benin City,
Nigeria
Tel 019-241054

Three letter code	IATA No.	ICAO Callsign
OKJ	-	Okadaair

A consortium of companies, led by Chief Igbenidian, founded Okada Air in 1983, in order to operate regional and international charter flights. Flight services were started using BAC One-Elevens followed by DC-8s and Boeing 707s. Its first foreign destination was London. There are also occasional charters to Frankfurt or Zürich. Okada also flies subcharters for other airlines as well as cargo. A network of domestic scheduled services is in being, joining such cities as Lagos, Kano, Kaduna and Port Harcourt. Over the years it has assembled the world's largest fleet of BAC One-Elevens. During the 1990s however larger Boeing 727s and a Boeing 747-100 have been added.

Routes

Charter flights to Europe, the Middle East and *ad hoc* to other destinations. Internal Nigerian services.

Fleet

20 BAC 1-11
3 Boeing 727-200
1 Boeing 747-100

Photograph: Airbus A300B4 TC-ONL (B.I.Hengi/Zürich)

ONUR AIR

Senlik Mah, Catal Sk. No. 3 Flora-Istanbul,
Turkey
Tel. 0212-6632300 Fax. 0212-5733696

Three letter code	IATA No.	ICAO Callsign
OHY	-	Onur Air

The airline, which was only founded in 1992, is a subsidiary of the Turkish tour operator 'TK Air Travel'. Flight operations started in May 1993 with new Airbus A320s. The airline intends to start scheduled services in addition to charter and inclusive tour flights. During the high season, further Airbus A320s are leased in addition to the airline's own aircraft. At the beginning of 1994 Ten Tours took over the company and put it on a stronger financial footing. Two Airbus A310s were added to the fleet at the beginning of 1996. At the beginning of 1997 a change in fleet acquisition policy was marked by an order for MD-88s, the first two of which were delivered in March 1997. From its home base at Istanbul Onur Air plans to build up a Turkish domestic network by the end of the 1990s.

Routes

From German, British, French, Italian and Swiss airports to the sunshine resorts of Turkey, plus flights to Israel.

Fleet

4 Airbus A320-200
3 Airbus A321-100
2 Airbus A300B4
2 McDonnell Douglas MD-88

Ordered

1 Airbus A321-100
3 McDonnell Douglas MD-88

Photograph: Boeing 737-200Adv SX-BCL (B.I.Hengi/Geneva)

OLYMPIC AIRWAYS

96 Snygrou Avenue, Athens,
Greece
Tel. 9267295 Fax. 9267123

Three letter code	IATA No.	ICAO Callsign
OAL	050	Olympic

Olympic Airways was founded on 6th April 1957 by no less a person than Aristotle Onassis. The well-known shipowner took over an airline called TAE Greek National Airlines which had been in existence since July 1951 and belonged to the Greek state. By the time of the first oil crisis Onassis had turned Olympic into a modern airline, but the oil situation caused the airline difficulties and it suspended flight operations for several months in 1974. In order to avert complete bankruptcy, the Greek state intervened and took over Olympic from 1st January 1976 when operations resumed. After the airline was completely restructured and unprofitable routes abandoned, things slowly took a turn for the better again. Right at the start of flight operations, in April 1957. Olympic had a fleet of 13 DC-3s and one DC-4 and a year later DC-6Bs started flying from Athens to London via Rome and Paris. Comet 4Bs went into service in 1960. Boeing 707s inaugurated a non-stop Athens to NewYork service on 1st June 1966 and later long-distance routes to New York, Johannesburg and Australia. Boeing 727s were introduced in 1969 and NAMC YS-11As in 1970 to replace DC-3s on local networks. Boeing 720s supplanted the DC-6Bs on long-haul routes from 1972. The first Boeing 747 came to Olympic while it was still under Onassis' control. As part of a fleet replacement policy, the airline's Boeing 707s and most Boeing 727s were replaced by new Boeing 737-400s and Airbus A300s by 1992, and all of these aircraft were painted in attractive colours. Olympic flies charters as well as schedules, especially during the summer, and there is an internal network operated by Olympic Aviation. (see page 229).

Routes

Amsterdam, Bangkok, Beirut, Berlin, Boston, Brussels, Dubai, Düsseldorf, Frankfurt, Geneva, Istanbul, Jeddah, Johannesburg, Copenhagen, Kuwait, London, Melbourne, Montreal, Munich, Nairobi, New York, Paris, Rome, Sydney, Tel Aviv, Toronto, Vienna and Zürich.

Fleet		Ordered
6 Airbus A300B4	11 Boeing 737-200Adv	2 Boeing 767
2 Airbus A300-600	7 Boeing 737-400	
4 Boeing 747-200		
3 Boeing 727-200Adv		

Photograph: ATR72-200 SX-BII (Andreas Witek/Graz)

OLYMPIC AVIATION

96 Snygrou Avenue, Athens,
Greece
Tel. 9362681 Fax. 9883009

Three letter code	IATA No.	ICAO Callsign
OAV	-	Olympic

Greece, with its numerous islands, and its fragmented and mountainous mainland, is dependent not only on a dense network of ferry connections but also on properly functioning regional flight services. In order to open up smaller islands for tourists and to save tourists long transfer times, Olympic Aviation was founded on 1st August 1971 with the objective of building up regional flight services. First of all runways had to be laid, extended or repaired on many islands. As many runways do not have a hard surface, robust aircraft such as Short Skyvans and Dornier 228s were used. Initially it was privately-owned but became Government-owned in 1974. Flights are operated to those places where the parent company, Olympic Airways, cannot operate its aircraft, plus the airline operates as a feeder service to international flights to Athens. It is also responsible for charter and air-taxi operations. ATR42s were first introduced in 1990. Since 1st January 1992, the airline has been operationally independent of Olympic Airways, of which it is a wholly-owned subsidiary. With the ATR72s which entered service in 1992/93, charters are also flown from smaller European airports to the Greek islands.

Routes

From Athens domestic airport to over 30 destinations in the Aegean, the Peleponnese and on the Greek mainland.

Fleet

7 ATR72
4 ATR42
7 Dornier Do228-200
5 Short 330

Photograph: Tupolev Tu-154B 4L-85430 (Björn Kannengiesser/Dubai)

ORBI GEORGIAN AIRWAYS

28,Rustavelli Pr, Tbilisi 3800D,
Georgia
Tel. 987328 Fax 990297

Three letter code	IATA No.	ICAO Callsign
DVU	819	Zena

In this country which is not spared from conflict, an independent and privately funded airline was established in 1991 from the former Georgian Directorate of Aeroflot. However only about half of the Soviet-built fleet is serviceable, and for economic reasons many aircraft have been retired. A Boeing 737-300 was in use for a while from October 1995 for international routes, but this has now been disposed of. The main base is at Tbilisi from which all flights are conducted. As well as scheduled services, charters are flown, these principally in the Middle East, to Dubai and Bahrein.

Routes

Batumi, Berlin, Istanbul, Kiev, Moscow, Paris, Prague, Tel Aviv, Vienna and Volgograd.

Fleet

4 Tupolev Tu-134A
4 Tupolev Tu-154B
6 Yakovlev Yak-40

Photograph: Airbus A300B4 AP-BAZ (Björn Kannengiesser/Dubai)

PAKISTAN INTERNATIONAL

PIA Building, Karachi-Airport,
Pakistan
Tel. 4572011 Fax. 7727727

Three letter code	IATA No.	ICAO Callsign
PIA	214	Pakistan

Pakistan Airlines was founded by the government in 1951 and began Super Constellation services on 7th June 1954 providing a valuable connection between East and West Pakistan. International routes to Cairo and London followed on 1st February 1955 and on 10th March the same year the airline was reorganised after formal amalgamation with Orient Airways, which had been founded on 23rd 1946 prior to the partitioning of India. On domestic flights Convair CV240s and DC-3s were used. They were replaced by Vickers Viscounts and later by HS Tridents. In 1960 long-distance flights changed over to Boeing 707s and in 1961 these aircraft were used for flights to New York for the first time. The airline's first widebody aircraft was a DC-10-30 in 1974. Two Boeing 747s were leased from TAP-Air Portugal in 1976, and then later bought, with further 747s added during the 1980s. In 1971 many flights and services had to be suspended due to the war situation and the secession of East Pakistan which became Bangladesh. After the airline was reorganised, flight operations picked up again in late 1972 and routes which had been abandoned, eg New York, were resumed. Airbus A310s for long-distance and A300B4s for high passenger volume short and medium length routes are the backbone of the fleet, which is growing steadily but surely. Fokker Friendships, the first of which was delivered in 1961 and Boeing 737s acquired from 1985 also have a significant role with PIA. Plans for privatisation have been put on hold, but a cost-cutting exercise is in progress, and fleet renewal plans must be made shortly.

Routes

From Karachi and Islamabad to Lahore, Dubai, Teheran, Amman, Copenhagen, Damascus, Cairo, Moscow, Istanbul, Athens, Rome, Frankfurt, Amsterdam, Paris, London, New York, Toronto, Tokyo, Beijing, Zürich, Manila, Singapore, Kuala Lumpur, Bangkok, Kathmandu, Nairobi, Jeddah, Bahrain and to over 20 domestic points.

Fleet

6 Airbus A310-300
10 Airbus A300B4
8 Boeing 747-200
2 Boeing 707-300F
7 Boeing 737-300
2 De Havilland DHC-6
13 Fokker F27

Photograph: Airbus A300B4 RP-C3003 (Josef Krauthäuser/Hong Kong)

PHILIPPINES

1, Legaspi Street, P.O. Box 954, Manila, Philippines
Tel. 02-8180111 Fax. 02-8109214

Three letter code	IATA No.	ICAO Callsign
PAL	079	Philippine

Philippine Air Lines was set up on 26th February 1941 but at the end of that year had to suspend operations as a result of the Japanese invasion. After the liberation of the Philippines services were restarted with five Douglas DC-3s on 14th February 1946. Far East Air Transport, which had routes to Hong Kong, Shanghai, Bangkok and Calcutta, was taken over with its five Douglas DC-4s in 1947. In the same year PAL began a scheduled service to San Francisco, but in 1954 all international routes with the exception of Hong Kong were suspended. However, that allowed the build up of domestic services to take place. In 1962, in co-operation with KLM, the international route to San Francisco was again opened. From May 1966 the first BAC One-Elevens were introduced, and in 1969 flights were started with Douglas DC-8s to Amsterdam, Frankfurt and Rome. In 1974 Air Manila and Filipinas were bought, and in the same year the first leased DC-10-30 arrived as a DC-8 replacement. By 1979 the Boeing 747 and the Airbus A300B4 (known as the 'love bus') were introduced. With the purchase of Fokker 50s from 1988, older HS.748s could be retired, and likewise the BAC One-Elevens were replaced with Boeing 737-300s from 1990 onwards. Alongside the Boeing 747-400, the newest jet in the fleet is the Airbus A340-300, which entered service in 1996. A further fleet expansion is envisaged until the end of 1998, notably with the addition of Airbus A320s.

Routes

Amsterdam, Frankfurt, London, Paris, Rome, Los Angeles, New York, San Francisco, Dharhan, Dubai, Bangkok, Brisbane, Ho Chi Minh City, Hong Kong, Seoul, Taipei, Tokyo, Sydney, Singapore, Kuala Lumpur, Karachi, and an intensive domestic network.

Fleet

12 Airbus A300B4
1 Airbus A330-300
8 Airbus A340-300
12 Boeing 737-300
8 Boeing 747-200
4 Boeing 747-400
10 Fokker 50

Ordered

12 Airbus A320
11 Airbus A330-300
7 Boeing 747-400

Photograph: McDonnell Douglas DC-10-30 PP-VMW (Uwe Gleisberg collection/Madrid)

PLUNA

Colonia 1021, P.O. Box 1360, Montevideo, Uruguay
Tel. 2-980606 Fax. 2-921478

Three letter code	IATA No.	ICAO Callsign
PUA	286	Pluna

Primeras Lineas Uruguayas de Navegazion Aera – PLUNA – was founded in September 1935 by the Marquez Vaeza brothers. Flight operations started on 20th November 1936 with two de Havilland DH.90 Dragonflies. The airline expanded and ordered a DH.86B, until operations had to be discontinued on 15th March 1943. After the end of the Second World War, the government of Uruguay acquired 83% of the shares in the airline, and on 12th November 1951 the remaining capital shares were also transferred to the state. Services were operated to neighbouring states using DC-3s, and a domestic network was built up. In addition to DC-3s, de Havilland Herons and Vickers Viscounts were employed. In late 1967 Pluna took over the route network and the aircraft belonging to CAUSA. Pluna acquired its first jet aircraft, a Boeing 737-200, in late 1969. Pluna's sole overseas route was a weekly connection to Madrid. Boeing 707s were used on this route from 1982 but Pluna entered into a co-operation agreement with Spanair in 1993 for the flights on this route; the latter airline operated the flights with Boeing 767s, as Pluna did not have any suitable aircraft of its own available. This was valid until the end of 1994, after which VARIG bought 51% of Pluna's shares and thus completed the anticipated privatisation. As a result a DC-10-30 leased from VARIG but in a new Pluna colour scheme, was rostered on the Spanish flights.

Routes

From its principal base at Montevideo to Asuncion, Buenos Aires, Madrid, Melo, Paysandu, Porto Alegre, Rio de Janeiro, Santiago de Chile, Sao Paulo, Tel Aviv.

Fleet

3 Boeing 737-200Adv
1 McDonnell Douglas DC-10-30

Photograph: Boeing 747-100F N853FT (Josef Krauthäuser/Miami)

POLAR AIR CARGO

100 Oceangate, Long Beach,
California 90802, USA
Tel. 310-4367471 Fax. 310-4369333

Three letter code	IATA No.	ICAO Callsign
PAC	403	Polar Tiger

Polar Air Cargo was set up in January 1993 and began scheduled freight services to Anchorage, Honolulu and New York in May of that year: Two Boeing 747-100 freighters were brought into service initially, with two more added later in the year. On 7th July 1994 the Federal Aviation Administration gave permission for the airline to carry out its own maintenance at its main base in New York and during the year more Boeing 747s were added, so that by the end of 1995 there were 12 in the fleet. Alongside FedEx and UPS, Polar is one of the fastest growing cargo airlines, with worldwide scheduled and charter flights. The airline works with cargo agencies worldwide and offers a dependable service. Plans are in hand for the further expansion of scheduled services to Europe, India Africa and the Middle East.

Routes

Anchorage, Atlanta, Auckland, Buenos Aires, Chicago, Columbus, Hong Kong, Honolulu, Los Angeles, Melbourne, Moscow, New York, Miami, Prestwick, Santiago, Seoul, Singapore, Sydney, Taipei.

Fleet	Ordered
13 Boeing 747-100F 1 Boeing 747-200F	4 Boeing 747-200F (conversions)

Photograph: Boeing 737-300 5W-ILF (Uwe Gleisberg/Sydney)

POLYNESIAN

Beach Road, P.O. Box 599, Apia,
Western Samoa
Tel. 20047 Fax. 20023

Three letter code	IATA No.	ICAO Callsign
PAO	162	Polynesian

After the collapse of its predecessor, Samoan Airlines, Polynesian Airlines Limited was founded on 7th May 1959. Its first flight was from Apia to Pago Pago, using a Percival Prince, in 1960. After state independence in 1962 further routes to the Cook Islands were opened on 5th July 1963 and a DC-3 was acquired. In 1968 Polynesian obtained a DC-4, and from January 1972 onwards modern turboprop aircraft were acquired in the form of two HS.748s. Modernisation became possible after the state acquired a 70% stake in the airline. Polynesian entered the jet age in 1981 with the delivery of a Boeing 737, followed by new routes to Australia. Various GAF Nomads, BN Islanders and DHC Twin Otters were also acquired for regional routes. In the early 1990s Polynesian acquired the latest Boeing 737-300. A Boeing 767 leased from Air New Zealand followed in 1993; it was used on routes to the US.This however turned out to be too large and it was returned. A close co-operation is maintained with Air New Zealand, and long-distance services are now operated under a code-share agreement with ANZ.

Routes

Apia, Auckland, Nadi, Nine, Noumea Pago Pago, Papeete, Sydney, Tongatapu, Vila, Vaṛa'u.

Fleet

1 Boeing 737-300
1 De Havilland DHC-6 Twin Otter
1 Pilatus BN 21 Islander

Photograph: Fokker 100 CS-TPF (Patrick Lutz/Lisbon)

PORTUGALIA

Avenida Almirante Gago Coutinho 88,
1700 Lisbon, Portugal
Tel. 8486693 Fax. 894862

Three letter code	IATA No.	ICAO Callsign
PGA	685	Portugalia

Portugalia was founded as a regional scheduled airline on 25th July 1989 and started flights a year later, on 7th July 1990, with Fokker 100s leased from Guinness Peat Aviation. In the first two years the airline made a loss of US$12 million. It made its first small profit in 1993. With the arrival of the sixth Fokker 100 in 1995, a new colour scheme was adopted. The new Embraer 145 regional jet has just been introduced to the fleet. Portugalia is based in Lisbon, where it has a maintenance base, and is also active in the charter business, particularly at holiday times when it serves European airports, and especially Faro.

Routes

Scheduled services to Brussels, Faro, Frankfurt, Hannover, Cologne/Bonn, Lisbon, Manchester, Madrid, Porto, Strasbourg, Stuttgart, Turin.

Fleet	Ordered
2 Embraer 145 6 Fokker 100	2 Embraer 145

Photograph: Airbus A320 OY-CNF (Uwe Gleisberg/Salzburg)

PREMIAIR

Hangar 276, Copenhagen Airport South,
2791 Dragoer, Denmark
Tel. 32454500 Fax. 32451220

Three letter code	IATA No.	ICAO Callsign
VKG	630	Viking

1st January 1994 marked the inauguration of a new airline which represented the amalgamation of two well-known charter companies. Conair had been founded in 1964 as Consolidated Aircraft Corp. and from the 1965 summer season had flown exclusively for the Spies holiday concern. First it used DC-7s, later Boeing 720s and Airbus A300B4s. Scanair meanwhile was started on 30th June 1961; SAS had a 45% holding in this company and provided the aircraft. After a reconstruction it was passed over to the SAS participants, DNL, DDL and ABA. As well as leased DC-8s, Boeing 727s and later DC-10s were used. In 1993 the pressure of competition for charter companies in Europe indicated that a merger would be a good idea. Spies had become the owner of Conair and over the years had also acquired a share in Scanair. The merger was decided upon in November 1993, executed in January 1994 and the aircraft all received a new colour scheme. The joint owners were Spies Holding and Scandinavian Leisure Group; the latter was acquired from SAS by the British group Airtours in July 1994, and the Spies group was also bought by Airtours in 1996. Thus Premiair has become fully owned by Airtours, and there was at the beginning of the 1997 season a mass exchange of A320 fleets with the Airtours UK fleet in order to achieve engine commonality for both airlines. Premiair's aircraft are now taking on a colour scheme almost identical to the Airtours 'sunburst' except for the titling, this no doubt to facilitate easy inter-operation. Premiair's main base is at Copenhagen, with subsidiary operations in Oslo and Stockholm.

Routes

Charter flights to the classic holiday regions of the Mediterranean, and winter sports in the Alps.

Fleet

3 Airbus A300B4
6 Airbus A320-200
7 McDonnell Douglas DC-10-10/30

Photograph: Boeing 737-400 VH-TJH (Uwe Gleisberg/Perth)

QANTAS

Qantas Centre, QCA9, 203 Coward Street, Sydney, NSW, Australia
Tel. 2-6913472 Fax. 2-6914547

Three letter code	IATA No.	ICAO Callsign
QFA	081	Qantas

Queensland and Northern Territory Aerial Service Limited – QANTAS for short – was formed on 16th November 1920. Two Avro 504s were stationed in Longreach; initially the airline operated taxi and sightseeing flights, and the first routes from Charleville to Cloncurry were flown in November 1922. Qantas aircraft were also used to set up the famous Flying Doctor Service in 1928 and in the same year began the first scheduled air service in Australia between Brisbane and Toowoomba, a distance of 80 miles. In co-operation with Imperial Airways, Qantas served the London-Brisbane route, with Qantas flying the last leg from Singapore to Brisbane from 1934. The airline called itself Qantas Empire Airways from 1934 to 1967. QEA employed Short Empire flying boats, because of their greater capacity, on this route, which went as far as Sydney from 1938 until the outbreak of the war. During the war, Qantas operated flights for the armed forces, while flights in Australia itself virtually came to a standstill. After the war Lockheed Constellations, DC-3s and DC-4s were acquired. In 1947 the Australian government acquired a controlling interest in Qantas. When seven Boeing 707s were delivered from 1959 Qantas entered the jet age, at the same time introducing new colours for the aircraft. Boeing 747s were introduced in 1973 and formed the backbone of the fleet for over 20 years. Boeing 767s, the second generation of widebody aircraft, were acquired starting in 1985 bringing another new colour scheme that is familiar today. In 1992 Australian Airlines was taken over and incorporated into the network in 1993, giving Qantas a new domestic dimension, having up to then operated international services only. In 1992, British Airways took a 25% stake, and the two airlines co-operate.

Routes

Extensive internal network. International flights to Auckland, Bangkok, Beijing, Boston, Chicago, Fukuoka, Frankfurt, Harare, Hong Kong, Honolulu, Jakarta, Johannesburg, Kuala Lumpur, London, Los Angeles, Manila, New York, Osaka, Papeete, Port Moresby, Rome, San Francisco, Seoul, Singapore, Toronto, Tokyo, Vancouver and Washington.

Fleet

4 Airbus A300B4
16 Boeing 737-300
22 Boeing 737-400
11 Boeing 747-200/300
18 Boeing 747-400
2 Boeing 747SP
24 Boeing 767-200/300ER

Photograph: Lockheed L-188 Electra N9744C (Josef Krauthäuser/Anchorage)

REEVE ALEUTIAN

4700 West International Airport Road,
Anchorage, Alaska 99502-1091, USA
Tel. 907-2431112 Fax. 907-249-2317

Three letter code	IATA No.	ICAO Callsign
RVV	338	Reeve

The airline was founded at Valdez, Alaska on 25th August 1932 by Bob Reeve, a famous Alaskan pilot and airline pioneer who had flown for PanAm in South America. The airline flew initially under the name of Reeve Airways and operated charter flights for various firms, using a single-engined Eaglerock biplane. Reeve's first owned aircraft was a Fairchild 51 with which he busied himself as a bush pilot. During the war years Reeve worked principally for the government and undertook relief flights using a Boeing 80 and a Fairchild 71. In 1946 he bought a DC-3 for $20,000 and established a 'real airline' in Anchorage. In 1948 the US government invited tenders for flights to the Aleutian Islands in the north-western part of the US. Reeve obtained the licence in January 1948, initially for a period of five years, on account of its experience on the 1,800 mile long route. The present title was adopted in April 1951. The DC-3 was the appropriate aircraft for use on flights to reach these inhospitable and sparsely populated places and the type was introduced in 1946 between Fairbanks, Anchorage and Seattle. DC-4s enabled the airline to open up the group of Pribilof Islands. DC-6s were added to the fleet in 1962; Lockheed Electras were introduced in 1968 and Boeing 727s in 1983. The only route outside Alaska is the link with Seattle, but this is flown only as a charter. As Reeve Aleutian flies combined cargo/passenger aircraft to supply the islands, the proportion of passengers is lower than with other airlines. Reeve also carries out charters including anglers during the season, and to neighbouring Siberia.

Routes

Schedules from Anchorage to Adak, Bethel, Cold Bay, Dillingham, Dutch Harbour, King Salmon, Port Heiden, St Paul Island and Sand Point.

Fleet

2 Boeing 727-100C
3 Lockheed L-188 Electra
2 NAMC-YS-11A

Photograph: McDonnell Douglas MD-82 N822RA (Josef Krauthäuser/Las Vegas)

RENO AIR

P.O. Box 30059, 220 Edison Way,
Reno NV 89520, USA
Tel. 702-686-3835 Fax. 702-6884181

Three letter code	IATA No.	ICAO Callsign
ROA	384	Reno Air

Reno Air was founded in 1990 and obtained permission to operate flights between Reno and Los Angeles in April 1992. It started flight operations to these destinations in June 1992.
Reno Air promoted its flights with low fares and good service and expanded its network of routes. There were seven MD-82s in use in late 1992, and by means of purchases and leasing the airline was able to more than double the fleet by late 1993. Unprofitable routes were consequently cancelled and abandoned in favour of new services. In August 1995 the airline succeeded in the issue of new shares to the value of $25 million, to ensure the further expansion of the company. The MD-90 is thus the latest addition to the entirely McDonnell Douglas fleet, which operates from a main base at Reno/Cannon International Airport and a hub at San Jose, California. There is co-operation with American Airlines, and Reno Air Express operates as a feeder carrier with Jetstream 31s.

Routes

Albuquerque, Chicago, Colorado Springs, Las Vegas, Los Angeles, Ontario, Orange County, Palm Springs, Phoenix, Portland, Reno, San Diego, San Jose, Seattle, South Lake Tahoe and Tucson.

Fleet	Ordered
21 McDonnell Douglas MD-82/83 4 McDonnell Douglas MD-87 3 McDonnell Douglas MD-90	10 McDonnell Douglas MD-90

Photograph: De Havilland DHC-8-100 OE-LRT (Author's collection)

RHEINTALFLUG

Bahnhofstr. 10a, 6900 Bregenz,
Austria
Tel. 48800 Fax. 488008

Three letter code	IATA No.	ICAO Callsign
RTL	915	Rheintal

Founded in 1977 as a non-scheduled airline, regular flights began in 1984 from Hohenems (Vorarlberg) to Vienna. Then in 1988 the airline was able to set up a new route, from the neighbouring airport of Altenrhein (in Switzerland) to Vienna using a Grumman Jetprop Commander 900. Rheintal also connected Friedrichshafen with Vienna from autumn 1989 with a daily off-peak return flight using a de Havilland DHC-8-100. Since then only DHC-8s have been used. There is an agreement with Austrian Airlines for through traffic from Bregenz/Altenrhein to Vienna. An order was placed early in 1997 for a single example of the stretched Dash 8-400 (plus an option on another) for delivery in the year 2000 for use on the Vienna-Altenrhein route.

Routes

Altenrhein, Frankfurt, Graz, Linz, Vienna, Zürich. Additionally there are charter and non-scheduled operations.

Fleet	Ordered
3 De Havilland DHC8-100 2 De Havilland DHC8-300	1 De Havilland DHC8-300 1 De Havilland DHC8-400

Photograph: Boeing 737-400 9M-MMX (Martin Bach/Singapore)

ROYAL AIR CAMBODGE

24-26 Kranuon Sar Avenue, 206A Nordodom Blvd., Phnom Penh, Cambodia
Tel. 23-428830 Fax. 23-428806

Three letter code	IATA No.	ICAO Callsign
RAC	658	Cambodge

The first Royal Air Cambodge was until 1970 known as the national airline of Cambodia. Its beginnings went back to 1956, stemming from the time when the country was French Indo-China. After the many years of war and political instability in the country, a new civil airline was established in 1994 – Air Cambodia – which however was only active for a few months before its licence was withdrawn. The Cambodian authorities had other plans and had already talked with MHS (the parent company of Malaysia Airlines) about setting up another airline. This was founded in December 1994, with Malaysia Airlines taking a 40% shareholding, It was therefore a joint venture of the government with MHS. At the beginning of 1995 service was started with a route to Kuala Lumpur using a leased Boeing 737-400. Further destinations followed, especially with an eye to the tourist markets, and ATR72s were acquired to carry passengers on internal routes. The famous ruins at Angkor Wat are the destination of thousands of tourists, mostly travelling from Thailand. Naturally there is close co-operation with Malaysia Airlines, and some flights are operated as code-shares. However, in mid-1997 a military coup in the country has cast doubt on the future of the airline, with the MAC-owned 737s grounded in Kuala Lumpur, many executives having fled to exile, and most international services suspended. The new government, whose principals were known not be sympathetic to the arrangement with Malaysian, have announced that they plan to form a new Kampuchea Airlines in partnership with Orient Thai Airlines.

Routes

Bangkok, Battambang, Ho Chi Minh, Hong Kong, Koh Kong, Kuala Lumpur, Mundulkiri, Ratanankiri, Siem Reap, Sihanoukville, Singapore, Stung Treng.

Fleet

3 ATR72
2 Boeing 737-400

Photograph: Boeing 737-500 CN-RMY (Frank Fielitz/Frankfurt)

ROYAL AIR MAROC

Aéroport Arifa, Casablanca,
Morocco
Tel. 2-912000 Fax. 2-912087

Three letter code	IATA No.	ICAO Callsign
RAM	147	Marocair

The name Royal Air Maroc was introduced on 28th June 1957, after Morocco had obtained its independence from Spain and France. The state-owned airline Royal Air Maroc emerged from the Société Air Atlas and Avia Maroc Aérienne, which together formed the Compagnie Chérifienne de Transport Aériens (CCTA) on 25th June 1953. At first there were only domestic services and some routes to France initially using Junkers Ju 52s but they were soon replaced by DC-3s. In 1957 a Lockheed Constellation came into use and was employed on the newly introduced international routes.

In July 1958 Air Maroc acquired its first Caravelle. Boeing 707s were bought in 1975 for long-distance routes. Boeing 727s came into service on regional and long-distance routes in 1970. When the first Boeing 757 was delivered in July 1986 a fleet replacement programme was carried out. The first ATR42 was received on 24th March 1989 and is used on domestic routes. In 1993 RAM acquired another widebody aircraft, a Boeing 747-400. Also from Boeing from 1994 came the 737-400s, replacing older 727s and 737s. RAM is controlled by the Moroccan Government.

Routes

To Europe, North Africa, the Middle East, USA, South America and numerous charter flights.

Fleet

2 ATR42
6 Boeing 737-500
7 Boeing 737-400
6 Boeing 737-200Adv
1 Boeing 747-200
1 Boeing 747-400
3 Boeing 727-200Adv
2 Boeing 757-200

Ordered

9 Boeing 737-800

Photograph: Boeing 757-200 V8-RBB (Josef Krauthäuser/Hong Kong)

ROYAL BRUNEI

P.O. Box 737, Bandar Seri Begawan, Brunei
Tel. 2-240500 Fax. 2-244737

Three letter code	IATA No.	ICAO Callsign
RBA	672	Brunei

Royal Brunei Airlines was founded on 18th November 1974 as the national airline of Brunei Negara Darussalam and began flight operations over the Bandar Seri Begawan to Singapore route on 14th May 1975. A few Boeing 737-200s were the mainstay of the airline until three Boeing 757s were acquired, the first arriving on 6th May 1986. When this aircraft was delivered Royal Brunei also painted all of its aircraft in attractive new colours, principally yellow and white. With the introduction of the Boeing 757s long-haul routes were launched and a London Gatwick service commenced. A leased Boeing 767 arrived in June 1990 and, with more aircraft of this type being added since then, they have taken over some 757 routes while the 737s have been disposed of. The Airbus A340 delivered in 1993 is used by the Sultan of Brunei (said to be the world's richest man) as his personal aircraft when needed. New routes for 1993 were Bahrain, Beijing, Cairo and Zürich. Since 1995 there has been a marketing alliance with United Airlines, and Malaysia Airlines has a 10% shareholding. Fokker 100s were introduced from 1996 for regional routes.

Routes

From Bandar Seri Bagawan to Bangkok, Darwin, Dubai, Frankfurt, Jakarta, Kota Kinabalu, Kuala Lumpur, Kuching, London, Manila, Hong Kong, Osaka, Perth, Singapore, Taipei and Zürich.

Fleet

2 Boeing 757-200
9 Boeing 767-300ER
2 Fokker 100

Photograph: Lockheed L-1011-500 JY-AGD (Oliver Krauthäuser/Amsterdam)

ROYAL JORDANIAN

P.O. Box 302, Amman,
Jordan
Tel. 6-679178 Fax. 6-672527

Three letter code	IATA No.	ICAO Callsign
RJA	512	Jordanian

King Hussein declared the establishment of the Jordanian national airline Alia on 8th December 1963. It succeeded Jordan Airways, also known as Jordanian Airways, which itself had succeeded Air Jordan of the Holy Land two years previously. Alia (meaning high flying) was named after King Hussein's daughter. Flight operations were started from 15th December 1963 Amman to Beirut, Cairo and Kuwait with two Handley Page Heralds and a DC-7. In 1964 a second DC-7 was added to the fleet. With the introduction of the SE210 Caravelle a European route to Rome was opened for the first time in 1965; Paris and London followed in 1966. The DC-7s were destroyed during the Israeli-Arab Six Day War and later replaced by F27s. The Jordanian Government assumed full control of Alia in 1968. In 1969 the network of routes was expanded to include Munich, Istanbul and Teheran, followed by Frankfurt in 1970. In 1971 Alia acquired its first Boeing 707; the Caravelle was replaced in 1973 by Boeing 727s and in 1977 two Boeing 747 'Jumbos' were bought. Flights to New York and Los Angeles commenced in 1984; Alia was the first of the Arab national carriers to commence schedules to the USA, using 747s. TriStars joined the fleet in 1981. When the Airbus A310 was introduced in 1986, a new colour scheme was introduced. The airline then took the name Royal Jordanian. During the Gulf War the airline suffered severe losses, so that some aircraft had to be leased. In 1992 Berlin, Jakarta and Aden were included for the first time in the scheduled network; flights to Athens were also resumed. With the arrival of the third Airbus A320 in March 1996 the last Boeing 727 was retired. By the year 2000 the TriStar should also have been replaced by the Airbus A340.

Routes

The Middle East, Europe with Amsterdam, Ankara, Athens, Berlin, Brussels, Frankfurt, London, Paris, Vienna and Zürich; Montreal, Toronto and New York, Bangkok and Singapore are served regularly.

Fleet	Ordered
4 Airbus A310-300 2 Airbus A310-200 3 Airbus A320-200 3 Boeing 707C 6 Lockheed L-1011-500	5 Airbus A340

Photograph: Boeing 757-200 9N-ACB (Josef Krauthäuser/Frankfurt)

ROYAL NEPAL AIRLINES

RNAC Building, P.O. Box 401, Kantipath,
Kathmandu 711000, Nepal
Tel. 1-220757 Fax. 1-225348

Three letter code	IATA No.	ICAO Callsign
RNA	285	Royal Nepal

Royal Nepal Airlines Corporation Limited was founded by the government on 1st July 1958, replacing Indian Airlines which had operated domestic services for some eight years on Nepal's behalf. External services to such points as Delhi and Calcutta continued to be operated by Indian Airlines until 1960 when Royal Nepal took over DC-3s and later, Fokker F27 Friendships, ideal aircraft for the harsh climate of Nepal because they are undemanding. Three HS.748s came into use in 1970, and the first Boeing 727 in June 1972. However, the airfield at mountainous Kathmandu had to be extended by that time, which was a difficult business; even today, it is not possible for jumbo jets to take off and land there. The Boeing 727 was used to open a route to Delhi. The delivery of the first Boeing 757s in 1987 and 1988 marked at the same time a fleet replacement programme and the expansion of services to European destinations. As passenger demand on the European routes has grown it has been possible to lease in an Airbus A310. Newly opened services in 1996 were to China and Japan.

Routes

Bangkok, Bombay, Calcutta, Delhi, Dubai, Frankfurt, Hong Kong, London, Osaka, Shanghai, Singapore and to some 10 internal destinations in Nepal.

Fleet

2 Boeing 757-200
1 BAe HS.748
7 De Havilland DHC-6
1 Pilatus PC-6 Turbo Porter

Photograph: Boeing 737-200 EI-CJH (Andrè Dietzel/Munich FJS)

RYANAIR

Corporate Building, Dublin Airport,
Republic of Ireland
Tel. 01-8444489 Fax. 01-8444400

Three letter code	IATA No.	ICAO Callsign
RYR	224	Ryanair

Founded in May 1985, Ryanair can be seen as a rival to Aer Lingus as far as regional services and flights to Britain are concerned. London European Airways were acquired in 1986. No airline has served more towns in Ireland, nine airports in all at one time, than Ryanair. It used ATR42s and BAC/Rombac One-Elevens but in 1994 introduced Boeing 737-200s on services from the UK mainland to Dublin. The route Dublin to Munich was taken over from Aer Lingus, a service which Ryanair has been serving since 1988 and the Liverpool to Dublin route was also taken over. Luton to Dublin services were a main route for Ryanair when it moved onto UK routes but, since the expansion of Stansted, it has increased its presence there to the detriment of Luton. Prestwick was served from May 1994 and Ryanair is the only operator flying scheduled services from the famous Scottish airport. Ryan Air UK was set up in 1995 as a 100% subsidiary, and operates from Stansted. The expanding fleet is now all Boeing 737-200, aircraft having been principally acquired from Lufthansa, Britannia, and Air Malta; it is planned to reach 20 aircraft by November 1997. A couple of aircraft have been painted in all over advertising 'billboard' schemes, in a similar manner to that adopted more widely by Western Pacific in the USA; one is in the house colours of Jaguar Cars, and another advertises the 'Sun' newspaper.

Routes

Regional services in Ireland and Great Britain. From nine Irish airports to Birmingham, Cardiff, Coventry, Glasgow, Leeds, Liverpool, London, Luton and Manchester. Charter flights to Germany and other European destinations.

Fleet	Ordered
13 Boeing 737-200	4 Boeing 737-200

Photograph: Boeing 727-100 N416EX (Josef Krauthäuser/Seattle SEA)

RYAN INTERNATIONAL AIRLINES

6800 West Kellogg, Wichita,
KS 67209, USA
Tel. 316-9420141 Fax. 316-9427949

Three letter code	IATA No.	ICAO Callsign
RYN	-	Ryan International

Ryan Aviation has been in existence since 1972 as an airline operating charter flights as a subcontractor for Emery Express and began operations on 3rd March 1973 as DeBoer Aviation. Ryan International was a division of these operations until it was sold in 1985 to the PHH group. In February 1989 Ronald Ryan bought the company back and started an airfreight service from Indianapolis for the US Mail using eight DC-9s and nine Boeing 727s. The airline operates on behalf of Emery Worldwide using further Boeing 727s. Ryan sought further activities in the Pacific. A Boeing 727 flies freshly caught fish from Saipan to Japan, and freight is flown between the islands of Micronesia. A Boeing 737-200 for passenger flights is on stand by in Cleveland and Cincinnati for a tour operator; this service was extended to Atlantic City in 1995. The fleet was also increased with the acquisition of further 727s in that year. Ryan International is not at present operating any aircraft in its own colours; all the aircraft have the colours of the particular client, and only some small lettering indicates the name of the operator.

Routes

Numerous freight services on behalf of the US Post Office, for Emery Worldwide and other companies.

Fleet

1 Boeing 737-200
38 Boeing 727
1 McDonnell Douglas DC-9-15F

Photograph: Airbus A340-300 OO-SCX (Patrick Lutz/Brussels)

SABENA WORLD AIRLINES

Avenue E. Mounier, 1200 Brussels,
Belgium
Tel. 02-7233111

Three letter code	IATA No.	ICAO Callsign
SAB	082	Sabena

The Société Autonyme Belge d'Exploitation de la Navigation Aérienne (SABENA) was founded on 23rd May 1923 to succeed the Syndicat National pour l'Etude des Transports Aériens (SNETA), formed in 1919. Sabena began revenue flights on 1st April 1924 over the Rotterdam to Strasbourg route via Brussels. The carrier was a pioneer in establishing many African services, and flights to the Congo began in 1925. In 1938 Sabena flew a network of 5,970 km in Europe. Between May 1940 and October 1945 European services were suspended, but African operations continued. After the war Sabena extended its network rapidly. DC-3s were used in Europe, and they were replaced in 1950 by Convair 240s. A route to New York was opened in 1947 using DC-4s and later DC-6s, and also from Brussels to the Congo. The famous DC-7 'Seven Seas' followed in 1957. There were drastic changes for Sabena in 1960, when the state of Zaire was founded and previous routes to the Congo had to be abandoned. The first Boeing 707s were also added to the fleet in 1960 and were used for flights to the US. SE210 Caravelles were used for the European routes, then from 1967 Boeing 727s and from 1973 Boeing 737s. The Boeing 737-200 was supplemented by the more modern Boeing 737-300 from 1987 onwards. Sabena acquired its first wide body aircraft in 1971 and 1974: DC-10s and Boeing 747s. The Airbus A310-300s added from 1984 are used on heavily frequented routes. Sabena entered a close partnership with Air France in 1993, with Air France acquiring a 49% stake but this did not last; in 1995 Swissair took a shareholding instead. There has been significant restructuring, and A340s have now joined the fleet. Orders for Avro RJ100s and Airbus A319/320s are expected by the end of 1997.

Routes

Particularly strong are the routes from Brussels to Africa, where 27 destinations are offered. The network also reaches to the Far East, USA and to all major European cities.

Fleet

3 Airbus A330-300
4 Airbus A340-200/300
2 Boeing 747-300
13 Boeing 737-200Adv
6 Boeing 737-300
3 Boeing 737-400
6 Boeing 737-500
4 De Havilland DHC-8-300

Ordered

4 Airbus A330-200

Photograph: Airbus A310-300 HC-BRP (Josef Krauthäuser/Miami)

SAETA

Avenida C.J.Arosemeria M 2.5, Guayaquil, Ecuador
Tel. 200277 Fax. 205115

Three letter code	IATA No.	ICAO Callsign
SET	156	Saeta

SAETA SA – Ecuatoriana de Transportes Aereos – started as a non-scheduled air carrier using DC-3s. The airline, which was founded in January 1967, entered the scheduled services business in 1969 with routes from Quito to Guayaquil, Esmeraldas and Tulcan. Two Vickers Viscounts were used, later replaced by SE 210 Caravelles in June 1975. A DHC-6 Twin Otter was used at times for short-distance routes. SAETA also started flights to neighbouring countries with a Boeing 727 delivered in 1981. Its latest aircraft is an Airbus A310-300, which came into use in 1992. In 1993 Saetatook over the routes to New York and Miami from Ecuatoriana. There is a shareholding in the Paraguayan airline Lapsa and Saeta aircraft fly services for this airline. As well as passenger schedules and charters, freight work is undertaken.

Routes

Bogota, Buenos Aires, Caracas, Curacao, Guayaquil, Esmeraldas, Lima, Los Angeles, Mexico City, Miami, New York, Panama, Quito, Santiago.

Fleet

1 Airbus A310-300
3 Airbus A320
1 Boeing 727-200Adv
2 Boeing 727-100
1 Boeing 737-200

Photograph: Lockheed L-1011-200 HZ-AHI (Josef Krauthäuser/Frankfurt)

SAUDI ARABIAN AIRLINES

P.O. Box 620, Jeddah,
Saudi Arabia
Tel. 2-6860000 Fax. 2-6864552

Three letter code	IATA No.	ICAO Callsign
SVA	065	Saudia

Saudia, the national carrier of the Kingdom of Saudi Arabia, was founded in late 1945 as the Saudi Arabian Airlines Corporation. Flights began on 14th March 1947 with a fleet of three DC-3s. In the early 1950s, five Bristol Freighter 21s, DC-4s and Convair 340s were used. The jet age began for Saudia in April 1962 with the introduction of the Boeing 720B, and with this aircraft the airline started operating long-distance flights. This opened up routes to Cairo, Karachi and Bombay, and in 1968 to destinations in Europe with London, Rome, Geneva and Frankfurt. In 1975 Saudia acquired its first widebody aircraft, the Lockheed L-1011, and in June 1977 it also obtained Boeing 747s. Its expansion policy has always been very cautious, making Saudia the largest airline in the Arab world for years, and with about 11 million passengers Saudia is one of the world's largest international airlines. The fleet age is very low and the aircraft manufacturers from Europe and the USA are always looking for lucrative contracts for fleet renewal; even state presidents can be involved in obtaining this business. As soon as a massive new order for US aircraft was announced at the beginning of 1996, a new corporate image was also unveiled, and this is being introduced with the delivery of these new aircraft. The name of the airline was also changed from Saudia to its present style. Also operated in airline colours and as part of their fleet are various royal household and government executive aircraft; these are operated by a separate division.

Routes

From its main base in Jeddah, the airline serves Dhahran and Riyadh, some 25 regional points and about 50 international destinations in Europe, Africa, Asia and the USA.

Fleet

11 Airbus A300-600
19 Boeing 737-200Adv
1 Boeing 747SP
20 Boeing 747-100/200/300
1 McDonnell Douglas DC-8-63F
17 Lockheed L-1011-200

Ordered

5 Boeing 747-400
23 Boeing 777-200
4 McDonnell Douglas MD-11F
29 McDonnell Douglas MD-90-30

Photograph: Fokker F28 SE-DGR (Uwe Gleisberg/Munich FJS)

SCANDINAVIAN - SAS

19587 Stockholm-Bromma,
Sweden
Tel 8-7970000 Fax. 8-857980

Three letter code	IATA No.	ICAO Callsign
SAS	117	Scandinavian

SAS – Scandinavian Airlines came into existence on 1st August 1946 after the merger of DDL (Denmark), DNL (Norway) and ABA/SLA (Sweden), all of which were formed in the early 1920s, except for DDL, formed in 1918. The realisation that these three countries could not operate flights independently meant that old plans from 1940 were revived after the war. SAS started scheduled flights on 9th September 1946, with a DC-4 from Stockholm to New York via Copenhagen. A route to Buenos Aires was opened in late 1946 and to Bangkok as early as 1949. SAS started flights to Johannesburg in 1953 for the first time with DC-6s. SAS's pioneering effort was to explore the polar routes to Los Angeles and Tokyo, which were opened on 15th November 1954 and 24th February 1957 respectively. In Europe, Saab Scandias and Convair 440s were used in addition to DC-3s. SAS's first jet aircraft was the SE 210 Caravelle, and the first of these was used in 1959 on the route Copenhagen to Beirut. The DC-8 followed in 1960 for intercontinental routes, replacing DC-6s and DC-7s. In early 1971 SAS acquired its first widebody aircraft, a Boeing 747. DC-10-30s and A300B4s were added to the SAS fleet in the late seventies. Structural changes to the airline and adjustment of capacity led to the sale of the Boeing 747s and Airbus A300s in the mid-'80s. MD-80s and Boeing 767 aircraft were ordered. A few MD-90s have been added in the mid-1990s, but the principal re-equipment for short to medium range will be the new Boeing 737-600. In 1993 the domestic airline Linjeflyg was completely taken over, and co-operation with other airlines increased. SAS has interests in several other airlines, including Spanair and British Midland, and has co-operation agreements including Lufthansa and United.

Routes

Dense network in the participant countries of Sweden, Norway and Denmark. To Los Angeles, New York, Washington in the USA; Bangkok, Beijing, Hong Kong, Osaka, Singapore in Asia, to South America, Africa and to the principal cities in Europe.

Fleet

16 Boeing 767-200/300ER
16 Fokker F28
29 McDonnell Douglas DC-9-21/41
69 McDonnell Douglas MD-81/82/83
18 McDonnell Douglas MD-87
6 McDonnell Douglas MD-90

Ordered

41 Boeing 737-600
2 McDonnell Douglas MD-90

Photograph: Airbus A300B4 PK-JID (Björn Kannengiesser/Jakarta CGK)

SEMPATI AIR

Terminal Building, Halim Perdanakusuma
Airport, Jakarta 13610, Indonesia
Tel. 21-8011612 Fax. 21-8094420

Three letter code	IATA No.	ICAO Callsign
SSR	821	Spirow

PT Sempati Air Transport was formed on 16th December 1968 by the PT Tri Usaha Bhakti concern. The first aircraft was a DC-3 which came into service in March 1969. Straight away work within Indonesia was undertaken on behalf of international oil companies, and to meet the demand further DC-3s and Fokker F27s were acquired for routes to Manila, Singapore and Kuala Lumpur. Between 1975 and 1978 scheduled services between Jakarta and Tokyo via Denpasar with a leased Boeing 707 were offered, but the government transferred this lucrative route to the state airline Garuda. The DC-3s were retired and further F27s acquired between 1977 and 1984, so that the fleet consisted of this type only. Restrictive measures applied to private airlines meant that it was not possible for them to use jet aircraft until the late 1980s. Thus it was that Sempati Air, as it was known following a restructuring and the introduction of a new shareholder in 1989, acquired its first Fokker 100 in 1990. With these aircraft more international routes were flown. More capacity for the longer Asian routes followed with Boeing 737s and from 1993 three Airbus A300B4s. A fourth A300 was added in the summer of 1996. Flights to Europe have been planned for a long time, but no approval has been forthcoming.

Routes

Sempati Air flies schedules to more than 25 destinations in South East Asia, and to Perth in Australia.

Fleet	Ordered
4 Airbus A300B4	6 IPTN N-250-100
7 Boeing 737-200	
5 Fokker F27	
2 Fokker 70	
7 Fokker 100	

Photograph: Boeing 757-200 B-2842 (Björn Kannengiesser/Beijing)

SHANGHAI AIRLINES

Hong Qiao International Airport, 200335
Shanghai, Peoples Republic of China
Tel. 21-2558558 Fax. 21-2559239

Three letter code	IATA No.	ICAO Callsign
CSH	774	Shanghaiair

As early as 1985 an airline was formed by the regional government of the Shanghai district. At this time it was not possible to fly aircraft in its own colours. It was however the first airline in China to become independent from CAAC. Five Boeing 707s were used in CAAC colours on internal services, but in 1988 one of these 707s appeared with Shanghai's own insignia. With the receipt of the first Boeing 757 in August 1989 the current colour scheme was introduced. Maintaining the all-Boeing fleet equipment stance, 767s were introduced from 1994 and used on flights to Beijing and other major cities. The airline flies scheduled and charter services within China, and freight flights also. The main operating and home base is at Shanghai, and 25% of the shares are in private hands.

Routes

Dense network to over 60 points in China.

Fleet	Ordered
7 Boeing 757-200 3 Boeing 767-300	2 Boeing 767-300

Photograph: Airbus A320-200 SU-RAA (Uwe Gleisberg/Munich FJS)

SHOROUK AIR

2, El Shaheed Ismail Fahmy, Heliopolis-Cairo, Egypt
Tel. 4172308 Fax. 4172311

Three letter code	IATA No.	ICAO Callsign
SHK	273	Shorouk

Shorouk Air is a Cairo-based joint venture set up by Egypt Air and Kuwait Airways in 1992 to operate charter flights from Western Europe to Egypt, as well as scheduled flights to the Middle East. It was intended to operate cargo flights for Kuwait Air using Boeing 757-200PFs, but because of poor business results these have not yet been put into service. Shorouk also flies subcharter for Air Sinai and Egyptair, particularly at Hadj time, with many flights to Jeddah.

Routes

Schedules from Cairo to Beirut, charters from various points in Europe to Hurghada, Cairo and Luxor.

Fleet

2 Airbus A320-200

Photograph: Tupolev Tu-154M B-2624 (Björn Kannengiesser/Beijing)

SICHUAN AIRLINES

9 Nan Sanduan Yihuan Road, Chengdu,
Sichuan 610041, Peoples Republic of China
Tel. 86285551161 Fax. 86285582641

Three letter code	IATA No.	ICAO Callsign
CSC	-	Chuanghang

In 1986 the regional government of the Sichuan province of China saw a need for its own airline. After bureaucratic squabbles with the almighty CAAC, services were able to commence in July 1988 with Yunshuji Y-7s.The first and for a while only service was from Chengdu to Wanxian on the Yangtse River. More Y-7s were added in 1990 and the company's own colours were applied to the aircraft. At the end of 1991 Tupolev Tu-154Ms were acquired for use on a new Beijing service. Western aircraft in the form of three Airbus A320-232s leased from ILFC appeared at the very end of 1995 and early 1996, leading to a further expansion. In spite of that the airline is still only active regionally and within the confines of China; international services are not planned for the time being.

Routes

Regional and Chinese domestic services to some 20 destinations.

Fleet	Ordered
3 Airbus A320 5 Tupolev Tu-154M 5 Yunshuji Y-7	3 Airbus A320

Photograph: Boeing 737-300 9V-TRA (Author's collection)

SILKAIR

P.O. Box 501, Singapore 9181,
Singapore
Tel: 5428111 Fax. 5420023

Three letter code	IATA No.	ICAO Callsign
SLK	629	Silkair

Tradewinds Charters was founded in October 1976 as a subsidiary of Singapore Airlines to carry out non-scheduled passenger flights. Its operations consisted of inclusive tour charters, oil-crew changes and *ad hoc* charters. Some flights were operated in the region from Seletar Airport until 1988. As a charter airline it leased its aircraft from SIA when needed. Using MD-87s on scheduled flights to five destinations in Malaysia and Brunei, Tradewinds became the second scheduled airline in Singapore. In 1991 the airline was renamed Silkair. New routes were opened to Cebu, Medan, Phnom Penh and Ho Chi Minh City. Apart from scheduled flights, the airline continues to offer charter services from its base at Singapore Changi airport. In 1990 the fleet was augmented by the Boeing 737, the type which now forms the mainstay of the fleet, and for a short while Airbus 310s from the parent company were also used. For the short-haul routes two Fokker 70s were acquired in 1995. In May 1997 it was announced that the Airbus A319/320 family has been chosen as Silkair's new narrowbody type, to replace the 737s and Fokker 70s, with an order for four A319s and four A320s for delivery beginning at the end of 1998. There are also options on ten more A319/320/321s.

Routes

From Singapore to Cebu, Chiang Mai, Jakarta, Kunming, Langkawi, Medan, Padang, Phnom Penh, Phuket, Vientiane and Yangon.

Fleet	Ordered
6 Boeing 737-300	4 Airbus A310
2 Fokker 70	4 Airbus A320

Photograph: Airbus A310-300 9V-STQ (Uwe Gleisberg/Perth)

SINGAPORE AIRLINES

P.O. Box 501, Singapore 9181,
Republic of Singapore
Tel. 5423333 Fax. 5455034

Three letter code	IATA No.	ICAO Callsign
SIA	618	Singapore

Singapore Airlines was formed on 28th January 1972 as the wholly Government-owned national airline to succeed the jointly operated Malaysia-Singapore Airlines. Operations began on 1st October 1972. Boeing 707s and 737s were taken over from MSA, but soon the changeover was made to Boeing 747-200s, in 1973. Since then Singapore Airlines has been undergoing continual expansion. An agreement with British Airways in 1977 saw the inauguration of a joint service using Concorde on the London-Bahrain-Singapore route, but it was not a success and ended in 1980. With the acquisition of further Boeing 747s, routes to Australia, New Zealand, the US and Europe were expanded. There were daily flights to San Francisco via Honolulu as early as 1979. In 1978, DC-10s arrived and between 1978 and 1983 up to six Boeing 727s were used. 1981 saw Airbus A300s being introduced on regional services and Boeing 757s were also acquired but SIA decided to rationalise its fleet on Airbus A310s and Boeing 747s. Its first two Boeing 747-400s were delivered in December 1988 and began non-stop services between Singapore and London Heathrow in early 1989. SIA's first pure 747 freighter entered service the same year. The airline's own new dedicated freight terminal was opened at Changi in 1995. Singapore Airlines flies each year more passengers than the total population of the country, and is well known for the quality of its service and always modern fleet. The latest addition is the Airbus A340 which entered service in Spring 1996. There is a Tri-lateral Alliance with Delta Airlines and Swissair, each airline having shares in the others. The main base is at Changi, where over 3,000 are employed in the massive SIA workshops.

Routes

Serves all continents with about 75 destinations eg: Auckland, Abu Dhabi, Amsterdam, Athens, Bangkok, Beijing, Berlin, Brussels, Cairns, Capetown, Dallas/Fort Worth, Darwin, Durban, Delhi, Dubai, Frankfurt, Hong Kong, Johannesburg, Kathmandu, Kuala Lumpur, Los Angeles, London, Paris, Seoul, Sydney, Vienna and Zürich.

Fleet		Ordered
23 Airbus A310-200/300	7 Boeing 747-200/400F	9 Airbus A340-300
8 Airbus A340-300	2 Boeing 777	9 Boeing 747-400
37 Boeing 747-400		28 Boeing 777
4 Boeing 747-300		

Photograph: Boeing 767-300ER OO-SBY (Patrick Lutz/Brussels)

SOBELAIR

131 Avenue Frans Courten, 1030 Brussels, Belgium
Tel. 2-7305211 Fax. 2-7235280

Three letter code	IATA No.	ICAO Callsign
SLR	-	Sobelair

Société Belge de Transports par Air SA was established on 30th July 1946 and operations began the following year with a DC-3. The intention was to operate charter flights, mainly to the Belgian Congo, with DC-4s. In 1948 Sabena acquired a controlling interest in Sobelair. From 1957 to 1962 a domestic network of routes was set up using Cessna 310s on behalf of Sabena within the Congo to supplement the main services operated by Sabena. Apart from a DC-6, Sobelair also obtained ex-Sabena SE 210 Caravelles as its first jet aircraft. Up to 1960 the major activity had involved scheduled passenger services between Belgium and Zaire but, since the early 1960s, the airline has been primarily operating charter flights to popular holiday areas in the Mediterranean. After the last Boeing 707 was sold in 1988, Sobelair used only Boeing 737s until the addition of the first of two Boeing 767-300ERs in the Spring of 1996. Following Sabena's introduction of new colours Sobelair also introduced a complementary new scheme in spring 1993. Aircraft are leased to meet seasonal demand. Sobelair also owns 35% of the shares of Air Belgium.

Routes

Destinations in the Mediterranean region, the Canary Isles and North Africa, California, the Caribbean and Thailand, plus special sub-charters or charter flights.

Fleet

2 Boeing 737-200
2 Boeing 737-300
3 Boeing 737-400
2 Boeing 767-300ER

Photograph: Boeing 737-300 VH-TJB (Author's collection)

SOLOMONS

P.O. Box 23, Honiara,
Solomon Islands
Tel. 677-20031 Fax. 677-23992

Three letter code	IATA No.	ICAO Callsign
SOL	193	Solomon

Solair, a subsidiary of Macair (Melanesian Airline Charter Company) was founded on 1st May 1968. This had been preceded by the takeover of Megopade Airways' routes; the latter was an airline serving the Solomon Island capital Honiara from Papua New Guinea since 1963. Solair's first flight was on 1st June 1968. In September 1975 Solair was bought by Talair, also an airline from Papua New Guinea following Talair's acquisition of Macair. It was only after some time that Solair became the property of the island administration, which acquired 49% of the shares in April 1979 and finally in 1982 and 1985 all of the Solair shares. In the mid-1980s a Brisbane service from the Solomon Islands was introduced in association with Air Pacific. The present name, Solomon Airlines, was introduced in early 1990. With a Boeing 737 now in the fleet, direct services to Nadi and Cairns started in 1993. The airline works closely with Qantas – who look after technical matters, Air Pacific, Air Nauru, Air Niugini and Air Vanuatu.

Routes

Auckland, Brisbane, Cairns, Honiara, Melbourne, Nadi, Port Moresby, Port Vila as well as some 20 destinations in the Solomon Islands.

Fleet

1 Boeing 737-300
2 De Havilland DHC-6
2 Pilatus BN2 Islander

Photograph: Boeing 747-300 ZS-SAT (Uwe Gleisberg/Munich FJS)

SOUTH AFRICAN AIRWAYS

SAA Towers, P.O. Box 7778, Johannesburg
2000, Republic of South Africa
Tel. 11-3561127 Fax. 11-3561126

Three letter code	IATA No.	ICAO Callsign
SAA	083	Springbok

South African Airways was founded on 1st February 1934, when Union Airways passed into government ownership and became a subsidiary of South African Railways. Operations started the same day with a fleet of single-engined Junkers F-13s, later supplemented by a large number of Ju 52s and Ju 86s. Numerous routes were operated, including to Nairobi, until the outbreak of the Second World War. South West African Airways had been acquired in February 1935 and gave SAA an extensive network of regional services. November 1945 saw the start of the 'Springbok' service to London, using DC-4s, DC-7s and Lockheed Constellations. The latter were used by SAA to open a route to Perth in Australia in November 1957. When the Boeing 707 was introduced in October 1960, this route was extended to Sydney, and a further long-distance route to Rio de Janeiro was opened in 1969. SAA had to restrict its routes to a few European points for political reasons: many African states withdrew its flyover rights. In order to be able to operate direct flights, Boeing 747SPs and later Boeing 747-300s with extreme ranges were ordered. Airbus A300s and Boeing 737s were ordered to expand the regional and domestic service, replacing the Vickers Viscounts and older aircraft. The first A320 was delivered to SAA in 1991, and in the same year the long-range Boeing 747-400 as replacement for the 747SP. After the shake-up of the government and the 1994 elections, SAA's situation was completely altered. All sanctions were lifted and it became possible to fly to any country, which resulted in new routes. SAA has stakes in regional airlines SA Airlink and SA Express. Its main bases are Johannesburg, Durban and Capetown.

Routes

Accra, Amsterdam, Atlanta, Bangkok, Blantyre, Bombay, Dar Es Salaam, Dubai, Düsseldorf, Frankfurt, Harare, Hong Kong, Kinshasa, Lilongwe, Lome, London, Luanda, Lusaka, Maputo, Mauritius, Miami, Munich, Nairobi, New York, Paris, Perth, Rio de Janeiro, Sal, Singapore, Sydney, Taipei, Tel Aviv, Windhoek, Zürich. Regional services are flown to about 15 destinations in southern Africa.

Fleet		Ordered
8 Airbus A300B4	5 Boeing 747SP	2 Boeing 747-400
7 Airbus A320-200	4 Boeing 747-300	4 Boeing 777-200
1 Airbus A300F	4 Boeing 747-400	
13 Boeing 737-200	1 Boeing 767-200ER	
6 Boeing 747-200		

Photograph: Boeing 747-200F N745SJ (Josef Krauthäuser/Miami)

SOUTHERN AIR TRANSPORT

P.O. Box 32-8988, 2255 Kimberly Park East,
Columbus, Ohio, USA
Tel. 614-7511100 Fax. 614-7519002

Three letter code	IATA No.	ICAO Callsign
SJM	351	Southern Air

This company was founded in Miami in 1947, and started operations in the same year with a Curtiss C-46 Commando, providing freight services in the Caribbean area for several years. There were scheduled services between San Juan and Miami, as well as to St Thomas in the Virgin Islands. Douglas DC-3s and DC-6s were brought into service, the latter especially on routes to Colombia and Venezuela. The civil version of the turboprop Lockheed Hercules freighter was used by Southern from mid-1960 first to supplement and then to replace the piston types. The first jet was the proven Boeing 707. The airline specialised in wet-leasing (aircraft inclusive of crews) to other companies. In 1984 the schedules were given up, in favour of concentration on world-wide charter flights, including work for the US military. In 1995 the base was suddenly moved from Miami to Rickenbacker Airport, Columbus, Ohio, which is thought to be a much better strategic departure point. In contrast to Miami, in Columbus there are almost no limitations to further expansion which was marked by the acquisition of Boeing 747 freighters in 1995. For the Lockheed Hercules equipment has been developed so that the aircraft can be used a sprayers of dispersants and pesticides, and a kit is also available for quick 'mixed passenger/freight' conversion. It is hoped that these adaptations will all make for more flexible use, and new tasks, for this versatile aircraft. Plans for the next three years focus on the acquisition of another five Boeing 747Fs.

Routes

Freight flights to South America and world wide charter services; special transport tasks and spraying.

Fleet

4 Boeing 747-200F
15 Lockheed L-100
4 McDonnell Douglas DC-8-71/73F

Photograph: Boeing 737-300 N538SW (Josef Krauthäuser/Las Vegas)

SOUTHWEST AIRLINES

P.O. Box 36611, Love Field, Dallas,
Texas 75235, USA
Tel. 214-3044000 Fax. 214-9045097

Three letter code	IATA No.	ICAO Callsign
SWA	526	Southwest

The airline first appeared on 15th March 1967 under the name of Air Southwest, but it took some time until flight operations could start. The established airlines tried their utmost to prevent the troublesome newcomer from flying, as the airline intended to set up a 'one-class service' with particularly low fares. A major legal controversy for many years involved Southwest's use of Love Field airport in Dallas. Other airlines and some municipal officials made attempts to force the carrier to shift operations to more distant Dallas-Fort Worth Regional Airport, which was then a small airport. In March 1971 the airline's name was changed to Southwest Airlines and in June 1971 Southwest flew for the first time from Dallas to Houston and San Antonio. After deregulation in the US, Southwest's fortunes soared. The airline bought Muse Air on 25th June 1985 and it was renamed TranStar airlines on 17th February 1986 but operations of this subsidiary stopped on 1st July 1987 due to mounting losses. The cost-conscious airline is considered to be one of the winners of this deregulation having expanded from its initial services within the state of Texas only, to cover a wide part of the continental USA. Using a homogeneous fleet of Boeing 737s, more and more passengers have been flown to an increasing number of destinations in the US every year. Utah-based Morris Air was acquired in December 1993, and integrated into Southwest in 1995. Areas in the south-east of the USA and Florida which had not previously been served were brought into the network in 1996. Large orders and future options for the newest model Boeing 737-700 mark continued expansion and fleet modernisation.

Routes

Over 40 points in 18 US states, but always with a blanket coverage, eg Austin, Dallas, Houston, Las Vegas, San Francisco, Los Angeles, San Antonio, San Diego, Seattle, Tampa, Tucson.

Fleet	Ordered
47 Boeing 737-200Adv	13 Boeing 737-300
173 Boeing 737-300	65 Boeing 737-700
25 Boeing 737-500	

Photograph: McDonnell Douglas MD-83 EC-FTU (Uwe Gleisberg/Salzburg)

SPANAIR

Airport P.O. Box 50086, Palma de Mallorca
07000, Spain
Tel. 71-492012 Fax. 71-492553

Three letter code	IATA No.	ICAO Callsign
SPP	680	Sunwing

The tour operators Vingresor AB and Scandinavia & Viajes Marsono SA founded their own charter airline by the name of Spanair in 1987. The airline is based on the holiday island of Majorca. Operations commenced during March 1988 and a fleet of new MD-83s were leased from Irish Aerospace and Guinness Peat Aviation and are used mainly to fly Scandinavian holidaymakers to the sunny beaches of Spain. Spanair also flies from UK and German airports, and from Zürich and Salzburg. The first revenue flight took place on 1st June 1988, from Palma to Bilbao. When Boeing 767-300ERs were acquired in 1992 flights were also operated to destinations in the USA, Mexico and the Caribbean. In 1993 Spanair carried 2 million passengers for the first time. As well as its traditional charter work, since 1993 Spanair has been operating an increasing number of schedules from Madrid and Barcelona.

Routes

Charter flights from Northern and Central Europe to Spain, the Balearics and Canary Islands. From Spain to New York, Orlando, Cancun, Puerto Plata, Punta Cona, Montevideo. Spanish domestic schedules.

Fleet

2 Boeing 767-300ER
15 McDonnell Douglas MD-83
2 McDonnell Douglas MD-87

Photograph: Airbus A310-300 F-GKTD (Stefan Schlick/Frankfurt)

SUDAN AIRWAYS

P.O. Box 253, Khartoum,
Sudan
Tel. 11-47953 Fax. 11-47978

Three letter code	IATA No.	ICAO Callsign
SUD	200	Sudanair

Sudan Airways was founded in February 1946 by the Sudanese government as a subsidiary of Sudan Railways System and a contract was signed for technical and flying assistance from the British company Airwork. Domestic service began in July 1947 with a fleet of four de Havilland Doves. In November 1954, the first foreign service was the route to Cairo, which was served using DC-3s. On 8th June 1959 a scheduled service was opened via Cairo-Athens-Rome to London using Vickers Viscounts, and Comet 4Cs from 1962 onwards. The first Fokker F27 was delivered in January 1962 and the first de Havilland Comet on 13th November 1962. The second jet generation was introduced in 1972 in the form of the Boeing 707, which was used for regular flights to Europe. For domestic services mainly F27s were used, replaced in spring 1990 by the modern Fokker 50s. Recent civil unrest has had its effect on air traffic; however new aircraft have been introduced to the fleet – the Airbus A320, A310 and A300-600 from 1993. These are used on the markedly reduced international network. Sudan Airways is also responsible for agricultural flying and other government work, and the aircraft used on these duties, and for training, can also be used for short domestic routes.

Routes

Abu Dhabi, Addis Ababa, Damascus, Dhahran, Doha, Dubai, Jeddah, Johannesburg, Kano, London, Muscat, Nairobi, Ndjamena, Riyadh, Rome, Sanaa, Sharjah and Tripoli.

Fleet

1 Airbus A310-300
1 Airbus A300-600
3 Boeing 707-300
2 Boeing 737-200
2 Fokker 50
1 De Havilland DHC-6

Photograph: McDonnell Douglas DC-10-15 N152SY (Albert Kuhbandner/Munich FJS)

SUN COUNTRY AIRLINES

2520 Pilot Knob Road, Suite 250 Mendota Heights, MN 55120, USA
Tel. 612-6813900 Fax. 612-6813972

Three letter code	IATA No.	ICAO Callsign
SCX	-	Suncountry

Sun Country was set up in Minneapolis on 1st July 1982. The airline was owned by a group of former employees of Braniff International Airlines, which had gone spectacularly bankrupt on 12th May 1982. After the issue of a licence as a charter operator in January 1993, flights were begun on 20th January with Boeing 727, and operating for MLT Tours. This organisation held 51% of the share capital, but this was given up in 1988 when there was a fundamental re-organisation of the company. In 1984 a scheduled service licence was issued and a route inaugurated between Minneapolis and Las Vegas. Further Boeing 727s came into the fleet over the years as the company made good progress. Flights were undertaken to Florida, Mexico and to the Caribbean. In 1986 Sun Country received its first widebody, a DC-10, and in 1994 the airline went heavily into scheduled services, with several US domestic routes. At the same time a new colour scheme was introduced for the aircraft. Additionally aircraft are leased out on an *ad hoc* basis, and thus Sun Country aircraft may be seen from time to time at many airports worldwide.

Routes

Schedules to 10 domestic US cities; charters to Florida, California, Mexico and the Caribbean.

Fleet

10 Boeing 727-200Adv
6 McDonnell Douglas DC-10-10/15

Photograph: Boeing 737-400 TC-SUS (Eduard Braun/Salzburg)

SUN EXPRESS

Fener Mahallesi Sinanoglu Cad, Oktay Airport,
07100 Antalya, Turkey
Tel. 3234047 Fax. 3234057

Three letter code	IATA No.	ICAO Callsign
SXS	-	Sunexpress

On 11th September 1989 Lufthansa (40% of the shares), Turkish Airlines (40% of the shares) and Turkish investors (20%) established the airline Sun Express with headquarters in Antalya. Flight operations started with a leased Boeing 737-300 on 4th April 1990. Its first flight was from Nuremberg to Antalya. Two further Boeing 737-300s were acquired in 1991; also, additional aircraft are leased from Lufthansa when needed. Because of the Gulf War, Turkish tourism came almost to a standstill in 1991, and the planned additional destinations could not be taken on. However, growth has resumed, and the fleet of Boeing 737s has been expanded. Sun Express is a typical niche carrier of the type to be found developing charter services to Turkey from Europe's smaller airports.

Routes

Charter traffic from airports in Germany, Czech Republic, Austria, Switzerland, England and other European countries to Antalya, Dalaman, Izmir and other Turkish destinations.

Fleet

3 Boeing 737-300
2 Boeing 737-400

Photograph: De Havilland DHC-8-300 N106AV (Author's collection)

SURINAM AIRWAYS

P.O. Box 2029, Paramaribo,
Surinam
Tel. 465700 Fax. 491213

Three letter code	IATA No.	ICAO Callsign
SLM	192	Surinam

Surinaamse Luchtvaart Maatschappij NV was set up in January 1955 with the objective of providing service from the capital, Paramaribo, to the little developed hinterland of Surinam. Initial service was commenced with DC-3s, and was at first scanty. Then in 1964 routes to neighbouring countries – to Georgetown, Port of Spain and Curacao – were begun with the help of KLM as a pool partner. With Surinam's independence from the Netherlands in 1975 came the introduction of a service to Amsterdam, for which leased Douglas DC-8s were brought into service. In 1980 the leap to Miami in the USA was also made. At the beginning of 1993 the Amsterdam route was given over to KLM, as Surinam had no suitable aircraft for this long-distance route. Since then the airline has concentrated on regional services, for which a DHC-8 (in 1993) and an MD-87 (in 1996) have been acquired. KLM remains an important partner, and there is a code-share agreement in place for the important tourist route to Amsterdam.

Routes

Barbados, Belem, Cayenne, Curacao, Georgetown, Miami, Port au Prince, Port of Spain.

Fleet

2 De Havilland DHC-6 Twin Otter
1 De Havilland DHC-8-300
1 McDonnell Douglas MD-87

Photograph: Airbus A320-200 HB-IJA (Uwe Gleisberg/Zürich)

SWISSAIR

Postfach, 8058 Zürich-Flughafen,
Switzerland
Tel. 1-8121212 Fax. 1-8108046

Three letter code	IATA No.	ICAO Callsign
SWR	085	Swissair

On 26th March 1931 Basler Luftverkehr (Balair) and Ad Astra Aero AG merged to form Schweizerischer Luftverkehrs AG. The company called itself Swissair and continued the routes of its predecessors. It used Fokker F VIIbs and the famous Lockheed Orion on the route Zürich-Munich from 1932 and Curtiss Condors were acquired in 1934. In 1935 Swissair acquired Douglas DC-2s and DC-3s in 1937, which were used on the route to London. Post-war services resumed on 30th July 1945 with DC-3s as the mainstay of the fleet, but DC-4s arrived in 1947 and transatlantic services started in 1949. Convair 240s were added to the fleet in 1949, with Convair 440s later. Alpair Bern was taken over in 1947 and from then on Swissair was the official carrier of Switzerland. DC-6Bs and DC-7s were the last propeller aircraft before Caravelles and DC-8s were introduced in 1960. Convair 990 Coronados were used for flights to the Far East from September 1961. The first DC-9 was delivered on 20th July 1966. Swissair's first jumbo jet was a Boeing 747 in January 1971, followed by the DC-10 a year later. Airbus A310s were also added from 1978, Swissair being a launch customer. The first MD-11s were acquired in early 1991. In 1995 Swissair acquired a 49% interest in the Belgian national airline Sabena, and on 25th January took delivery of its first Airbus A321, followed on 1st June by the first A320, replacing the MD-81s. 1995 saw a major re-structuring of the airline, with subsidiary Balair/CTA being integrated into Swissair and Crossair. On 1st March 1996 a new group structure was introduced, and another type, the A319 added, making Swissair the first operator of all three small Airbus types – 319, 320 and 321. There is close co-operation with Delta, Austrian, Sabena and Singapore Airlines.

Routes

Swissair connects Switzerland with over 100 destinations in North and South America, Asia, Africa, the Middle East and Europe. Zürich-Vienna is flown in co-operation with AUA. There are flights from Geneva and Basle as well as the principal base at Zürich.

Fleet

8 Airbus A319-100
18 Airbus A320-200
8 Airbus A321-100
8 Airbus A310-300
5 Boeing 747-300
14 McDonnell Douglas MD-11

Ordered

9 Airbus A330-200
2 McDonnell Douglas MD-11

Photograph: Tupolev Tu-134B YK-AYD (Author's collection)

SYRIANAIR

P.O. Box 417, Damascus,
Syria
Tel. 223434 Fax. 2214923

Three letter code	IATA No.	ICAO Callsign
SYR	070	Syrianair

The airline was founded in October 1961 by the Syrian government, after its predecessor Syrian Airways (founded on 21st December 1946) had formed United Arab Airlines with Misrair. However, this union only held for less than two years. Egyptian carrier Misrair had been renamed UAA in February 1958 and Syrian Airways merged with it on 23rd December 1958. After the break with Egypt, Syrian Arab Airlines, to give the airline its full name, took back its fleet and routes from UAA. Syrian Airways had operated domestic and regional routes from Damascus; Syrian Arab inherited these and started operating into Europe with DC-6Bs, serving Paris and London from 1964 and also flying east to Karachi and Delhi. Depending on the political orientation of the particular government, both Western aircraft and Soviet-built aircraft are used. SE 210 Caravelles were introduced in 1965, and Boeing 747SPs in 1976. The first Boeing 727 was delivered in March 1976 to supplement the Caravelles, the latter only being retired at the beginning of 1996. In the early 1980s Tu-134s were acquired followed by Tu-154s. The only other fleet acquisition since then has been three Boeing 727-200s which came from Kuwait in 1994: thus the fleet is relatively old.

Routes

From Damascus internal Syrian services to Aleppo, Latika, Kameschli. Internationally the network spans from Delhi via various points in the Middle East and North Africa to Europe, where Munich, Frankfurt, Berlin/Schönefeld, Moscow, Rome, Prague, Copenhagen and Paris are served.

Fleet

1 Antonov An-24
5 Antonov An-26
2 Boeing 747SP
6 Boeing 727-200Adv
4 Ilyushin IL-76M
6 Tupolev Tu-134B
3 Tupolev Tu-154M
6 Yakovlev Yak-40

Photograph: Ilyushin IL-62M D2-TIF (Henrique Belinha/Lisbon)

TAAG ANGOLA AIRLINES

R. da Missao, C P 3010, Luanda,
Peoples Republic of Angola
Tel. 332485 Fax. 393548

Three letter code	IATA No.	ICAO Callsign
DTA	118	DTA

Direccao de Exploracao dos Transportes Aereos (DTA – Angola Airlines) was established by order of the Portuguese government in September 1938. Flight operations could only begin in 1940, as the infrastructure was completely lacking. With an initial fleet of three de Havilland Dragon Rapides, scheduled services were started on 17th July 1940 on domestic routes and also on an international route between Luanda and Pointe Noire in the Congo Republic (then French Equatorial Africa), where connections were available to various European destinations. In that year the airline's name was changed to DTA Linhas Aereas de Angola and remained unchanged until 1973. For political reasons flight operations were suspended between 1973 and the country's independence from Portugal in November 1975, with a few exceptions. When the airline was renamed TAAG – Linhas Aereas de Angola it became the flag carrier of the new people's republic. Boeing 707s and 737s were acquired in the late 1970s/early 1980s and were the types used on its longer routes with Fokker F27s used on domestic services. A TriStar 500 has been leased from TAP since 1990 for long range services, and a Boeing 747-300 Combi from Singapore Airlines was due to be added in mid-1997. Around a million passengers a year are carried. Angola Aircharter and Aviaco Nigeria are subsidiary companies for freight and regional flights.

Routes

From Luanda to Benguela, Brazzaville, Cabinde, Dundo, Harare, Havana, Huambo, Johannesburg, Kinshasa, Kuito, Lisbon, Lubango, Lusaka, Malange, Menongue, Moscow, Pointe Noire, Rio de Janeiro, Sal, Sao Tome, Soyo, Windhoek.

Fleet

1 Boeing 707-300
5 Boeing 737-200Adv
6 Fokker F27
2 Ilyushin IL-62M
1 Lockheed L-1011-500

Ordered

1 Boeing 747-300

Photograph: Boeing 767-300ER N769TA (Josef Krauthäuser/Miami)

TACA

Edifico Caribe 2, Piso San Salvador,
El Salvador
Tel. 2985055 Fax. 2233757

Three letter code	IATA No.	ICAO Callsign
TAI	202	Taca

TACA International Airlines was founded in November 1939 in El Salvador as TACA El Salvador, at that time as a division of TACA – Airways SA, a powerful multinational organisation in Central America. The well-known airline pioneer, Lowell Yerex had formed TACA originally in Honduras in 1931. Operations began on the Salvador-Tegucigalpa-Managua-San Jose trunk route. In 1942 flights started with DC-3s to Bilbao in the Panama Canal Zone, and a year later to Havana. TACA International succeeded TACA El Salvador in 1950, and acquired all remaining assets of the original TACA Corporation in 1960. The airline also made use of DC-4s, Vickers Viscounts and DC-6s until the first jet aircraft, a BAC One-Eleven, was taken into service in 1966. Twenty years later TACA acquired its first widebody aircraft, a Boeing 767. The relatively modern all-Boeing fleet is all leased in, and aircraft are further leased out to other airlines, and to other members of the TACA group, comprising Aviateca, LACSA, NICA and Sahsa. A change from Boeing equipment will however occur from the fourth quarter of 1997 when the first three of five Airbus A320s are due to be delivered.

Routes

From San Salvador to Belize, Guatemala, Houston, Los Angeles, Mexico City, Miami, Montego Bay, New Orleans, Panama, San Francisco, San Jose and Tegucigalpa.

Fleet	Ordered
5 Boeing 737-300	5 Airbus A320
10 Boeing 737-200	
1 Boeing 767-200	
1 Boeing 767-300	

Photograph: Boeing 737-300 XA-SNC (Frank Litaudon/Mexico City)

TAESA AIRLINES

Zona C DE Hangares No. 27 Mexico City,
International Airport 15620, Mexico
Tel. 5-2270727 Fax. 5-7569205

Three letter code	IATA No.	ICAO Callsign
TEJ	838	Transejecutivos

The truly exotic story of Transportes Aereos Ejecutivos SA began on 27th April 1988 when Capitano Albert Abed started the company as an air taxi operator with two Lear Jets. Only a year later two Boeing 727s were added for charter and freight work. Then it was one thing after another; and the airline grew very rapidly, in spite of a business crisis which had affected Mexico; in spite of accusations in the US and German press that the owner was active in the world of drugs cartels, and in spite of accusations about the airline's safety standards – none of which allegations could be shown to have any concrete basis. Soon TAESA had become Mexico's third largest airline, and was also strong in charter operations. The fleet grew so quickly and so often, the move from old to new equipment was so rapid, and leased aircraft were quickly returned if they cost too much that the actual status of the fleet was difficult to ascertain. Boeing 767s and 737-300s and 500s came into service, as well as 737-200s and 757s, but the fleet continues to change rapidly. TAESA has diverse operations, and TAESA Express Division looks after cargo operations, helicopter and business aircraft. There is a considerable maintenance facility in Mexico City and another in Toluca.

Routes

Scheduled services to 27 Mexican internal points, to Chicago, Orlando and Laredo. Charters to over 60 cities in Europe, USA, Canada, the Caribbean and Japan.

Fleet

1 Boeing 757-200
4 Boeing 737-200/300
7 Boeing 727-100
5 McDonnell Douglas DC-9-14/15
2 McDonnell Douglas DC-10-30

Photograph: Tupolev Tu-154M EY-85717 (Björn Kannengiesser)

TAJIK AIR

31/2 Titov, Dushanbe Airport,
734006 Tajikistan
Tel. 3772-223283 Fax. 3772230768

Three letter code	IATA No.	ICAO Callsign
TJK	502	Tajikistan

Known as Tajikistan Airlines or Tajikair, the former Aeroflot regional directorate was taken over from the state in 1990 and re-organised. It was anticipated that the airline would operate schedules, cargo and charter flights, and special flights for members of the government. Mil-8 helicopters are used to provide passenger and emergency service in inaccessible mountain areas, where they are often the only means of speedy connection with a major town. There is an alliance with Tajikistan International Airlines, which has no aircraft of its own, and thus relies for its aircraft and flights on Tajik Air. Because of economic difficulties in the country and a weak foreign exchange position, part of its extensive but ageing ex-Soviet fleet is unserviceable, and new routes are seldom added. However, in spite of this, there are plans to increase the number of international services.

Routes

Almaty, Bombay, Delhi, and Frankfurt are international destinations; to some 20 regional cities.

Fleet

12 Antonov An-28
6 Antonov An-24/26
12 Mil-Mi-8
9 Tupolev Tu-134A
14 Tupolev Tu-154B/M
20 Yakovlev Yak-40

Photograph: Fokker 100 PT-MRO (Antònio del Pintos/Sao Paulo CGH)

TAM

Rue Monsenhor Antonio Pepe 94,
CEP 04357 Sao Paulo, Brazil
Tel. 5777711 Fax. 5332469

Three letter code	IATA No.	ICAO Callsign
TAM	877	TAM

TAM is Brazil's principal third-level airline, set up by VASP Brasilian Airlines and Taxi Aereo Marilia on 12th May 1976 to operate scheduled services in the interior of Sao Paulo State. Operations began on 12th July 1976 and 'domestic' routes have been added within the state and to other states of Brazil using Fokker F27s from the start. For less frequented routes, aircraft built in Brazil were used, Embraer 110 Bandeirantes. In October 1990 the first jet aircraft, Fokker 100s, were put into service. The airline continues to expand with a mixed fleet composed of Fokker 50s, 100s and F27s, but following the collapse of Fokker a new aircraft supplier has to be found, and several aircraft which had been on order will not now be delivered. In 1995/96 15 new aircraft were received and 10 new routes opened with the result that passenger totals for 1996 exceeded three million, a 19% increase on 1995. The airline ordered 5 Airbus A330-200s in June 1997, with options on a further five. TAM is based at Congonhas airport in Sao Paulo.

Routes

Dense internal network from Sao Paulo to Brasilia, Merilla, Porta Pora, Rio de Janeiro, Belo Horizonte and Asuncion. Shuttle service between Rio de Janeiro and Sao Paulo downtown airports.

Fleet	Ordered
7 Fokker F27 9 Fokker 50 28 Fokker 100	5 Airbus A330-200

Photograph: Airbus A340-300 CS-TOB (Patrick Lutz/Brussels)

TAP AIR PORTUGAL

Edifico 25, Aeroporto Lisboa, 1704 Lisboa, Portugal
Tel. 01-8415000 Fax. 01-8415095

Three letter code	IATA No.	ICAO Callsign
TAP	047	Air Portugal

Transportes Aereos Portugueses – TAP was established on 14th March 1945 by the Portuguese government. Flight operations began on 19th September 1946 with a converted C-47 (DC-3) from Lisbon to Madrid, and Casablanca was served by a Lockheed L-18 Lodestar. Routes were also opened to Luanda and Laurenco Marques in Mozambique on 31st December 1946, followed in 1947 by London and Paris. All these flights were operated using DC-4s. TAP became a joint-stock company, partly with private shareholders, on 1st June 1953. Lockheed L-1049 Constellations were used for long-distance routes. When Caravelles were commissioned in 1962, followed by Boeing 707s in 1966 as well as Boeing 727s a year later, this provided TAP with a completely jet fleet. In 1972 TAP obtained its first widebody aircraft, a Boeing 747. The confusion of the revolution in Portugal brought flights partly to a standstill in 1975, and it was only in 1977, after reorganisation, that it was possible to operate flights to their full extent. In 1975 the airline's aircraft were given their present colours, the TAP logo also being altered. Its present name was adopted in 1979. Two new aircraft were integrated in 1984: the Lockheed L-1011 TriStar for long-distance routes and the Boeing 737 for short and medium-distance routes. The first Airbus A320-200s arrived in 1992 and the TriStars are now largely replaced by Airbus A340s the first of which was delivered at the end of 1994. The Airbus A319 has been chosen as a partial replacement for the older Boeing 737s, with delivery to commence at the end of 1997. TAP has shareholdings in Air Macau and Air Sao Tome.

Routes

TAP serves some 10 internal destinations as well as points in Africa, South America, USA and Europe including Frankfurt, London, Munich, and Zürich.

Fleet		Ordered
6 Airbus A320-200	3 Lockheed L-1011-500	21 Airbus A319-100
5 Airbus A310-300		1 Airbus A320-200
4 Airbus A340-300		
10 Boeing 737-300		
6 Boeing 737-200		

Photograph: Airbus A310-300ET YR-LCA (Albert Kuhbandner/Zürich)

TAROM

OTP A/P SOS Bucuresti Ploesti km 16,5
Bucharest, Romania
Tel. 3152747 Fax. 3140524

Three letter code	IATA No.	ICAO Callsign
ROT	281	Tarom

Transporturi Aeriene Romana Sovietica (TARS) was established as a Romanian-Soviet airline in 1946 to succeed the pre-war state airline LARES. Operations began with a fleet of Lisunov Li-2s provided by its Russian partner.The Romanian state acquired the shares in 1954 and it was renamed TAROM (Transporturile Aeriene Romane). Tarom flew IL-14s from 1958 to destinations in eastern and western Europe and the first IL-18s were placed in service in 1963. In 1968 Tarom acquired its first BAC One-Eleven (they were later built in Romania under licence). IL-62s and Boeing 707s were commissioned in 1973 and 1974, and the Boeing 707s were used to open a route to New York. The IL-62s allowed extension of services to Africa and the Far East. Two Airbus A310s for long-distance routes were delivered at the end of 1992, and Boeing delivered five 737-300s in late 1993 and 1994. The intention was to bring the entire fleet up to 'Western' standard by the mid-90s, but this aim has been hindered by the poor economic progress of Romania. Some of the older Soviet types which are more or less unsaleable have been simply mothballed. Two ATR42-300s were however added at the beginning of 1997. LAR – Liniile Aeriene Romane was formed in 1975 as the charter subsidiary of Tarom using BAC One-Elevens. It was re-formed in 1991 as a joint-stock company, one third owned by the Romanian Government. Its fleet is leased from Tarom or other Romanian operators as required.

Routes

Abu Dhabi, Amsterdam, Athens, Beijing, Berlin, Casablanca, Chicago, Copenhagen, Düsseldorf, Frankfurt, Cairo, Karachi, Lisbon, London, Madrid, Moscow, New York, Paris, Prague, Rome, Tel Aviv, Warsaw, Vienna, Zürich.

Fleet

2 Airbus A310-300
14 Antonov An-24
2 ATR42-300
2 Boeing 707-300
5 Boeing 737-300
2 Ilyushin IL-62M
3 Ilyushin IL-18
13 Rombac 1-11
3 Tupolev Tu-154

Photograph: Boeing 737-200 F-GGCP (Andrè Dietzel/Munich FJS)

TAT EUROPEAN AIRLINES

BP 0237, 37002 Tours Cedex,
France
Tel. 47423000 Fax. 47423202

Three letter code	IATA No.	ICAO Callsign
TAT	930	TAT

Founded in 1968 as Touraine Air Transport, the company grew from a local air taxi service into an important French regional airline maintaining schedules throughout France and to Corsica. It began scheduled operations in March 1969 with a Tours to Lyon service. Over the years various companies such as Air Alpes, Air Alsace, Taxi Avia France, Air Paris and Air Languedoc were taken over. The airline also entered into a contract with Air France to provide feeder services for the national airline. A subsidiary, TAT Export, was created in 1984 to undertake international charters and a scheduled service was operated between West Berlin and Saarbrucken. Transport Aérien Transregional, as the airline was subsequently called, had a mixed fleet for the various tasks, but this has been rationalised over the past three years. The important change came with British Airways taking a 49.9% stake in the carrier in January 1993 as a result of which some aircraft (mostly Fokker F28s and 100s) now have a BA/TAT livery, and operate on behalf of BA on newly opened European routes. using BA flight numbers. A further change of name came about in 1995 when the airline became TAT European Airlines, reflecting the greater emphasis on its European services. At the same time TAT gave up its 20% holding in l'Aéropostale, dropped several routes, and introduced two Boeing 737-200s for charter work. British Airways had an option to buy the remaining shares, and this was taken up in 1996, so that TAT is now a 100% subsidiary of the British national carrier, and following losses of about FFr. 2 billion ($360m) in 1996 is being merged with Air Liberté. Some services are operated by Flandre Air using Beech 1900s and Embraer 120s in full TAT colours and using TAT flight numbers.

Routes

TAT flies to some 20 French internal destinations, and in co-operation with British Airways to Athens, Bergamo, Berlin, Frankfurt, Geneva, Helsinki, Copenhagen, London, Milan, Munich, Stockholm, and Vienna. Charters are also flown to seasonal destinations.

Fleet

10 ATR42
6 ATR72
2 Boeing 737-300
6 Fairchild FH227
16 Fokker F28
13 Fokker 100

Photograph: Boeing 737-300 HB-IIB (Patrick Lutz/Faro)

TEA - SWITZERLAND

Postfach 238, 4030 Basel,
Switzerland
Tel. 061-3253348 Fax. 061-3253947

Three letter code	IATA No.	ICAO Callsign
TSW	-	Topswiss

As a part of the pan-european airline group TEA, a Swiss operation was established in 1988 in Basle. The first of the new Boeing 737-300s was delivered in March 1989, and the first service flown on 23rd March 1989 from Zürich to Lisbon. From November 1989 to mid-March another aircraft was leased out to Australia. Thus the first year was concluded without making any loss, and the new airline had carried 200,000 passengers. Real profits were shown for the first time in 1993. TEA-Basle also set up a subsidiary in Cyprus, and established TEA-Hellas. In 1994 it took on the TEA-Switzerland name and has continued to grow. One of the growing fleet of Boeing 737s has been leased out long-term to Pacific Air in Vietnam, and two of the newest model Boeing 737-700 are on order for delivery at the end of 1997. Zürich now features more and more as an departure point for TEA as well as Basle.

Routes

Principally from Basle and Zürich to 25 destinations around the Mediterranean, to Mombasa, Recife and Goa plus *ad hoc* charters.

Fleet	Ordered
6 Boeing 737-300	2 Boeing 737-700

Photograph: Airbus A300B4 HS-THW (Josef Krauthäuser/Hong Kong)

THAI AIRWAYS INTERNATIONAL

89 Vibhavachi Rangit Road,
Bangkok 10900, Thailand
Tel. 02-5130121 Fax. 02-5130183

Three letter code	IATA No.	ICAO Callsign
THA	217	Thainter

Thai Airways was established on 24th August 1959 as a joint venture between SAS and the Thai Airways Company, which operated regionally, to take over Thai Airways international routes. Thai had a 70% stake and SAS 30%. Flights started in May 1960 to neighbouring countries, to Hong Kong and Tokyo, using DC-6Bs. As early as 1963 the airline changed over to jet aircraft, to Caravelles, and in 1969 to DC-9-41s. When DC-8-33s arrived Thai expanded its network to Australia in April 1971, and then to Copenhagen from June 1972. A route to Frankfurt was opened in 1973. In May 1975, when a DC-10-30 was delivered, Thai also introduced a new colour scheme. Thai has been in state ownership since April 1977 after SAS gave up their 15% shareholding to the Thai Government on 31st March. The fleet is being continually expanded, with Airbus A300s and Boeing 747s being introduced to the fleet in 1975 and 1979 respectively. The United States was served from April 1980. On 1st April 1988 Thai International and Thai Airways merged in preparation for the privatisation of the airline. Thai Airways had originally been formed on 1st November 1951 by the merger of Siamese Airways and Pacific Overseas Airlines (Siam). By taking over Thai Airways, Thai International somewhat surprisingly had taken over the airline of which it was once a subsidiary. Thai is one of the world's largest operators of the Airbus A300/310 which are used on regional routes, the fleet having been built up from 1979 to 1993. New Airbus A330s were delivered from 1994 to 1996, and Boeing 777-200s are being delivered from early 1996, with the larger 777-300s on order for delivery from late 1997. New Boeing 737s and 747s are also still in course of delivery.

Routes

Destinations on four continents including Amsterdam, Brisbane, Copenhagen, Dallas, Düsseldorf, Frankfurt, Hong Kong, Melbourne, Paris, Perth, Rome, Seattle, Seoul, Sydney, Stockholm, Tokyo, Vienna, Zürich. More than 10 internal Thai destinations are also served.

Fleet

2 Airbus A310-200
7 Airbus A300B4
16 Airbus A300-600
8 Airbus A330-300
2 ATR42
2 ATR72
5 BAe 146-300
7 Boeing 737-400
6 Boeing 747-200
2 Boeing 747-300
12 Boeing 747-400
4 Boeing 777-300
3 McDonnell Douglas DC-10-30ER

Ordered

4 Airbus A330-300
5 Airbus A300-600
4 Boeing 777-300
3 Boeing 747-400
4 Boeing 737-400

Photograph: BAe 146-200 QT EC-ELT (Author's collection)

TNT INTERNATIONAL AVIATION SERVICE

Archway House, 114-116 St Leonards, Windsor, Berkshire, SL4 3DG, Great Britain
Tel. 1753-842168 Fax. 1753-858172

Three letter code	IATA No.	ICAO Callsign
NTR	-	Nitro

TNT, which originated in Australia, is one of the largest cargo organisations in the world. TNT Express Worldwide is part of the TNT Group which began operations in 1968. TNT came to Europe in 1984 and in 1987 the European airfreight system was established and a special version of the BAe 146, the QT (or 'quiet trader'), was ordered. This particularly quiet aircraft is not subject to night-flight restrictions and can therefore be used on overnight flights. TNT does not operate its own aircraft but charters them to partners such as Air Foyle, Hunting Cargo, Mistral Air, Eurowings, Pan Air, Sterling European and Pacific East Asia Cargo. The cargoes are flown in a star-shaped pattern from around 30 European cities to the central hub at Cologne/Bonn (though this is expected to move to a purpose-built superhub at Liège in Belgium in 1998 because of German environmental restrictions and because it offers the space for long-term growth). There the freight is distributed, transferred, and sorted, when the aircraft then leave the hub again. All this takes place at night-time. A further hub was established in Manila in 1993 covering the Far East region, in conjunction with Pacific East Asia Cargo Airlines (formerly Air Philippines). The BAe 146 fleet now numbers 19, but has been supplemented since 1995 by a growing number of hushkitted Boeing 727Fs, which offer greater capacity. Three more of these are expected to be added in the next year, but will probably be retired by 2002 by which time there will be a widebody type in the fleet. At the end of 1996, TNT was purchased by the Dutch postal service, KPN. Further expansion is planned with a doubling of capacity by the year 2000.

Routes

Some 40 destinations in Europe and Brunei, Manila, New York, Singapore, Taipei.

Fleet

19 BAe 146-200/300 QT
6 Boeing 727-200F

Photograph: Boeing 747-100 N609FF (Josef Krauthäuser/Las Vegas)

TOWER AIR

Hangar 17, JFK International Airport, Jamaica, New York 11430 USA
Tel. 718-5534300 Fax. 718-5534312

Three letter code	IATA No.	ICAO Callsign
TOW	305	Tee Air

Tower Air was founded as a pure charter airline in August 1982. Flights were marketed to Europe and Israel without the airline possessing its own aircraft; the flights were carried out by Metro International Airways on Tower Air's behalf. By Spring 1983, Tower became the general sales agent for Metro International's scheduled services and on 1st November 1983 Tower Air took over from Metro on the New York-Brussels-Tel Aviv route with its only Boeing 747. One year later the airline entered the domestic American scheduled business as a 'low fare operator'. It entered competition with PeoplExpress with flights between New York and Los Angeles, but with little success, and so these loss-making schedules were dropped in 1984. Two more Boeing 747s were delivered in 1985 and a fourth in 1988. During the rest of the 1980s charters were flown between the USA and a number of European destinations. In 1992 scheduled flights to Berlin and Cologne/Bonn were offered for the first time. At the end of 1995 and early in 1996 further Boeing 747-200s were added and charter work further increased. Special contract and troop charters for the US military have also been flown on a regular basis, either in support of exercises, or to war zones such as Yugoslavia and the Gulf.

Routes

Amsterdam, Athens, Berlin, Bombay, Buenos Aires, Hong Kong, Los Angeles, Milan, Miami, New York, Paris, Rome, Sao Paulo, San Juan, Taipei, Tel Aviv are regularly served.

Fleet

8 Boeing 747-100
10 Boeing 747-200

Photograph: Boeing 757-200 EI-CLU (Stefan Schlick/Frankfurt)

TRANSAERO AIRLINES

Gos NIGA, Sheremetyevo Airport,
Moscow 103340, Russia
Tel. 9264633 Fax. 9280637

Three letter code	IATA No.	ICAO Callsign
TSO	670	Transaero

Transaero was founded in late 1991 as one of the first private joint-stock companies in Russia and the first non-Aeroflot company approved for scheduled passenger services in Russia. The shareholders are Aeroflot and aircraft manufacturers Ilyushin and Yakovlev. Flight operations commenced in early 1992 with Tu-154s. Thousands of emigrants were flown from Russia to Israel in a spectacular action which caught the media's attention and gave the airline publicity. Two Boeing 737-200s were leased in late 1992 and two IL-86s acquired, as well as IL-76s for cargo flights. In April 1994 Transaero received its first Boeing 757 and was also admitted as a member of IATA. Further 757s were added during 1995, allowing even more routes to be opened up. In 1996 the first flights to the USA in competition with Aeroflot were started. Leased ex-American Airlines DC-10-30s are used for the the Moscow-Los Angeles route, with a further route to Orlando being added in the Autumn. Further international routes are anticipated, including New York with Boeing 767s, three of which are planned to be added later in 1997. Also later in 1997 it is planned to add 6 Boeing 737-400s.

Routes

Adler, Almaty, Baku, Berlin, Eilat, Ekaterinburg, Frankfurt, Irkutsk, Kiev, Los Angeles, Minsk, Nizhnvartovsk, Norilsk, Novosibirsk, Odessa, Orlando, Riga, St Petersburg, Tel Aviv, Vladivostok, Yuzhno Sakhal.

Fleet

5 Boeing 737-200
5 Boeing 757-200
1 Ilyushin IL-86
3 McDonnell Douglas DC-10-30

Photograph: Airbus A320-200 B-22302 (Stefan Hartmann/Taipei)

TRANSASIA AIRWAYS

139 Cheng Chou Road, Taipei,
Republic of China
Tel. 5575767 Fax. 5580240

Three letter code	IATA No.	ICAO Callsign
TNA	170	Foshing

Founded in 1951 as Foshing Airlines, this airline experienced more downs than ups and returned its licence in 1965. It was then reactivated by the Gold Sun Group in 1990 and since then it has made rapid progress. It was renamed Transasia Airways in 1992 in order to better reflect the airline's ambitions with regard to an international network of routes. Its first jet aircraft was an A320, which was delivered in August 1992. The airline also opened international routes to Cambodia and the Philippines in 1992. The fast-growing company took delivery of more A320s in 1995 as well as the first of its six longer A321s. The shorter range services are flown by a fleet of ATR42s (introduced in 1989) and ATR72s (from November 1990). The main hubs are at Taipei/Sung Shan and Kaoshiung in Taiwan.

Routes

Cebu, Hualien, Kaoshiung, Kinmen, Makung, Manila, Surabaya, Phnom Penh, Taihan, Taipei.

Fleet	Ordered
3 ATR42	2 Airbus A320
12 ATR72	2 Airbus A321
6 Airbus A320-200	3 ATR72
4 Airbus A321-100	

Photograph: Boeing 737-300 PH-HVI (Josef Krauthäuser/Amsterdam)

TRANSAVIA

Postbus 7777, 1118 ZM Schiphol,
Netherlands
Tel. 020-6046518 Fax. 020-6015093

Three letter code	IATA No.	ICAO Callsign
TRA	979	Transavia

Transavia Airline, which was formed as Transavia Limburg in 1965 and changed its name to Transavia Holland in 1967 and to Transavia Airlines in 1986, has been operating flights since 16th November 1966 when it operated a charter service to Naples. Initially, flights to the Mediterranean were offered with DC-6s. The airline acquired its first jet aircraft, a Boeing 707, followed by an SE 210 Caravelle, as early as 1969; this aircraft was replaced by the Boeing 737 in 1974 as the airline operated a large share of the Dutch market in holiday flights. Transavia introduced a scheduled service from Amsterdam to London on 26th October 1986 and also has schedules to Spain; otherwise, the airline operates charters and provides aircraft leasing with a fair-sized fleet of 737s, supplemented from early 1993 by Boeing 757s. Boeing 737-800s have been ordered, with delivery scheduled to commence in Spring 1998. Transavia is a subsidiary of KLM which since 1991 has an 80% shareholding and its base is Amsterdam/Schiphol. The current colour scheme was adopted during the summer of 1995.

Routes

Charter flights to the Mediterranean area, North Africa, Canary Islands, and in winter to the Alpine resorts, plus *ad hoc* charters. Schedules to London and to Spain.

Fleet	Ordered
13 Boeing 737-300 4 Boeing 757-200	8 Boeing 737-800

Photograph: Boeing 767-200ER PT-TAG (Josef Krauthäuser/Miami)

TRANSBRASIL

Rua General Panteleao Telles 40,
CEP 04355-040, Sao Paulo, Brazil
Tel. 11-5254600 Fax. 11-5438048

Three letter code	IATA No.	ICAO Callsign
TBA	653	Transbrasil

The Brazilian meat wholesaler Sadia started flight operations as Sadia SA Transportes Aereos on 5th January 1955 with a DC-3, primarily to transport freight from Concordia to Sao Paulo. The airline entered the passenger business on 16th March 1956 and then proceeded to develop routes in Brazil's south east. Close co-operation with REAL and Transportes Aeros Salvador began in 1957; the latter was taken over by Sadia in 1962 and thereby expanded services into north-eastern Brazil after the collapse of REAL. The aircraft they used were Handley Page Heralds and, from 1970, BAC One-Elevens: Boeing 727s were used from 1974 onwards. Sadia changed its name to Transbrasil in June 1972 and transferred its headquarters to Brasilia. In June 1976, Transbrasil joined with the government of the state of Bahia to form the regional Nordeste airline which took over many local routes, allowing Transbrasil to concentrate on mainline route development. A cargo service to Miami was introduced in March 1978. Fleet replacement began in July 1983 with the purchase of Boeing 767s; the Boeing 727s were replaced by modern Boeing 737-300s and 400s starting in 1987. The airline divides up its scheduled and charter routes with Varig. In 1994 a new regional subsidiary, Interbrasil Star, was set up, operating Embraer Brasilias. With bases at Sao Paulo and Brasilia it has suitable departure points for unlimited internal services, though international schedules depart from Sao Paulo-Guarulhos. In co-operation with VARIG and VASP, an 'air bridge' is operated between the city airports of Rio de Janeiro and Sao Paulo in a pool arrangement.

Routes

Schedules to over 30 points in Brazil, to Amsterdam, Buenos Aires, Miami, New York, Orlando, Vienna and Washington.

Fleet

11 Boeing 767-200/300
11 Boeing 737-300/400

Photograph: Boeing 757-200 D4-CBG (Stephan Jansen/Amsterdam)

TRANSPORTES AEREOS DE CABO VERDE

Caixa Postal 1, Praia, Ilha do Santiago, Republic of Cape Verde
Tel. 613215 Fax. 613585

Three letter code	IATA No.	ICAO Callsign
TCV	696	Transverde

Transportes Aereos de Cabo Verde (TACV) was founded on 27th December 1958 to succeed a local flying club which had served internal points from May 1955 using de Havilland Doves until its bankruptcy in 1958. TACV began flights in January 1959. In 1971 the first of three Britten-Norman Islanders was commissioned. Operations were suspended for a time in 1967, while re-organisation took place with the help of the Portuguese national carrier TAP. After the country gained its independence from Portugal on 5th July 1975, TACV became the flag carrier of the recently established republic. After the acquisition of a BAe HS.748 in 1973, a weekly flight to Dakar in Senegal was set up; this remained TACV's sole foreign destination for many years. In association with TAP Air Portugal there is a direct service to Lisbon with a TCV flight number, but flown by a TAP Airbus. As a more modern supplement to the HS.748 two ATR42s were delivered at the end of 1994, and the arrival in March 1996 of the airline's own Boeing 757-200 allowed the route to Lisbon, and new routes to Frankfurt and Amsterdam to be flown by TACV. There are plans for a service to the USA.

Routes

From the capital Praia to Banjul, Bissau, Dakar and to the islands which form the republic, such as Boa Vista, Sal, Sao Vincente, Sao Nicolau; also to Amsterdam, Frankfurt, Lisbon, Milan and Paris.

Fleet

2 ATR42
2 BAe HS.748
1 Boeing 757-200
2 De Havilland DHC-6

Photograph: Fokker 100 SE-DUC (Andreas Hainzel/Salzburg)

TRANSWEDE AIRWAYS

P.O. Box 530, 19045 Stockholm-Arlanda,
Sweden
Tel. 59365000 Fax. 59360705

Three letter code	IATA No.	ICAO Callsign
TWE	-	Transwede

The present-day Transwede was founded on 1st April 1985 under the name of Aerocenter Trafikflyg AB. Initially it operated charter flights throughout Europe using F27s. The next aircraft in the fleet were three SE 210 Caravelles, used to operate inclusive tour charters from Sweden and Norway to the Mediterranean area. At the same time as these aircraft were acquired the airline's name was changed and the aircraft were painted blue, yellow and white. In 1986 two further MD-83s were added to the fleet, which was continually expanded in the following years. As well as Boeing 737s, new MD-83s and MD-87s were added to the fleet, while the Caravelles were sold to the airline's Turkish subsidiary, Sultan Air. The decision was taken to acquire more MD-83s, and Fokker 100s were bought for short-distance routes and domestic services in 1993, as changes in the market situation had made this necessary. In June 1996 Braathens bought 50% of Transwede's shares in order to acquire its scheduled services, and the 'leisure' activities have been phased out, with the airline operating as a Braathens subsidiary with a fleet reduced to Fokker 100s only.

Routes

Internal Scandinavian services.

Fleet

5 Fokker 100

Photograph: Boeing 767-200ER N604TW (Patrick Lutz/Paris CDG)

TRANS WORLD AIRLINES

One City Centre, 515 North 6th Street, St Louis, MO 63101, USA
Tel. 314-5893101 Fax. 314-5893125

Three letter code	IATA No.	ICAO Callsign
TWA	015	TWA

Founded on 1st October 1930, TWA made aviation history as a leading US airline for many years. It was the first airline to operate scheduled service from coast to coast in the USA, it opened up California for flights and was the joint initiator of such famous aircraft as the DC-1/2 and the DC-3. DC-2s started to arrive in 1934 and the larger DC-3 in 1936, followed by the first of five Boeing 307 Stratoliners in 1940. Howard Hughes, who had a controlling interest in TWA, placed an order with Lockheed in 1939 for an aircraft which would fly coast to coast in less than nine hours; the Constellation went into service in 1944. TWA's first overseas service operated on 5th December 1945 between Washington and Paris. On 21st May 1950 the airline changed its name to Trans World Airlines. London and Frankfurt became part of the network of routes as early as September 1950. On international flights the Constellation was used, and in the US DC-3s and Martin 404s. The first jet, a Boeing 707, came into service in March 1960. In August 1969 a round-the-world service was set up. TWA acquired its first Boeing 747 in December 1969. A second widebody type, the L-1011 TriStar, was added in 1972, and Boeing 767s from 1982. Ozark Airlines was acquired in 1986. In recent years TWA has hit hard economic times, but emerged from Chapter 11 bankruptcy protection in 1995, now part owned by its employees. It had been drastically slimmed down, notably with the sale in 1991 of routes to London to American Airlines. The opportunity was taken to introduce a new corporate identity and colour scheme. The latest type in the fleet is the Boeing 757, with deliveries commencing in July 1996, and Airbus A330s have been ordered for delivery from 1998. However, the airline continues to show poor economic performance.

Routes

Main hub is St Louis, with internal US services, and internationally to Europe and the Middle East.

Fleet

48 Boeing 727-100/200
14 Boeing 767-200/300ER
8 Boeing 747-100/200
12 Boeing 757-200
58 DC-9-15/32/41
14 Lockheed L-1011
56 McDonnell Douglas MD-82/83

Ordered

10 Airbus A330
8 Boeing 757
4 McDonnell Douglas MD-83

Photograph: Boeing 737-500 TS-IOH (Dieter Drabsch/Leipzig)

TUNISAIR

Boulevard 7 Novembre, 1012 Tunis,
Tunisia
Tel. 700100 Fax. 700472

Three letter code	IATA No.	ICAO Callsign
TAR	199	Tunair

Tunisair was founded in 1948 as a subsidiary of Air France by agreement with the Tunisian Government. Flight operations started in 1949 with DC-3s, initially from Tunis to Corsica and Algiers. In 1954 Tunisair acquired its first DC-4 for flights to Paris. By 1957 the government had acquired a controlling 51% interest. Air France's shareholding has gradually reduced. In 1961 the airline entered the jet age with the start of flights using SE 210 Caravelles. As a successor to the Caravelle was not available from France, the airline decided to buy Boeing 727s, and the first of these was added to the fleet in 1972; most are still in service. After the Caravelles had been taken out of service in late 1977, the smaller Boeing 737-200s were taken into service for the first time in 1979. European aircraft were purchased again, in 1982 with the single Airbus A300 and the first A320 in 1990, the latter delivery prompting the introduction of the present, modern colour scheme. More A320s were added in 1994/95, with Boeing 737-500s between 1992 and 1995. The Tunisian government now holds 45.2% of the shares, with the rest in private hands. Tunisair has a shareholding in Tuninter, which operates domestic services with ATR42s. Both airlines are based at Tunis-Carthage.

Routes

Amsterdam, Athens, Bahrein, Baghdad, Brussels, Budapest, Casablanca, Copenhagen, Damascus, Dakar, Düsseldorf, Frankfurt, Geneva, Istanbul, Jeddah, Cairo, London, Munich, Warsaw, Vienna, Zürich. Seasonal charter flights also to Europe.

Fleet

1 Airbus A300B4
8 Airbus A320
4 Boeing 737-200Adv
7 Boeing 727-200Adv
4 Boeing 737-500

Ordered

4 Airbus A320

Photograph: Avro RJ 100 TC-THG (Uwe Gleisberg/Munich FJS)

TURKISH AIRLINES

Atatürk Hava Limani, 34830 Yesilköy Istanbul, Turkey
Tel. 6634740 Fax. 6634763

Three letter code	IATA No.	ICAO Callsign
THY	235	Turkair

THY stems from Turkiye Devlet Hava Yollari (DHY), founded in 1933, and taken over by the state in 1956. Aircraft including DC-3s were taken over, with the first new acquisition, the Vickers Viscount, delivered from January 1958. In 1960 the first services to western Europe were started, including Frankfurt. In August 1967 the first DC-9 arrived, and on 1st December 1972 the first widebody in the form of the DC-10. For regional services the Fokker F27 and F28 were used. Boeing 727-200s were taken on from 1974, and from 1984 the first Airbus A310. For a long time THY concentrated on the development of domestic rather than international routes; only in the late 1960s were services to the most important European cities developed. A significant factor here was the need to serve the numerous Turks working throughout Europe. The Airbus A310 was brought into service from 1985. The first overseas destination was New York from 1990, in which year a new colour scheme was also adopted. Capacity continued to be increased, with the Airbus A340 arriving in 1993, along with further Boeing 737s. Also from 1994 the Avro RJ100 was added to the fleet for short and medium range services, replacing the older DC-9s and Fokker F28s. THY is well equipped for the rest of this century with a modern fleet. The airline has holdings in Sun Express and Kibris Cyprus Turkish Airlines and also conducts freight and charter flights.

Routes

Over 25 Turkish domestic destinations; and to Abu Dhabi, Almaty, Amman, Amsterdam, Athens, Bahrain, Baku, Bangkok, Barcelona, Basle, Beirut, Berlin, Bishkek, Brussels, Bucharest, Copenhagen, Dubai, Düsseldorf, Frankfurt, Geneva, Hamburg, Hannover, Jeddah, Cairo, Cologne, Kuwait, London, Lyon, Madrid, Milan, Munich, New York, Nice, Nürnberg, Osaka, Paris, Riyadh, Rome, Singapore, Stockholm, Stuttgart, Tashkent, Teheran, Tel Aviv, Tokyo, Tunis, Vienna and Zürich.

Fleet		Ordered
14 Airbus A310-200/300	3 Boeing 727-200Adv	6 Airbus A340-300
4 Airbus A340-300	30 Boeing 737-400	
14 Avro RJ 70/100	2 Boeing 737-500	

Photograph: Fokker 70 OE-LFK (Andrè Dietzel/Innsbruck)

TYROLEAN AIRWAYS

Postfach 58, Flughafen, 6026 Innsbruck, Austria
Tel. 22220 Fax. 293490

Three letter code	IATA No.	ICAO Callsign
TYR	734	Tyrolean

Founded in 1958 as Aircraft Innsbruck, it operated until 1980 as a non-scheduled airline, when it acquired the rights to operate scheduled flights from Innsbruck to Vienna. Before starting flight operations in April 1980 with DHC-7s, the name was changed to Tyrolean Airways in 1979. In that same year further routes were opened to Zürich and Frankfurt. Tyrolean also operates from its Innsbruck base, as a holiday airline and also operates *ad hoc* charters and air ambulance flights. In 1994 the domestic arm of Austrian Airlines, Austrian Air Services, was integrated with Tyrolean following Austrian taking a 42.85% stake in the regional airline. Since then Tyrolean has expanded strongly. New aircraft types in the shape of the Fokker 70 (from May 1995) and Canadair Regional Jet (from May 1996) have been added to the previously all de Havilland Canada fleet of DHC-7s and DHC-8s. With the aid of the Austrian Airlines marketing partners, the network has also been widened and intensified.

Routes

Tyrolean serves some 30 destinations in Europe from Innsbruck, Linz and Salzburg. Charter flights to holiday regions in the northern Mediterranean.

Fleet

7 Canadair Regional Jet
1 De Havilland DHC-7
22 De Havilland DHC-8-100/300
3 Fokker 70

Ordered

1 Canadair Regional Jet
4 De Havilland DHC-8-400

Photograph: Boeing 737-200Adv UR-GAD (Christian Dougett/London LHR)

UKRAINE INTERNATIONAL AIRLINES

Prospekt Pere Mogy 14, 252300 Kiev, Ukraine
Tel. 2218135 Fax. 2167994

Three letter code	IATA No.	ICAO Callsign
AUI	566	Ukraineinternational

This airline was formed in October 1992 as a subsidiary of Air Ukraine (which operates extensive domestic services with a large fleet of Soviet-built types) to operate international services. The young state of the Ukraine holds 90% of the shares. Flights were started to western Europe with a leased Boeing 737-400. In contrast with Air Ukraine, it was decided to operate modern aircraft which would appeal to western business travellers. In late 1994 the expensive 737-400 was returned to the lessor and replaced with an older 737-200, to which a further 737-200 was added in early 1995. The initial hopes of this airline have not been met, and so the company, which was renamed as Ukraine International Airlines in 1995, is developing but slowly. The main base is at the airport at Kiev, where there is a maintenance facility.

Routes

Almaty, Amsterdam, Barcelona, Berlin, Brussels, Frankfurt, Kiev, Larnaca, London, Milan, Manchester, Munich, Paris, Riga, Rome, Vienna, Zürich.

Fleet

2 Boeing 737-200Adv

Photograph: Boeing 777-200 N777UA (Albert Kuhbandner/Brussels)

UNITED AIRLINES

P.O. Box 66100, Chicago, IL 60666, USA
Tel. 847-7004000 Fax. 847-7007680

Three letter code	IATA No.	ICAO Callsign
UAL	016	United

United Airlines Inc of Chicago was founded on 1st July 1931 as the new holding company of the former Boeing Air Transport, Varney Air Lines, National Air Transport and Pacific Air Transport. All four had started operations in either 1926 or 1927. United flew with Boeing 247s but decided to buy DC-3s, using over 100 in the 1940s. After the war DC-4s and DC-6s were used, mainly on the airline's route from New York to Chicago. In 1946 Hawaii was served for the first time, and in 1959 the airline's first jet aircraft, a DC-8, was commissioned. United was the only US airline to order Caravelles, with 20 for short and medium-distance routes. There were no follow-up orders, however, and Boeing 727s were bought. On 1st June 1961 Capital Airlines, one of the largest airlines at that time, was taken over, making United the largest airline in the free world, a position which was only bettered by American Airlines in the late 1980s. Route rights were acquired in the Pacific, as were Lockheed TriStars, from PanAm in 1986. At the same time aircraft were bought from Boeing in order to renew the fleet. Boeing 737-300s and 767s are the backbone of the fleet, with Airbus A320s and now A319s also significant. United has been flying to Europe since 1990; in autumn 1993 it became a Lufthansa partner. The present colours were introduced early in 1994. United was the launch customer for the Boeing 777, introduced on services to Europe in June 1995. Air Wisconsin, Aspen Airways, Atlantic Coast, Mesa Airlines and West Air all operate feeder and regional services as United Express. 'Shuttle by United' is a dedicated division operating 30 Boeing-737-222s on 'no-frills' services. United, which flew 81 million scheduled passengers in 1996, has large aircraft orders with Boeing, with deliveries well into the 21st century.

Routes

United's main hubs are San Francisco, Chicago, Denver and Washington/Dulles with flights to over 150 destinations in the USA, South and Central America, Europe, the Middle East, Asia and Australia.

Fleet

2 Airbus A319
40 Airbus A320
64 Boeing 737-200
57 Boeing 737-500
75 Boeing 727-200
100 Boeing 737-300
92 Boeing 757-200
19 Boeing 767-200
23 Boeing 767-300
27 Boeing 747-100/200
31 Boeing 747-400
23 Boeing 777-200
30 McDonnell Douglas DC-10-10/30

Ordered

26 Airbus A319
13 Airbus A320
16 Boeing 747-400
12 Boeing 777
6 Boeing 757

Photograph: Boeing 767-300F N305UP (Björn Kannengiesser/Miami)

UNITED PARCEL SERVICE

1400 North Hurstbourne Parkway,
Louisville, Kentucky 40223, USA
Tel. 502-3296500 Fax. 502-3296550

Three letter code	IATA No.	ICAO Callsign
UPS	-	UPS

UPS – United Parcel Service was founded in 1907, and today it is the largest company in the world in its area of business. In 1953 the two-day 'UPS-Air' service was set up. In 1982 UPS entered the overnight small package market and now serves more US points than any other carrier. Flights to Europe were introduced in October 1985. It was only in 1987 that UPS established its own flight operations. Up to that point other airlines had been commissioned to carry out the flights. (Even today a large number of outside companies operate on behalf of UPS). There are also regular flights to the European hub in Cologne. Further hubs are in Hong Kong, Singapore, Miami and Montreal, with the main centre at Louisville. Dedicated DC-8 freighters were initially the mainstay of the long-range fleet, and many are still in service today. There are also a number of Boeing 747 freighters which have been acquired between 1984 and 1996. UPS induced Boeing to build a cargo version of the 757-200 and was the first customer to receive them from 1987. Older Boeing 727s are being equipped with new, more powerful and more environmentally friendly Roll-Royce Tay engines. These modified aircraft were first used in 1993, mainly to Europe, as a result of stronger environmental regulations there. As with the 757, UPS was also the launch customer for the larger Boeing 767-300F, the first of 30 of which was delivered in October 1995.

Routes

Scheduled freight/parcel services in the USA and Canada, to Hong Kong, Japan, Singapore, Korea, Cologne, London and Mexico.

Fleet	Ordered
14 Boeing 747-100F	14 Boeing 767-300F
61 Boeing 727-100/200F	15 Boeing 757-200F
60 Boeing 757-200F	
16 Boeing 767-300F	
50 McDonnell Douglas DC-8-70	

Photograph: Boeing 737-300 N508AU (Josef Krauthäuser/Fort Lauderdale)

US AIRWAYS

2345 Crystal Drive, Arlington, Virginia 22227, USA
Tel. 703-418-7000 Fax. 703-418-5437

Three letter code	IATA No.	ICAO Callsign
USA	037	US Air

Founded on 5th March 1937 as All-American Aviation, it initially provided postal services over a network of routes from Pittsburgh. Mail services were discontinued in 1949 and the airline changed its name to All American Airways on 7th March 1949, when scheduled passenger services commenced from Pittsburgh via Washington to Atlantic City using DC-3s. Martin 2-0-2s and Convair 340/440s replaced the DC-3s, the name was changed in 1953 to Allegheny Airlines and new routes were opened, especially in the eastern United States. Lake Central Airways was taken over on 1st July 1968, and on 7th April 1972 Mohawk Airlines followed, with its large route network and its BAC One-Eleven aircraft. After deregulation, Pacific Southwest Airlines and the much larger Piedmont Airlines were taken over. On 28th October 1979 the airline's new name, US Air, was a sign of its new size. Its first services to London were in 1988, followed in 1990 by Frankfurt and Zürich. After the integration of Piedmont the airline took on new colours. Fokker 100s were introduced in 1989, enabling this aircraft to make a breakthrough on the American market. US Air took over the shuttle service from New York to Washington and Boston from Trump. In January 1993 British Airways made a $400 million investment and operated joint transatlantic services, but this partnership became acrimonious, and BA sold its holding in early 1997, at which time the airline took on the new identity of US Airways. A $14 billion 'order' for 120 Airbus A319/320/321s plus options is deferred awaiting union agreements over pay, and cost-cutting moves in May 1997 include cutting domestic routes and the grounding of 5 F28s and 17 DC-9s. Several smaller carriers operate regional and feeder services in US Air Express colours.

Routes

Main US Airways hubs are Washington, Baltimore, Pittsburgh, Philadelphia, Indianapolis, Dayton and Charlotte. Outside the USA it flies to Cancun, Nassau, San Juan, Bermuda, Frankfurt, Madrid, Montreal, Munich, Ottawa, Paris, Rome and Toronto. Of the total of about 150 destinations, about 130 are within the USA.

Fleet

64 Boeing 737-200Adv
85 Boeing 737-300
54 Boeing 737-400
34 Boeing 757-200
12 Boeing 767-200ER
30 Fokker F28
40 Fokker 100
62 McDonnell Douglas DC-9-30
31 McDonnell Douglas MD-80

Ordered

40 Boeing 737-300
7 Boeing 757-200

Photograph: Airbus A310-300 F-OGQZ (Patrick Lutz/Hamburg)

UZBEKISTAN AIRWAYS

Proletarskaya 41,
700100 Tashkent, Uzbekistan
Tel. 3712-911490 Fax. 3712-327371

Three letter code	IATA No.	ICAO Callsign
UZB	250	Uzbek

In 1992 the government of the newly formed government of Uzbekistan assumed the air sovereignty over its national territory. At the same time the aircraft of the former Tashkent directorate of Aeroflot became the property of Uzbekistan, with Uzbekistan Airways being founded as the national airline. The routes were partly taken over and continued. Particular attention was paid to the new routes from western Europe via Tashkent to the Far East, and it was here that the airline with its particularly low priced tariffs entered into competition with established airlines. In order to be able to meet the sophisticated needs of travellers from Western countries, Uzbekistan leased two Airbus A310-300s. The first of these aircraft arrived in Tashkent in July 1993 and services started to London and Middle Eastern cities. In 1995 New Delhi and Kuala Lumpur were added as destinations, and in 1996 Jeddah and Tel Aviv came on line. As well as schedules, there are numerous charters to Arab countries. A modernisation and re-equipment programme with western aircraft has been started with the delivery in early 1997 of two leased Boeing 767-300s and with an order for three Avro RJ85s being delivered during the second half of 1997. Uzbekistan is by far the largest airline operating in the country, and it has additional responsibilities for government work such as patrol and agricultural work for which helicopters such as the Mil-8 are also used.

Routes

Aleppo, Amsterdam, Athens, Bahrain, Bangkok, Beijing, Denpasar, Frankfurt, Hong Kong, Istanbul, Karachi, London, Male, Manchester, New Delhi, New York, Seoul, Sharjah and 30 more domestic and CIS destinations.

Fleet

1 Avro RJ85
2 Airbus A310-300
23 Antonov An-24
2 Boeing 767-300(ER)
8 Ilyushin IL-62
15 Ilyushin IL-76TD
10 Ilyushin IL-86
24 Tupolev TU-154
25 Yakovlev Yak 40

Ordered

1 Airbus A310-300
2 Avro RJ85

Photograph: McDonnell Douglas DC-9-32 N930VV (Josef Krauthäuser/Fort Lauderdale)

VALUJET

1800 Phoenix Boulevard, Suite 126, Atlanta, Georgia 30349, USA
Tel. 404-9072580 Tel. 404-9072586

Three letter code	IATA No.	ICAO Callsign
VJA	-	Critter

Valujet was founded in June 1993 and operated its first service a few months later on 26th October, from Atlanta to Tampa in Florida. The business expanded very quickly and was liked by its customers on account of its low fares. With a fleet made up entirely of DC-9-32s, after only a year 20 cities in the east of the USA were being served, and the network built up on a permanent basis. Following the example proven by other 'no-frills' airlines, no special services were offered. As the market for used DC-9-32s was practically exhausted, other types such as the MD-80 or DC-9-20 were bought. A launch order for 50 aircraft was agreed with McDonnell Douglas for the new MD-95. Following some minor transgressions over maintenance, the Federal Aviation Administration decided to keep an eye on Valujet and the airline was kept under closer management control. This had consequences including a reining in of the rapid route expansion. However, following the well-publicised loss of a Valujet DC-9 on 11th May 1996, the airline's operating licence was withdrawn, even though the cause of the accident had not been properly established. The FAA had succumbed to press and political pressure. However, Valujet was allowed to restart operations from September 1996 on a restricted basis. During the grounding several aircraft had been sold or taken out of service. In July 1997 a merger was agreed with the small, Orlando-based Boeing 737-200 operator Air Tran Airways, which will rid the carrier of its stigmatised name. The aircraft will be painted in the Air Tran colours, and it is expected that the MD-95 order will be taken on.

Routes

Atlanta, Boston, Charlotte, Chicago, Columbus, Dallas, Detroit, Fort Lauderdale, Fort Myers, Hartford, Indianapolis, Jackson, Jacksonville, Kansas City, Louisville, Miami, Mobile, Nashville, New Orleans, New York, Orlando, Philadelphia, Pittsburgh, Raleigh-Durham, Savannah, Tampa, Washington and West Palm Beach.

Fleet	Ordered
35 McDonnell Douglas DC-9-32	50 McDonnell Douglas MD-95

Photograph: McDonnell Douglas MD-11 PP-VOQ (B.I.Hengi/Zürich)

VARIG

Avenida Almirante Silvio de Noronha 365,
CEP 20021, Rio de Janeiro, Brazil
Tel. 21-2725000 Fax. 21-2725700

Three letter code	IATA No.	ICAO Callsign
VRG	042	Varig

Founded on 7th May 1927 by German immigrant Otto Ernst Meyer, Varig developed initially in the south of Brazil. Its first aircraft was a Dornier Wal flying boat which operated the first service on 3rd February 1928 on the Porto Alegre to Rio Grande route. Lockheed 10A Electras were introduced in 1943 after Montevideo had become the first international destination in 1942, followed later in the decade by a Buenos Aires service. After the Second World War, Varig acquired 35 C-47s (DC-3s) and expanded its network of routes considerably. In 1951 Aero Geral was taken over as well as its routes to Montevideo and Buenos Aires. A scheduled service to New York was started on 2nd August 1955 using Lockheed Super Constellations. The switch was made to Caravelles on 2nd October 1959 and in late 1960 Boeing 707s came into service on this route. A further airline, REAL, was taken over in 1961. The much smaller Varig airline under its famous president Ruben Berta thus acquired new types of aircraft such as CV990s, Lockheed L-188s and C-46s, plus a large network of routes. Its network was also expanded internationally by order of the government in 1965, when it was ordered to take over Panair do Brasil. DC-10-30s came into service in May 1971, a further airline, Cruzeiro do Sul, was bought in 1975 (and integrated in 1993) and in 1981, Airbus A300s and Boeing 747-200s were acquired. Boeing 767s, Boeing 747-400s and MD-11s are the latest aircraft in the Varig fleet, with more 747-400s on order for delivery over the next three years. Varig has majority shareholdings in Rio Sul and Nordeste Linhas Aereas, both Brazilian regional operators. A two year $40m fleet refurbishment, including a new colour scheme, was begun in October 1996. A codeshare with United was added in 1997.

Routes

Varig has a dense network in South America, and flies to the USA , Canada, South Africa, Hong Kong and Japan. In Europe Amsterdam, Copenhagen, Frankfurt, Lisbon, London, Madrid, Paris, Rome, and Zürich are served. In Brazil itself 35 points are connected.

Fleet

17 Boeing 737-200Adv
25 Boeing 737-300
5 Boeing 727-100F
5 Boeing 747-300
10 Boeing 767-200/300ER
10 McDonnell Douglas DC-10-30
7 McDonnell Douglas MD-11

Ordered

11 Boeing 737-300
6 Boeing 747-400

Photograph: McDonnell Douglas MD-11 PP-SPE (Josef Krauthäuser/Miami)

VASP

Edifico Sede VASP 4 andar Congonhas,
Airport Sao Paulo, CEP 04695, Brazil
Tel. 011-5337011 Fax. 011-5420880

Three letter code	IATA No.	ICAO Callsign
VSP	343	VASP

Viacao Aerea Sao Paulo SA was founded on 4th November 1933 by the regional government of Sao Paulo and the Municipal Bank of Sao Paulo. Flight operations started on 16th April 1934, using two 3-seater Monospar ST-4s and in 1935 a scheduled route was opened between Rio de Janeiro and Sao Paulo using two Junkers Ju 52/3s acquired in 1935. When it took over the Brazilian-German Aerolloyd Iguassu on 28th October 1939 the network of routes included numerous destinations. VASP had six Saab Scanias in use from 1950 onwards, and later all the aircraft of this type ever built were in VASP's service, a total of 18 aircraft, and the last of the type in service was retired in 1966. VASP obtained its first Vickers Viscounts in October 1958. Two airlines, Loide Aereo Nacional (LAN) and Navegacao Aerea Braziliero (NAB), were taken over in 1962 as part of the general nationalisation of air services in Brazil. The first jet aircraft was a BAC One-Eleven in December 1967. Eight NAMC YS-11As were bought in late 1968 as replacement for the Vickers Viscounts and DC-4s. VASP evolved over the years into Brazil's second largest airline and continually modernised its fleet, adapting to the market situation. The first four Boeing 737s were introduced in July 1969. In the late 1970s the Brazilian-built Embraer 110 Bandeirante regional aircraft came briefly into service until the entire fleet was changed over to jet aircraft. The three Airbus A300s in the fleet are used on the high density Sao Paulo routes to Rio de Janeiro and Brasilia as well as on other routes. The airline has been in a severe financial crisis for some time, which it is seeking to overcome by means of reorganisation. VASP has majority holdings in LAB – Lloyd Aéreo Boliviano and Ecuatoriana.

Routes

Dense internal Brazilian network serving over 30 points such as Belem, Belo Horizonte, Brasilia, Campo Grande, Florianapolis, Iguacu, Maceio, Manaus, Porto Alegre, Recife, Rio de Janeiro, Sao Paulo, Vitoria. Internationally to Aruba, Brussels, Buenos Aires, Los Angeles, Miami, New York, Seoul, Toronto.

Fleet

3 Airbus A300B2
2 Boeing 727-200F
2 Boeing 737-300
22 Boeing 737-200
9 McDonnell Douglas MD-11

Photograph: Boeing 737-300 OO-VEB (Author's collection/Brussels)

VIRGIN EXPRESS

Building 116, Melsbroek Airport
B-1820 Melsbroek, Belgium
Tel. 2-7520511 Fax. 2-7520506

Three letter code	IATA No.	ICAO Callsign
EBA	665	Belstar

In November 1991 EuroBelgian Airlines was set up by the City Hotels Group, and it began operations from 1st April 1992 with Boeing 737-300s as a general European charter airline. Richard Branson, founder and head of the British airline Virgin Atlantic (see page 304) took over EBA in April 1996 as the basis for his European expansion plans, renamed it Virgin Express and set about building up a low-cost airline operating scheduled services within Europe. The existing Boeing 737-300 fleet and network were taken over as a nucleus. A strong partnership was quickly established with Sabena, and the national airline's London service taken over; it is flown by Virgin Express aircraft on a codeshare basis. The first brand new Boeing 737-300 for the new company – painted in an unmistakeable red colour scheme complementary to that of Virgin Atlantic – was delivered at the end of 1996. The 737-300 fleet has grown rapidly, and is presently augmented by a single 737-400 and, as a trial of the type for possible more extensive future use in the fleet, an Airbus A320 on wet-lease from Constellation International Airways. It is used for charters from Brussels, this type of work still forming about 40% of the airline's activity. Two Boeing 737-800s are on order for delivery in mid-1998.

Routes

Barcelona, Brussels, Copenhagen, London/Heathrow and Gatwick, Milan, Nice, Rome and Vienna.

Fleet	Ordered
14 Boeing 737-300 1 Boeing 737-400	2 Boeing 737-800

Photograph: Fokker 50 OO-VLN (Martin Bach/London City Airport)

VLM

Luchthaven Gebouw B50, Antwerp Airport
B-2100 Deurne, Belgium
tel. 3-2309000 Fax. 3-2813200

Three letter code	IATA No.	ICAO Callsign
VLM	978	Rubens

Vlaamse Luchttransportmaatschappij NV was set up in Antwerp in February 1992. A year and a quarter later on 15th May 1993 the first schedule was successfully flown from Antwerp to London. VLM is a typical niche carrier offering scheduled services from regional airports, with services also operated from Rotterdam. Since April 1996 VLM has flown to the airport at Mönchengladbach (which also now calls itself Düsseldorf Express). For a while the service to London City was extended to Liverpool, providing an internal UK service, but this was not successful and was dropped. All the routes are operated on a several flights a day basis, and the airline is also active with charter work. A careful expansion foresees a build up of destinations and of the fleet.

Routes

Antwerp, Mönchengladbach, Rotterdam, London City Airport.

Fleet

5 Fokker 50

Photograph: Boeing 767-200ER VH-RMA (Stefan Hartmann/Hong Kong)

VIETNAM AIRLINES

Gialem Airport, Hanoi,
Socialist Republic of Vietnam
Tel. 271643 Fax. 25922

Three letter code	IATA No.	ICAO Callsign
HVN	738	Vietnam Airlines

After the end of the Vietnam war and the coming together of North and South Vietnam, a new airline also came into existence in 1976: Hang Khong Vietnam. It took over the aircraft and staff of the former CAAV and partly those of Air Vietnam. However the fleet was very quickly changed over to Soviet standard, as spare parts could not be obtained for western aircraft. Air Vietnam had been 92.75% owned by the old government in 1975, shortly before the fall of Vietnam. It had been formed to take over the services of Air France in the area. In the early and mid-1980s Tu-134As operated several weekly services from Hanoi to Ho Chi Minh City (ex-Saigon), Phnom Penh, Bangkok, and Vientiane. It was only when the country opened up politically towards the West and towards the US that it was possible in 1990 to place an order for western aircraft. As a replacement for the IL-18s two ATR72s were ordered. A slow expansion of the network of routes is planned for the 1990s. In 1990 some Tu-134s were bought from Interflug stocks, the name was changed to Vietnam Airlines and new colours were introduced. The fact that the country had opened up politically made it possible for Air France to acquire a stake in Vietnam Airlines; Air France provided A320s for international flights and took over training and service from late 1993 on. As part of the plan to phase out the Russian-built airliners in favour of western aircraft Boeing 767s and ATR72s have been acquired.

Routes

Bangkok, Hanoi, Ho Chi Minh City, Hong Kong, Melbourne, Phnom Pen, Singapore, Sydney, Vientiane and several destinations within Vietnam.

Fleet

10 Airbus A320
6 ATR72
7 Boeing 767-200/300ER
2 Fokker 70
1 Ilyushin IL-18D
4 Tupolev Tu-134
1 Yakovlev Yak-40

Photograph: Boring 747-400 G-VFAB (Frank Schorr/London LHR)

VIRGIN ATLANTIC

Ashdown House, High Street, Crawley,
RH10 1DQ, Great Britain
Tel. 1293-562345 Fax. 1293-561721

Three letter code	IATA No.	ICAO Callsign
VIR	932	Virgin

Virgin Atlantic can trace its history back to British Atlantic Airways, set up in 1982 with Richard Branson involved, to operate services between Britain and the Falklands and then between Gatwick and New York. However the CAA declined a licence and subsequently Branson decided to set up Virgin Atlantic, through the Virgin Group. The collapse of Laker Airways encouraged Branson to establish an airline along the same lines, as there was obviously a need for a 'cheap airline' from London. Virgin Atlantic obtained a licence for London to New York (Newark) and the first flight was on 22nd June 1984. In November a daily connecting flight to Maastricht in Holland using BAC One-Elevens was started. This flight later changed over to Vickers Viscounts but was discontinued in 1990. With imaginative advertising this airline, offering only cheap flights, attracted more sophisticated passengers. New routes to New York (JFK) and Los Angeles were awarded to Virgin following the British Airways/British Caledonian merger. Approval for a new service to Tokyo was granted in August 1988 for scheduled flights to begin on 1st May 1989. Steady expansion continued with the launch of London Heathrow services (to where Virgin transferred all its long-haul routes apart from/to Boston) to Hong Kong on 21st February 1994 and to San Francisco from May 1994. Miami and Tokyo via Moscow were also added. The first Airbus A340s were delivered in Spring 1994, and the first Boeing 747-400 in May 1994. Further routes were added to Hong Kong and Australia, with Johannesburg following in 1996. Also in 1996 the Belgian charter operator EuroBelgian Airlines was bought and transformed into Virgin Express (see page 301). Virgin expects to take eight A340-600s plus eight options from 2002.

Routes

From London to Hong Kong, Johannesburg, Los Angeles, Miami, Moscow, New York/JFK, New York/Newark, Orlando, Sydney, and Tokyo.

Fleet	Ordered
8 Airbus A340	2 Airbus A340-300
6 Boeing 747-100/200	
5 Boeing 747-400	

Photograph: Boeing 737-300 EC-FLG (Klaus Brandmaier/Zürich)

VIVA AIR

Camiro de la escollera 4, 07012 Palma de Mallorca, Spain
Tel. 717188 Fax. 718268

Three letter code	IATA No.	ICAO Callsign
VIV	728	Viva

Viva Air, initially a German-Spanish charter airline belonging to Iberia and Lufthansa, was founded on 24th February 1988 and started its first flight from Nuremberg to Palma de Mallorca on 15th April 1988. The airline started the first season with three Boeing 737-300s, and two more Boeing 737s were acquired in 1989. In addition to the purely charter business Viva Air flew supplementary flights for Iberia. In 1993 the leased DC-9s were taken out of service and further Boeing 737s were acquired. Following some differences between the owners Viva Air is now 98% owned by Iberia. For a while it had its own independent scheduled domestic services, operating them instead of Iberia, but these were taken back by Iberia in 1995 and Viva now operates as the Iberia group's leisure and charter specialist.

Routes

Charter flights from European and Middle East airports to destinations on the Spanish mainland and to Palma de Mallorca.

Fleet

9 Boeing 737-300

Photograph: Tupolev Tu-204 RA-64011 (Heinz Kolper/Farnborough)

VNUKOVO AIRLINES

B 121 Reysovaya, Vnukovo AP,
Moscow 103027, Russia
Tel. 095-4367995 Fax. 095-4362626

Three letter code	IATA No.	ICAO Callsign
VKO	442	Vnukovo

Vnukovo is Moscow's third airport, and here this airline was founded in 1993 as Vnukovskie Avialinii. The former Aeroflot Vnukovo Production and Central Test Division provided material and personnel. Vnukovo quickly developed to be a leading airline, run to western standards. Punctuality and quality of service are outstanding points compared with other airlines from the former Soviet Union. Also the fleet, though all Soviet-built, is relatively young and well cared-for. Routes are flown from Moscow to destinations in the south of the CIS and the airline is also active with worldwide charters. In October 1993 the airline received the first of Russia's new-generation production, the Tupolev Tu-204, which it used for extensive tests under normal airline operating conditions. Two further aircraft are for use as freighters initially, and then for passenger work after certification.

Routes

Schedules from Moscow to Anapa, Aktau, Antalya, Athens, Barcelona, Dunai, Hurghada, Igarka, Istanbul, Kaliningrad, Kambala, Kemerovo, Krasnodar, Novosibirsk, Norilsk, Odessa, Samarkand, Sochi, Tblisi, Thessaloniki, Ulan Ude, Yerevan.

Fleet

22 Ilyushin IL-86
26 Tupolev Tu-154
3 Tupolev Tu-204

Photograph: Boeing 737-300 N950WP (Author's collection)

WESTERN PACIFIC AIRLINES

3 South Tejon Street, Suite 400,
Colorado Springs, CO 80903, USA
Tel. 719-4737737 Fax. 719-3891999

Three letter code	IATA No.	ICAO Callsign
KMR	318	Komstar

Edward R. Beauvais is well known in airline circles having founded the famous America West Airlines in 1981 and leading it to great success until he left the airline in 1992. In September 1994 he announced the formation of Commercial Air. The operating base was not to be the new Denver International Airport, but the smaller Colorado Springs Airport to the south. This airport, with its long Colorado runway until now used more or less only by the military, was newly built and offered good conditions. And so on 28th April 1995 Western Pacific Airlines – a better sounding name adopted for marketing reasons – began service with eight Boeing 737s, initially to Oklahoma, Los Angeles, Las Vegas and Phoenix. Further destinations from the east to the west coast of the USA were added quickly. A particularly eyecatching feature of WP's aircraft is that they are painted all over as advertising billboards The aircraft are colourful and promote for instance a casino or hotel in Las Vegas, a TV series, car rental or a rodeo. This has brought not only advertising revenue but public attention to the airline. In July 1996 Mountain Express was set up, with WestPac as a shareholder, and there is a marketing alliance between the two operators. As not enough of the preferred Boeing 737-300s are available for acquisition for expansion of the routes, rented Boeing 727s have been used for some services, pending the delivery of new Boeing 737-700s which are on order from the manufacturer. The 1997 network has expanded to 20 cities. A merger was proposed with Frontier (see page 163), to be effective by October 1997.

Routes

Atlanta, Chicago, Dallas/Fort Worth, Houston, Indianapolis, Kansas-City, Las Vegas, Los Angeles, Nashville, Newark, Oklahoma City, Phoenix, San Antonio, San Diego, San Francisco, San Jose, Seattle, Tulsa, Washington, Wichita.

Fleet	Ordered
15 Boeing 737-300	6 Boeing 737-300 12 Boeing 737-700

Photograph: De Havilland DHC-8 LN-WIB (Patrick Lutz/Hamburg)

WIDEROE

P.O. Box 247, 8001 Bodoe,
Norway
Tel. 116000 Fax. 116195

Three letter code	IATA No.	ICAO Callsign
WIF	701	Wideroe

Viggo Widerøe founded his Widerøe's Flyveselskap A/S on 19th February 1934. First he obtained a licence to open a route from Oslo to Haugesund. On behalf of DNL, the established airline of the time and the predecessor of SAS, he opened a postal service in 1936 to Kirkenes in the north of Norway. After the Second World War Widerøe started charter and supply flights again. It took over the Narvik-based Polarfly in 1950. Widerøe made a particular contribution to the opening up of northern Norway. The first DHC-6 Twin Otters were received in 1968 which was the year scheduled services using Twin Otters were introduced on local routes. With the support of the government a network of routes from Bodø and Trondheim was built up, and this was followed over the years by around 30/40 smaller airfields, all of them standardised with similar landing aids and a runway between 800 and 1000 metres long. In this way the necessary infrastructure was created in this inaccessible area criss-crossed with fjords. Towns like Kirkenes and Hammerfest had only been accessible by ship until flights started. Fred Olsen,. SAS and Braathens SAFE have stakes in Widerøe, the oldest Norwegian airline still in existence. From 1993 to 1996 almost the entire fleet, including the DHC-7s which had served for some years, was replaced by modern DHC-8s and international service was opened for the first time to Sumburgh in the Shetland Islands and to Copenhagen. Additionally Wideroes flies charters.

Routes

Alta, Andenes, Batsfjord, Bervelag, Bodø, Bromnoysund, Copenhagen, Hammerfest, Kirkenes, Leknes, Mo i Rana, Mosjoen, Namsos, Narvik, Oslo, Rost, Skolvaer, Stokmarknes, Sumburgh, Tromso, Trondheim, Vadso, Vardoe.

Fleet	Ordered
1 De Havilland DHC-6-300	1 De Havilland DHC-8-400
21 De Havilland DHC-8-100/300	

Photograph: McDonnell Douglas MD-11 N272WA (Andrè Dietzel/Munich FJS)

WORLD AIRWAYS

13873 Park Center Road, Herndon,
Virginia 22071, USA
Tel. 703-8349200 Fax. 703-8349212

Three letter code	IATA No.	ICAO Callsign
WOA	468	World

World Airways was founded on 29th March 1948 and started charter flights with a Boeing 314 flying boat from the east coast of the United States. One year later the flights were moved from water to land; Curtiss C-46s were used. In 1950 Edward Daly acquired an 81% interest in the airline and made it into one of the large, well-known supplemental charter airlines in the next few years. From 1960 onwards World Airways took over an increasing number of flights for the Military Airlift Command of the United States Air Force, and DC-4s, DC-6s and Lockheed 1049 Constellations were bought or leased. The first Boeing 707s were acquired in 1963, and regular flights to and from Europe were introduced using these aircraft, as well as services to the Caribbean and South America. In May 1973 charter flights to London from Oakland started using Boeing 747s. CAB approval for low-cost, coast-to-coast scheduled services was granted in early 1979. World commenced linking Newark and Baltimore/Washington with Los Angeles and Oakland in April 1979 Scheduled flights were further expanded with the introduction of the DC-10s, and the Hawaii-Los Angeles-Baltimore-London-Frankfurt flights were the lowest priced charter flights to these destinations for many years. After restructuring in 1988 World Airways withdrew from scheduled flights. Malaysian Helicopter took over 25% of the shares in 1994 and invested in the company. From 1993 passenger services were again started to Israel and charters were resumed under its own name to Great Britain and elsewhere in Europe. But these flights were again withdrawn after the 1996 summer season, to concentrate on freight and *ad hoc* charter work. Aircraft are loaned to and from Malaysian Airlines as required.

Routes

Worldwide charter and freight flights from its New York (Newark) base.

Fleet

4 McDonnell Douglas DC-10-30
9 McDonnell Douglas MD-11

Photograph: Boeing 757-200 B-2819 (Martin Bach/Hong Kong)

XIAMEN AIRLINES

Gaoqi Airport, 361009 Xiamen,
Peoples Republic of China
Tel. 592-622961 Fax. 592-6028263

Three letter code	IATA No.	ICAO Callsign
CXA	731	Xiamen Airlines

Xiamen Airlines was founded in 1991 by China Southern Airlines (with 60% of the shares) and the regional governments of Xiamen and Fujian, and is virtually a subsidiary of CSA but with its own aircraft fleet and operating area. Flight operations were begun in 1992 with a leased Boeing 737. More 737s have been added, including -500 series from 1992 onwards, and Boeing 757s have been in the fleet since the first was delivered in August 1992. There are services to the south and east of the People's Republic. In late 1992 a route to Hong Kong was opened. The base is Xiamen where there is a maintenance facility, and where the airline works closely with China Southern.

Routes

Dense network in co-operation with China Southern in the south and east of the People's Republic of China, and to Hong Kong.

Fleet

5 Boeing 737-200Adv
7 Boeing 737-500
5 Boeing 757-200

Photograph: Boeing 737-200Adv 7O-ACQ (Author's collection)

YEMENIA

P.O. Box 1183, Sanaa,
Republic of Yemen
Tel. 232380 Fax. 252991

Three letter code	IATA No.	ICAO Callsign
IYE	635	Yemeni

The 'new' Yemenia is the result of the amalgamation of the former Alyemen and Yemenia, respectively the two national airlines of the North and South Yemen, now merged into one country again. Saudi Arabian Airlines is a 40% shareholder in the new airline. The two precursor airlines were completely dissolved, bringing aircraft, routes, handling etc all completely into the new airline. The origin of the airline can be traced back to 1961 when it was started up under the name of Yemen Airlines. Alyemen established itself soon after the split of the country into North and South in 1971. Several of the aircraft are also used as transports by the country's air force. The mixed fleet arising from the merger includes two DHC-7s delivered in 1996 to augment two earlier examples, and two Airbus A310s, newly leased in Spring 1997 to give a modern image to international routes.

Routes

Abu Dhabi, Addis Ababa, Aden, Albuq, Al Gaydah, Amman, Ataq, Bahrain, Bombay, Damascus, Djibouti, Doha, Dubai, Frankfurt, Hodeidah, Jeddah, Cairo, Karachi, Khartoum, Larnaca, London, Paris, Riyadh, Rome, Seiyun, Sharjah, Taiz.

Fleet

2 Airbus A310-300
3 Boeing 737-200Adv
5 Boeing 727-200Adv
2 De Havilland DHC-6 Twin Otter
4 De Havilland DHC-7
2 Lockheed L-382 Hercules

Airline Three-letter codes (IATA codes in parentheses)

AAA Ansett (AN)
AAG Atlantique Airways (KI)
AAH Aloha Airlines (AQ)
AAL American Airlines (AA)
AAR Asiana (OZ)
AAT Austrian Air Transport (SO)
AAU Australia Asia Airlines (IM)
ABB Air Belgium (AJ)
ABD Air Atlanta Iceland (CC)
ABG Abakan-Avia
ABL Air BC (ZX)
ABR Hunting Cargo Airlines(AG)
ABW Albanian Airlines (7Y)
ABX Airborne Express (GB)
ACA Air Canada (AC)
ACF Air Charter (SF)
ACI Air Caledonie Intl. (SB)
ACU Aero Cancun (RE)
ADK ADC Airlines
ADR Adria Airways (JP)
AEA Air Europa (KX)
AEF Aero Lloyd (YP)
AES ACES Colombia (VX)
AFE Airfast Indonesia
AFG Ariana Afghan Airlines (FG)
AFL Aeroflot Russian Airlines (SU)
AFM Affretair
AFR Air France (AF)
AGN Air Gabon (GN)
AGO Angola Air Charter (C3)
AGU Air Guadeloupe (OG)
AGV Air Glaciers
AGX Aviogenex (JJ)
AHK Air Hong Kong (LD)
AHR Air Holland (GG)
AHY Azerbaijan Airlines (J2)
AIB Airbus Inter Transport
AIC Air India (AI)
AIE Air Inuit (3H)
AIG Air Inter Gabon
AIH Airtours International (VZ)
AIJ Air Jet (BC)
AIN African International Airways
AIZ Arkia (IZ)
AJM Air Jamaica (JM)
AJT Amerijet (JH)
AKC Arca Colombia (ZU)
AKH Turkmenistan/AKHAL Air-company (T5)
ALK Air Lanka (UL)
ALM ALM Antillean Airlines (LM)
AMC Air Malta (KM)
AMF Ameriflight
AMI Air Maldives (L6)
AML Air Malawi (QM)
AMM Air 2000 (DP)
AMT American Trans Air (TZ)
AMU Air Macau (NX)
AMC Aeromexico (AM)
ANA ANA-All Nippon Airways (NH)
ANG Air Niugini (PX)
ANK Air Nippon (EL)
ANT Air North (4N)
ANZ Air New Zealand (NZ)
AOM AOM French Airlines (IW)
APT LAP Colombia
APW Arrow Air (JW)
ARG Aerolineas Argentinas (AR)
ARN Air Nova (QK)
ARU Air Aruba (FQ)
ASA Alaska Airlines (AS)
ASD Air Sinai (4D)
ASE ASA-Delta Connection (EV)
ASH Mesa Airlines (YU)
ASN Air Straubing (IU)
ASU Aerosur
ASW Air Southwest
ATC Air Tanzania (TC)
ATL Air Atlantic (9A)
ATT Aer Turas Teorante
AUA Austrian Airlines (OS)
AUB Augsburg Airways (IQ)
AUI Air Ukraine International (PS)
AUR Aurigny Air Services (GR)
AUT Austral (AU)
AVA Avianca Columbia (AV)
AVE Avensa (VE)
AVN Air Vanuatu (NF)
AWA Ansett W.A. (MV)
AWC Titan Airways
AWD Airworld (RL)
AWE America West Airlines (HP)
AWI Air Wisconsin-United Express
AYC Aviaco (AO)
AZA Alitalia (AZ)
AZE Arcus Air Logistic (ZE)
AZM Aerocozumel (AZ)
AZW Air Zimbabwe (UM)
AZX Air Bristol/Air Belfast (7L)
BAG Deutsche BA (DI)
BAL Britannia Airways (BY)
BAR Bradley Air Service
BAW British Airways (BA)
BBC Biman Bangladesh (BG)
BCS European Air Transport
BEN Business Air
BER Air Berlin (AB)
BFC Basler Airlines
BFL Buffalo Airways
BFS Constellation Intl. (CQ)
BHO Bhoja Airlines (B4)
BHS Bahamasair (UP)
BIM Binter Mediterraneo (AX)
BKL Baikal Airlines (X3)
BKP Bangkok Airways (PG)
BLI Belair
BMA British Midland (BD)
BOI Aboitiz Airtransport
BOT Air Botswana (BP)
BOU Bouraq Indonesia (BO)
BRA Braathens S.A.F.E. (BU)
BRU Belavia (B2)
BRY Brymon European Airw. (BC)
BSK Miami Air (GL)
BTI Air Baltic (BT)
BUR Businessair
BVA Buffalo Airways Inc. (BV)
BWA BWIA International (BW)
BWL British World Airlines (VF)
BZH Brit Air (DB)
CAA Carnival Air Lines (KW)
CAL China Airlines (CI)
CAV Calm Air (MO)
CAW Comair (MN)
CAY Cayman Airways (KX)
CBE Aerocaribe (QA)
CBF China Northern Airlines (CJ)
CCA Air China (CA)
CCS Canarias Cargo
CDG Shandong Airlines (SC)
CDN Canadian (CP)
CES China Eastern Airlines (MU)
CFE City Flyer Express (FD)
CFG Condor Flugdienst (DE)
CFP Faucett Peru (CF)
CGW Air Great Wall (G8)
CHG Challengair
CHH Hainan Airlines (H4)
CHP Aviacsa (6A)
CIM Cimber Air (QI)
CJG Zhejiang Airlines
CKS Kalitta American International Airways (CB)
CKT Caledonian Airways (KG)
CLC Classic Air
CLH Lufthansa Cityline (CL)
CLI Air Club International (HB)
CLX Cargolux (CV)
CMI Continental Micronesia (GS)
CMM Canada 3000 (2T)
CMP Copa Panama (CM)
CNJ Nanjing Airlines (3W)
CNW China Northwest Airl. (WH)
COA Continental Airlines (CO)
COM Comair (OH)
CPA Cathay Pacific (CX)
CRC Conair Aviation
CRL Corse Air (SS)
CRN Aero Caribbean
CRQ Air Creebec (YN)
CRX Crossair (LX)
CSA CSA (OK)
CSC Sichuan Airlines (3U)
CSH Shanghai Airlines (SF)
CSN China Southern Airl. (CZ)
CSZ Shenzhen Airlines (4G)
CTH China General Aviation (GP)
CTN Croatia Airlines (OU)
CUA China United Airlines (HR)
CUB Cubana (CU)
CUS Cronus Airlines (X5)
CWC Challenge Air Cargo (WE)
CWU Wuhan Air Lines (WU)

CXA Xiamen Airlines (MF)
CXH China Xinhua Airlines (X2)
CXJ China Xinjiang Airlines (XO)
CXN China Southwest Airl. (SZ)
CXP Casino Express (XP)
CYH Yunnan Airlines (3Q)
CYP Cyprus Airways (CY)
DAH Air Algerie (AH)
DAL Delta Air Lines (DL)
DAN Maersk Air (DM)
DAO Daallo Airlines (D3)
DAT DAT Belgian Regional
DHL DHL Airways (ER)
DLA Air Dolomiti (EN)
DLH Lufthansa (LH)
DMO Domodedovo Airlines (E3)
DOA Dominicana de Aviacion (DO)
DRK Druk Air (KB)
DSB Air Senegal (DS)
DSL Diamond Sakha Airlines (D8)
DSR DAS Air Cargo (SE)
DTA TAAG Angola Airlines (DT)
DVU Orbi Georgian Airways (NQ)
EBA Virgin Express (BQ)
ECA Eurocypria Airlines (UI)
EDW Edelweiss Air
EEA Ecuatoriana (EU)
EIA Evergreen Intl. Airlines (EZ)
EIN Air Lingus (EI)
ELG Alpi Eagles
ELL Estonian Air (OV)
ELN Nordic East Airways (N7)
ELY EL AL Israel Airlines (LY)
ERT Eritrean Airlines
ETH Ethiopian Airlines (ET)
EUL Euralair (RN)
EVA Eva Air (BR)
EWG Eurowings (EW)
EWW Emery Worldwide (GJ)
EXS Channel Express (LS)
EZY Easyjet Airlines
FAB First Air (7F)
FAJ Air Fiji
FAT Farner Air Transport
FBF Fine Air (FB)
FCN Falcon Aviation (IH)
FDX Fed Ex (FX)
FEA Far Eastern Air Transp. (EF)
FFT Frontier Airlines (F9)
FIN Finnair (AY)
FJI Air Pacific (FJ)
FLI Atlantic Airways
FOF Fred Olsen Airtransp. (FO)
FOX Jetair
FRS Flandre Air (IX)
FUA Futura Intl. Airways (FH)
FWL Florida West Airlines (RF)
GAA Bex-Delta Connection (HQ)
GAW Gambia Airways
GBL GB Airways (GT)
GBU Air Bissau (YZ)
GCB Lina Congo (GC)
GDI Grandair (8L)
GEC Lufthansa Cargo (LH)
GFA Gulf Air (GF)
GHA Ghana Airways (GH)
GIA Garuda Indonesia (GA)
GIB Air Guinee (GI)
GIL Gill Airways (9C)
GMI Germania Fluggesellschaft
GRL Groenlandsfly (GL)
GRO Allegro Air
GTI Atlas Air (5Y)
GUG Aviateca (GU)
GYA Guyana Airways (GY)
HAL Hawaiian Air (HA)
HAS Hamburg Airlines (HX)
HDA Dragonair (KA)
HJA Air Haiti
HLA Heavylift Cargo Airlines (NP)
HLD Holiday Air (HW)
HLF Hapag-Lloyd Flug (HF)
HMS Hemus Air (DU)
HRH Royal Tongan Airlines (WR)
HVN Vietnam Airlines (VN)
HZL Hazelton Airlines (ZL)
IAC Indian Airlines (IC)
IAW Iraqi Airways (IA)
IBB Binter Canaris (NT)
IBE Iberia (IB)
ICE Icelandair (FI)
ICN Intercanadian (QB)
IMX Zimex Aviation (MF)
IRA Iran Air (IR)
IRB Iran Airtours
IRC Iran Asseman Airlines
IRK Kish Air (KN)
ISS Meridiana (IG)
IST Istanbul Airlines (IL)
ITF Air Inter Europe (IT)
IYE Yemenia Airways (IY)
JAA Japan Asia Airways (EG)
JAC Japan Air Commuter (JN)
JAI Jet Airways Ltd (9W)
JAL Japan Airlines (JL)
JAS Japan Air System (JD)
JAT Yugoslav Airlines (JU)
JAZ Japan Air Charter (JZ)
JEA Jersey European Airw. (JY)
JTA Japan Transocean Air
JEX Midway Airlines (JI)
KAC Kuwait Airways (KU)
KAL Korean Air (KE)
KBA Kenn Borek Airlines (4K)
KDA Kendell Airlines (KD)
KGA Kyrghyzstan Airlines (K2)
KHA Kitty Hawk Air Cargo (KR)
KIA Kiwi Internl. Air Lines (KP)
KIS Contact Air (3T)
KJC Kras Air
KKB Air South (WV)
KLC KLM Cityhopper (HN)
KLM KLM Royal Dutch Airl. (KL)
KOR Air Koryo (JS)
KQA Kenya Airways (KQ)
KRE Aerosucre
KYV Kibris Turkish Airlines (YK)
KZA Kazakhstan Airlines
LAA Libyan Arab Airlines (LN)
LAI Lesotho Airways (QL)
LAJ British Mediterranean (KJ)
LAM Linhas Aereas Mocambique (TM)
LAN LAN Chile (LA)
LAO Lao Aviation (QV)
LAP Lineas Aereas Paraguayas (PZ)
LAZ Balkan Bulgarian Airlines (LZ)
LBC Albanian Airlines (7Y)
LBH Laker Airways (7Z)
LCO Ladeco (UC)
LDA Lauda Air (NG)
LDE LADE (LD)
LEI Air UK-Leisure (UK)
LGL Luxair (LG)
LHN Express One Intl. (EO)
LIA Liat Caribbean Airlines (LI)
LIB Air Liberté (VD)
LIC LAC Colombia (LC)
LIL Lithuanian Airlines (TE)
LIT Air Littoral (FU)
LLB Lloyd Aéreo Boliviano (LB)
LOG Loganair (LC)
LOT LOT Polish Airlines (LO)
LPR LAPA (MJ)
LRC Lacsa (LR)
LSS Lone Star Airlines (AD)
LTE LTE Intl. Airways (XO)
LTL Latavio Latvian Airlines (PV)
LTS LTU-Süd Intl. Airways (LT)
LTU LTU Intl. Airways (LT)
MAB Millardair
MAH Malev Hungarian Airl. (MA)
MAK Macedonian Airlines (M7)
MAS Malaysia Airlines (MH)
MAU Air Mauritius (MK)
MDA Mandarin Airlines (AE)
MDG Air Madagascar (MD)
MDJ JARO International (JT)
MDL Mandala Airlines (RI)
MEA Middle East Airlines (ME)
MEP Midwest Express (YK)
MES Northwest Airlink-Mesaba Airlines
MGL Miat Mongolian Airl. (OM)
MLD Air Moldova (9U)
MLH Mahalo Air (8M)
MNA Merpati (MZ)
MNX Manx Airlines (JG)
MON Monarch Airlines (ZB)
MOZ Air Salzburg
MPH Martinair Holland (MP)
MRS Air Marshall Islands (CW)
MRT Air Mauritanie (MR)
MSR Egypt Air (MS)

MTM MTM Aviation
MTQ Air Martinique (PN)
MXA Mexicana (MX)
NAC Northern Air Cargo (HU)
NAM Air Manitoba (7N)
NAO North American Airl. (XG)
NCA Nippon Cargo Airlines (KZ)
NGA Nigeria Airways (WT)
NIS Nica (6Y)
NMB Air Namibia (SW)
NOP Novair
NOV Avianova (RD)
NSE Satena (ZT)
NWA Northwest Airlines (NW)
NWT NWT Air (NV)
NZM Mount Cook Airline (NM)
OAC Oriental Airways
OAL Olympic Airways (OA)
OHY Onur Air (8Q)
OIR Slov Air
OKJ Okada Air (9H)
OLT Ostfriesische Lufttransport (OL)
OLY Olympic Aviation (7U)
OMA Oman Air
ONT Air Ontario (GX)
ORB Orenburg Airlines
OXO Millon Air (OX)
PAC Polar Air Cargo (PO)
PAL Philippines (PR)
PAO Polynesian Airlines (PH)
PAR Spair Air Transport (S4)
PAS Pelita Air Service (EP)
PBU Air Burundi (PB)
PEG Pelangi Air (9P)
PFC Pacific International Airlines
PGA Portugalia (NI)
PGT Pegasus Airlines
PIA Pakistan Intl. Airlines (PK)
PLA Polynesian Airways (PH)
PLI Aero Peru (PL)
PMK Palair Macedonia (3D)
PUA Pluna (PU)
QFA Qantas (QF)
QNK Kabo Air (9H)
QSC ASA African Safari
QTR Qatar Airways Co (Q7)
QXE Horizon Air (QX)
RAM Royal Air Maroc (AT)
RAT Ratioflug
RBA Royal Brunei (BI)
RIA Rich Intl. Airways (JN)
RJA Royal Jordanian (RJ)
RKA Air Afrique (RK)
RME Armenian Airlines (R3)
RMV Romavia (VQ)
RNA Royal Nepal Airlines (RA)
ROA Reno Air (QQ)
RON Air Nauru (ON)
ROT Tarom (RO)
RPB Aerorepublica
RQX Air Engiadina (RQ)
RSN Royal Swazi National Airways
RTL Rheintalflug (WG)
RVV Reeve Aleutian Airways (RV)
RWD Air Rwanda (RY)
RYR Ryanair (FR)
SAA South African Airways (SA)
SAB Sabena (SN)
SAI Shaheen International (NL)
SAM Sam Columbia (MM)
SAS Scandinavian (SK)
SAT Sata Air Acores (SP)
SAY Suckling Airways (CB)
SBE Sabre Airwys (TJ)
SBZ Scibe Airlift Zaire (ZM)
SCH Schreiner Airways (AW)
SCW Malmö Aviation (6E)
SCX Sun Country Airlines (SY)
SER Aero California (JR)
SET SAETA (EH)
SEY Air Seychelles (HM)
SFR Safeair (FA)
SGL Senegal Air
SHI Seoul Air
SHK Shoruk Air (7Q)
SIA Singapore Airlines (SQ)
SJM Southern Air Transport (SJ)
SKW Skywest-Delta Connection (OO)
SLK Silkair (MI)
SLM Surinam Airways (PY)
SLR Sobelair (S3)
SNB Sterling European Airl. (NB)
SOL Solomon Airlines (IE)
SPA Sierra Pacific Airlines (SI)
SPP Spanair (JK)
SSR Sempati Air (SG)
SUD Sudan Airways (SD)
SVA Saudi Arabian (SV)
SVV Servivensa (VC)
SWA Southwest Airlines (WN)
SWG Spirit Airlines (NK)
SWR Swissair (SR)
SXS Sunexpress (XQ)
SYR Syrian Arab Airlines (RB)
TAB Taba (TT)
TAE Tame (EQ)
TAI TACA Intl. Airlines (TA)
TAJ Tunisavia
TAM TAM Transportes Aereos Regional (KK)
TAP TAP Air Portugal (TP)
TAR Tunis Air (TU)
TAT TAT European Airlines (IJ)
TBA Transbrasil (TR)
TCV TACV Cabo Verdes (VR)
TEJ TAESA (GD)
THA Thai Airways Intl. (TG)
THY Turkish Airlines (TK)
TJK Tajik Air (7J)
TLA Translift Airways (T8)
TLE Air Toulouse
TMA TMA of Lebanon (TL)
TNA Transasia Airways (GE)
TOW Tower Air (FF)
TPA TAMPA Columbia (QT)
TPC Air Caledonie (TY)
TQA Transwede Airways
TRA Transavia Airlines (HV)
TRJ AJT Air International (E9)
TRK Air Truck
TSC Air Transat (TS)
TSO Trans Aero (4J)
TSW TEA Basel (BH)
TTR Tatra Air (QS)
TUI Tuninter (UG)
TUN Air Tungaru (VK)
TWA Trans World Airlines (TW)
TWE Transwede Leisure
TYM Tyumen Airlines
TYR Tyrolean Airways (VO)
UAE Emirates (EK)
UAL United Airlines (UA)
UBA Myanma Airways (UB)
UCA USAir Express-Commutair
UGA Uganda Airlines (QU)
UKA Air UK (UK)
UKR Air Ukraine (GU)
ULA Zuliana de Aviacio
UPA Air Foyle (GS)
UPS United Parcel Service (5X)
USA US Air (US)
USS USAir Shuttle (TB)
UVL Orel Avia (SP)
UYC Cameroon Airlines (UY)
UZB Uzbekistan Airways (HY)
VBW Air Burkina (VH)
VCT Viscount Air Service
VDA Volga Dnepr Cargo Airl. (VI)
VER Venus Airlines
VGD Vanguard Airlines (NJ)
VIR Virgin Atlantic Airways (VS)
VIV Viva Air (FV)
VJA Valujet (J7)
VKG Premiair (DK)
VKO Vnukovo Airlines (V5)
VLM VLM (V4)
VRG Varig (RG)
VSP VASP (VP)
VTA Air Tahiti (VT)
VTR Air Ostrava (8K)
VUN Air Ivoire (VU)
WDL WDL Aviation
WIA Winair
WIF Wideroe (WF)
WLO Willowair
WOA World Airways (WO)
YRR Scenic Airlines (YR)

International Aircraft Registration Prefixes

AP	Pakistan
A2	Botswana
A3	Tonga Islands
A40	Oman
A5	Bhutan
A6	United Arab Emirates
A7	Qatar
A9C	Bahrain
B	China, Peoples Republic of, and Taiwan (Republic of China)
C	Canada
CC	Chile
CN	Morocco
CP	Bolivia
CS	Portugal
CU	Cuba
CX	Uruguay
C2	Nauru
C3	Andorra
C5	Gambia
C6	Bahamas
C9	Mozambique
D	Germany
DQ	Fiji
D2	Angola
D4	Cape Verde
D6	Comores
EC	Spain
EI	Ireland
EK	Armenia
EL	Liberia
EP	Iran
ER	Moldovia
ES	Estonia
ET	Ethiopia
EW	Belarus
EX	Kyrghyztan
EY	Tadjikistan
EZ	Turkmenistan
E3	Eritrea
F	France
F-O	France Overseas
G	Great Britain
HA	Hungary
HB	Switzerland (and Lichtenstein)
HC	Ecuador
HH	Haiti
HI	Dominican Republic
HK	Colombia
HL	South Korea
HP	Panama
HR	Honduras
HS	Thailand
HZ	Saudi Arabia
H4	Solomon Islands
I	Italy
JA	Japan
JY	Jordan
J2	Djibouti
J3	Grenada
J5	Guinea Bissau
J6	St Lucia
J7	Dominica
J8	St Vincent and Grenadines
LN	Norway
LV	Argentina
LX	Luxembourg
LY	Lithuania
LZ	Bulgaria
MI	Marshall Islands
MT	Mongolia
N	USA
OB	Peru
OD	Lebanon
OE	Austria
OH	Finland
OK	Czech Republic
OM	Slovak Republic
OO	Belgium
OY	Denmark
P	North Korea
PH	Netherlands
PJ	Netherlands Antilles
PK	Indonesia
PP	Brazil
PZ	Surinam
P2	Papua New Giunea
P4	Aruba
RA	Russia
RDPL	Laos
RF	Russia
RP	Philippines
SE	Sweden
SP	Poland
ST	Sudan
SU	Egypt
SU-Y	Palestine
SX	Greece
S2	Bangladesh
S5	Slovenia
S7	Seychelles
S9	Sao Tome
TC	Turkey
TF	Iceland
TG	Guatemala
TI	Costa Rica
TJ	Cameroon
TL	Central African Republic
TN	Congo
TR	Gabon
TS	Tunisia
TT	Chad
TU	Côte d'Ivoire
TY	Benin
TZ	Mali
T2	Tuvalu
T3	Kiribati
T7	San Marino
T9	Bosnia-Herzogovina
UK	Uzbekistan
UN	Kazakhstan

UR	Ukraine
VH	Australia
VN	Vietnam
VP-B	Bermuda
VP-C	Cayman Islands
VP-F	Falkland Islands
VP-G	Gibraltar
VP-LA	Anguilla
VP-LM	Montserrat
VP-LV	British Virgin Islands
VQ-T	Turks and Caicos Islands
VR-A to VR-Q	China (Hong Kong)
VT	India
V2	Antigua and Barbuda
V3	Belize
V4	St Kitts and Nevis Islands
V5	Namibia
V6	Micronesia
V7	Marshall Islands
V8	Brunei
XA, XB	Mexico
XT	Burkina Faso
XU	Cambodia
XY	Myanmar
YA	Afghanistan
YI	Iraq
YK	Syria
YL	Lithuania
YN	Nicaragua
YR	Romania
YS	El Salvador
YU	Serbia-Macedonia
YV	Venezuela
Z, Z2	Zimbabwe
ZA	Albania
ZK	New Zealand
ZP	Paraguay
ZS, ZU	South Africa
Z3	Macedonia
3A	Monaco
3B	Mauritius
3C	Equatorial Guinea
3D	Swaziland
3X	Guinea
4K	Azerbaijan
4L	Georgia
4R	Sri Lanka
4U	United Nations
4X	Israel
5A	Libya
5B	Cyprus
5H	Tanzania
5N	Nigeria
5R	Madagascar
5T	Mauretania
5U	Niger
5V	Togo
5W	West-Samoa
5X	Uganda
5Y	Kenya
6O	Somalia
6V	Senegal
6Y	Jamaica
7O	Yemen
7P	Lesotho
7Q	Malawi
7T	Algeria
8P	Barbados
8Q	Maldives
8R	Guyana
9A	Croatia
9G	Ghana
9H	Malta
9J	Zambia
9K	Kuwait
9L	Sierra Leone
9M	Malaysia
9N	Nepal
9Q, 9T	Zaire
9U	Burundi
9V	Singapore
9XR	Rwanda
9Y	Trinidad and Tobago

Space for notes

Other Airline and Airliner books

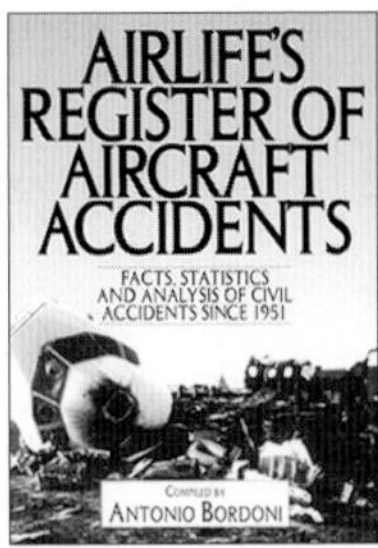

Midland Counties Publications is probably the world's leading mail-order supplier of aviation books of all kinds, with many years experience of world-wide business, thousands of satisfied customers and extensive stocks. Telephone, fax or e-mail orders to be charged to MasterCard or Visa accounts are gladly accepted. Very careful attention is paid to packaging. Sterling cheques and US dollar checks are also accepted. Free illustrated catalogues on request.

Amongst the thousands of titles in stock are hundreds on the various aspects of civil aviation, airlines and airliners . Here are just a few:

abc American Airlines (Simon Forty) . . . **c.£7.99**
abc Boeing 777 (Bruce Campian-Smith). . . . **£7.99**
abc British Airways (Leo Marriott / Second edition) . . . **£7.99**
abc Civil Airliner Recognition (P R March / 5th edition) . . . **£8.99**
abc United Airlines (Simon Forty) . . . **c.£7.99**
Air Transport: First Fifty Years (John Cook) Archive Photograph series . . . **£9.99**
Airlife's Register of Aircraft Accidents (A Bordoni) civil accidents s.1951. . . . **£19.95**
Airline Fleets 1997 (ed C Chatfield / Air-Britain) . . . **£17.50**
Airline Markings 14: Airbus A320 (Robbie Shaw) . . . **£9.95**
Airlines and Airliners 4: Bristol Britannia (Phil Lo Bao) . . . **£8.95**
Airliners of Asia since 1920 (R E G Davies / Putnam) . . . **£40.00**
Airliners at LAX (Robert D Archer) Los Angeles International Airport 1956-76 . . . **c£17.95**
Airliners in Flight (N Veronico & G Hull) Air-to-Air photos . . . **£15.95**
Airport of the Nine Dragons (Capt Charles Eather) Kai-Tak, Kowloon . . . **£18.95**
Boeing 367/377: Stratocruiser, Stratofreighter & Guppies (Martin Bach)
German text, English Summary . . . **£11.95**
Boeing 747 (Guy Norris & Mark Wagner) . . . **£12.95**
Boeing 747SP (Brian Baum / Great Airliners vol.3) . . . **due Nov c.£17.95**
Boeing 777 (G Norris & M Wagner / Enthusiast Color Series). . . . **£9.95**
Boeing Jetliners (G Norris & M Wagner / Enthusiast Colour Series) . . . **£9.95**
Boeing Jetliners (Robbie Shaw). . . . **£10.99**
British World Airlines Story (A J Wright) 50 years of service & achievement. . . . **£9.95**
Business Jets International 1997 (Terry Smith et al / Air-Britain, 12th edn) . . . **£15.00**
Capital Airlines: A Nostalgic Flight into the Past (Charles Baptie) . . . **£21.95**
Cargo Airlines (Oliver Scharschmidt) 140 colour photos of air freighters . . . **£16.95**
Colours in the Sky (G M Simons) Story of Autair & Court Line. . . . **due Oct £24.95**
Concorde and the Americans (K Owen) . . . **£24.95**
The Concorde Story (C Orlebar / new edition) 21 years of service. . . . **£14.99**

from Midland Counties Publications

Dream Schemes: Exotic Airliner Art (Stuart Spicer) **£16.95**
Emergency: Crisis on the Flightdeck (Stanley Stewart / softback edition) **£10.95**
Flights of Terror (D Gero) Aerial hijack and sabotage since 1930 . . . . **£17.99**
Flights to Disaster (Andrew Brookes) examines many different factors **£14.99**
Flying the Big Jets (Stanley Stewart / 3rd edition) **£16.95**
From Flying Boats to Flying Jets (Eric Woods) post-war air travel **£19.95**
Geneva International Airport (Aram Gesar) colour pictorial **£10.95**
Giant Jetliners (Guy Norris & Mark Wagner) **£12.99**
Hong Kong Aircraft Handbooks (Danny Chan) parts 1, 2 and 3. . . . . **each £12.00**
Is it on Auto Pilot (J Evans) all you wanted to know about flying **£10.95**
Jet Engines: Theory, Design and Operation (Klaus Hunecke) **£20.00**
Jetliner Colours (John Morton) new volume of airliner liveries **£16.95**
Jetliners (Clinton Groves / Enthusiast Colour Series) **£9.95**
JP Airline Fleets International 1997/98 (Ulrich Klee / 31st edn) **£34.95**
Kai Tak: The Final Decade (Robbie Shaw) colour pictorial **£12.95**
Line Up in Sequence – Amsterdam Airport, Schiphol: 100 colour photos **£10.95**
The One-Eleven Story (R J Church) Air Britain production history **£24.95**
Saudia: Saudi Arabian Airlines – an airline and its aircraft (R Davies) **£24.95**
The Stansted Experience (John F Hamlin). **£19.95**
Survivors '97 (Vince Horan) lists extant propliners/early jetliners **£6.95**
Transbrasil: An Airline and its Aircraft (R E G Davies) **£24.95**
Turboprop Airliners & Military Transports of the World 1997 (Air-Britain) **£15.00**
Twilight of Pistons: Air Ferry – A Manston Airline (Malcolm Finnis). **£26.95**
Viscount, Comet & Concorde (S Wilson / Legends of the Air Series) **£14.95**
Wings to the Orient (S Cohen) Pan Am clippers 1935-45 pictorial history **£14.95**
World Directory of Airliner Crashes (Terry Denham) over 10,000 listed **£19.95**

Post and packing: UK Please add 10% (minimum £1.50, maximum £3.00) orders over £40.00 sent post-free; **Overseas:** Please add 15% (minimum £2.00), or 10% of order over £150. MasterCard and Visa welcome.

Midland Counties Publications
Unit 3 Maizefield, Hinckley, Leicestershire, LE10 1YF, England
Tel: 01455 233 747 Fax: 01455 233 737
E-mail: midlandbooks@compuserve.com

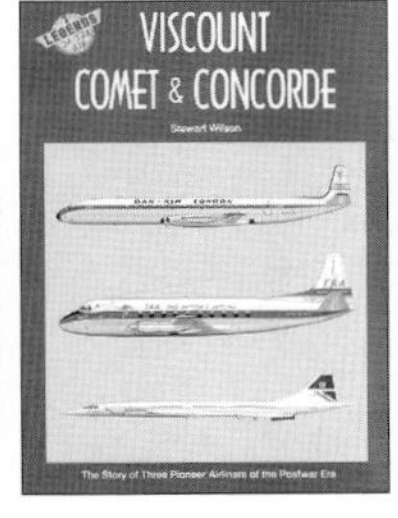

We hope you enjoyed this book . . .

Midland Publishing titles are edited and designed by an experienced and enthusiastic trans-Atlantic team of specialists.

Further titles are in preparation but we welcome ideas from authors or readers for books they would like to see published.

In addition, our associate company, Midland Counties Publications, offers an exceptionally wide range of aviation, spaceflight, astronomy, military, naval and transport books and videos for sale by mail-order around the world.

For a copy of the appropriate catalogue, or to order further copies of this book, or any of the titles mentioned on pages 318 to 320, please write, telephone, fax or e-mail to:

Midland Counties Publications
Unit 3 Maizefield,
Hinckley, Leics, LE10 1YF, England

Tel: (+44) 01455 233 747
Fax: (+44) 01455 233 737
E-mail: midlandbooks@compuserve.com

US distribution by
Specialty Press – details on page 2

An indispensible companion volume –

AIRLINERS
WORLDWIDE
Over 100 Current Airliners Described and Illustrated in Colour
TOM SINGFIELD

Interest in the airliners of the world continues to grow and with it demands for better reference material. Now, following on from the highly popular full colour format of *Airlines Worldwide,* comes a companion volume, devoted to the wide variety of types that ply the world's airways.

Ranging from the humble 15 seat feederliner to the huge Boeing 747-400, the book provides full colour illustrations of the major types, and roams the planet for rare and colourful examples. Detail given includes development, conversions and sub-series, number built and number in service. Also included is a listing of the airlines using each type.

The author, an air traffic controller, has scoured the world for the illustrations for this book and provided an informative but highly readable reference to each aircraft. From Anglo-French Concorde to DHC Twin Otter, Airbus A340 to Beech 1900D, Douglas Dakota to Boeing 777 – full details of the airliner workhorses of the late 1990s are all there.

An excellent reference, providing at-a-glance information on how widespread a type is, how long it has been in service and operators worldwide. With all of the illustrations in full colour, it also provides a lavish catalogue of colour schemes and logos.

Softback, 240 x 170 mm, 128 pages.
134 full colour photographs
1 85780 056 7 published August 1997
UK £11.95 / US $19.95